ROOTS OF ENTANGLEMEN

Essays in the History of Native-Newcomer Relations

Edited by Myra Rutherdale, Whitney Lackenbauer, and Kerry Abel

Roots of Entanglement offers a historical exploration of the relationships between Indigenous peoples and European newcomers in the territory that would become Canada. Various engagements between Indigenous peoples and the state are emphasized and questions are raised about the ways in which the past has been perceived and how those perceptions have shaped identity and, in turn, interaction both past and present.

Specific topics such as land, resources, treaties, laws, policies, and cultural politics are explored through a range of perspectives that reflect state-of-the-art research in the field of Indigenous history. Editors Myra Rutherdale, Whitney Lackenbauer, and Kerry Abel have assembled an array of top scholars including luminaries such as Keith Carlson, Bill Waiser, Arthur Ray, and Ken Coates. *Roots of Entanglement* is a direct response to the Truth and Reconciliation Commission's call for a better appreciation of the complexities of history in the relationship between Indigenous and non-Indigenous peoples in Canada.

MYRA RUTHERDALE was a professor in the Department of History at York University.

WHITNEY LACKENBAUER is a professor in the Department of History and co-director of the Centre on Foreign Policy and Federalism at the University of Waterloo.

KERRY ABEL is a professor in the Department of History at Carleton University.

Roots of Entanglement

Essays in the History of Native-Newcomer Relations

EDITED BY MYRA RUTHERDALE, KERRY ABEL, AND P. WHITNEY LACKENBAUER

UNIVERSITY OF TORONTO PRESS
Toronto Buffalo London

Toronto Buffalo London
www.utorontopress.com
Printed in Canada

ISBN 978-1-4875-0318-9 (cloth) ISBN 978-1-4875-2137-0 (paper)

♾ Printed on acid-free, 100% post-consumer recycled paper with vegetable-based inks.

Library and Archives Canada Cataloguing in Publication

Roots of entanglement : essays in the history of native-newcomer relations / edited by Myra Rutherdale, Kerry Abel, and P. Whitney Lackenbauer.

Includes bibliographical references and index.
ISBN 978-1-4875-0138-9 (cloth). – ISBN 978-1-4875-2137-0 (paper)

1. Native peoples – Canada – History. 2. Native peoples – Canada – Government relations. 3. Native peoples – Education – Canada. 4. Native peoples – Legal status, laws, etc. – Canada. 5. Native peoples – Canada – Historiography. I. Rutherdale, Myra, 1961–2014, editor II. Abel, Kerry M. (Kerry Margaret), editor III. Lackenbauer, P. Whitney, editor

E78.C2R66 2018 971.004'97 C2017-905046-X

University of Toronto Press acknowledges the financial assistance to its publishing program of the Canada Council for the Arts and the Ontario Arts Council, an agency of the Government of Ontario.

Canada Council for the Arts Conseil des Arts du Canada

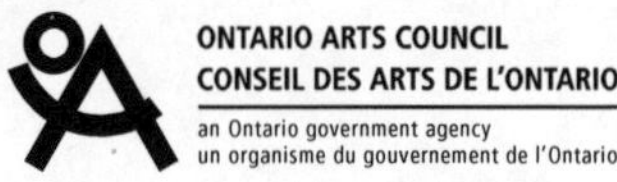

Funded by the Government of Canada Financé par le gouvernement du Canada Canada

This book is dedicated to Myra Rutherdale (1961–2014), accomplished scholar, colleague, and dear friend.

Contents

A Note on Terminology

"Indian" is a loaded word, reflecting racist assumptions held by the Europeans who coined it; those assumptions were then dug deeply into the English language. It is also, of course, historically and culturally inaccurate and misleading. Its use has been avoided here, except in cases drawing directly on the written historical record in which it was used. Instead, the term "Indigenous" is used to refer to all peoples who trace their ancestry to the original populations of this continent. "First Nations" has been used for those people once known as "Indians," and "Métis" and "Inuit" refer to the other major groups of Indigenous peoples in Canada. The term "Aboriginal" is used to refer to legal concepts.

PART ONE

Introduction

Introduction

MYRA RUTHERDALE, P. WHITNEY LACKENBAUER, AND KERRY ABEL

Reconciliation is about establishing and maintaining a mutually respectful relationship between Aboriginal and non-Aboriginal peoples in this country. In order for this to happen, there has to be an awareness of the past.

Truth and Reconciliation Commission of Canada[1]

In 2007, the largest class-action lawsuit ever pursued in Canada was settled. Among the provisions of the agreement was the requirement that the Canadian government establish a commission to inquire into the experiences of thousands of Indigenous children who had passed through the residential school system that had been established and maintained as part of the official policy to assimilate First Nations into the social, political, and economic systems of the settler-society that was Canada. The result was the creation of the Truth and Reconciliation Commission in 2008, loosely modelled on the commission of that name in South Africa. It would work for six years, travelling the country, hearing from nearly 7,000 witnesses, and gathering the heart-wrenching stories of residential school "survivors." Late in the spring of 2015, the final report was presented during a week of ceremony and symbol in the nation's capital.

Fundamental to the commission's mandate was a project of historical research and interpretation: in the words of the commission, to "reveal to Canadians the complex truth about the history and ongoing legacy" of the schools.[2] And there was no doubt that during the course of its hearings, the commission succeeded in capturing media attention and generating concerns and questions among that segment of the population who follows public affairs. Many Canadians were shocked by the stories of physical and sexual abuse; younger people who had grown up believing Canada was an inclusive and multicultural society were perplexed by the obvious disjuncture. How could this have happened? "History" became a convenient shorthand explanation. For example, sociologist James S. Frideres proposed this idea in a text for use in introductory university courses:

> The view that First Nations played no significant part in Canada's history was first set in place when non-Aboriginals began to write the history of Canada. Today we find that the majority of written historical sources, from which First Nations history is constructed, are from elites who had an interest in representing First Nations social life in negative terms ... The dynamic of concealment (consciously and unconsciously) has ultimately served the settler population in covering up the violence ... that has been visited upon First Nations people.[3]

Such a view of the role of history and historians certainly applies to generations past, but since the 1970s, the writing of Canadian history has undergone a profound series of changes. One of the most significant has been a reappraisal of the role of Indigenous peoples in the national narrative. Throughout the 1970s, a growing list of publications provided insight in many new directions: studies of the processes of early contact by both historians and anthropologists such as Robin Fisher, Cornelius Jaenen, and Bruce Trigger; analyses of economic interaction in the fur trade by Arthur Ray and others; an influential examination of the ideas of European colonizers by Olive Dickason; and studies of the social dimensions of the fur trade by Sylvia Van Kirk and Jennifer Brown.[4] Clearly, the growing interest was influenced by the constitutional debates and Indigenous rights activism that were reshaping the political and legal landscape.

Universities began to respond, and in the 1980s, a few across Canada began to offer undergraduate courses in what was then called "Native history." One of the early courses was offered at the University of Saskatchewan, where historian J.R. Miller developed a survey course to study the interaction between Indigenous peoples and the Canadian state. Although he had grown up in Cornwall, Ontario, next to the Akwesasne Mohawk territory, it was not until he moved to Saskatoon as a young scholar to take a position at the university there that he became acutely aware of the troubled relations between Indigenous peoples and newcomers. He began to ask questions about why that was the case. Miller's graduate work at the University of Toronto, under the renowned Donald Creighton and then–rising star Ramsay Cook, had been in the field of political history with a particular interest in Quebec – hardly surprising given his roots in the Ontario-Quebec borderlands and the Quiet Revolution that was dominating the headlines at the time.[5]

In the early 1980s, Miller decided to apply his expertise in political history to the question of Native-newcomer relations. During a year in Japan, he had been struck by the extent to which the Japanese education system transmitted social values and class systems to Japanese children, and he began to wonder about the role of the residential school system in Canada. What part had public policy played in establishing the roots of the modern problems? The question turned into a lengthy and challenging research project. It required extensive searching through government and church archives, and then many interviews with federal public servants, former students, and former residential school staff. In a 1987 essay, "The Irony of Residential Schooling," he observed that the federal government and the churches in fact failed in their objectives of Christianizing and assimilating First Nations children. That failure was marked by irony. First, the schools not only failed to convert Indigenous people into "model Canadians" but actually succeeded in educating a cadre of Indigenous leaders who eventually challenged the government from many directions. Second, Miller proposed that Indigenous leaders successfully made use of the Euro-Canadian education system itself to create Indigenous space in Canadian society. "Ironically," Miller concluded, "it was the residential school, which was designed to be the benign exterminator of Indian identity, that indirectly played a role in its perpetuation and revitalization."[6]

While working on his residential school research, Miller decided that he needed a textbook for his undergraduate course in Native history; in 1989, he published *Skyscrapers Hide the Heavens: A History of Indian-White Relations in Canada.*[7] It was the first comprehensive survey in the field that has come to be known as Native-newcomer history, and today it remains perhaps the most influential, among both general readers and the scholarly community. Still in print (in an updated edition) with well over 20,000 copies sold, it is in part a compelling synthesis of the rich array of scholarship of the preceding decade. But it is not merely a summary of the literature. Miller proposed a periodization scheme to help readers understand the history of Indigenous-European interaction. He used the term "cooperation" to cover the era from initial contact through the fur trade and military alliances in the eighteenth century, in which both sides forged relationships based upon self-interest. He labelled the next period "coercion," in which European perceptions shifted from alliance to an image of Indigenous people as "irrelevant" – obstacles to the march of agrarian and industrial progress. During this era, Miller argued, the colonizers pushed Indigenous peoples to the margins both physically (through their confinement on reserves) and culturally (through the policies of assimilation through residential schools, Indian Act governance, and other tools). Miller's third period was the era of "confrontation," marked by the emergence of Indigenous political organizations, concerted campaigns for recognition of Aboriginal rights, and movements seeking redress for land claims. Miller dated this third era from the end of the Second World War to the present.

However, for Miller, the story of Native-newcomer relations was not a narrative with a single trajectory. Within each period, he devoted chapters to specific regions – a reminder that there was no single pattern of Native-newcomer relations across the country and an affirmation of the need to understand history in its temporal and spatial contexts. And above all, he emphasized Indigenous *agency*: "that the Native peoples have always been active, assertive contributors to the unfolding of Canadian history."[8] This was no one-sided history of the imposition of settler colonialism on a passive Indigenous population of victims. Thus, while his work studied Native-newcomer history through the perspective of government policy, he never lost sight of Indigenous responses to those policies.

Meanwhile, Miller continued his study of residential schools and, in 1996, published the award-winning book *Shingwauk's Vision: A History of Native Residential Schools*.[9] Some time later, a prize citation recorded Miller's recollections of the work that led to this publication:

> While the abuse that occurred at many residential schools is now well known, when Miller began his research residential school survivors had yet to come forward and tell their stories. He says when he first uncovered written evidence that there had been serious abuse at a certain school, he was shaken and upset. Soon after, he did his first interview with a Cree woman who told him about the abuse her husband had suffered as a residential school student. "It was my first indication of how horrific these schools really were," says Miller.[10]

In spite of the profoundly disturbing stories he uncovered, the book did not stop at describing the victimization of those subjected to the school system. As with his *Skyscrapers* history, he took care to address the fact that Indigenous pupils and their families were also active "agents" to the extent that was possible. It was a "subtle and shifting interplay of forces," he wrote. And while "it would be misleading to suggest, for example, that Native groups were able to force schools to operate as they wished," he explained, "it is important to understand that protest and resistance could and did have some effect."[11]

Of course, Miller's interpretation of the "subtle and shifting interplay of forces" did not go unchallenged. Two graduate students at the University of Toronto, Robin Jarvis Brownlie and Mary-Ellen Kelm, chastised Miller and other historians who had taken a similar approach to Indigenous "agency" as amounting to defenders of colonialism. Brownlie and Kelm argued that these interpretations actually used "evidence of Native resilience and strength to soften, and at times to deny, the impact of colonialism, and thus, implicitly, to absolve its perpetrators."[12] The result was a lively debate, both within the field of Native-newcomer history and from without, among those who argued that the focus needed to shift entirely because the history of the Indigenous peoples of Canada was more than the history of their relations with the European newcomers. When historian Kerry Abel wrote a review essay on the state of the literature at that time, she entitled it "Tangled, Lost, and Bitter?" drawing on the titles of three important studies of the day.[13]

The ground did, indeed, begin to shift in the late 1990s. Instead of examining what actually happened in the encounter between Indigenous peoples and the colonizing state, historians began to ask questions about how those encounters had been perceived. Myth, memory, and imagery became the focal points as historians drew on critical theory and culture studies. Canada's history was no longer only the history of colonization of lands and peoples but now also the colonization of mental spaces, memories, and history itself.[14]

More recently, culture studies and anthropological theory have shifted ground again, and in some cases, new questions are being asked, while in others, old approaches have been given a facelift. A growing field of Indigenous studies, with its global framework and search for international patterns and comparisons, has become influential across the older disciplines. Australian anthropologist Patrick Wolfe – in revisiting the myth of the pioneer, the frontier, and the march of civilization through

Australian history – coined the term "settler colonialism" to describe that variant of colonialism in which settlers remove Indigenous populations from the land and replace the Indigenous world view with a new one. "Invasion is a structure, not an event," Wolfe proposed,[15] in which "the primary motive is not race (or religion, ethnicity, grade of civilization, etc.) but access to territory."[16] The most widely recognized theorist of settler colonialism, Lorenzo Veracini (influenced by semiotics, literary theory, and the psychology of Jacques Lacan), explored the minds of settler-colonizers and argued that settler colonialism was the "most invisible" form of colonization because of the historical narratives that settlers create and transmit, constructing fantasies about the process of settlement and dispossession. According to Veracini, the central fact of conquest is obscured by a process of mimesis (making an illusion seem real) in which "settler colonialism obscures the conditions of its own production."[17] The central concern for Veracini and his followers is no longer Native-newcomer relations but the ways that newcomers erased the Native from the land and from the mind.

A second important recent trajectory has been the emerging literature from outside traditional scholarly circles: Indigenous voices heard through literature, history, and the arts more generally are challenging historians who work within academic conventions. These voices are calling for (among other things) a recognition that the process of colonization did not succeed in erasing the Indigenous – resistance and resilience must be understood in order to appreciate the continuing presence of Indigenous peoples within settler-states. Activist Roxanne Dunbar-Ortiz opens her recent *Indigenous Peoples' History of the United States* by noting that, although she has two graduate degrees in history, her book focuses on a perspective that "came from outside the academy," generated in lived experience, community, and resistance.[18] That perspective has been very much a part of public discourse in Canada in recent years, reflected in the work of the Truth and Reconciliation Commission, discussions of the issue of missing and murdered Indigenous women, and calls for social justice more broadly. Reconciliation has become an international call, one possible yet problematic solution. Veracini was suspicious of it, proposing that it is potentially just another guise for assimilation.[19]

For historians, these debates resonate with familiar echoes. Thirty years ago, research in Canadian "Native history" began to rewrite the national narrative. Indigenous peoples were recognized as active agents in their engagement with colonizers, not passive victims of a faceless process. Resilience and the retention of identity were recognized as central to the story. Some attempts have been made to write Indigenous histories that tell stories beyond the colonization narrative, although that approach has not been as fully developed as it might have been. Arguably the most fruitful reconsideration of Canadian history has come through the influence of J.R. Miller, whose studies of "Native-newcomer" relations continue to shape our understanding of Canada's past and to impact public policy, hence shaping Canada's future. The argument can and should be made that historians are no longer complicit in the construction of an imagined narrative of colonialism. Indeed, historians and history can and should be playing a central role in addressing the legacies of colonization and helping all Canadians find a way forwards.

This book is a collection of essays that represent the variety of directions taken in the field inspired and shaped by Miller. The relationships between Indigenous peoples and (largely) European newcomers remain the focal point, while topics at the heart of Miller's work – land, treaties, laws, policies, and agency – remain here, too. However, these essays also reflect new preoccupations and perspectives as scholars respond to both earlier historical writing and twenty-first-century politics.

Readers will notice an emphasis on the role of the individual in history through a number of these essays. At one level, the biographical approach is an attempt to put a human face on historical processes that all too often appear to be amorphous and impersonal. At another level, it is an attempt to put names and individual stories into a narrative that for too long classified all Indigenous people as "Indians" and denied the humanity that individual recognition can bring. J.R. Miller urged his readers and students to recognize "agency" and the varieties of experience; the biographical approach is one possible response to that lesson.

Another theme of this collection is the surprising variety of engagements between Indigenous peoples and the state, reflecting cultural, geographical, and temporal differences. There is no single narrative of "Native-newcomer relations," and to generalize in this way does a disservice to all involved. If we want true reconciliation, we need to be aware of the full complexity of the past and not base our efforts on a single storyline.

Several of the contributors to this volume raise questions about how we have *perceived* the past, or the role that perceptions have played in that past. The question of identity has become a foundational approach in historical studies more generally in the twenty-first century, as historians explore topics of memory, myth, and the role of historical consciousness in shaping social and political behaviour around the globe. The writing of Indigenous history in Canada has not been immune to the influence of this important development, and it is reflected here in this collection as well. How did Native and newcomer *see* one another, and was it really just a simple dichotomy of "us" and "them"? What roles did personal and collective identities play in our interaction?

The essays in this collection have been divided into four groups. In the first section, "The Crown, Colonial Spaces, and Aboriginality," the authors address a conventional topic – state intervention in Indigenous affairs – in new ways. Kerry Abel focuses on the role of the first lieutenant governor of Upper Canada (John Graves Simcoe), who attempted to protect the land interests of the various First Nations within the new province but ultimately failed because of the successes of greedy land grabbers, corrupt officials, and an international power game. Donald Smith juxtaposes the perspectives of two men in a later generation: the mid-nineteenth-century superintendent general of Indian Affairs in the Canadas and Kahkewaquonaby (Peter Jones), a leading Mississauga. Their lives intersected at a crucial moment in the transfer of imperial authority over Indigenous lands. Brendan Edwards explores the often-surprising views of John Buchan, Lord Tweedsmuir (who served as governor general of Canada from 1935 to 1940), through a careful rereading of Buchan's novels and correspondence. Whitney Lackenbauer traces the impact of Cold War militarization on Inuit and notes the anxiety of some *qallunaat* (non-Inuit) about the impacts of an expanding military footprint on northern residents. Myra Rutherdale studies different protagonists in the North but finds similar anxieties. The Westernized doctors and nurses sent to the Arctic by the Indian and Northern Health Services Branch soon learned of their limitations and began to appreciate more traditional medical practices. Both Lackenbauer and Rutherdale challenge the "totalization" framework of earlier studies; the process of interaction was not entirely controlled by the colonizers in a "total" imposition of European cultural norms.

The second section of this collection is called "Interraciality and Education." Here, the contributors raise questions about categories and categorization, past and present, in the context of the residential school system. In the process, they remind us that the schools were not exclusive to "Indian" children. Jean Barman looks at three schools in British Columbia, each run by a different religious denomination, to tell the story of how "interraciality" was negotiated. Who was "Indian" and who was "Métis" and what purpose(s) did different identities serve the various actors on the stage? Jonathan Anuik examines the range of lifelong impacts that prairie residential schools had on identity and self-image through the stories of four former pupils in the post–Second World War era. Their experiences are sometimes surprising.

The third section, "Law, Legislation, and History," includes essays on the role of the courts in both specific issues about Aboriginal rights and the more general questions of how the legal process shaped historical understanding. Bill Waiser revisits the myth of "Indian" participation in the 1885 Rebellion through the notorious court cases brought against Poundmaker and Big Bear. Frank Tough studies the legal proceedings concerning hunting and trapping rights of First Nations in the Ontario region covered by the Robinson Treaties to demonstrate the behind-the-scenes process by which treaty rights were eroded. Hamar Foster prods his readers to reconsider the Euro-Canadian assertion that there was no such thing as Indigenous law or Indigenous legal systems. Understanding the principles and practices of Indigenous law will lead to a far more reasonable appreciation, both in the courts and in Canadian society, of the history of Native-newcomer interaction. Ken Coates uses the 1999 Supreme Court decision in the *Marshall* case over Mi'kmaq fishing rights to demonstrate how a court case can provide both a platform for public engagement and a vehicle to "reclaim Indigenous history."

The final section in this collection is entitled "Anthropologists, Historians, and Indigenous Historiography." Keith Carlson uses an appreciation of the cultural dimensions of the history of Coast Salish peoples in British Columbia and a careful re-evaluation of the sources to challenge a number of scholarly conclusions about the Coast Salish and their responses to the arrival of Europeans. Dianne Newell and Arthur Ray consider how the ideas of early anthropologist Diamond Jenness remain influential in today's courts, eighty years after Jenness first published them and long after they have been challenged by other scholars. Anthropology, like history, is a tool that can serve many purposes.

The collection concludes with an essay by Alan Cairns, in which he reflects on the increasing politicization and polarization that has shaped the field of Indigenous history over the past generation. In his provocative assessment, he addresses the debate about whether non-Indigenous scholars can or should write about Indigenous pasts, and reflects on the need for reconciliation in an intellectual space where men and women, regardless of race or ethnicity, can exchange ideas. It is the hope of the contributors to this volume that it might help to open some windows on that intellectual space. For, as J.R. Miller once said,

> All my research on Native-newcomer relations has been motivated by one question: Why don't we get along? I'm always searching for the roots of this. Because if we can figure out the roots, we can work towards a solution.[20]

NOTES

1 Truth and Reconciliation Commission, *Final Report*, vol. 1, *Summary* (Toronto: James Lorimer, 2015), 6.

2 Ibid., 23.

3 James S. Frideres, *First Nations in the Twenty-First Century* (Oxford: Oxford University Press, 2011), 2–3.

4 Robin Fisher, *Contact and Conflict: Indian-European Relations in British Columbia, 1774–1890* (Vancouver: UBC Press, 1977); Cornelius Jaenen, *Friend and Foe: Aspects of French-Amerindian Cultural Contact in the Sixteenth and Seventeenth Centuries* (Toronto: McClelland and Stewart, 1976); Bruce Trigger, *The Children of Aataentsic: A History of the Huron People to 1660* (Montreal: McGill-Queen's University Press, 1976); Arthur Ray, *Indians in the Fur Trade: Their Role as Trappers, Hunters, and Middlemen in the Lands Southwest of Hudson Bay* (Toronto: University of Toronto Press, 1974); Arthur Ray and Donald Freeman, *"Give Us Good Measure": An Economic Analysis of Relations Between the Indians and the Hudson's Bay Company Before 1763* (Toronto: University of Toronto Press, 1978); Sylvia Van Kirk, *"Many Tender Ties": Women in Fur Trade Society in Western Canada, 1670–1870* (Winnipeg: Watson & Dwyer, [1980]); Jennifer Brown, *Strangers in Blood: Fur Trade Company Families in Indian Country* (Vancouver: UBC Press, 1980).

5 Miller's early publications include *Equal Rights: The Jesuits' Estates Act Controversy* (Montreal: McGill-Queen's University Press, 1979).

6 J.R. Miller, "The Irony of Residential Schooling," *Canadian Journal of Native Education* 14, no. 2 (1987): 3–14. See also Scott Trevithick, "Native Residential Schooling in Canada: A Review of the Literature," *Canadian Journal of Native Studies* 18, no. 1 (1998): 73–4.

7 The first edition was published in 1989, the second in 1991, and the third in 2000, all by the University of Toronto Press.

8 *Skyscrapers Hide the Heavens*, 3rd ed. (Toronto: University of Toronto Press, 2000), xiii, from the preface to the first edition.

9 *Shingwauk's Vision: A History of Native Residential Schools* (Toronto: University of Toronto Press, 1996). The book was awarded prizes by the Dafoe Foundation, the Canadian Association of Foundations of Education, the Canadian Historical Association, the Association for Canadian Studies, the Saskatchewan Writing Awards, and the Gustavus Myers Center for the Study of Bigotry and Human Rights.

10 Quoted on Social Sciences and Humanities Research Council (SSHRC), SSHRCC Impact Awards, Previous Winners, http://www.sshrc-crsh.gc.ca/results-resultats/prizes-prix/2010/gold_miller-or_miller-eng.aspx (consulted 24 August 2015).

11 Miller, *Shingwauk's Vision*, 345.

12 Robin Jarvis Brownlie and Mary-Ellen Kelm, "Desperately Seeking Absolution: Native Agency as Colonialist Alibi?" *Canadian Historical Review* 75, no. 4 (December 1994): 543–56. See also J.R. Miller and Douglas Cole, "Desperately Seeking Resolution: Responses and a Reply," *Canadian Historical Review* 76, no. 4 (December 1995): 628–43.

13 Kerry Abel, "Tangled, Lost, and Bitter? Current Directions in the Writing of Native History in Canada," *Acadiensis* 26, no. 1 (autumn 1996): 92–101. The books she discussed were Dianne Newell, *Tangled Webs of History: Indians and the Law in Canada's West Coast Fisheries* (Toronto: University of Toronto Press, 1993); Sarah Carter, *Lost Harvests: Prairie Indian Reserve Farmers and Government Indian Policy* (Montreal: McGill-Queen's University Press, 1990); and Denis Delâge, *Bitter Feast: Amerindians and Europeans in Northeast North America, 1600–64* (Vancouver: UBC Press, 1993).

14 For example, see William C. Wicken, *The Colonization of Mi'kmaw Memory and History, 1794–1928: The King v. Gabriel Sylliboy* (Toronto: University of Toronto Press, 2012); Julie Cruikshank, *Do Glaciers Listen? Local Knowledge, Colonial Encounters, and Social Imagination* (Vancouver: UBC Press, 2005); Cole Harris, *Making Native Space: Colonialism, Resistance, and Reserves in British Columbia* (Vancouver: UBC Press, 2002); Patrice Groulx, *Pièges de la mémoire: Dollard des Ormeaux, les Amérindiens et nous* (Hull, Quebec: Vents d'Ouest, 1998); Mary-Ellen Kelm, *Colonizing Bodies: Aboriginal Health and Healing in British Columbia, 1900–1950* (Vancouver: UBC Press, 1998); Sarah Carter, *Capturing Women: The Manipulation of Cultural Imagery in Canada's Prairie West* (Montreal: McGill-Queen's University Press, 1997).

15 Patrick Wolfe, *Settler Colonialism and the Transformation of Anthropology* (London: Cassell, 1999), 163.

16 Patrick Wolfe, "Settler Colonialism and the Elimination of the Native," *Journal of Genocide Research* 8, no. 4 (December 2006): 388.

17 Lorenzo Veracini, *Settler Colonialism: A Theoretical Overview* (Basingstoke: Palgrave Macmillan, 2010), particularly 14–15. It should be noted that some historians find the concept of settler colonialism an unnecessary affectation. See Nancy Shoemaker, "A Typology of Colonialism," in *Perspectives on History* (newsletter of the American Historical Association), October 2015.

18 Roxanne Dunbar-Ortiz, *An Indigenous Peoples' History of the United States* (Boston: Beacon Press, 2014), xi.

19 Veracini, *Settler Colonialism*, 15.

20 Quoted in a 2010 interview on Social Sciences and Humanities Research Council (SSHRC), SSHRCC Impact Awards, Previous Winners, http://www.sshrc-crsh.gc.ca/results-resultats/prizes-prix/2010/gold_miller-or_miller-eng.aspx (consulted 24 August 2015).

PART TWO

The Crown, Colonial Spaces, and Aboriginality

The Simcoes and the Indians

KERRY ABEL

It was a cheerful group that gathered at Navy Hall near Niagara on a fresh day in early June 1794 to celebrate the birthday of a dark-haired little boy who had charmed both the ladies and the officers of the garrison as much on his own account as for the fact that he was the lieutenant governor's son. One of the company had given the lad a miniature cannon that was used to good effect to fire a 21-gun salute, delighting the birthday boy with its sharp retorts. The adults in the assembly, however, were more taken with the boy's costume, a shirt and sash "which gave him somewhat the air of an Indian," in the words of his adoring mother.[1] It would not be the only time little Francis cut such a figure. "At Montreal," wrote his father to an older sister in England, "he thought himself so fine in his red stockings or Leggins & Indian cloak that he strutted as if he was twenty years old."[2] "He attends all their councils in his blanket and silver arm bands," reported his mother, adding that he did so "with great solemnity."[3] The chief justice of Upper Canada referred to him fondly as "the Great Chieftain,"[4] and when the lad, in high spirits, accurately imitated the dancing and singing of a visiting delegation of Seneca, his family was delighted, apparently at the innocence and exuberance. Others saw the performances differently. "The Governor is very anxious to oblige and please the Indians," recorded a French traveller. "His only son, a child four years old, is dressed as an Indian and called TIOGA, which name has been given him by the Mohawks. This harmless farce may be of use in the intercourse with the Indians."[5]

Indeed, the clothing worn by a toddler and his public performances as an "Indian" should be seen as neither "farce" nor "harmless." They represent an intersection of the public and private, a visible manifestation of the complex network of ideas and events into which John and Elizabeth Simcoe presented themselves. The role that they played would become both seminal and irrelevant to the working out of the relationship between Native and newcomer in British North America. As the first lieutenant governor of the new province of Upper Canada at a time when authority was still highly personal, John Graves Simcoe was in a position to mould the foundations for generations to come. There was more to him, the devoted husband of an educated, talented, and highly intelligent woman, than he presented to the public. Elizabeth Posthuma (Gwillim) Simcoe's observations of and participation in the events of the 1790s must also be considered if we are to understand fully their dynamics and why they continue to influence relations between Native and newcomer in the twenty-first century.[6] Their sympathies towards First Nations and their land rights were eventually lost in a tangle of local and international power struggles.

When the Simcoes stepped ashore at Quebec in November 1791, Indigenous affairs were already much on their minds. Before leaving England, Colonel Simcoe had consulted with Secretary of State Henry Dundas, who had been instructing Lord Dorchester, governor of the Canadas, to pay careful attention to the "Indian Nations": an "indispensable necessary." Indeed, Simcoe had determined to make that attention a top priority. He told Dundas that he intended to take up residence within easy access of Detroit, "where that discretion appears now most necessary to be exercised," a point that met with Dundas's approbation and was conveyed to Dorchester without request for comment or approval.[7] Simcoe had also consulted with his friend Hugh Percy, the Duke of Northumberland, and carried with him a letter of introduction from Northumberland to Joseph Brant of the Six Nations in Upper Canada. The gift of a brace of pistols accompanied the letter, in which Northumberland praised Simcoe earnestly and highly:

> I must particularly recommend the Colonel to you and the nation. He is a most intimate friend of mine, and is possessed of every good quality which can recommend him to your friendship. He is brave, humane, sensible, and honest ... He loves and honours the Indians, whose noble sentiments so perfectly correspond with his own. In short, he is worthy to be a Mohawk.[8]

The new lieutenant governor was, in fact, already well acquainted with some of the "Indian nations" of eastern North America. During the American Revolutionary War, he had served for nearly five years in command of the Queen's Rangers, a light infantry unit of colonial volunteers who patrolled, escorted, and fought in the countryside of Pennsylvania, New Jersey, South Carolina, and Virginia. There he learned the techniques of camouflage and surprise, strategies that more resembled Indigenous warfare than the battlefield order of Europe in which he had been trained. His men had fought both with and against Indigenous warriors; in his memoirs, Simcoe wrote of them as "excellent marksmen" and "gallant" fighters, noting by name the "chieftain" Nimham who succeeded in wounding him in an ambush at Kingsbridge in August 1778.[9] One American popular legend even has it that Simcoe refused to permit his men to cut down a certain elm tree for firewood because it was reputed to be the site where William Penn had made a treaty with a local nation in 1682.[10]

What Simcoe had learned about Indigenous Americans during that war and later in conversations with colleagues in England seems to have been interpreted through the filter that coloured so much of his world view: an admiration for the philosophy and values of ancient Rome. As were so many of his generation and class, he was fascinated by the art, architecture, history, ethos, and literature of the ancient world, admiring any vestiges of it that he believed he saw in his contemporary surroundings. He modelled himself after the military governors of ancient Rome and memorized endless Latin poetry. He sought out archaeological vestiges of the Roman Empire in Britain and purchased one property solely on the conviction that the ruins on it were of Roman origin. And in the leading chiefs of eastern North America, he saw the same values of dignity, honour, courage, and martial bearing that he fancied had shaped the Roman Empire. Simcoe's savage was noble because he was Roman. His wife Elizabeth shared his admiration for things ancient and was also a reader of Jean Jacques Rousseau, even following him in the rearing of her children. Undoubtedly she had formed some preconceptions of the "Indian" long before she actually met the real thing. And once she did, she too was quick to find parallels with the ancient world. "I have often observed," she recorded in 1794, "that when the Indians speak their air & action is more like that of Greek or Roman Orators than of Modern Nations. They have a great deal of impressive action, & look like the figures presented by the Old Masters."[11] She likened the sad scene of two Indian widows and their children lamenting their loss to the story of Sisygambis, a Persian princess who starved to death in her grief after the death of Alexander the Great.[12]

Because of his haste to take on the position of lieutenant governor, Simcoe arrived at Quebec long before the rest of his entourage, which consisted in part of members of his executive council. Without a quorum, he decided to winter at Quebec and took advantage of the time to read and consult. He struck up a close relationship with Alexander McKee, who had been a member of the Indian Department since 1760 and was married to a Shawnee woman through whom he had extensive contacts and influence in the Detroit hinterland. Simcoe found McKee's ideas about "Indian" policy much closer to his own than those of Governor Lord Dorchester, with whom Simcoe had maintained a long acrimony both personal and professional. Even before his swearing-in ceremony, Simcoe's first official act (after a proclamation outlining his land grant plans) was to send a surveyor to investigate complaints from the Mississauga people regarding the boundaries of a tract they had sold in 1784 north of Lake Erie.[13] He proposed an immediate trip to the American Congress to mediate "for the Indians" whose rights Simcoe felt were being abused in the new republic.[14] He also responded quickly to correspondence from Joseph Brant, who had been pressuring Lord Dorchester (without success) for a title deed to the lands along the Grand River that had been set aside for the Six Nations in the Haldimand Grant of 1784. Simcoe assured Brant that he was prepared to arrange a deed,[15] but the matter would have to wait until his executive councillors arrived from England and the new administration had been formally constituted. As he would write shortly to his counterpart in Lower Canada, "the giving of the Indians legal title to their possessions will be one of the first objects of the consideration of this Government."[16] When Simcoe and his family finally arrived at Niagara on 26 July 1792, he intended to leave immediately to investigate Indigenous affairs in the western districts. The trip was briefly delayed because of a visit by Prince Edward to Niagara; as soon as the royal entourage departed, Simcoe was on his way to Detroit.

Detroit was then at the centre of a maelstrom, stormy waves from which were threatening to engulf all of what was left to the British in North America. As the supply and distribution point for an extensive network of trade and alliance in the Ohio country between traders operating out of Montreal and a dozen powerful Indigenous nations, it was economically vital to British Quebec. Perhaps more important to those in the London halls of power, it was politically vital as well. Without Indigenous allies, the British realized they could not hold the territories that remained to them after the American Revolutionary War, and those allies were reliable only so long as the British protected their Ohio lands from rapacious American settlers. In 1778, an American army had seized British posts along the Ohio River and the Americans now claimed the Ohio country on the grounds that they had defeated the British and their Indigenous allies in war. The British realized that if they handed over the Ohio country, they would not only lose their Indigenous alliances but also potentially find warriors turning on the British settlements and scattered garrisons. So London stalled. British soldiers and Indian Department personnel continued to occupy strategic northwest posts on the pretext that the Americans had not yet returned property seized from Loyalists as had been promised in the Treaty of Paris (1783). The British would remain until Loyalist property was returned or the state of Indigenous affairs in the Ohio country was otherwise resolved.

The Ohio country was a vital centre to Indigenous political interests as well. Native refugees from the Revolutionary War had been spilling into the region, where they were now working to establish new farms and villages and rebuild their lives. The mid-1780s found Miami, Shawnee, Delaware, Ottawa, Chippewa, Potawatomi, Huron (Wyandot), some Six Nations, and others in an uneasy alliance. Arrayed against them were American settlers who refused to recognize their federal government's authority in Indian Affairs and particularly its attempt to regulate land sales and surrenders.[17] Small-scale warfare had become endemic as the Americans tried to assert control of the lands. Joseph Brant, the Mohawk who had risen to prominence during the revolution, was playing a game of his own in the region, promoting a general confederacy largely as a means to maintain the sphere of influence that the Haudenosaunee had extended there in the seventeenth century. The Algonkians in Ohio mistrusted Brant for that reason but also realized the necessity of unity in the face of the American threat, and they recognized the value of the Haudenosaunee's long history with (and better knowledge of) both American and British politics.[18] Between 1783 and 1786, the seeds of a new confederacy had been planted and nurtured in the Ohio country but it was a contentious arrangement at best.

In 1784, the infant American government decided to try diplomacy to gain control of the Ohio country. It quickly learned that the various nations were not willing to negotiate away their lands. The "Treaty" of Fort Stanwix was all the Americans could obtain, "negotiated" at gunpoint, signed after key players such as Joseph Brant had walked out, and formally rejected within two years by the Haudenosaunee. Yet the Americans claimed they had obtained peace with the Six Nations, who had allegedly ceded their interests in the western lands in return for a reservation in New York. The following year, American delegates attempted to make a similar agreement with the Wyandot, Delaware, Ottawa, and Chippewa at Fort McIntosh; again the "treaty" was quickly repudiated by those who had not signed. In 1786, American commissioners met with the Shawnee of the Miami (Maumee) country; the third "treaty" had all the same problems as its predecessors. Nothing had been resolved, yet the American government and local settler populations alike proceeded as if the territory was now rightfully theirs. The Haudenosaunee and Ohio nations continued to pressure the British to come to their aid, as one would expect from an ally. Officials in London were well aware of the calls but were in no position financially or militarily to risk a renewal of war with the Americans. Subtle diplomacy and secret aid were all the ministry in London was willing to offer.

Obedient to orders as any good army officer should be, Simcoe was nonetheless personally concerned about the complex net of relationships in the Ohio country. In the fall of 1790, American general Josiah Harmar had been soundly defeated in an attempt to destroy the main Miami village, and in early November 1791, Indigenous warriors had routed American general Arthur St Clair and his army at Fort Recovery (near Fort Jefferson).[19] Now the various Indigenous nations were converging at a Shawnee village known as "the Glaize" at the confluence of the Maumee and Auglaize Rivers in northwestern Ohio (now the site of Defiance, Ohio, near Toledo). Here, they debated their response to American peace overtures. Hardliners among the Algonkian nations (particularly the Shawnee, Miami, and Delaware) would settle for nothing less than American recognition that the lands west and north of the Ohio River were Indian Territory, as guaranteed in the Proclamation of 1763 and recognized by an agreement at Fort Stanwix in 1768. The Six Nations, including Joseph Brant, were willing to compromise with a boundary farther west. Simcoe learned of a formal conference to be held at the Glaize and made haste to attend it himself. There on 30 September 1792, he heard speakers such as the Shawnee leader Painted Pole and the Delaware Buckongahelas call for unity among all the nations and the rejection of American ideas about "civilization" programs. They called for instead the "recapture" of "sacred power." Not all agreed. When Seneca chief Cowkiller called for peace with the Americans, he was taken to task by Elder Brother of the Six Nations.[20]

The assembly eventually addressed Simcoe directly, requesting a copy of the 1783 treaty between the British and Americans "to vindicate our claims" and asking Simcoe to attend the forthcoming council with the Americans at Sandusky as a stand-in for the king. Simcoe replied that he would do his utmost to assist and would obtain permission from the king to attend the council provided that the Americans agreed. He also encouraged the assembly to make peace with the Americans because he realized that another American war would be disastrous for the still undefended Upper Canada. His answer was deliberately vague because he appreciated the delicacy of the situation. He needed to maintain the alliance by offering some semblance of support, but he also needed to keep the Americans happy by not appearing to meddle too far in the issue. Indeed, the Americans were already alarmed at his movements, and protests were being raised officially, unofficially, and in the press. Simcoe had also become convinced of the value of an Indigenous buffer state in the Ohio country as a sort of shield against American aggression at least until such time as his plans for the defence of Upper Canada had materialized.[21]

Simcoe was impressed by what he witnessed at the Glaize; the encounter reinforced his developing ideas about Indian policy. Historian Alan Taylor has proposed that Simcoe "meant to treat Indians as military auxiliaries rather than autonomous peoples,"[22] but even if Simcoe had originally considered that position, it had clearly changed. With the particularity of a soldier-strategist, Simcoe had researched the legal arguments, which he explained in a letter to Henry Dundas. The Treaty of Utrecht (1713) was, for Simcoe, the "definitive construction" of relations between European powers and the Indigenous peoples of North America. He read the treaty as recognizing the Indians as *"free Nations,"* thereby acknowledging that they had the same rights and liberties as all independent nations.[23] Indeed, he considered the Seven Years' War to have been occasioned in America by the French violation of one of these rights – that of the commercial freedom of the Indigenous peoples to trade with whomever they chose. Simcoe believed that the Proclamation of 1763 had reinforced the concept of independent nations and that Indian Superintendent Sir William Johnson had acknowledged it formally that same year. Furthermore, Simcoe was well aware that the Indigenous people themselves had a strong "sense of their own Independency," and quoted a Seneca chief who told the British commanding officer at Niagara, "We are a free people and accustomed to sell whatever we have to whom and where we like best."[24]

Of course, there was a strong measure of self-serving rationalization here. The Canadian merchants at Montreal were lobbying hard to encourage the British to maintain the Ohio country posts, so the right of the nations to trade freely also implied the right of the British to trade with those nations. More important to Simcoe personally was his determination that an Indigenous buffer state between the United States and British North America made military sense, and he was, after all, a military man. He urged his superiors to call on the Americans to recognize the Indigenous boundary claims as soon as possible. Otherwise, he wrote, "I am convinced Great Britain will sooner or later be forced into a contest deprived of assistance in the Indians being subdued and probably turned against her."[25] Simcoe was extremely disappointed by the ministerial decision to remain silent on the issue.

After the Glaize council, Simcoe set to work to address issues closer to home. He was outraged to discover that a woman named Sally (Sarah) Ainse had been trying unsuccessfully to obtain title to a large tract of land she had purchased on the Thames River in 1788 from the "Ochique" (Mississauga). Sally Ainse was a wealthy trader of probable Shawnee or Oneida ancestry, widow of an interpreter for the British, and a woman with a considerable network of relatives and influence among both the Delaware and Six Nations. The land board at Detroit had been holding up her petition for a title deed on the grounds that the sale had not followed the requirements of the Proclamation of 1763[26] and that Indian Agent Alexander McKee (who was also a member of the land board) had purchased the land on behalf of the British government for other purposes. Ainse argued that her claim was supported by all the local headmen, who later told McKee "that their sister, Sarah Ainse, had always used them well and this tract must be reserved for her."[27] Simcoe stepped in and directed an order-in-council (17 October 1792) to approve her application for eight lots in the tract. When the land board refused to act on the order, Simcoe and his executive council attempted to settle the issue through negotiation. Unfortunately, by the time he left the province in 1796, little had changed. The Ainse affair pitted Simcoe against his trusted advisor Alexander McKee; Simcoe demonstrated by his actions that he was prepared to put his principles against the pressures of a personal connection. Clearly, too, Simcoe recognized the necessity of keeping Sally Ainse's network of supporters happy at a time when British interests relied so heavily upon their support.

Believing that the Sally Ainse affair was settled, Simcoe turned his attention to the situation of the Mississauga, a branch of the Chippewa/Ojibwe who lived in the lands along the north shores of Lakes Ontario and Erie. Governor Haldimand's officials had negotiated with some of them in 1784–5 to release lands for the settlement of refugees from the American Revolutionary War. Simcoe realized that his plans for a provincial capital on the River la Tranche (now the Thames River), as well as other plans for military defences and transport routes, would require new negotiations with bands living farther inland. But even as he was making plans for these talks, word reached him of extensive dissatisfaction with the earlier agreements. He began to deal with those first.

In May 1784, the Mississauga had agreed to sell a tract of land from Niagara to La Tranche; surveyors had subsequently discovered the description in the agreement was geographically impossible. So on 7 December 1792, Simcoe convened a grand council at Navy Hall (Niagara) to renegotiate with a corrected description. This time, the Mississauga also agreed to allow the king's representatives to make roads and have free passage of the waterways through Mississauga lands for both trade and "king's purposes." A sum of slightly more than £1180 was to be paid (apparently as had been promised in the original), with an additional five shillings presumably in consideration of the delay and additional provisions. The document would later be designated as Treaty No. 3.[28] The event did not register in Elizabeth Simcoe's diary, although a dinner at which she hosted Joseph Brant a few days later did. Undoubtedly the domestic setting provided a convivial opportunity to discuss recent developments.

Shortly afterward, Simcoe finalized (or so he thought) two agreements in which the Crown granted land instead of receiving it. On 14 January 1793, Treaty No. 4 was signed at Navy Hall, conveying lands along the Grand River to the Six Nations to formalize the promises made in the 1784 Haldimand Grant. The agreement included a proviso that the Six Nations could not sell these lands except to themselves or to the Crown at a public meeting, following the principles laid down in the Proclamation of 1763. Three months later, Simcoe met another Six Nations delegation at Navy Hall to grant a tract of land on the Bay of Quinte under terms similar to those of the Grand River grant. Later designated Treaty No. 3½, it guaranteed the lands to be free of "Rents, Fines, or Services" in perpetuity and promised them for the "sole use and behoof" of the Six Nations "for ever."[29]

Simcoe, a stickler for both precision and justice, was very concerned that all these arrangements be clear, accurate, fair, and satisfactory to all concerned. With tension rising in the Ohio country, he could ill afford to alienate the Six Nations or anger the Mississauga and Ojibwe on his doorstep. Indeed, the latter were already growing restive. As historian Robert Allen put it, "By the mid-1790s, the Mississauga had come to the painful realization that the loss of their lands, combined with the rapid growth of settlement, was destroying the basic economic and cultural fabric of their lives."[30] There were several immediate manifestations of the growing unrest.

One of Simcoe's central plans for the defence of Upper Canada involved the development of a route from Lake Ontario to the inland lake he had modestly chosen to rename for his father, then on to Georgian Bay at Penetanguishene harbour. He believed these lands had been ceded through a purchase in 1784–5. However, surveyors at Lake Simcoe in the winter of 1793–4 were accosted by a group of Chippewa and Mississauga who said "they had no knowledge of the sale of these lands" and insisted that they accompany the survey party to keep an eye on its activities.[31] That summer, a similar problem arose with the surveyors sent to the Thames River to begin mapping in preparation for the laying out of Simcoe's new capital. When the surveyors explained that the sale there had been signed by Wabagonoing, the people there dismissed him as "an old woman" whose band had "no right to those lands."[32]

Concerned, Simcoe began an investigation. He spoke with (among others) a "Mr. Ferguson," likely John Ferguson, the Indian agent at Kingston who was also the son-in-law of respected Mohawk matron Molly Brant. Simcoe discovered that there were no documents at hand pertaining to any of these agreements and, worse, the deed to the sale of lands at Matchedash Bay (at the southern end of Georgian Bay) appeared to consist of a blank piece of paper with only the headmen's signatures affixed thereto.[33] Simcoe repeatedly sent to Lord Dorchester for copies of any documents that might be found "in the Archives of Lower Canada" or in the Indian Department files at Montreal; in particular, he wanted original or authenticated copies.[34] There was no response. Increasingly annoyed, Simcoe demanded at one point that Dorchester order Superintendent of Indian Affairs Sir John Johnson "to proceed without loss of time to settle these disputes, which … might be the ruin of this province."[35] Significantly, Simcoe seemed to have been coming to the conclusion that the First Nations' allegations about these "treaties" were true, and the fault lay with the Indian Department and its officials.

Simcoe was by now utterly frustrated with the system of managing Indian Affairs in the Canadas. He had concluded that "incompetence," "abuses," and outright fraud were at the root of these and other complaints. The Indian Department was rotten from the roots to the tip, and no one (by whom he meant Governor Dorchester) had been willing to take the situation in hand. Part of the problem was personal animosity between Simcoe and Dorchester, and between Simcoe and Johnson – the last in particular hated Simcoe because Johnson had expected to be appointed lieutenant governor of Upper Canada himself. The awkward division of authority and power was also a problem. The superintendent general of Indian Affairs was based at Montreal, did little travelling in Upper Canada, and was disinclined to report to or coordinate with the Upper Canadian administration. But Simcoe was also correct to note that incompetence, sloppiness, and the pursuit of personal gain at the expense of the public good ran rampant.

In early September 1794, he wrote a lengthy memorandum to the Committee of the Privy Council for Trade and Plantations on the subject, in which he detailed specific proposals for reorganizing the administration of Indian Affairs. Colonial laws needed to be passed to prevent "encroachments" on Indigenous lands and "abuses" of Indigenous traders. The Indian Department in Upper Canada should be relegated to the care of "lesser duties" such as supervision of the department stores and the annual ceremony to renew the Covenant Chain agreement.[36] A senior official in the Indian Department (he recommended Alexander McKee as the deputy superintendent general) should have a seat on the Legislative Council to ensure that high-level communications were maintained at all times. The custom of renewing alliances with gifts should be regularized, with gifts delivered "at stated times" to all nations, not simply a select few. The ceremonies should be structured so as to make clear to the participants that the king was the provider, not local officials. These annual ceremonies should also serve as an opportunity for the invited chiefs "to reconcile their respective differences, to receive advice, and to renew their Friendship with the King's People." Traders had to be regulated, and Canadians from Montreal or Detroit should not be placed in positions of authority in the department because their loyalty to Britain was "doubtful." Furthermore, agents should be paid regular and sufficient salaries to ensure their loyalty to the Crown and lessen the temptation to profit on the side.[37] A few months later, Simcoe expanded on some of these ideas in a long letter to Lord Dorchester. The lieutenant governor should personally superintend "the various concerns of the Indian Nations," oversee expenditures, and manage "the delivery of the annual presents."

He also proposed that a permanent "Council House" be built in London, his proposed government seat, where the annual councils and gift-giving ceremonies could be held, and where the various nations could discuss and reconcile their problems (both among themselves and with the Crown). Local magistrates from across the province should attend these councils so as to get to know the First Nations in their districts and to act as witnesses to help prevent fraud. In short, a "uniform system" should replace the current "casual and fluctuating system." The goal was to promote unity among the First Nations, cement the alliance with the king, eliminate fraud and improper spending, and bring the agents and superintendents under control.[38] As Simcoe explained to the Duke of Portland, because "the power exercised by the Superintendants [*sic*]" was "unknown to the British Constitution," they could act too easily without "the King's authority." He went on:

> I need not enter into the detail of Indian Superintendants [*sic*]; their Want of Education, Ignorance of all but the sperate [*sic*] Nations, upon an interest with whom, their own consequence is grafted, their immoral Habits, and the Indolence and depravity which in them, seems to ... disable them from *unnecessary* confidence.[39]

It may have appeared to Simcoe that Lord Dorchester was utterly passive regarding Indigenous affairs, but in February 1794, Dorchester took a decisive step that created shockwaves back and forth across the Atlantic. Matters in the Ohio country were not going well. The frontier war continued while, after much manoeuvring and debate both in public and behind the scenes, a great council had finally been held between the First Nations and three high-level American commissioners at the Glaize in the summer of 1793. Still the nations were divided about land policy, with the majority of the more southerly groups deciding to take a hard line on their ownership of the Ohio lands, while Joseph Brant and his supporters continued to promote a compromise boundary. In the end, all that everyone could agree upon was to meet again in the spring.[40] Through the fall and winter, councils were held by various groups to try to reach agreement on strategies and positions, while British Indian agents and military officers did their best to reinforce the idea that the British were doing all they could (short of a military expedition) to live up to their side of the alliance.[41]

Dorchester appears to have decided that the subtle approach was insufficient. On his own initiative, he delivered a speech to the Seven

Nations of Canada on 11 February 1794 in which he claimed that war between the British and Americans was inevitable and left the clear impression that in the event of such a war, the First Nations could rely on British support for their aims.[42] Dorchester conveyed a copy of this speech to Simcoe and instructed Simcoe to begin shoring up positions in the Detroit hinterland, starting with the reoccupation of abandoned posts along the Maumee River. This was to be no casual deployment of Indian Department personnel. Simcoe was instructed to

> order such Force (as you think of the proper size) from Detroit to the Miamis River ... as soon as the Season & other Circumstances will permit ... it may not be amiss to consider what Reinforcements you may draw from other Parts within your Command ... and what Assistance you may have from the Militia; also whether by collecting all the Force in your power to assemble you would be in a condition to resist [American general] Wayne's attack should he attempt by Force to take possession of the country.[43]

Simcoe was outraged. For months without success, he had been trying to convince Dorchester of the necessity of building a defensive strategy for Upper Canada. Now Dorchester was ordering a plan that Simcoe considered strategically foolish. So Simcoe bypassed the chain of command (almost unthinkable for a military man of his ilk) and wrote immediately to Secretary of State Henry Dundas, complaining that if he were to follow Dorchester's instructions, "it would effectually disable me in case of hostilities ... for the safety of the Colony entrusted to my charge." Simcoe was tormented by the dilemma. He was, he wrote, "anxious ... on the one hand not to incur the censure of a breach of subordination; and on the other being determined not to abandon the Province to a merciless enemy."[44] A few weeks later, Simcoe had resolved the problem in his own conscience: he would obey Dorchester's orders but under protest.[45]

Simcoe was not the only person to be highly agitated by Dorchester's sudden and unexpected moves. A good number of American newspapers reprinted the text of Dorchester's speech, and American secretary of state Edmund Randolph wrote an official diplomatic note of protest to George Hammond (first British minister to the United States of America). He also demanded to know whether the president's intelligence was correct that "Governor" Simcoe and the good part of a British regiment were proceeding to the Maumee to build a fort. Hammond acknowledged Dorchester's speech but was evasive on Simcoe's whereabouts.[46] Almost simultaneously, the US *Gazette* published a letter conveying intelligence from Sandusky that Simcoe and two Indian agents "were visiting all the Indian towns in that quarter and exciting them there to continue their opposition to the Americans" while promising support from the king. "They were preparing for fighting Gen. Wayne the moment he moved," the writer added, and "the British were erecting garrisons on the Miami River."[47] The affair mushroomed suddenly into an international incident, raising the war fever more than a few degrees on both sides of the Atlantic. Simcoe would later be vilified by his opponents in England for his actions, which pained him greatly because he had disagreed with the plan from its inception.

In deference to Dorchester's instructions, Simcoe and his party arrived at Detroit on 2 April, then headed upriver to the site of a former post at the Maumee Rapids, which he had determined to rebuild and garrison in hopes that he could at least cut off the supply lines of an advancing American army. While his men were at work, he held extensive private consultations with Alexander McKee, whose home and family were nearby, and presented Dorchester's speech to the area First Nations. While he may have doubted the military wisdom of Dorchester's actions, he could not deny that their impact was quick and "positive" on the Indigenous people, who were finally beginning to see the kind of concrete response they had long been demanding. Within weeks, warriors had begun to gather at the Glaize, united in their determination to prevent an American advance (which local intelligence suggested was being prepared) and hopeful of British military support. An important Seneca named Cornplanter declared Simcoe "his best *Friend*."[48] And the lieutenant governor eventually received a letter from Henry Dundas that seemed to approve Simcoe's "very prudent and pacific line of Conduct," a curious phrase that, as historian Reginald Horsman has pointed out, scarcely reflected the operations of the British Indian Department out of Detroit.[49] Perhaps it was code for approval of Simcoe's dealings with Dorchester, who had come under attack in London for his very *imprudent* line of conduct.

At any rate, by midsummer, Simcoe was anxious again about his own activities, having learned of the public row they had generated in the United States and having received a note from Colonel R.G. England (officer commanding at Detroit) reporting that recent letters he had received from across the Atlantic were troubling. "Entre nous," wrote England, "We don't see anything from home that justifies His

Excellency's Speech to the Indians."[50] Simcoe then wrote to Henry Dundas, complaining about Lord Dorchester and pointing out that, in constructing the Miami fort and taking other controversial actions, he had only been following Dorchester's orders.[51] He wrote directly to Dorchester several times, asking for clarifications and explanations of the orders, expressing his concerns about the American response, and pointing out that he considered the situation now to be "peculiar and unpleasant."[52]

Indeed it was. Four days after that comment was written, General Wayne led his army towards the new fort at the rapids of the Maumee and routed the Indigenous warriors at a place known as Fallen Timbers, mutilating the bodies of their dead, then laying waste the homes and crops in the vicinity in a wild rampage that further drove in the point. The name of the battle site was oddly appropriate. The great forest of pan-Indian forces was knocked to the ground and hope for a First Nations territory northwest of the Ohio River was laid waste. Relations between the nations and the British were profoundly damaged as well. While senior British agents had been present at the battle, they had taken care to act as observers only. And when the retreating Indigenous warriors clamoured for safety within the walls of Fort Miami, they had been refused admission. As historian Reginald Horsman observed, the people "were long to remember the British closing of Fort Miami."[53] The representatives of the English king had made it clear that their interests lay more in preventing war between Britain and the United States than in assisting the First Nations in their goal of preserving Indigenous territory. It is hardly surprising that Simcoe failed in subsequent meetings with various Ohio nations to convince them to remain united and allied to the British interests.

Even as General Wayne was using military might to pursue American policy goals, John Jay was in London wining and dining on the diplomacy circuit. The news of his momentous treaty was sent to Simcoe on 19 November 1794, although an American "privateer" captured the ship carrying it,[54] so it was not until the spring of 1795 that Simcoe was fully aware of the provisions of Jay's Treaty and the requirement that all British troops be withdrawn from American territory by 1 June 1796. Lieutenant Governor Simcoe now turned his energies to appeasing the First Nations.[55] He attempted to put matters in the best possible light by claiming the new treaty reiterated the principles of the Treaty of Paris (1763), which he claimed recognized the rights of all First Nations as independent peoples, and thereby guaranteed them the right to trade with whomever they pleased. Jay's Treaty reinforced the point by guaranteeing them the right to cross the new borders with their own goods without having to pay duty or tax. Although Simcoe was addressing only issues of trade and commerce, it is not difficult to see how the First Nations audience, including Joseph Brant, heard in his words a recognition of much broader principles. As Brant put it, "We are happy to hear that the late Treaty has preserved our rights as a free and Independent people entire."[56]

Having been ordered out of the Ohio country, Simcoe was now more than ever concerned about keeping the nations within the borders of Upper Canada content, and it seemed his biggest problem was with the Six Nations settlement along the Grand River. In Joseph Brant, Simcoe recognized a man of subtle strategic mind, a man who could be extremely valuable as an ally and friend, but also a man who could be utterly formidable as an opponent. "It is difficult to deal with him," wrote Simcoe in 1793, "but I shall leave no method untried to conciliate his regard which is not only due to his many good qualities, his former services, and the real influence he has, but in a more especial manner to the very high opinion that the people of the United States most certainly entertain of him."[57] Perhaps it helped that Brant was as contemptuous of Sir John Johnson and his cohorts in the Indian Department as Simcoe was.[58] Elizabeth Simcoe shared her husband's mixed feelings about Brant. While she admired his bearing and social skills and always referred to him respectfully as "Captain Brant," she also wrote, "He has a countenance expressive of art or cunning." The Simcoes' courting of Brant included regular visits with Brant's two younger sons, who were encouraged to play with little Francis Simcoe. The Brant boys sometimes stayed overnight without their parents in the Simcoe household. They were "fine children" according to Mrs Simcoe.[59]

Land along the Grand River had been granted to the Six Nations through Governor Haldimand and something called a "licence of occupation" in 1784. Joseph Brant had begun petitioning almost immediately for a regular land title deed; nothing had materialized for a decade. So when Simcoe arrived at Quebec, Brant corresponded with him urgently on the subject. Simcoe assured Brant that he would give the matter his full attention, and indeed, when he arrived in Upper Canada, he convened a council (on 14 January 1793) to ratify in public a deed drawn up in accordance with instructions from Haldimand and Dorchester. In it, Simcoe offered "the sole use ... for ever freely and clearly of all and from all and all manner of Rents, fines, and services whatever" the "full and entire possession use benefit and advantage" of the defined district. However, lands could be alienated only to the Crown in accordance with the provisions of the Proclamation of 1763.[60] The council did not go well. "This Deed was peremptorily refused by Captain Brant," reported Simcoe, "as it did not contain within it a power for the Indians to lease their lands." As Brant explained, his people could no longer support themselves by hunting, while farms alone could not support the elderly and the very young. Income from leased land was a necessity. Others among the Six Nations petitioned Simcoe to sell some of the lands but Simcoe refused, fearing that Sir John Johnson was manipulating them because he wanted the land for himself. "Very improper," sniffed Simcoe.[61]

Lord Dorchester told Simcoe that Brant's call for a full and regular title deed could not be met. It would be wrong "to suffer this Tract to get into the hands of Land Jobbers," he explained. "If it must be resold, the Crown should repurchase it."[62] At the same time, both Dorchester and Simcoe fully realized the need to keep Brant and his people satisfied, given their central place in the delicate international situation. The matter stalled.

The winter of 1794–5 was so mild that deer could not be tracked and the Grand River settlement suffered. Brant decided to take matters into his own hands and at the beginning of March sold a tract of twelve square miles to a group of white men from Fort Erie. Provincial secretary and registrar William Jarvis duly recorded the sale.[63] Not long afterward, Brant also held a public auction to sell more land,[64] quite possibly a strategy to force the British officials into compliance, since a public sale implied community consent, negating concerns that Brant was acting in his own interests. Simcoe attended a council at Grand River that October and promised to resubmit the question to Lord Dorchester. At the end of January 1796, Dorchester sent Simcoe the draft of yet another deed for the Six Nations. This one conceded the right of the people to lease land in the tract, but required them to give notice of their intentions to the governor and reserve what was essentially the right of first refusal to the Crown. "I must say that I see no reason why the Indians being patentees of these lands, may not lease them," explained Dorchester, "as those of the Sault St. Louis have done theirs."[65] It seems that the attorney general of Lower Canada had considered and rejected another option: "to Grant the Tract to the Superintendent General of Indian Affairs to be held by him and his successors in office in fee, but in Trust to the use of the Six Nations." The idea directly foreshadowed post-Confederation

Canadian government thinking on the subject of Indian reserve lands. But in 1796, the attorney general had rejected the idea. "This plan upon reflection I do not think advisable," he had written.[66] Instead, the idea was to prevent the Grand River people from selling the land by offering a compromise: they could lease it for 999-year terms.

Simcoe received the new deed and duly promised to present it to the Six Nations but was now himself highly dissatisfied with it. The chief justice of Upper Canada advised him that "such a power of leasing" was probably "incompatible with the laws of England"; Simcoe concluded that a special act of the British Parliament would be required to enable it.[67] Nevertheless, he believed that promises made to the Six Nations must be fully carried out, and policy regarding them "rather enlarged than diminished."[68] Accordingly he conveyed the new deed to Brant for his consideration with a very positive recommendation and no mention of the possible legal issues. "It is unnecessary for me to observe," he wrote, "that a lease for nearly one thousand years is full as valuable in the market as an absolute sale."[69]

Joseph Brant found fault with this latest proposal because a new complication had arisen. He had recently learned that some Seneca living on the American side of the border were expressing their opposition to his plans to lease Six Nations' land. They believed that the Haudenosaunee as a whole had to be consulted in such matters, and any revenues should accrue to the entire Confederacy, not just to those living at Grand River.[70] So Brant now demanded that the deed recognize only the Grand River settlers as owners of the tract, not the Six Nations as a whole. Frustrated, he hinted not so subtly, "if something is not done more satisfactory than has been hitherto, he will not mention the matter again, but take it wholly into their own hands, and do what they think best with the Land."[71] Simcoe responded with a new compromise proposal. Deeds would be formally prepared for those who had made land deals with Brant if these tracts were first formally surrendered to the king (as required by the Proclamation of 1763) and properly surveyed. Brant reluctantly agreed.

By now, the question of ownership rights had become intertwined with the issue of exactly which lands had been set aside for the Six Nations. A survey of the tract had been completed shortly before Simcoe's appointment as lieutenant governor, but from the beginning, there had been disagreements over whether the Haldimand Grant included a tract of land at the northern headwaters of the Grand River, and whether the boundaries were supposed to follow the natural curves of the river or run in straight lines down to the lake. So in the summer of 1796, Brant seized the opportunity of the surveyors' presence to request a survey of the controversial northern section. Now it seemed that Simcoe, not Dorchester, was in favour of limiting the interests of the Six Nations. "The survey of the lands at the Grand River during Colonel Gordon's command was at that time made with the perfect acquiescence of Brant and the Chiefs of the Grand River," Simcoe observed.[72] In his view, Brant was simply being querulous. The tract should stand as originally surveyed. Why Simcoe's apparent about-face on the general principle of liberal interpretation?

In part, it was because Simcoe was concerned that Brant wanted these lands for hunting purposes and Simcoe believed that such a large, uncultivated tract would be bad for the interests of the province as a whole.[73] Equally important was Simcoe's increasing concern about Brant's various activities. "I have long been acquainted with Brant's views of setting up an Indian Interest, separate from the controul or influence of His Majesty's Servants," he explained to Lord Dorchester. He was concerned that Brant wanted to make the Grand River settlement a barrier between the British and the "western" (Ohio) Indians for Brant's own strategic interests.[74] Being well aware of the animosity between the Ohio nations and Brant, he feared both a loss of British political influence in Ohio (still believing it might someday be returned to the fold) and a loss of the economic value of the trade there if the Six Nations became middlemen or worse. Simcoe also knew that Brant did not have the full support of the Six Nations both at Grand River and elsewhere for the land-lease program. Indeed, in 1794, Simcoe had devoted some considerable energy to encourage better relations between Brant and the Seneca.[75] Finally, Simcoe had come to see Brant as a power threat. "He prefers the British, in a certain degree, to the people of the United States," he explained, "yet I cannot but consider the use He has made of his Power to be the subject of just alarm and that it is necessary by degrees and on just principles that it should be diminished." He went on to note that Brant had "made an Artful use" of his position by "the almost guidance of the Superintendant [*sic*] General's Office as far as the Six Nations have been concerned," and had made it appear to his people that he alone was "the dispenser of His Majesty's Bounty."[76] The First Nations would never be firm allies to the British if they believed that Joseph Brant had more to offer.

It may well be that Simcoe's own strategic and diplomatic manoeuvring succeeded in keeping something of a check on Brant, for it was not until after Simcoe left Upper Canada that the Grand River lands issue exploded. Mere weeks after the Simcoes set sail, Brant obtained the signatures of a number of Six Nations chiefs to a power of attorney authorizing him to sell lands at Grand River on their behalf. The plan was to create a fund for the general welfare. Over 380,000 acres were "sold," then Brant attempted to obtain a transfer deed from William Claus of the Indian Department. Claus refused on the grounds that the Six Nations were not indigenous to the area and so had no "right of soil" in Upper Canada, being only "loyal subjects" under the protection of the Crown. Besides, the sale had not been conducted according to the provisions of the Proclamation of 1763.[77] Peter Russell, administering the government in Simcoe's absence, wrote urgently to London for instructions. Fears of an imminent Indigenous uprising along the Mississippi meant that the Six Nations had to be pacified. With no reply from London and Brant in Philadelphia making ominous overtures to the Americans, the Executive Council urged Russell to act. Russell decided to issue the deeds that Brant had requested. They were being drawn up at the very moment that the instructions from London finally arrived – Russell was *not* to acquiesce to Brant's demands, but rather to offer the Six Nations an annuity to compensate for their loss of permission to sell the land. Brant refused and upped the ante, demanding full legal title to *all* the Grand River lands, not simply the ones he had sold. Finally, early in February 1798, a compromise was arranged. Following the procedures of the Proclamation of 1763, Brant agreed to surrender to the Crown the Six Nations' interests in the lands already "sold," then the Crown re-conveyed those lands to the non-Native buyers whom Brant had produced.[78] Of course, the "solution" was only temporary and the issue has festered for generations among those who argue Brant had no right to dispose of lands that were held in common by the Six Nations as a whole. As for the contested land at the head of the Grand River, the government of Upper Canada purchased it from the Mississauga after the War of 1812 and sold it to non-Native settlers over Six Nations' protests.[79]

These land disputes were not the only ones that Simcoe faced. As has been noted, the Mississauga were increasingly dissatisfied about alleged agreements made before his arrival as lieutenant governor, and Simcoe did what he could to hear and address their concerns, taking matters into his own hands. He arranged a meeting in the spring of 1795 with the Lake Huron people at York to discuss the purchase of lands at Penetanguishene harbour, in spite of an order from Dorchester that no purchases were to be made without the presence of superintendent general Sir John Johnson – who was out of the country having a temper tantrum in England.[80] Simcoe decided to disobey instructions. "As I apprehend not many of the former purchases required the presence of Sir John Johnson," he wrote the governor, his pen dripping with vitriol, "in eminent cases, I shall by no means suffer his absence from this Continent to impede His Majesty's Service in the Province for which I am responsible."[81] Accordingly, on 29 September 1795, British army officers and Indian Department officials made an agreement with six Chippewa chiefs for a 12-mile-square tract bordering on the St Clair River (intended as a residence for any of the Ohio nations who wished to leave American soil),[82] and a month later, lands at Burlington Bay were purchased from the Mississauga in what was later designated Treaty No. 3¾.[83] Simcoe had advised Dorchester that "these lands should be purchased so as to leave the Mississauga in full possession of their rivers and fishing grounds,"[84] but the historical record has yet to speak on how (or whether) such an agreement was incorporated.

Lest one conclude that Simcoe's sympathies lay entirely with the needs of the Indigenous population, however, it must be noted that at the same time, he was asking Dorchester's permission to purchase part (or all) of an area known as the Huron Reserve across from Detroit to facilitate a new townsite for the non-Natives who wished to remain in the area after the British evacuation of that garrison.[85] It was clear where his priorities ultimately lay. Indeed, Simcoe seems to have assumed that treaty "negotiations" were pro forma and took for granted the First Nations' willingness to sell. For example, he gave the go-ahead for surveys of the townships of Russell and Montague (in what is now eastern Ontario) before "the final Adjustment of the claims of the Indians on the St. Lawrence" had been made. The surveyors in the field were more hesitant and were advised by their supervisor to go ahead only "provided the same shall not give offence to the Indians."[86]

Some dilemmas for Simcoe's administration involved matters other than land. Early in 1796, a man named Oliver Jaffray requested that his and other families at "the Head of the Lake" be inoculated against smallpox, which many believed would appear amidst the population upheaval to follow the British evacuation of the Ohio posts. Elizabeth Simcoe was an advocate of inoculation (a method predating the vaccination pioneered by Edward Jenner); indeed, Lady Mary Wortley Montague, who had brought the idea to England in the 1720s, was a relative. Simcoe's own children in England had been inoculated. However, this early technique was risky because it involved the use of pus from a human sufferer with an active case of smallpox. Not only could the recipient die, but contagion could easily spread through the community.[87] In fact, one of Simcoe's own children would later die of complications following inoculation. Understandably, Simcoe was hesitant. Principles of "humanity and justice" dictated that every measure possible must be used to protect the Indigenous population "from any dangers resulting from introducing this disorder which might otherwise prove fatal to them."[88] In the end, Simcoe decided the wisest course would be to wait until (or if) a case of smallpox actually appeared and then provide the expertise and services for inoculation.

Simcoe's judgment was also called upon in a difficult case involving the murder of a white man by an Indigenous man in the spring of 1795. How far did the principle of "independent nations" really extend?

The matter was complicated by the fact that the accused was Karaguantier, also known as Isaac, Joseph Brant's eldest son. By all accounts, Isaac was a troubled soul with a violent temper and an alcohol problem. The victim, apparently a deserter from General Wayne's army, was shot at Grand River in a dispute with the young Brant in full view of two witnesses. Because the victim was a harness-maker, he had "promised to be of great use to the Settlement" and his death became a public issue. Simcoe proceeded cautiously. He learned that Sir William Johnson had made an agreement with the Mohawk to turn over any murderer to the British for their justice, so he petitioned Governor Dorchester for a copy of that treaty before taking action.[89] When no copy could be found, Simcoe asked Dorchester for instructions (from the king if necessary), writing, "I shall not take any steps and shall restrain the Attorney General from applying to the Indian Department for obtaining the delivery of the accused Person" until such instructions were received.[90] Simcoe believed that Joseph Brant and the Grand River people were willing to hand Isaac over, but that members of the Haudenosaunee elsewhere (notably the Cayuga) opposed the move because of the principle involved. Isaac Brant remained a free man until the autumn, when in a drunken rage he attacked his own father with a knife. Tragically, Joseph killed his son in self-defence.[91] The issue of whether the British felt that their law could be applied to the First Nations went untested.[92]

While the Simcoes' relations with Joseph Brant and his family were fraught with tension, relations with Brant's sister Molly (Mary or Gonwatsijayenni) were very different. Elizabeth Simcoe crossed paths with her regularly at Niagara. She and her daughters attended a ball hosted by the Simcoes in 1793, for example, and the women came to know one another more closely in the autumn of 1794, when Elizabeth Simcoe invited Molly Brant to share her boat on a trip from Niagara to Kingston. Elizabeth Simcoe recorded, "She speaks English well & is a civil & very sensible old woman."[93] She would later have good reason to value Molly Brant's friendship. In the spring of 1795, John Graves Simcoe was seriously ill for over a month, unable to leave his room with agonizing headaches and a violent cough. Finally, Molly Brant advised the use of a medicinal root that "really relieved his Cough in a very short time," according to his grateful wife.[94] The regard between families was made tangible some years later when a great-grandson of Molly Brant's named his son William Simcoe Kerr (who eventually served as chief of the Six Nations confederacy in Canada).[95]

There were other individuals with whom the Simcoes developed particular connections. One was Keenees, chief of a village on Lake Simcoe, for whom John Graves Simcoe held a particular admiration and whom he mourned deeply at his untimely death.[96] Another was Egushwa, an influential Chippewa/Ojibwe man (probably from a settlement on Lake Huron) who was wounded at the battle of Fallen Timbers and who shared Simcoe's interests in promoting unity among the First Nations.[97] It is important to note that Simcoe recorded in his letters and memoirs the personal names of many of the Indigenous people with whom he worked, unlike most of his contemporaries for whom "Indians" were simply anonymous props on the stage of European action. Elizabeth Simcoe, too, mentioned many by name: Canise, Walbekanine, Jacob Lewis, Great Sail, Cowkiller, Wable Casigo, Man of the Snakes, and Aaron Hill among them.[98]

During their sojourn in Canada, the Simcoes developed a complex set of attitudes towards Indigenous people. Historians have tended to focus on the negative, such as Elizabeth Simcoe's description of the Mississauga at Kingston as an "idle, drunken, dirty tribe" or John Graves Simcoe's reference to "indolence" among the trading nations of Upper Canada.[99] Yet it is clear that the couple found much more that they admired: the "ease and grace" of Jacob the Mohawk's dancing, the beauty of "that inexpressible ease & composure" with which birch canoes were conducted, the "superior air" and handsome appearance of the Lake Huron Ojibwe, the rich and "excellent" gravy in an Indian recipe for elk, the "Martial Science & Spirit" and "passion for Glory" that infused their culture, and the "well expressed fine sentiments" in their speeches.[100] Elizabeth Simcoe fully appreciated the exquisite needlework of the Indigenous women and purchased quite a few articles of their manufacture for her family's use, including moccasins (which she sent home to her children in England), carved wooden bowls, and woven baskets. She was fascinated by their fine physique and sketched people such as Great Sail but (tellingly) never the Europeans who surrounded her. She made an effort to learn a little of their languages and something of their ideas about the cosmos. She communicated a good deal of this information to her closest friend in England, who studied it carefully and concluded (most perceptively) in one letter, "It appears to me that in some of the Indian sayings repeated by Charlevoix as nonsense, he only thought them so, because he took them literally, & that metaphorically, as they meant them, they were exceedingly reasonable & proper."[101] This was no superficial tourist impression but a reflection of a thoughtful and sophisticated appreciation of the First Nations of eastern North America.

The Simcoes' legacy to Indigenous affairs was similarly complex. While historian S.F. Wise could dismiss John Graves Simcoe's policies as "amateurish," "abortive," and lacking in judgment,[102] they could equally be described as subtle, sophisticated, and sympathetic to many Indigenous people's own goals. His sense of duty and honour led to his insistence on recognizing the Indigenous peoples as nations and respecting all that entailed. His outrage at the incompetence and greed of many Indian Department officials led to his detailed proposals for a new system that would better serve the interests of both First Nations and the Crown, proposals not unlike some of those expressed more recently to the Royal Commission on Aboriginal Peoples. His recognition of the value of a First Nations alliance with the British led to his attempts to repair the damage of the 1784–5 Mississauga land secessions and to put the land title situation at Grand River on a sound legal footing.

That John Graves Simcoe failed in most of these endeavours is hardly surprising, nor is it entirely his fault. He was caught in the midst of a complex and shifting situation. There were the almost infinite conflicting interests: American, British, Upper Canadian, Lower Canadian, Haudenosaunee, Ojibwe, Delaware, Shawnee, Mississauga, Miami, Huron, settlers, Kingston merchants, the Indian Department, and on and on. There were the endless personal conflicts: Simcoe, Dorchester, Johnson, Brant, McKee, Cartwright, and others, to say nothing of the personal politics in London. There was the issue of his poor health:

Simcoe was forced into absences at crucial times and had to leave for England in 1796 before these issues could be resolved. And ultimately, they were handled at councils where new interests prevailed. As Upper Canadians filled government positions in the province, the interests of land speculators and businessmen who knew nothing of the old "Indian" trade were given priority. The Mississauga were only the first among the nations to lose their lands, with even the determined Six Nations at Grand River seeing a steady erosion of their territory.[103] And as J.R. Miller has argued, the years following the War of 1812 put an end to the most powerful reasons for the British to acquiesce to Indian agendas: the need for their economic and military support.[104] The detailed plans and lofty hopes of Colonel and Mrs Simcoe would no longer speak to those who came after them.

NOTES

1 Elizabeth Simcoe, *Mrs. Simcoe's Diary*, ed. Mary Quayle Innis (Toronto: Macmillan, 1965), 127. This version of the diary is more complete and reliable than the earlier John Ross Robertson edition, *The Diary of Mrs. John Graves Simcoe* (Toronto: William Briggs, 1911).

2 John Graves Simcoe to "My Dear Charlotte," Niagara, 9 November [179-], microfilm reel A606, Simcoe Papers, Library and Archives Canada [LAC].

3 Letter probably by Mary Ann Burges, quoting a letter from Elizabeth Simcoe, 18 October [1795], Simcoe Papers, LAC, microfilm reel A606, folder 24.

4 William Osgoode to Simcoe, [Quebec], 24 July 1799, in William Colgate, "Letters from the Honourable Chief Justice William Osgoode," part 2, *Ontario History* 46, no. 3 (summer 1954): 159.

5 Duc de la Rochefoucauld Liancourt, as quoted in the introduction to John Graves Simcoe, *Simcoe's Military Journal: A History of the Operations of a Partisan Corps, called the Queen's Rangers* (New York: Bartlett and Wolford, 1844), xv. "Tioga" is now the name of counties in New York and Pennsylvania, where it is believed to mean "at the forks" of a stream.

6 The term "Indian" is frequently used in this paper because (1) many of the people descended from those mentioned here still prefer the term, and (2) it was the term used at the time studied in this paper.

7 Dundas to Dorchester, Whitehall, 16 September 1791, in E.A. Cruikshank, ed., *The Correspondence of Lieut. Governor John Graves Simcoe with allied documents …*, vol. 1 (Toronto: Ontario Historical Society, 1923), 66–8 (hereafter, Simcoe Correspondence).

8 Duke of Northumberland to "My Dear Joseph," 3 September 1791. The letter is signed "Northumberland/Thorighwegari." Quoted in Simcoe, *Simcoe's Military Journal*, 328. Northumberland had known Brant while serving as a senior officer in the American Revolutionary War. He was one of England's wealthiest men; he and his father had been friends and patrons of Simcoe's family for some time. One of John Graves Simcoe's brothers was named Percy in his honour. Brant and Simcoe were both Masons, and Brant was well known to others of Simcoe's circle, including Lord Francis Rawdon and Evan Nepean. See Isabel Thompson Kelsay, *Joseph Brant 1743–1807: Man of Two Worlds* (Syracuse, NY: Syracuse University Press, 1984), 182, 385.

9 Simcoe, *Simcoe's Military Journal*, 85–6.

10 William Tegg, *Tegg's Dictionary of Chronology: or, Historical and Statistical Register etc. …*, 5th ed. (London: William Tegg & Co., 1854), 698.

11 *Mrs. Simcoe's Diary*, entry for 9 January 1794 (at Toronto), 114.

12 Ibid., 25 October 1793 (Toronto), 108.

13 Simcoe to surveyor Samuel Holland, Quebec, 17 March 1792, Simcoe Correspondence, 126. Simcoe's letter dated the sale to 2 May 1784, but later government sources give 22 May.

14 Simcoe to Evan Nepean, 16 March 1791, Simcoe Correspondence, vol. 1, 21. The trip to Congress never materialized.

15 Kelsay, *Joseph Brant*, 556–7. See also John Graves Simcoe to Henry Dundas, 10 March 1792, in Simcoe Correspondence, vol. 1, 119.

16 Simcoe to Alured Clarke, [Niagara?], 23 August 1792, Simcoe Correspondence, vol. 1, 205.

17 See Richard White, *The Middle Ground: Indians, Empires, and Republics in the Great Lakes Region, 1650–1815* (Cambridge: Cambridge University Press, 1991), 413–21; Helen Hornbeck Tanner, ed., *Atlas of Great Lakes Indian History* (Norman, University of Oklahoma Press, 1987).

18 White, *Middle Ground*, 433, 441.

19 See Gregory Evans Dowd, *A Spirited Resistance: The North American Indian Struggle for Unity, 1745–1815* (Baltimore: Johns Hopkins University Press, 1992), 106–7.

20 Ibid., 103–5, and the report of the conference in Simcoe Correspondence, vol. 1, 218–30.

21 See S.F. Wise, "The Indian Diplomacy of John Graves Simcoe," Canadian Historical Association *Annual Report* (1953): 36–44.

22 Alan Taylor, *The Divided Ground* (New York: Vintage Books, 2007), 263.

23 For an overview of the relevant section of this treaty (Article 15), see Dale Miquelon, *New France, 1701–1733* (Toronto: McClelland and Stewart, 1987),

52–3. Miquelon reads the article quite differently from Simcoe, writing that it "carpentered together a host of contradictory notions" about British and French relations with the Indian nations. Emphasis in the original.

24 Simcoe to Henry Dundas, Quebec, 28 April 1792, in Simcoe Correspondence, vol. 1, 140.

25 Simcoe to Alured Clarke, Niagara, 20 August 1792, in Simcoe Correspondence, vol. 1, 204.

26 The Proclamation of 1763 prohibited private individuals from purchasing land directly from First Nations. The latter could sell only to the Crown at a public ceremony. The intention was to prevent unscrupulous non-Native buyers from profiting.

27 Simcoe Correspondence, vol. 4, 196n1. For more on the Sally Ainse story, see John Clarke's entry on her in the *Dictionary of Canadian Biography*, http://www.biographi.ca/en/bio/ainse_sarah_6E.html; Kelsay, *Joseph Brant*, 544–5; and John Clarke, *Land, Power, and Economics on the Frontier of Upper Canada* (Montreal: McGill-Queen's University Press, 2001), 139–41.

28 The numbers of these early treaties should not be confused with the post-Confederation "Numbered Treaties" series that are better known. See Canada, *Indian Treaties and Surrenders*, vol. 1 (Ottawa: Queen's Printer, 1891). Reprinted 1992 by Fifth House Publishers, Saskatoon.

29 See *Indian Treaties and Surrenders*, vol. 1, 7. The treaty was dated 1 April 1793.

30 Robert S. Allen, *His Majesty's Indian Allies: British Indian Policy in the Defence of Canada, 1774–1815* (Toronto: Dundurn Press, 1992), 92. The best study of the Mississauga surrenders is Donald B. Smith, "The Dispossession of the Mississauga Indians: A Missing Chapter in the Early History of Upper Canada" (1981), reprinted in J.K. Johnson and Bruce Wilson, eds., *Historical Essays on Upper Canada* (Ottawa: Carleton University Press, 1989), 23–52. See also Robert J. Surtees, "Indian Land Cessions, 1763–1830," in Edward S. Rogers and Donald B. Smith, eds., *Aboriginal Ontario* (Toronto: Dundurn Press, 1994), 92–121.

31 William Chewett to E.B. Littlehales, Newark, 31 August 1794, in Simcoe Correspondence, vol. 3, 24.

32 Ibid.

33 Simcoe to Dorchester, Navy Hall, 6 September 1794, in Simcoe Correspondence, vol. 3, 45.

34 Ibid.

35 Simcoe to Dorchester, Navy Hall, 9 or 19 September 1794, in Simcoe Correspondence, vol. 3, 51.

36 For more on the history and meaning of the Covenant Chain, see Daniel K. Richter, *The Ordeal of the Longhouse: The Peoples of the Iroquois League in*

the Era of European Colonization (Chapel Hill: University of North Carolina Press, 1992).

37 Simcoe to the Committee of the Privy Council for Trade and Plantations, Navy Hall, 1 September 1794, in Simcoe Correspondence, vol. 3, 61–5.

38 Simcoe to Dorchester, Kingston, 9 March 1795, in Simcoe Correspondence, vol. 3, 319–24. Simcoe sent a copy of this letter to the Duke of Portland.

39 Simcoe to the Duke of Portland, Johnstown Upper Canada, 17 February 1795, in Simcoe Correspondence, vol. 3, 302. Emphasis in the original.

40 For an account of the council proceedings, see Kelsay, *Joseph Brant*, 490–504. Joseph Brant's "Journal of the Proceedings at the General Council Held at the Foot of the Rapids of the Miamis" is in Simcoe Correspondence, vol. 2, 5–17. The best interpretation is Reginald Horsman, "The British Indian Department and the Abortive Treaty of Lower Sandusky, 1793," *Ohio Historical Society Quarterly* 70, no. 3 (July 1961): 189–213.

41 See, for example, the account of a council held 7 February 1794 with the Delaware and Six Nations in Simcoe Correspondence, vol. 2, 141–6.

42 See Reginald Horsman, "The British Indian Department and the Resistance to General Anthony Wayne," *Mississippi Valley Historical Review* 49, no. 2 (September 1962): 269–90.

43 Dorchester to Simcoe, Quebec, 17 February 1794, Simcoe Correspondence, vol. 2, 154.

44 Simcoe to Henry Dundas, York, 23 February 1794, Simcoe Correspondence, vol. 2, 157, 163.

45 Simcoe to Dorchester, York, 14 March 1794, Simcoe Correspondence, vol. 2, 179.

46 Edmund Randolph to George Hammond, Philadelphia, 20 May 1794, Simcoe Correspondence, vol. 2, 238–9; Hammond's reply, Philadelphia, 22 May 1794, Simcoe Correspondence, vol. 2, 240.

47 US *Gazette*, 3 June 1794, letter dated 23 May 1794, Simcoe Correspondence, vol. 2, 245.

48 Simcoe to Henry Dundas, Navy Hall, 21 June 1794, Simcoe Correspondence, vol. 2, 285. Emphasis in the original.

49 Horsman, "The British Indian Department," 278–9.

50 R.G. England to Simcoe, Detroit, 22 July 1794, Simcoe Correspondence, vol. 2, 334.

51 Simcoe to Henry Dundas, Navy Hall, 10 August 1794, Simcoe Correspondence, vol. 2, 382.

52 Simcoe to Dorchester, Navy Hall, 16 August 1794, Simcoe Correspondence, vol. 2, 382.

53 Horsman, "The British Indian Department," 282.
54 See Simcoe Correspondence, vol. 4, 7–8, 16.
55 See, for example, his speech to the Six Nations at Fort Erie, 28 August 1795, in Simcoe Correspondence, vol. 4, 83–8.
56 Simcoe Correspondence, vol. 4, 88.
57 Simcoe to Alured Clarke, Niagara, 1 April 1793, Simcoe Correspondence, vol. 1, 309.
58 Ibid., 308–9.
59 *Mrs. Simcoe's Diary*, 12–13 and entry for 15 June 1796, 185.
60 This version of the deed is sometimes referred to as the Simcoe Patent. See a discussion of it in Sidney L. Harring, *White Man's Law: Native People in Nineteenth-Century Canadian Jurisprudence* (Toronto: University of Toronto Press for Osgoode Society for Canadian Legal History, 1988), 38–9.
61 Simcoe to Lord Dorchester, York, 6 December 1793, Simcoe Correspondence, vol. 2, 114–16.
62 Dorchester to Simcoe, Quebec, 27 January 1794, Simcoe Correspondence, vol. 2, 137.
63 Peter Russell to Simcoe, Niagara, 5 April 1795, Simcoe Correspondence, vol. 3, 342.
64 See Kelsay, *Joseph Brant*, 555–95, for a fuller account of this story.
65 Dorchester to Simcoe, Quebec, 25 January 1796, Simcoe Correspondence, vol. 4, 182.
66 Jonathan Sewell to Dorchester, Quebec, 25 January 1796, Simcoe Correspondence, vol. 4, 184.
67 Simcoe to the Duke of Portland, York, 27 February 1796, Simcoe Correspondence, vol. 4, 201; Simcoe to Dorchester, York, 28 February 1796, Simcoe Correspondence, vol. 4, 204.
68 Simcoe to Dorchester, York, 28 February 1796, Simcoe Correspondence, vol. 4, 204.
69 Simcoe to Joseph Brant, York, 2 March 1796, Simcoe Correspondence, vol. 4, 206.
70 Joseph Brant to Joseph Chew, Niagara, 17 May 1796, Simcoe Correspondence, vol. 4, 268. Another objection regarding reversionary rights to the Crown is noted in Kelsay, *Joseph Brant*, 566.
71 William Johnson Chew to Joseph Chew, Niagara, 14 May 1796, Simcoe Correspondence, vol. 4, 265.
72 Simcoe to Dorchester, York, 28 February 1796, Simcoe Correspondence, vol. 4, 204.
73 Ibid.

74 Simcoe to Dorchester, York, 22 December 1795, Simcoe Correspondence, vol. 4, 165.
75 Simcoe to Henry Dundas, Navy Hall, 21 June 1794, Simcoe Correspondence, vol. 2, 286.
76 Simcoe to Henry Dundas, York, 20 September 1793, Simcoe Correspondence, vol. 2, 55.
77 Allen, *His Majesty's Indian Allies*, 94.
78 See the account in Allen, *His Majesty's Indian Allies*, 93–6; and Kelsay, *Joseph Brant*, 570–95. It seems highly likely that Simcoe was behind these policy decisions.
79 Kelsay, *Joseph Brant*, 633–4. The history of the Haldimand Tract and post-Simcoe era controversies over it and other lands have been explored through a number of windows. See the relevant sections in Alan Taylor, *The Divided Ground: Indians, Settlers, and the Northern Borderland of the American Revolution* (New York: Vintage Books, 2006), and the work of Mohawk scholar Rick Monture, *We Share Our Matters: Two Centuries of Writing and Resistance at Six Nations of the Grand River* (Winnipeg: University of Manitoba Press, 2014). The issue is, of course, the subject of a contemporary land claim and litigation. See, among others, Laura DeVries, *Conflict in Caledonia: Aboriginal Land Rights and the Rule of Law* (Vancouver: UBC Press, 2011). For a broader historical perspective on the role of the Covenant Chain, see Bruce Morito, *The Ethic of Mutual Respect: The Covenant Chain and Aboriginal-Crown Relations* (Vancouver: UBC Press, 2012), or the older Francis Jennings, *The Ambiguous Iroquois Empire* (New York: W.W. Norton, 1984).
80 Simcoe to Dorchester, Kingston, 15 March 1795, Simcoe Correspondence, vol. 3, 326. Dorchester's instructions were dated 26 December.
81 Simcoe to Dorchester, [Niagara], 31 October 1794, Simcoe Correspondence, vol. 3, 164.
82 See details of the purchase in Simcoe Correspondence, vol. 4, 96, and Alexander McKee to Joseph Chew, Detroit, 24 October 1795, Simcoe Correspondence, vol. 4, 111.
83 *Indian Treaties and Surrenders*, dated 24 October 1795.
84 Simcoe to Dorchester, York, 9 April 1796, Simcoe Correspondence, vol. 4, 239.
85 Simcoe to Dorchester, Navy Hall, 5 June 1796, Simcoe Correspondence, vol. 4, 289. The Huron Reserve had been set aside in 1790. A subject of considerable controversy generated by non-Natives who wanted to settle or speculate in these lands, it was not officially recognized as sold, however, until 1835. See Clarke, *Land, Power, and Economics*, 122–31.

86 E.B. Littlehales to David William Smith (acting surveyor general), York, 19 March 1796, Simcoe Correspondence, vol. 4, 220.
87 See Christina Hole, *English Home Life 1500 to 1800* (London: B.T. Batsford, 1947), 162–4.
88 E.B. Littlehales to Oliver Jaffray, York, 20 March 1796, Simcoe Correspondence, vol. 4, 220–1, and Alexander McKee to Joseph Chew, Detroit, 20 June 1796, in Simcoe Correspondence, vol. 4, 312.
89 Peter Russell to Simcoe, Niagara, 5 April 1795, Simcoe Correspondence, vol. 3, 342; William Johnson Chew to Joseph Chew, Niagara, 11 April 1795, Simcoe Correspondence, vol. 3, 344; Simcoe to Dorchester, Kingston, 5 May 1795, Simcoe Correspondence, vol. 5, 140; Simcoe to Dorchester, Navy Hall, 9 July 1795, Simcoe Correspondence, vol. 4, 38. See also Duncan Campbell Scott, *John Graves Simcoe* (Toronto: Morang, 1910), 191–2.
90 Simcoe to Dorchester, Navy Hall, 9 July 1795, Simcoe Correspondence, vol. 4, 38.
91 William Johnson Chew to Joseph Chew, Niagara, 23 November 1795, Simcoe Correspondence, vol. 4, 145.
92 Another case involved the murders of four people in a Lake Erie settlement, apparently by some Chippewa in a revenge feud dating back to the 1770s. See Matthew Elliott to Joseph Chew, Detroit, 28 October 1795, Simcoe Correspondence, vol. 4, 114. I have not attempted to trace details of this case.
93 *Mrs. Simcoe's Diary*, 136 (entry for 13 September 1794).
94 Ibid., 155 (entry for 24 April 1795).
95 See the *Dictionary of Canadian Biography* entry on his father, William Johnson Kerr (1787–1845).
96 Alexander Macdonell, "Diary of a Journey from Matchedash Bay," entry for 10 October 1793, Simcoe Correspondence, vol. 2, 72, 77.
97 See Simcoe's "Diary of a Journey to the Miamis River," entry for 28 September 1794, Simcoe Correspondence, vol. 3, 99–100, and Simcoe to Dorchester, York, 18 June 1796, Simcoe Correspondence, vol. 4, 304.
98 *Mrs. Simcoe's Diary*, 107, 182, 97, 114, 81, 104, 113, 97.
99 Ibid., 3 July 1792, 72; Simcoe to Henry Dundas, Quebec, 28 April 1792, Simcoe Correspondence, vol. 1, 141.
100 *Mrs. Simcoe's Diary*, 19 February 1796, 174; 14 September 1793, 107; 9 August 1793, 103; 19 December 1791, 42; Simcoe to Dundas, 26 August 1791, Simcoe Correspondence, vol. 1, 51; Simcoe to Dundas, 30 June 1791, Simcoe Correspondence, vol. 1, 29; *Mrs. Simcoe's Diary*, 4 November 1792, 81.

101 Mary Ann Burges to Elizabeth Simcoe, Bath, 12 October 1793, MS 517, reel #4, Series B-1–2, Devon Record Office. Microfilm courtesy of Donald B. Smith.
102 Wise, "Indian Diplomacy of John Graves Simcoe," 43.
103 See the essays in Rogers and Smith, *Aboriginal Ontario*.
104 J.R. Miller, *Skyscrapers Hide the Heavens* (Toronto: University of Toronto Press, 1989, 1991, and 2000).

Lord Bury and the First Nations: A Year in the Canadas

DONALD B. SMITH

A decade ago, the Alberta 2005 Centennial History Society published a two-volume history of the province, *Alberta Formed Alberta Transformed*, with a novel approach. Editors Michael Payne, Donald Wetherell, and Catherine Cavanaugh asked the thirty-five contributors to "write a lively, engaging and personal study of a particular year in Alberta's history."[1] That innovative approach has inspired this essay in honour of Jim Miller, a scholar who has made an outstanding contribution to our understanding of the relationship between Indigenous and non-Indigenous peoples in Canada. By considering a particular year (1855), and by focusing on Lord Bury and Peter Jones, two major figures in Canadian Indian Affairs, one gains an extraordinary vantage point on Native-newcomer relations in the last phase of imperial government control. A cornucopia of available source materials exists on the life of William Coutts Keppel (1832–94), styled Viscount Bury, or often Lord Bury (pronounced "Berry"). In 1855, he served as the superintendent general (administrative head) of Indian Affairs, in charge of the 15,000 First Nations individuals in today's Quebec and Ontario. Decide on your setting as the novelists do, and then tell the story. 15 November 1855 marks the best point of departure. The wedding of Lord Bury, a young English aristocrat, to Sophia MacNab, daughter of the Canadian prime minister, Sir Allan Napier MacNab, attracted wide media interest. The *New York Times* described their marriage as "the most prominent event of recent date in Canada."[2]

The wedding was held at Dundurn Castle, Sir Allan's baronial mansion on Burlington Heights in Hamilton, located on the southeast end of the long, narrow peninsula high above the harbour.[3] Only half a century earlier, the site was still at the heart of the hunting territory of the

Head of Lake Ontario sketched by Elizabeth Simcoe in the mid-1790s. Archives of Ontario, F 47-11-1-0-199.

Mississauga (Ojibwe) chief Wahbanosay and his extended family. Wahbanosay's grandson, Kahkewaquonaby ("Sacred Feathers") – known in English as Peter Jones, son of his daughter Tuhbenahneequay – was born on Burlington Heights in a wigwam in 1802.

Jim Miller includes prominent references to Peter Jones, the Mississauga chief, in five of his major books: *Skyscrapers Hide the Heavens: A History of Indian-White Relations in Canada* (1989), *Shingwauk's Vision: A History of Native Residential Schools* (1996), *Reflections on Native-Newcomer Relations* (2004), *Lethal Legacy: Current Native Controversies in Canada* (2004), and *Compact, Contract, Covenant: Aboriginal Treaty-Making in Canada* (2009). Literary scholar Niigonwedom James Sinclair, associate professor of Native Studies and English at the University of Manitoba, has seconded Jones's importance. The First Nations leader, he writes, was "one of the fiercest and bravest advocates for Anishinaabeg community

An aerial view of Dundurn Castle on Burlington Heights, overlooking Burlington Bay. Courtesy of Local History and Archives, Hamilton Public Library, 32022189091784.

who have ever lived. He deserves a place amongst our greatest narrative voices."[4]

Let's experience the event in the fullness of the moment that mid-November day. In the morning it rained, but the showers ended by noon, an hour or so after the wedding guests arrived.[5] The white-haired father of the bride, now a little physically bent, welcomed the visitors. Horse-drawn cabs passed one after another through the estate's impressive pair of entrance gates, recently put in place for the occasion. Under the shelter of the portico, well-dressed men and women in procession stepped out of carriages. Because of the late fall chill, fireplaces and stoves blazed in the mansion's large public rooms. Dundurn, with its forty rooms and public spaces, had on the east a spectacular vista of Burlington Bay and of Lake Ontario beyond.[6]

To the west, the craggy outline of the Niagara escarpment dominated. On the south, the rapidly growing commercial city of Hamilton, founded by land developer George Hamilton four decades earlier, expanded farther inland.[7] In 1855, Hamilton had a population of 25,000.[8] The city at the Head of the Lake strongly rivalled Toronto, with its population of about 40,000, for economic leadership of Canada West.[9] Sir Allan had fought for years to build the Great Western Railway with the aid of government credit, loans, and outright grants, and that railway now reached south to Niagara Falls and west from Hamilton to London, then on to Windsor. That December, it would reach Toronto. The Great Western's yards and shops were visible from Sir Allan's estate, looking eastward towards Burlington Bay.[10]

Two-thirds of a century earlier, European settlement had not yet begun in earnest. Until the first land survey in 1791, Burlington Heights was a First Nations' homeland, as it had been for over 9,000 years or roughly 400 generations.[11] The first non-Indigenous settlers initially regarded the Head of the Lake, the area immediately around Burlington Bay, as undesirable. In summer, the swarms of mosquitoes that bred in the swamps near the lakeshore deterred them, as did the Head of the Lake's large population of rattlesnakes, bears, and wolves.[12] This isolation allowed the young Mississauga (Ojibwe) boy who would be known in English as Peter Jones to have a full Mississauga boyhood.

Within two generations, the British displaced the Mississauga from their traditional territory at the west end of Lake Ontario. Initially the Mississauga had little idea of the British system of land tenure.[13] They experienced great difficulty in comprehending the newcomers' concept of absolute ownership by individuals. The land belonged to the community, to the future yet-to-be-born members as well as to its present members. In 1784, the British obtained three million acres of the Niagara Peninsula for gifts worth £1200 (sterling). Twenty-one years later, the British obtained a large section of the Mississauga's only remaining tract of land between present-day Toronto and Hamilton.[14] By one modern historian's estimate, the British paid in 1805 about 2.5 per cent of what was, at the time, its market value.[15] Evidence exists that these First Nations regarded the early treaties as merely a series of useful and profitable rental agreements for the newcomers' use of their land.[16]

Peter Jones was the younger son of Tuhbenahneequay and her Welsh American lover, Augustus Jones, who had completed many of the early surveys at the western end of Lake Ontario. In a Christian service in 1798, Jones had married Sarah Tekarihogen, an Iroquois convert to Christianity, and lived with her at their farm at Stoney Creek at the south end of Burlington Beach. Augustus's intimate relationship with Tuhbenahneequay ended shortly after Peter's birth. In her own Mississauga community, Tuhbenahneequay raised her two sons by Jones, with the help of her brother, Sloping Sky (known in English as Joseph Sawyer), and other family members.[17] The Mississauga at the western end of Lake Ontario spent as much as eight months of the year at encampments at the Head of the Lake. Before the War of 1812, this district stood at the centre of their seasonal round of hunting and trapping, collecting maple sap, fishing, planting corn, and gathering wild rice.[18] Peter Jones later described his birthplace this way:

> Perhaps I may be partial in my judgment, as it was on the romantic Burlington Heights I first drew my breath, and, in my youthful days, was accustomed to traverse the shores of its clear waters in the light birchbark canoe; here I ranged the forest, and shot many a partridge, squirrel, and pigeon, where now may be seen the fine brick or stone house, and the productive farm of the white man.[19]

The 1810s proved a grim decade for the Mississauga. The battles fought in their territory during the War of 1812 ruined the remaining Mississauga hunting grounds at the western end of Lake Ontario. Their population continued to decline. In two treaties arranged in 1818 and 1820, the British obtained almost all of the Mississauga's remaining lands between Toronto (then known as York) and Hamilton.[20] By the mid-1820s, the Mississauga numbers at the western end of the lake had fallen in a single generation by nearly two-thirds, from roughly 500 to 200, due to the ravages of disease and poor nutrition. Newcomers occupied their old hunting grounds.[21] The Indian Department failed to protect their fisheries. Alcohol abuse tore away the fabric of Mississauga society.

In 1816, Augustus Jones took his Mississauga son Peter to live with his Iroquois family on the Grand River, just north of Brantford and west of Hamilton, where they had relocated immediately after the War of 1812. The young man, raised within Mississauga culture and tradition, now mastered English and some Mohawk and learned how to farm.

Sent to school by his father, he intended to become an accountant in the fur trade, but his conversion in 1823 to Methodism completely changed his direction.[22] Instead, he became a Methodist church worker among his mother's people and, later, an ordained minister. With the help of non-Indigenous Christians and the colonial government, Peter Jones established a successful Methodist agricultural mission at the Credit River, just twenty kilometres west of Toronto. But the pressures of the newcomers on the First Nations relentlessly continued. As Peter Jones informed a Scottish audience in 1845, "the Indian territories have been taken away till our possessions are now so small that you would almost require a magnifying glass to see them. We are surrounded on all sides by white settlers, still encroaching on us."[23] In 1847, the Mississauga moved from the Credit River to land adjacent to the Six Nations or Iroquois Territory on the Grand River. They called their new home New Credit.

It is interesting to compare the parallel lives of contemporaries Allan MacNab and Peter Jones. Born in York in 1798, Allan was the son of a British army officer who had fought in the Revolutionary War. Never financially well off, the MacNab family compensated by making much of their Scottish Highlander origins. Young Allan grew up intensely proud of his clan and its history. The family crest was adorned with a severed head and the motto, "Let fear be far from all": *timor omnis abesto*. The severed head was a gory trophy, representing the head of the chief of the rival MacNeish clan, taken in a 1612 raid. Young Allan, powerfully built, dark-haired, and taller than average, cultivated the image of the fierce Highland Scot.[24] With determination, he relentlessly strove to become a major participant in both the business and political worlds of Upper Canada.

MacNab first made his mark during the War of 1812. Only 14 years old at the war's outbreak, the "Boy Hero" fought with conspicuous bravery. Called to the bar in 1826, the young lawyer set up office in Hamilton, which then had a total population of 200.[25] Peter Jones became a Christian minister and Allan MacNab a land speculator. Within a decade, MacNab had cornered much of the best land in the centre of the expanding town.[26] In 1830, the young lawyer gained a seat in the provincial assembly. Anxious to impress his fellow citizens, he began to build his "castle" in 1833 and completed it in 1835.[27] MacNab's military prowess proved an asset to the ruling conservative forces. In the Rebellion of 1837, he rode at the head of the column that routed rebel leader William Lyon Mackenzie and his followers north of Toronto.[28]

Sir Allan MacNab, photograph taken in Montreal, 1861. McCord Museum I-25492.0.1.

After the suppression of the Rebellion, Colonel MacNab was knighted for services to the Crown.

Sir Allan became premier in 1854, 13 years after the union of Upper and Lower Canada (now renamed Canada West and Canada East). With John A. Macdonald's help, he assembled a centralist coalition that combined Conservatives from Canada West and moderate members of the Parti bleu of Canada East. The ambitious 39-year-old Conservative politician from Kingston became the central figure in MacNab's cabinet. As Tory insider John Langton (the Conservative member of Parliament from Peterborough, Canada West) wrote, "Macdonald was looked upon as the soul of the ministry."[29] The MacNab administration passed important pieces of legislation, including the restructuring of the militia, secularization of the clergy reserves in Canada West, and the abolition of seigneurial tenure in Canada East.[30]

In this age of religious extremism, Sir Allan, a Protestant, was an unusual man: he favoured Christian unity. In one of his early historical articles, Jim Miller expertly probed the depth of anti-Catholic thought in Victorian Canada, exploring the extent of hostility towards Roman Catholicism.[31] Surprisingly, MacNab was free of anti-Catholicism. After his first wife's death, he married Mary Stuart, whose maternal grandmother was a French Canadian Roman Catholic.[32] They had a very happy marriage, despite their different faiths.[33] After Mary Stuart's death in 1846, MacNab continued to respect his promise to Mary that middle daughter Sophia and her younger sister would be raised as Roman Catholics.

The lively, intelligent Sophia became her father's delight. She did well at her studies. A surviving diary written by her as a girl of thirteen confirms how observant she was. Her entries show her discipline and attention to detail.[34] As a young woman, she studied music and learned to dance and to write in an elegant hand. She learned the art of gracious entertaining. After her schooling in a good convent school in Montreal, Sophia also spoke conversational French. Her father devoted a great of time to her and her younger sister. As an acquaintance wrote of Sir Allan shortly after his death, "In his habits, he was extravagant, always living beyond his means, but a kind husband and an indulgent father."[35] In Quebec City, the accomplished Sophia assisted her widowed father as his official hostess after he became prime minister in September 1854.

On 15 November 1855, Sophia married William Coutts Keppel, Lord Bury, heir to the earldom of Albemarle. The world traveller had arrived in Canada in mid-June 1854. As a member of an aristocratic family that owned a vast estate in Norfolk, England, he belonged to the patrician power elite of England.[36] A contemporary engraving of the viscount in his mid-20s shows a good-looking, self-assured young man.

He was a wonderful raconteur. A reference to him later appeared in the reminiscences of Algernon West, a prominent British civil servant. Both men, old Etonians, had served as captains in the Middlesex Rifles shortly before Bury's departure for Canada. West recalls his friend:

Lord Bury, 1857. Reproduced with kind permission of Suffolk Record Office, Ipswich, England, ref. HA67/D4/10/1857.

> In these happy days he used to keep the mess table in a roar of laughter, not only by his wit and stories, but by the humour of his telling; the glory fades in their repetition, and, though fifty stories spring to my mind, I could not tell one without losing the salt and the sparkle with which he ornamented them all so well.[37]

Because of his own genuine ability, and even more importantly thanks to his family connections, the young viscount had a multitude of career opportunities. After he left Eton, he joined the elite Scots Fusilier Guards as a lieutenant. A year later, in 1850, he took a leave from the Guards to serve as a secretary to the British prime minister, Lord John Russell, a second cousin of his father's.[38] Young Bury circulated within the top echelons of British political life. His social calendar in 1851 included a dinner at the mansion of Viscount and Viscountess Palmerston, an official assembly held by Lady John Russell at Downing Street, a state ball at Buckingham Palace, and a grand ball at the old Tower of London honoured by the presence of the Constable of the Tower, the Duke of Wellington – the "Iron Duke" himself.[39]

Shortly after his twentieth birthday in April 1852, Bury made one false step. He announced to his parents that he wished to marry a "Miss Dashwood."[40] *Faute majeure*, as the earl and countess regarded the young woman as totally unsuitable. They acted quickly. The offer of a prestigious overseas placement in India enticed their only son to leave Britain. Viscount Bury accepted the invitation of Lord Frederick FitzClarence, Commander-in-Chief of Her Majesty's Forces in Bombay, India, to become his aide-de-camp.[41] Lord FitzClarence was one of the illegitimate sons of King William IV, Queen Victoria's uncle and her predecessor in office.

In early 1853, the adventurous Lord Bury chose to ride across Asia from the Mediterranean to the Persian Gulf, in preference to the infinitely safer Red Sea route to India. His father's Asian journey nearly 30 years earlier inspired him. His father had travelled through the Middle East and Russia on his return from service as aide-de-camp to the governor general of India and later wrote about his travels in two volumes: *Personal Narrative of a Journey from India to England, by Bussorah, Baghdad, the Ruins of Babylon, Curdistan, The Court of Persia, The Western Shore of the Caspian Sea, Astrakhan, Nishney Novogorod, Moscow, and St Petersburgh in the year 1824.*[42] The younger Bury's travel choice in 1853 was a hazardous one. While journeying through Kurdistan, he narrowly escaped being kidnapped, as he wore a fez and the Kurds mistook him for a Turk, their deadly enemies. In Baghdad, the young Englishman attended a grand hunting party on the plains where Babylon once stood. After sailing down the Tigris on a British gunboat, he embarked on a pilgrim ship across the Persian Gulf that took him to Muscat, part of the way to Mecca. From Muscat, he sailed to India. Unfortunately, shortly after his arrival in Bombay, Bury fell seriously ill, forcing an immediate return to England in the late summer of 1853 and his subsequent retirement from the regular army.[43]

The viscount remained in London until early May 1854. He attended Her Majesty's levee at St James's Palace, graced by an appearance of both Her Majesty and Prince Albert,[44] and the next day acted as the best man at Lord Suffield's wedding.[45] A few days later, he attended an assembly at the mansion of Viscountess Palmerston.[46] Then Bury left for Canada, where his friend Laurence Oliphant had just become civil secretary to Lord Elgin, governor general of the Province of Canada. Oliphant, an accomplished writer, had won the appointment through his mother's friendship with Elgin's sisters Lady Charlotte Locker and Lady Augusta Bruce.[47] The father of Lord Elgin and his sisters was the British ambassador in Athens, best known for his removal half a century earlier. Before his appointment, 25-year-old Laurence Oliphant had never stepped foot in North America, never seen a North American Indian. His appointment is surprising, for in his post as civil secretary, he would assist the governor general with his administrative duties and, most importantly, would also serve as the superintendent general for Indian Affairs for the Canadas.

In Quebec, Lord Elgin invited Viscount Bury on his arrival to stay at his residence Spencer Wood, three kilometres from the city itself. Of independent means, the young man appeared to be in search of a New World experience. The governor general was most impressed by the young viscount, scion of a distinguished English family. On inspection, he proved to be an agreeable, sporting young gentleman with political ambitions.[48] Elgin wrote his wife on 24 June 1854 to say that he found Bury "a very nice & clever young man."[49] Certainly Bury had unlimited self-confidence. In July he decided, after only a few weeks in the colony, to investigate the possibility of running for the colonial assembly. The viscount chose the County of Victoria, near Peterborough. But he was a realist. Once he discovered that electoral chances were, well, somewhat remote, he left the contest, and joined Laurence Oliphant on a rigorous six-week trip to visit First Nations communities in the Upper Great Lakes.[50] On their way to Lake Superior, the two athletic young men canoed, shot rapids,

James Bruce, 8th Earl of Elgin. Library and Archives Canada, C-291.

and swam every morning and evening.[51] His First Nations guides gave him the Ojibwe name "Wahbah Tik," which he translated in his diary as "white rein deer" but which actually means "white elk."[52] The viscount had a wonderful time, even writing in his diary the French words of the voyageurs' ballads. They returned by the Mississippi to Chicago, and then to Niagara Falls.[53] Once in Quebec City, Lord Bury himself joined Lord Elgin's staff and lived again at Spencer Wood.[54]

In the fall of 1854, the governor general's seven-year term of office drew to a close. The skilled diplomat had just successfully negotiated the Reciprocity Treaty of 1854. That sought-after agreement, now ratified by the provincial legislatures of British North America, allowed for free trade in natural products with the United States. Elgin left his post in late December 1854. Upon his return to England he was made a special envoy to China. There, in 1860, Elgin achieved great infamy by burning the emperor's summer palace in Beijing to the ground. Tales of his action still elicit Chinese indignation.[55] He later served in Japan and ended his career as the viceroy and governor general of India.

Six years earlier, Elgin, on behalf of the British government, had given the colonists of the Province of Canada the responsibility to govern their own affairs. One of the few powers held back was Indian Affairs, which remained under the jurisdiction of the British government through the governor general until 1860. Elgin initially had selected his brother, Robert Bruce, as his first appointee as superintendent general of Indian Affairs. Laurence Oliphant replaced Bruce in 1854. After Oliphant left with Lord Elgin in late 1854, the post became vacant. Lord Bury obtained his appointment as civil secretary from Sir Edmund Head. In-depth knowledge of the First Nations was not a requirement to run the Indian Department. Good social skills and connections counted for a great deal.

Sir Edmund mentioned the viscount in a letter written 15 November, one month before he succeeded Elgin, as a possible replacement for Oliphant. "Lord Bury is staying in the house & whom I like much. He is clever & has learnt a great deal about the country during the last 5 or 6 months."[56] In December, Bury replaced his friend Oliphant in office of the Indian Department at the Hôtel Union on the Place d'Armes.[57] The fact that the viscount wrote and conversed comfortably in French was a definite advantage.[58] Few Anglophones in government had fluent French; Prime Minister MacNab and Attorney General Macdonald did not speak it.[59] Although it might seem absurdly young by our standards today, Viscount Bury at the tender age of twenty-three assumed administrative control over approximately 15,000 First Nations people in the Canadas.[60] Responsibility at a young age was not unusual for Victoria's servants of empire. In India, district officers not much older than the viscount himself ran the lives of up to three million Indians spread over 17,000 square miles.[61]

Canada remained pre-industrial in 1854. Most people lived on farms. The Canadas in the mid-1850s had roughly two million people. The French-speaking population of the St Lawrence Valley, fed by a high birth rate, had doubled every 30 years after the British conquest in 1760.

Sir Edmund Head. Archives and Special Collections, University of New Brunswick Libraries, UA PC 13 no. 43.

The population of Lower Canada (Canada East), predominantly French-speaking, now reached almost one million. A stream of immigration from the British Isles, attracted largely by the availability of good agricultural land, had caused the population of Upper Canada (Canada West) to soar. It had risen from only 35,000 in 1800 to just under a million at mid-century. Cleared farmland replaced dense forests along the thousand kilometres or so of river- and lakefront from the border of Lower Canada (Quebec) to the St Clair River and the border with the United States at Detroit.[62] British culture was transplanted and its population took over large areas of southern Ontario at the complete expense of the First Nations inhabitants. The new settlers who moved into Upper Canada were unaware of the history and culture of the original inhabitants. The newcomers believed that the land belonged to them, even if they themselves were only recent arrivals.

The biggest cities were, by today's standards, small. Quebec was the second-largest city in British North America with a population of approximately 50,000, after Montreal with about 80,000 people.[63] Quebec City then served as the capital of the Province of Canada. It remained so until October 1855, when Toronto again become the seat of government, part of the clumsy alternation that continued until finally Queen Victoria selected Ottawa as the permanent capital in 1857. Quebec City's population was one-third English-speaking and two-thirds French. In the elite Upper Town, both language groups mixed socially. In the Lower Town lived the "little people": *les gagne-petits*, who worked on the wharfs and in the timber trade. They and their families suffered from poor housing, inadequate sanitation, and seasonal unemployment. What a contrast, noted Isabella Bird, a young middle-class English visitor in late 1854. With all her class-bound prejudices, she wrote,

> The little world in the upper part of the city is probably the most brilliant to be found anywhere in so small a compass. But there is a world below, another nation, seldom mentioned in the aristocratic quarter of St. Louis, where vice, crime, poverty, and misery jostle each other, as pleasure and politics do in the upper town.[64]

In Quebec City, Bury met Sophia MacNab, at twenty-two exactly his age. He found the outgoing woman attractive, physically and personally. A sketch that he drew of the belle in government circles confirms her beauty, as well as his own artistic gift in recording it.[65] Unfortunately, no record of Sophia's first impressions survives. The testimony of Lady Harriet Sarah Wantage, the wife of his lifelong friend and cousin Robert Lindsay, Lord Wantage, does provide a female impression: "Bury was clever, versatile, light-hearted, brilliant in talk, endowed with quick perception and the power of rapid mastery of any subject he took up, and full of life and energy."[66] Years later a gentleman who knew the

Sophia MacNab, drawn by her husband during their courtship. Courtesy of Dundurn National Historic Site, Hamilton, Ontario.

viscount at the time of his arrival in Canada recalled, "He was then the handsomest young man, by all odds in the country. He was in great demand at social events, and was a particular favorite with young ladies."[67]

In late October 1854, Isabella Bird neared the end of her grand tour of North America. The young Englishwoman won invitations to the affable Lord Elgin's dinners and parties at his viceregal residence. In her published memoir, *The Englishwoman in America*, Miss Bird recalled the splendour of parties at Spencer Wood, "glittering epaulettes, scarlet uniforms, and muslin dresses whirled before my dizzy eyes." The dancing continued to two or three in the morning.[68] At the ball she attended on the evening of 25 October, Miss Bird met Lord Bury. Unlike the reaction of other females to him, hers was negative. She noted in her unpublished journal that his free easy unrestricted behaviour, his total freedom, aggravated her. The Anglican clergyman's daughter noted, "There was far too much riot and freedom at this party for my quiet taste and I greatly blame Lord Elgin for lowering the tone of Quebec manners." Isabella continued, "I saw Lord Bury sit for some time on the sofa with his arm round a young lady's waist and this was by no means a solitary instance of impropriety."[69]

Lord Bury's friendship with Sophia did come with a complication. Miss MacNab belonged to the Roman Catholic Church. Many Protestants in Canada feared and distrusted Rome.[70] Moreover, Lord Bury descended directly from Arnold Joost van Keppel from the Netherlands, an adherent of William of Orange, the champion of Protestantism in Britain in the late seventeenth century. Indeed, the Keppel family's English title, Albemarle, had been given for the first earl's services to the Protestant Crown.[71] Yet the free-spirited William Coutts Keppel failed to see her faith as an impediment, for, as he wrote in his diary in 1854, "universal tolerance in religion is most important."[72]

The viscount's friendship with Sophia deepened in the winter of 1854/55. The new superintendent general of Indian Affairs loved Canada's cold, bracing winter, as did the outgoing Sophia. They found the air quality in Quebec City oppressive, with thousands of coal and wood fires pouring carbon into the air. The young couple sought refuge on sleighing parties. The regular clip-clop, clip-clop sounded and sleigh bells rang as their horses raced along the glistening tracks. The handsome, tall Englishman sat beside the bright-eyed, petite Sophia, all warmly wrapped within furs and carriage rugs.[73] During their courtship, he told her stories of England and of faraway lands in Asia.[74]

Sophia was part of an influential family network in Quebec City. The Stuarts, her relatives on her mother's side, were well integrated into both English and French worlds. Her first cousin, prominent Quebec lawyer Andrew Stuart, had married Charlotte-Elmire Aubert de Gaspé, a member of an old French Canadian seigneurial family.[75] Their household was so bilingual that they once trained a parrot to greet Andrew in English and Elmire in French.[76] Another first cousin, George Stuart, had served as the first English-speaking mayor of the city in the late 1840s.[77]

Sophia also had a family tie to the First Nations, as her maternal grandfather was the Reverend John Stuart, an Anglican missionary at Fort Hunter in the Mohawk Valley immediately before the outbreak of the American Revolution. The famous Mohawk war chief Joseph Brant helped the Rev. John Stuart to learn Mohawk. After the rebels occupied Fort Hunter, they turned the Anglican chapel into a tavern and later put the chapel to use as a stable and finally as a fort. Disgusted by the confiscation of his property and persecution by the populace, Stuart left and joined the British in Montreal. In Kingston, he became a prominent Anglican clergyman and occasionally ministered to his old Mohawk flock.[78]

Bury liked his job. First, it was straightforward, thanks to new structures recently put in place, structures that allowed an amateur like himself to run the department. The Bagot Commission, named by the governor general who established it in 1842, had laid down many of the key elements that would govern Indian Affairs to and beyond Confederation. No longer needed as military allies after the War of 1812, the First Nations must be "civilized" and assimilated.[79] Second, another advantage of his post, the pay, by Canadian standards, was lucrative. The young viscount earned £675 (sterling) a year.[80] In comparison, the five visiting Indian superintendents who travelled among First Nations communities throughout the Province of Canada collected only a total of £963, or roughly £200 each.[81] Another great advantage of the position was that it carried with it both prestige and importance. As the governor general's civil secretary, he associated "with public men of all parties" and was called upon to "maintain intimate relations with politicians of all shades of opinion."[82] Disliking formality, the young Englishman, now totally relaxed, urged friends and close colleagues to stop calling him "Lord Bury."[83] He wanted simply to be known as "Bill Bury." The governor general lacked such warmth. Although more than double the viscount's age, Sir Edmund had travelled little. His knowledge of the world came from books. An outstanding linguist, he knew the Greek and Latin classics intimately. The former Oxford don wrote poetry and articles on art criticism. He loved language. In 1855, the viceregal representative prepared an essay on the proper use of the future auxiliary verbs, "shall" and "will."[84] He had a slight stoop, indicating the long hours he spent huddled over a desk.[85]

The fact that Sir Edmund liked Bury was remarkable, as his subordinates did not always please him. When lieutenant governor in New Brunswick he had written to a friend that his private secretary, one Richard Theodore Pennefather, could only talk about work:

"He is young – about 21 – well informed & a gentleman – but I cannot say that he is particularly agreeable to me." Apparently the scholarly governor once tried to discuss with Pennefather the play *Agamemnon* by the ancient Greek dramatist Aeschylus: "I tried at first to get intimate with him and read some of the Agamemnon with him, but I soon found that he was so shy and reserved that I could do nothing."[86] He was disappointed after Pennefather married a young New Brunswick woman, writing to a friend in England, "her people are respectable in every way & I dare say *he* thinks her pretty – which I do not."[87]

Sir Edmund liked the viscount on account of his intellect. Bury's social status as a man of noble birth no doubt also contributed. But that being said, Sir Edmund came to dislike what he regarded as his civil secretary's recklessness. The problem manifested in mid-May 1855, when the governor general refused to meet a delegation of angry First Nations people from the Saugeen or "Indian" Peninsula (later named the Bruce Peninsula for James Bruce, Lord Elgin) between Lake Huron and Georgian Bay.[88] In New Brunswick he had urged that the First Nations be treated as children, and their demands, on account of their diminishing numbers, need not be given great attention. By refusing to see this delegation he followed his previous policy in New Brunswick.[89] Except for five small reserves, the Saugeen First Nations had surrendered the peninsula in October 1854. Six months later, they voiced several important concerns about the government's fulfilment of the agreement's terms. (Today the First Nations in the Bruce Peninsula still seek redress for irregularities in the Saugeen Peninsula Treaty of 1854, No. 72 – Surrender of the Saugeen Peninsula.)[90] Four chiefs were delegated to visit Quebec City with the missionary from Owen Sound, Conrad Van Dusen. The Methodist missionary later wrote, "With all the ample and courteous qualifications of His Excellency in the plenitude of his kindness, he utterly refused to give them an audience to hear their complaints, redress their grievances, or allow them money, from their own funds, to pay their expenses." In contrast, Viscount Bury allowed the visitors to meet him unofficially.[91] Two months later, on an official trip in July 1855 to the Bruce Peninsula, the superintendent general of Indian Affairs went further. He made a small alteration in the 1854 treaty boundary near Southampton to meet First Nations' objections. The Ojibwe interpretation held that they were entitled to increased frontage on Lake Huron. At Floodwood Crossing (now Allenford), Bury accepted their understanding of the correct boundary line and immediately removed a major source of friction.[92]

A 1969 Ontario Archaeological and Historic Sites Board plaque commemorates "The Allenford Pow-Wow" of 1855. It recognizes Lord Bury's contribution. Photo courtesy of Karin Noble, taken 13 May 2016.

Although both his meeting with a First Nations delegation and his alteration of a reserve boundary showed some compassion, Bury remained as culture-bound as anyone of his own time or ours. He neither understood nor valued the First Nations' old way of life, terming it "primitive barbarism."[93] This assessment was used to justify completely the Euro-Canadian efforts to subjugate and convert the original inhabitants of the Canadas to Christianity. As did others, he looked upon assimilation into the non-Indigenous community as a most laudatory goal. In early December 1855, the viscount carefully ranked the First Nations in respect to their degree of "civilization." Top grades went to the Hurons at Lorette, near Quebec City, who had adjusted well to the surrounding French Canadian society. Dedicated Roman Catholics, a great number had lost their Huron language and spoke only French.

At the bottom end of the scale, he consigned the migratory Algonquian fishers and hunters northeast of Quebec and on the north shore of the St Lawrence to the status of "savages."[94]

When Lord Bury visited the Mount Elgin Industrial School at Muncey, Canada West, he found his ideal. The discipline of the institution no doubt attracted him, for was he not himself a product of Eton, the most distinguished of the English public (i.e., private) schools, in which strict discipline was the unalterable rule? Laurence Oliphant, his predecessor as superintendent of Indian Affairs, had urged that the First Nations boarding schools be run with a "salutary system of discipline," which would train the young men "to steady habits of thought and action."[95] Neither Oliphant nor Bury had any idea of how differently the First Nations raised their young. Great Lakes First Nations cultures neither understood nor valued regimentation.[96] Parents were appalled by the corporal punishment of children. Bury knew nothing of this. He left Mount Elgin after a short visit very impressed, writing, "There is no want of mental capacity in an Indian. In one, at least, of the schools which I have visited, the scholars are fully equal, if not superior, to the average pupils of the common schools of the whites." His visit only served to confirm that full assimilation was indeed the road to follow. The former Etonian went on: "The pupils are generally intelligent, clean and orderly; some young men who have completed their course of education there, are now perfectly ready and able to take their places as members of the general population."[97]

By the mid-1850s, Indigenous peoples constituted less than 1 per cent of the province of Canada's total population of roughly two million people. Non-Indigenous people outnumbered the Indigenous by over one hundred to one. All groups had grown rapidly in the first half of the nineteenth century, with the exception of the First Nations, which had declined. Even the African Canadian population now exceeded that of the First Nations.[98] The accepted wisdom held that within two or three generations this "vanishing race" would assimilate or die off. Bury believed this. As he wrote in 1857, "notwithstanding all the care now bestowed," the result "is fast coming to pass – the extermination of the Red Man."[99] In view of their eventual extinction, Bury argued, "The only course which remains for the friend of the aborigines, is to watch jealously the conduct pursued towards them by the authorities, and to protest again unnecessary tyranny or injustice."[100]

Here, our story returns to Peter Jones. Several months before Bury's appointment, a scandal had broken in the Indian Department. It was discovered that Joseph B. Clench, the western superintendent of Indian Affairs, had embezzled from the sale of First Nations' lands an enormous sum, later estimated at £9000.[101] Clench's immediate dismissal now left his position, as visiting superintendent to the First Nations west of London, vacant. Egerton Ryerson, chief superintendent for education for Canada West (and now considered the founder of the Ontario public school system), had served as the first Methodist minister to the Mississauga on the Credit River in the mid-1820s. He strongly recommended Peter Jones for the post. In his letter to Laurence Oliphant on 21 November 1854, Ryerson wrote, "I know of no man whom I think better qualified for the office lately vacated by the removal of Colonel Clench."[102] After Oliphant's departure several weeks later the decision rested with Lord Bury. He did not follow Ryerson's advice, and in hindsight, we can see that he missed an opportunity to contribute to fundamental change.

For three decades, Peter Jones had advocated a new approach to Indigenous affairs: secure titles to the First Nations reserves, a viable economic land base for each First Nation community, a first-class system of education, and self-government for the Indigenous population.[103] The Mississauga leader wanted First Nations communities to become self-sufficient and stable, permanent safe places for the First Nations. As he wrote, "I cannot suppose for a moment that the Supreme Disposer has decreed that the doom of the red man is to fall and gradually disappear, like the mighty wilderness, before the axe of the European settler."[104] But the Indian Office wanted Indigenous people to assimilate, to leave their communities and fully integrate into the dominant Canadian society. Peter Jones had no chance. John A. Macdonald, the most powerful cabinet minister, lobbied Oliphant and then his successor, Viscount Bury, to give the job of civil secretary to John Langton, member of Parliament for Peterborough. Macdonald secured the appointment for his friend, but Langton, whose interest was really in fiscal policy, declined it, as the post of chair of the colony's Board of Audit had also just become available.[105] In late January 1855, the viscount passed over Peter Jones and chose Froome Talfourd, a politically safe English magistrate in Sarnia, Canada West.[106]

In July 1855, Lord Bury toured First Nations communities in Canada West. Shortly after his return, an ugly scandal seriously weakened his conduct of Indian Affairs.[107] In mid-August, young Bury had allegedly embarked on a St Lawrence excursion steamer to Rivière du Loup with a "female of bad character." Worse still, it was said, he had tried to

The last known image of Peter Jones, sketched probably in the early 1850s. The illustration appears as a frontispiece in his *Life and Journals of Kah-ke-wa-quo-na-by (Rev. Peter Jones), Wesleyan Missionary* (Toronto: Anson Green in the Wesleyan Printing Establishment, 1860).

bring his *compagnonne de voyage* to dine at the captain's table. Newspapers throughout the Canadas took up the charges, in English and in French: the woman had been in his stateroom that day for "a reason." The *Brockville Recorder* thundered, "No virtuous woman can meet Lord

Bury without damage to her reputation."[108] A vitriolic attack also issued forth from the Chatham *Planet* in Canada West. "We are glad to see that the press is dealing with him in a proper manner, – castigating him in the right style without gloves. If he be allowed to set an example of immorality to Canadian youth, mock at common decency, openly and unblushingly violate public morality, and trample under foot all respect for those he should honor, what may we expect will eventually be its fruits."[109]

We know that interpretations of events can be multiple and conflicting and that no historical interpretation is final in any respect. In a tone of self-contained aristocratic rage, Bury, heir to the earldom of Albemarle, defended himself: "None of these statements are true." The lady, whom he did not know at all, had been refused a stateroom. To protect the "defenceless woman," he gave up his own, to her and her female servant. They had not gone together to the "table of the steamer at all."[110] Sophia MacNab sided entirely with the viscount. He had acted nobly, in total moral purity. Some papers also accepted his defence. Montreal's French-language *La Patrie* noted his politeness, his distinguished manners, and his conduct as a"vrai gentilhomme," a true gentleman.[111] Others did not.[112] Over a decade later, for instance, the Toronto *Daily Telegraph* still thundered forth against his conduct as "a Commissioner among the Indians." The paper alleged that his behaviour at times "ought to have driven him for ever beyond the bounds of decent society."[113]

When the centre of government in early October 1855 returned to Toronto from Quebec, the governor general took the opportunity to tour Canada West. Bury travelled with Sir Edmund and Lady Head. Premier MacNab and Sophia MacNab came too, as did, among the other dignitaries, John A. Macdonald. In Kingston, all went well. Ladies joined the gentlemen at Kingston's banquet for Sir Edmund. A contributor to the Kingston *Daily British Whig* later noted that "Lord Bury had been the lion of the Kingston party."[114] The "Bury Affair" surfaced with a vengeance at the next stop of the viceregal party, the town of Cobourg, located roughly halfway between Toronto and Kingston on the north shore of Lake Ontario. Cobourg's ladies refused outright to "grace the festive board" because the viscount was there.[115] Throughout, the governor general stood loyally by his secretary. So did Sophia, unflinchingly. In her opinion, the ugly accusations had absolutely no substance. None of Bury's alleged accusers, neither the steamer captain nor any of the passengers, had signed their names to a letter of protest.[116]

The prime minister's daughter courageously defied the hostile eyes of the Cobourg women by leaning on the arm of the notorious Lord Bury as they walked through the fairgrounds of the provincial agricultural fair.[117]

After visiting Hamilton, the governor general and entourage travelled to London. En route, the train stopped briefly in the town of Ingersoll. Only one week earlier, the *Ingersoll Chronicle* had repeated the now well-known charges: "The stateroom occupied by Lord Bury and his companion on board the Saguenay, appeared on the Passenger List as taken by George Brown and lady." Bury, the paper continued in hushed tones, entered first, then his companion "crossed the saloon and joined him in his stateroom, where they spent a considerable part of the afternoon together, alone."[118] The Toronto *Globe* referred to the province's superintendent general of Indian Affairs on 30 October as "one who has outraged all the laws of propriety."[119] The weight of public attention on him, the stares, the continuing "talk" – all took their toll. Although he was expected, Bury failed to appear at the public banquet in London in Sir Edmund's honour.[120]

On the way back from London, the governor general stopped in Brantford, where, at last, he met Peter Jones. A few days later, the Mississauga leader wrote of their meeting, "I was introduced to His Excellency who said he was glad to see me and hoped that my health had improved." Sir Edmund added "that he would be happy to see me in Toronto when settled as he wished to have a conversation with me."[121] The viscount might have been present at the Brantford meeting with Peter Jones. If not, Sir Edmund must have mentioned the meeting to his secretary and superintendent general of Indian Affairs. But Bury, clearly destabilized by the scandal, retained no memory of it. Nearly two years later, he would write,

> Justice to the full extent the aborigines will not obtain; they are too feeble to assert their right to it – too ignorant even to demand it intelligibly: but they lament our broken faith and violated treaties with a simple pathos that makes one's heart ache, and submit to their inevitable fate with the stoicism that a savage alone can exhibit.[122]

In such a statement, Bury completely overlooked Peter Jones, whose voice had thundered against the injustices of the Indian Department for three decades. The superintendent general of Indian Affairs was not well briefed on the Mississauga. He knew little, for instance, about

Peter Jones's uncle, Joseph Sawyer. In late 1855, Bury wrote that he was chief at Port Credit, or the Credit River.[123] Actually, the Mississauga had moved nearly a decade earlier to New Credit.

The newspapers continued to show an interest in Bury's private life. Late in October, the Toronto correspondent of the *Montreal Gazette* wrote,

> Rumor says Lord Bury has resolved on a wise course to silence the scandal circulated respecting him. I say scandal, but there are many here who believe it perfectly true, and some of our best families were resolved to treat his lordship coldly accordingly. But now he is to be married, and so become respectable again.[124]

The well-informed circles proved correct. In early November Bury drew up his marriage settlement with Sophia and their wedding was announced for 15 November.[125] The respectable Hamilton wedding silenced almost all the Canadian newspapers.[126] John A. Macdonald himself pronounced the Bury Affair "dead and gone" in a letter written to a Montreal journalist in January 1856.[127]

Lord Bury and Sophia MacNab had two marriage ceremonies at Dundurn Castle. As the *Hamilton Spectator* delightfully phrased it, "The Roman Catholic marriage ceremony, rendered necessary by the bride's adherence to that faith, was performed at an early hour in the morning."[128] The second, more formal, Anglican ceremony followed the arrival of Sir Edmund Head and Lady Head and the numerous other distinguished guests, including several cabinet members, the powerful Montreal politician George-Etienne Cartier, and the Anglican archdeacon of Toronto, John Strachan. The latter assisted Sophia's uncle, George Okill Stuart, the Anglican archdeacon of Ontario, with the Anglican service in Dundurn's principal reception area, the fully carpeted drawing room.[129]

The day of his wedding, Lord Bury kept his own views on First Nations to himself. He had been seriously destabilized by the uproar over his alleged conduct on the St Lawrence steamer. Yet this is one of the redeeming attributes of the young man. He had seen injustice to the First Nations, and he did record it. In his 1855 summary report on Indian Affairs to the British government, submitted just three weeks after his wedding, he wrote of how the "whites" "forcibly squat upon their lands and plunder their timber."[130] This was embarrassing as several years earlier, his own father-in-law, now the prime minister of the

Canadas, had defended the rights of squatters who had illegally taken up residence on the Six Nations' territory along the Grand River.[131]

A lunch followed the Anglican wedding. The governor general made an "exceedingly happy" speech to the health of the newly married pair, to which Viscount Bury responded. After the lunch, the 150 or so guests dispersed to return by cab that evening around eight for a dance. The drawing room of Dundurn, so recently the chapel, was now transformed into a ballroom. Dancing began at 9 p.m. and continued to 1 a.m., when a huge supper followed, marked by a fusillade of champagne corks. The popping of so many bottles, one journalist commented, made all imagine that Dundurn actually stood "in the neighbourhood of Sebastopol,"[132] a reference to the Russian fortress in the Crimea that had recently fallen to the Anglo-French and Turkish forces. The newly married couple spent their honeymoon at Spencer Wood at the invitation of His Excellency and Lady Head.[133]

In January 1856, Lord Bury announced his intention to return to England with his Canadian bride. Sir Edmund accepted his resignation.[134] From within his staff he now elevated the dull but predictable Richard Theodore Pennefather to become his civil secretary. Pennefather would be the last imperial appointee to head the Indian Department. Head welcomed tranquillity. Bury had provided far too much excitement, from the viscount's reception of the Saugeen chiefs to the charges of Bury's improper conduct on a St Lawrence steamer. As His Excellency wrote to his friend George Cornewall Lewis in England, the young aristocrat had gotten into several "scrapes," situations "which have bothered me considerably." Nevertheless, he added this final comment about the future 7th Earl of Albemarle: "I hope he will do well yet. He has great abilities."[135]

Viscount Bury's involvement in the complex world of Native-newcomer relations in Canada was fleeting at just one year. In his year-end report on Indian Affairs submitted in early December, he called for the retention of the Indian Department in the Province of Canada. To do away with it as some suggested would amount to "a breach of faith" with the First Nations, who had, through the treaty process, given up their lands for British protection and support.[136] He recommended that the Indian Department be retained, and it was. The imperial authorities then made sure they did not pay for it. They transferred all financial and political responsibility for the First Nations to the Province of Canada in 1860.

In 1857, a little over a year after Bury's departure, Attorney General John A. Macdonald advanced the Canadian policy of full integration.

He introduced in the Canadian assembly the Act for the Gradual Civilization of the Indian Tribes, legislation designed to speed up the assimilation of the First Nations. In effect, it further curtailed First Nations' control over their population, land, and finances. It aimed to integrate a settled, educated First Nations population with full citizenship into the larger society. It would give the vote to qualifying First Nation males who were at least 21 years old. They would receive as well 50 acres of reserve land in their own names, land that subsequently would be removed from the reserve. Those who applied must meet the test of a special board, to prove they were of good moral character and educated, as well as debt free. Those who qualified ceased to be wards of the Crown, ceased to be legal Indians. No long members of their First Nations communities, those who were "enfranchised" became full British subjects.[137] This objective enjoyed widespread support among the political elite of the Canadas. In the nineteenth and twentieth centuries, this policy was described as assimilation. In the twenty-first century, particularly after the release of *The Final Report of the Truth and Reconciliation Commission of Canada* in 2015, the phrase "cultural genocide" has now entered into wide usage.

The Canadian legislature quickly passed the bill. In response, the First Nations from across the province of Canada met at an important council on the Six Nations territory on the Grand River west of Hamilton in 1858. Their protest against the breakup of their remaining land base and the campaign to end their Indian status went largely unnoticed.[138] An editorial in the Toronto *Globe* a few years later summarized the opinion of many non-Indigenous Canadians: "[The Indians] cannot be permitted to stand in the way of the advance of civilization on this continent."[139]

In the same year that imperial control of Indian Affairs finally passed to the Canadas, the 18-year-old Prince of Wales (the future Edward VII) travelled across British North America on a goodwill mission. Throughout the tour, First Nations groups presented petitions. Exactly one decade earlier, the Province of Canada had rejected the Mississauga land claims submitted by Chief Peter Jones and his uncle, Head Chief Joseph Sawyer. Their petition of 8 June 1847 had specifically mentioned among the "tracts of land, which to the best of their knowledge and belief have never been surrendered … Burlington Heights, containing about 200 acres, near Sir Allan MacNab's house."[140] Peter Jones had died in June 1856, but Joseph Sawyer, still head chief of the Mississauga of New Credit, sent a second list of land claims in September 1860, including "the peninsula forming Toronto harbour [now Toronto Islands]" and "Burlington Beach and a portion of Burlington Heights."[141] But the Mississaugas' petition to the imperial government, and those of the other communities, went unheeded. Britain had just transferred complete authority over the First Nations to the Province of Canada. The site of Dundurn Castle would not be returned to the Mississauga, or any compensation provided.

Back in England, William Coutts Keppel did well. The viscount was elected to the House of Commons. In London commercial circles, he became a strong advocate of the practicability, and of the imperial importance, of a railway from the Province of Canada to the Pacific Coast.[142] Bury served in the House of Commons for over a dozen years, then the House of Lords for nearly two decades. His love of writing led to four articles on Canadian affairs in *Fraser's Magazine* in 1857 and 1858. His big book on the British Empire, *The Exodus of the Western Nations*, his magnum opus at nearly 1,000 pages, followed in 1865. The *Times* praised his examination of three centuries of settlement in the Americas as a work that "shows very great research with honourable industry."[143] The several articles he published on electricity, and an essay on modern philosophy, reveal his remarkably wide range of interests. His co-authored handbook on bicycling that came out in 1887 enjoyed the greatest commercial success. It ran through five editions before his death in 1894.[144]

A serious accident in 1867 handicapped Bury's political career. He was permanently injured when a rifle that he was firing exploded and the breech bolt entered his forehead. His doctors prescribed "absolute surcease from any mental or political activity."[145] Nevertheless, he recovered well, even if he thereafter was supposed to avoid strenuous political activity. He founded in 1868 the Colonial Society in London, which later evolved into the Royal Commonwealth Society. In 1876, he was called up to the House of Lords as Baron Ashford during his father's lifetime, although customarily only one member of a family at a time can be a peer. On two occasions in the Lords, he acted as the undersecretary for war.[146]

Twice Bury returned to Canada: in 1858 and in 1883.[147] On his 1883 visit, he travelled with Sophia and two of their daughters, accompanied by his valet and his wife's maid.[148] A highlight of the trip was his visit to Ottawa in late October. He met twice with Sir John A. Macdonald, who in addition to serving as prime minister was now also superintendent general of Indian Affairs.[149] Macdonald had become one of the foremost statesmen of the British Empire. Three decades earlier, Bury recalled, he had managed his cabinet portfolio as attorney general quite informally. On occasion, what Macdonald biographer Richard Gwyn has called "his best known personal habit" went completely out of control.[150] Bury recalled that one day, Governor General Head dispatched him to find Attorney General Macdonald, who had not been seen for a week. Bury located him, pushed his way past the old housekeeper, and walked into Macdonald's bedroom, where he found him sitting on his bed, reading a novel with a decanter of sherry on the table beside him. Bury said, "Mr. Macdonald, the Governor-General told me to say to you that if you don't sober up and get back to business, he will not be answerable for the consequences." Macdonald fired back: "Are you here in your official capacity, or as a private individual?" "What difference does that make?" replied Bury. "Just this," snapped the inebriated politician, "if you are here in your official capacity, you can go back to Sir Edmund Head, give him my compliments, and tell him to go to hell; If you are here simply as a private individual, you can go yourself!"[151]

The year 1883 marked Lord Bury's last trip to Canada. It included a short visit in mid-November with Sophia to Hamilton and to Dundurn Castle, the site of their wedding exactly 28 years earlier.[152] They had had a happy family life. Of their ten children, one had died in infancy, but three boys and six girls had grown to healthy adulthood.[153] Since their marriage, Sophia had acted as her husband's private secretary, writing letters in her large, clear hand.[154] They were extraordinarily close, so close, in fact, that on Easter Day 1879, the viscount converted to her faith and became a Roman Catholic.[155] Bury succeeded to the family earldom of Albemarle on his father's death in 1891, but he himself died just three years later. The 7th Earl of Albemarle was buried at the family seat of Quidenham, Norfolk.[156] Sophia survived her husband for nearly a quarter of a century. The dowager countess of Albemarle died in 1917.[157] Today many descendants of the 7th Earl of Albemarle and the dowager countess live in the United Kingdom. One of their great-great-granddaughters is Camilla, Duchess of Cornwall, consort of Prince Charles, Prince of Wales.

Lord Bury had an extremely varied and interesting year and a half in the Canadas. A study of his sojourn in Canada provides both an entertaining snapshot of life in the higher echelons of Canadian life in the mid-1850s and a glimpse into the administration of Indian affairs in 1855, one of the last years of imperial control. On occasion, he showed true humanity, such as his welcoming of the First Nation delegation in

John A. Macdonald, Attorney General for Canada West, about 1857. Library and Archives Canada, C-4154.

Quebec City after the governor general refused meet them, and his readjustment of a reserve boundary in the Saugeen Peninsula. The viscount also raised the alarm in his 1855 report of the rapacity of land squatters and timber robbers on First Nations lands. Yet clearly there were also lost opportunities. Most significantly, Bury passed over an opportunity to improve the status of the First Nations when he failed to appoint Peter Jones as western superintendent of Indian Affairs. How truly ironic that through his mother, Peter Jones was directly linked to at least 10,000 years of occupancy in North America, while Viscount Bury could claim less than two years; yet this newcomer to Canada became the senior administrator for all 15,000 Indians in the Canadas, while Peter Jones could not obtain even the position of western superintendent.

NOTES

This essay expands upon an after-dinner talk given at the Dundurn Castle Coach House Restaurant, Wednesday, 19 November 2008, hosted by the L.R. Wilson Centre for Canadian History, Department of History, McMaster University. I thank Professor Viv Nelles, chair of the Wilson Centre, for his invitation to give this address. I thank also Agnes Bongers and Kevin Cavanagh of the *Hamilton Spectator* for publishing a short excerpt on 15 November 2008, the 154th anniversary of the wedding of Lord Bury and Sophia MacNab, under the title "Hamilton's Special Moment: Sophia MacNab's Wedding Attracted Canada's Elite to Dundurn Castle." Thanks are due to many others who assisted, including, in Hamilton, Janet Forjan of the Dundurn National Historic Site, who helped in so many ways with images and additional documentation; Tom Minnes of the Dundurn National Historic Site; Margaret Houghton, archivist, Local History and Archives, Hamilton Public Library; Michael McAllister of the Hamilton Military Museum; David Lopeke, liturgy coordinator and archivist, St Mary's Pro Cathedral, Hamilton. I thank in the Owen Sound area Stephanie McMullen, heritage interpreter, Grey Roots Museum and Archives, and Stephanie's father, Cliff McMullen; Bill Fitzgerald; Elizabeth Cockburn; Charles Meanwell; and Frances Cockburn. Others elsewhere in Ontario who assisted include John Leslie of Ottawa; Elene Ftohogiannis of the Archives of Ontario; Jennifer Toews of the Thomas Fisher Rare Book Library at the University of Toronto; Neville Thompson of the Department of History, Western University; Sally Bowen of Amherst Island; Nadia Bock, reference librarian, Cobourg Public Library; and David Beasley of Simcoe. In Quebec City, I thank Pierre-Louis Lapointe, Jean-Marie Lebel, and Frédéric Smith. For accommodation and good cheer on two research trips to Quebec City I am grateful to Fernand Harvey and Sophie Laurence Lamontagne, Richard Jones and Lilianne Plamondon. In England, I thank Miranda Villiers, secretary of the Keppel Association; Louise Clark and Sue Lodwick, Suffolk Record Office, Ipswich

Branch; Charles Barber of Kings Lynn; Barry Johnson of Birmingham; the staff of the British Library; and Andrew Bethell and Claire Widgery for lodging and good conversation in London. Others assisted: Edward Beasley of San Diego, California; Ged Martin of Shanacoole, Ireland; and Emily Earley of Madison, Wisconsin. Kerry Abel of Ottawa provided excellent comments on the final draft of this essay. Most important of all, I thank my wife, Nancy Townshend, for the time taken from family activities to tell this story for this Festschrift in honour of Jim Miller.

1 *Alberta Formed Alberta Transformed*, 2 vols., eds. Michael Payne, Donald Wetherell, and Catharine Cavanaugh (Calgary: University of Calgary Press, and Edmonton: University of Alberta Press, 2006), 1:xii.

2 On 30 November 1855, the *New York Times* described the wedding as "the most prominent event of recent date in Canada." See the article "Canada: Correspondence of the New-York Daily Times, Toronto, Saturday, Nov. 24, 1855."

3 D.R. Beer, "Sir Allan Napier MacNab," *Dictionary of Hamilton Biography*, vol. 1 (Hamilton, Ontario: Dictionary of Hamilton Biography, 1981), 135, and Marion MacRae, *MacNab of Dundurn* (Toronto: Clarke, Irwin & Company Ltd., 1971), are invaluable resources on both Allan MacNab and Dundurn. Beer's piece is wonderfully researched and MacRae's superbly written. Also useful is the beautifully illustrated *Dundurn Castle: Sir Allan MacNab and His Hamilton Home* (Toronto: James Lorimer & Company, 2007), by Edward Smith.

4 Niigonwedom James Sinclair, "Nindoodemag Bagijiganan: A History of Anishinaabeg Narrative" (PhD thesis, University of British Columbia, 2013), 186 and 190.

5 "Register, Thermometer, Barometer," *Hamilton Spectator*, 5 December 1855.

6 Beer, *MacNab*, 55; Peter Baskerville, "Sir Allan Napier MacNab," *Dictionary of Canadian Biography* (hereafter *DCB*), vol. 9, *1861–1870* (1976), 520. Both state that Dundurn has 72 rooms, but actually it has 40 rooms and public spaces. Interview with Tom Minnes, Dundurn National Historic Site, 18 November 2008.

7 John Weaver, *Hamilton: An Illustrated History* (Toronto: James Lorimer & Co., 1982), 16. Hamilton became the name of the settlement at the Head of the Lake in 1816. Few Hamiltonians then, and fewer today, know that their city's namesake, by today's usage, is a Métis. George Hamilton's maternal grandmother, Catharine Askin Robertson Hamilton, was the daughter of the fur trader and merchant John Askin and his Indigenous wife. His mother's brother, John Baptist Askin, the clerk of the peace in the London District, was recognized as "Indian." See Cl. T. Campbell, *Pioneer Days in London* (London: Advertiser Job Printing Company, 1921), 26–7.

8 Isabella Lucy Bird, *The Englishwoman in America* (Toronto: University of Toronto Press, 1966; first published 1856), 191. Weaver, *Hamilton*, supplies the figures of 14,112 for 1852 and 25,000 for 1857 (p. 196).
9 J.M.S. Careless, "Table IV: Population Growth in Central Canadian Cities, 1851–1921," in *Toronto to 1918: An Illustrated History* (Toronto: James Lorimer & Co., 1984), 200. In 1851 Toronto had 30,775 residents and in 1861, 44,821; hence, I use the estimate of 40,000 for 1854.
10 The baronial castle on Burlington Heights, now a National Historic Site, has been beautifully restored to its original appearance in the mid-nineteenth century. A virtual reality tour is available on the Dundurn website at http://museumshamilton.com/#/pano/dundurn-main-frontentrance.
11 Michael Fitzpatrick McAllister, "A Very Pretty Object: The Socially Constructed Landscape of Burlington Heights 1780–1815" (MA thesis, McMaster University, 2002), 7; Smith, *Dundurn*, 10.
12 Donald B. Smith, *Sacred Feathers: The Reverend Peter Jones (Kahkewaquonaby) and the Mississauga Indians*, 2nd ed. (Toronto: University of Toronto Press, 2013), 2.
13 Ibid., 26.
14 Donald B. Smith, *Mississauga Portraits: Ojibwe Voices from Nineteenth-Century Canada* (Toronto: University of Toronto Press, 2013), 44–50.
15 Leo A. Johnson, "The Mississauga – Lake Ontario Land Surrender of 1805," *Ontario History*, 83/3 (September 1990): 249.
16 Donald B. Smith, "The Dispossession of the Mississauga Indians: A Missing Chapter in the Early History of Upper Canada," *Ontario History* 73/2 (1981): 67–87; see in particular pages 74–6.
17 Donald B. Smith, "Nawahjegezhegwabe," *DCB*, 9:592–3.
18 McAllister, "Heights," 10–11.
19 Peter Jones, *History of the Ojebway Indians* (London: A.W. Bennett, 1861), 51. Partridge can also here mean "ruffed grouse."
20 Smith, *Mississauga Portraits*, 44–50.
21 Smith, *Sacred Feathers*, 39.
22 Peter Jones, *Life and Journals of Kah-ke-wa-quo-na-by* (Toronto: Anson Green at the Wesleyan Printing Establishment, 1860), 8. Eliza Field Jones, entry for 23 August 1835 in "Diary, April 13, 1834–September 13, 1835," Peter Jones Collection, Victoria University Library.
23 Peter Jones, quoted in the *Banner* [Aberdeen, Scotland], 15 August 1845. A copy of the clipping is in the United Church Archives, Toronto.
24 Smith, *Dundurn Castle*, 49–55.
25 Beer, "Sir Allan Napier MacNab," 1:135. Sir Allan MacNab, quoted in, "The MacNab Testimonial," *Hamilton Spectator*, 1 December 1855.
26 Baskerville, "MacNab," 520.

27 Smith, *Dundurn Castle*, 7. Marion MacRae, *MacNab of Dundurn* (Toronto: Clarke, Irwin & Company Ltd., 1971), comments in the opening section of the book, entitled, "Why."
28 William Kilbourn, *The Firebrand: William Lyon Mackenzie and the Rebellion in Upper Canada* (Toronto: Clarke, Irwin & Co., 1956, repr. 1967), 179, 182–6.
29 John Langton, copy of a letter fragment entitled "J. Langton's estimate of Cayley 1855," B 1965–0014/004(09), University of Toronto Archives.
30 Baskerville, "MacNab," 525.
31 J.R. Miller, "Anti-Catholic Thought in Victorian Canada," *Canadian Historical Review* 66/4 (1985): 474–94.
32 Two excellent sources of information on the Stuart family are A.H. Young, *The Rev. John Stuart D.D., U.E.L. of Kingston, U. C. and His Family: A Genealogical Study* (Kingston: Whig Press, 1920); and Doris Mary O'Dell, "Launching Loyalist Children. The Stuart Family of Early Kingston" (MA thesis, Queen's University, 1984).
33 Beer, *MacNab*, 42.
34 Charles A. Carter, "Sophia Mary MacNab," *Dictionary of Hamilton Biography*, vol. 1 (Hamilton, Ontario: Dictionary of Hamilton Biography, 1981), 144–5; and Charles Ambrose Carter and Thomas Melville Bailey, eds., *The Diary of Sophia MacNab*, 6th ed. (Hamilton, Ontario: Seldon Griffin Graphics, 2003).
35 Amelia Ryerse Harris, "Diary," in *The Eldon House Diaries: Five Women's Views of the 19th Century*, ed. Robin S. Harris and Terry G. Harris (Toronto: Champlain Society, 1994), 208.
36 Cecil Woodham-Smith, *The Reason Why* (New York: McGraw-Hill, 1954), 8. See, as well, the "Prologue" of David Cannadine's *The Decline and Fall of the British Aristocracy* (New Haven, CT: Yale University Press, 1990), 1–31. I thank Warren Elofson for this reference.
37 Sir Algernon West, *Recollections 1832 to 1886* (London: Smith, Elder, & Co., 1899), 75–6.
38 Earl of Albemarle, M.C., "Foreword," in Carter and Bailey, *The Diary*, 4; and Georgiann Blakiston, *Woburn and the Russells* (London: Constable London, 1980), 141–2, 261.
39 "Viscount and Viscountess Palmerston Entertained," *Times*, 24 March 1851; "Lady John Russell's Assembly," *Times*, 5 June 1851; "Town Edition: Her Majesty's Costume Ball," *Era* (London, England), 15 June 1851; "Ball in the Tower," *Freeman's Journal and Daily Commercial Advertiser* (Dublin, Ireland), 22 December 1851.
40 "Episodes in the Life of Wm. Coutts, Viscount Bury, afterwards 7th Earl," HA67/D2/5, pp. 204, 213, Suffolk Record Office, Ipswich Branch. William Coutts Keppel turned 20 on 15 April 1852. He was aide-de-camp to Lord

Frederick FitzClarence in India, 1852–3, according to Frederic Boase, *Modern English Biography*, 6 vols. (1909; London: Frank Cass & Co., 1965), 5:62. Bury landed in India only on 27 March 1853. See "India and China," *Daily News* (London, England), 15 April 1853.

41 A.F. Pollard, rev. H.C.G. Matthew, "William Coutts Keppel, Seventh Earl of Albemarle and Viscount Bury (1832–1894)," *Oxford Dictionary of National Biography*, vol. 31 (Oxford: Oxford University Press, 2004), 373.

42 Published in London by Henry Coulburn in 1827. A delightful review of the book appears in *The Eclectic Review* 27 (May 1827): 385–405; available through Google Books.

43 C.A. Manning Press, *Norfolk Notabilities: A Portrait Gallery* (London: Jarrold and Sons, 1893), 41–2. Bury was back in England by late August 1853, as he attended an election dinner at Norwich 25 August. See the *Times*, 27 August 1853.

44 "Her Majesty's Levee," *Morning Chronicle* (London), 4 May 1854.

45 Suffield to Arnold Keppel, dated Gunton Park, Norwich, 29 August 1894, HA67: 461/422, Suffolk Record Office, Ipswich Branch. Lord Suffield married Cecilia Annetta Baring on 4 May 1854; Geoffrey H. White, ed., "Suffield," *The Complete Peerage*, vol. 13, pt. 1 (London: St Catherine Press, 1953), 427.

46 "Political Reunion," *Morning Chronicle* (London), 8 May 1854.

47 Leslie Stephen, rev. Anne Taylor, "Laurence Oliphant," *Oxford Dictionary of National Biography*, vol. 41 (Oxford: Oxford University Press, 2004), 725–30; and Philip Henderson, *The Life of Laurence Oliphant: Traveller, Diplomat and Mystic* (London: Robert Hale, 1956), 43.

48 MacRae, *MacNab of Dundurn*, 156.

49 Lord Elgin to Lady Elgin, dated [Quebec City, Spencer Wood], 24 June 1854, Mikan no. 4030109, Library and Archives Canada.

50 Lord Bury, Diary 1854, 17–24, Albemarle Manuscripts, microfilm reel A-305, Library and Archives Canada; "The Canadian Elections," *Times* (London), 25 July 1854.

51 Laurence Oliphant, *Minnesota and the Far West* (Edinburgh: William Blackwood and Sons, 1855), 52–5.

52 Bury, Diary 1854, 33. Ojibwe speaker Cecil King points that the reindeer is not an animal familiar to the Ojibwe. "Wah-bah" is the form used for a semi-tone of white, that is, pale whitish. The word "tic" is not Ojibwe. What is meant here is actually the word *adik* or "elk." The English lord's name, he writes, best translates as "pale or white (even) Elk," e-mail from Cecil King to Donald Smith, 6 November 2008.

53 Bury, Diary 1854. The trip began in Peterborough on 21 July and ended at Niagara Falls, 4 September 1854. On p. 31 he states that after he decided

not to enter the contest he briefly canvassed "for Boyd who when I left July 22 had an excellent chance of success." The lumberman Mossom Boyd lost.

54 Isabella Lucy Bird, an English traveller, described Lord Bury as one of Lord Elgin's aides-de-camp, "who, on a tour through North America, became enamoured of Quebec." Isabella Lucy Bird, *The Englishwoman in America* (Toronto: University of Toronto Press, 1966; first published 1856), 262. "Foreign Intelligence," *Liverpool (England) Mercury*, 13 October 1854. "The guests now at Spencer Wood are the Hon. Miss Murray, maid of honour to her Majesty, and Lord Bury."

55 David C. Wright, *The History of China* (Westport, CT: Greenwood Press, 2001), 106.

56 Sir Edmund Head to Sir George Cornewall Lewis, dated Spencer Wood, Quebec, 15 November 1854, Sir Edmund Head Papers, microfilm reel M194, Library and Archives Canada. I thank Ged Martin for bringing this quotation to my attention and for his transcription of Head's almost totally unintelligible handwriting.

57 Marc Vallières et al., *Histoire de Quebec et de sa region, tome II: 1792–1939* (Quebec: Les Presses de l'Université Laval, 2008), 778; Pierre-Georges Roy, "L'hôtel Union ou Saint-George à Québec," *Bulletin de recherches historiques* 43/1: 3–17. Today the building stands directly across the Place d'Armes from the Château Frontenac at 12 and 14, rue Sainte-Anne. It is now the *Centre Infotouriste de Québec*. For Laurence Oliphant's description of the view from his office window in late 1854, see Margaret Oliphant W. Oliphant, *Memoir of the Life of Laurence Oliphant and of Alice Oliphant, His Wife*, 2 vols, 2nd ed. (Edinburgh: Blackwood and Sons, 1891), 1:155.

58 See, for example, copies of his letters in French to the Mother Superior of the Ursulines in Quebec City, the Superior of the Sulpician Order in Montreal, and Bishop Charbonnel of Toronto, 4 January 1855, in Governor General's Office, Letterbooks, Canada, Civil Secretary's Letterbook, 1847–1855, RG 7 G17 C, vol. 14, microfilm reel H-1204, Library and Archives Canada.

59 See Beer, *MacNab*, 191–2; and Richard Gwyn, *John A.: The Man Who Made Us: The Life and Times of John A. Macdonald*, vol. 1, *1815–1867* (Toronto: Random House, 2007), 130–1.

60 Isabelle Bird estimated there were "fourteen thousand Indians in Canada." Bird, *Englishwoman*, 288, 312. Laurence Oliphant wrote that the entire number "does not exceed 15,000." Oliphant, *Minnesota and the Far West*, 49. Smith, *Sacred Feathers*, 329n55.

61 Niall Ferguson, *Empire: How Britain Made the Modern World* (London: Penguin, 2004), 184.

62 R. Cole Harris, "Peopling," in *Encyclopedia of Canada's Peoples*, ed. Paul Robert Magocsi (Toronto: University of Toronto Press, 1999), 1049.
63 John Hare, Marc Lafrance, and David-Thiery Ruddel, "Tableau 10: La population de Quebec, 1608–1871," in *Histoire de la ville de Québec 1608–1871* (Montreal: Boréal, 1987), 324. In 1851 the population was 45,940 and in 1861 57,375; hence I use the estimate of 50,000 for 1854. For Toronto, see Careless, "Table IV: Population Growth in Central Canadian Cities, 1851–1921," in *Toronto to 1918*, 200.
64 Bird, *Englishwoman*, 265.
65 The "belle in Government circles." I love Marion MacRae's description in *MacNab of Dundurn*, 157.
66 Lady Harriett Sarah Wantage, *Lord Wantage, V.C., K.C.B.: A Memoir*, 2nd ed. (London: Smith, Elder & Co., 1908), 12.
67 Unidentified "gentleman" quoted in "The Parliamentary Buildings: Visited by Distinguished Personages," *Ottawa Daily Free Press*, 27 October 1883.
68 Bird, *Englishwoman*, 273.
69 Two pages of the manuscript diary are reproduced in Bird, *Englishwoman*, 273 and 274. The reference to Lord Bury appears on 274.
70 J.R. Miller, "Anti-Catholic Thought in Victorian Canada," *Canadian Historical Review* 66/4 (1985): 474–4.
71 James Falkner, "Arnold Joost van Keppel," *Oxford Dictionary of National Biography*, vol. 31 (Oxford: Oxford University Press, 2004), 360–6. I also thank Mary Eggermont-Molenaar for background information on Arnold Joost van Keppel.
72 Bury, Diary 1854, 19.
73 He was six feet tall. Special Correspondent of the *N.Y. Times*, "Incidents at Sea – Voyage of the Asia – Amusements on Board – Poem by Lord Bury," *New York Times*, 11 February 1859; reprinted in the *Hamilton Times*, 14 February 1859. I thank Janet Forjan for this reference.
74 Albemarle, "Foreword," 4.
75 Celine Cyr, "Sir Andrew Stuart," *DCB*, vol. 12, *1891–1900* (1990), 999–1000.
76 Louisa Blair, *The Anglos: The Hidden Face of Quebec City*, vol. 1, *1608–1850* (Québec: Commission de la capitale nationale du Québec, 2005), 60; also Jacques Castonguay, *Au temps de Philippe Aubert de Gaspé: Lady Stuart* (Montreal: Editions du Méridien, 1986), 94.
77 Kenneth S. Mackenzie, "George Okill Stuart," *DCB*, vol. 11, *1881–1890* (1982), 861.
78 Barbara Graymont, *The Iroquois in the American Revolution* (Syracuse: Syracuse University Press, 1972), 148; and John Wolfe Lydekker, *The Faithful*

Mohawks (Port Washington, NY: Ira J. Friedman, 1968; first published 1938), 132, 165, 187–8. Also see Earle Thomas, "Missionary to the Mohawks: John Stuart's Early Career," in *St. George's Cathedral: Two Hundred Years of Community*, ed. Donald Swainson (Kingston, ON: Quarry Press, 1991), 136.

79 J.R. Miller, *Skyscrapers Hide the Heavens: A History of Indian-White Relations in Canada*, 3rd ed. (Toronto: University of Toronto Press, 2000), 132–3. John Leslie, "The Bagot Commission: Developing a Corporate Memory for the Indian Department," *Historical Papers, Ottawa 1982* 17/1: 31–52.

80 Two estimates appeared in the press. The Montreal *Commercial Advertiser*, as reported in *Le Pays* (Montreal), 21 August 1855, claimed that the figure was £750. The *New Brunswicker* quoted in the Halifax *Tri-Weekly British Colonist*, 26 February 1856, reported £800 (sterling). I thank Janet Forjan for the *Colonist* reference. Actually, the sum listed in the Blue Books contains the exact figure £675 (sterling). My thanks to both Lorraine Gaboury and Patricia Kennedy of Library and Archives Canada for this information: e-mail to the author, 23 February 2009.

81 Lord Bury to Sir Edmund W. Head, dated Indian Department, Toronto, 5 December 1855, in Indian Department, Canada: Return to an Address of the Honourable The House of Commons, dated 28 April 1856, 23, CIHM fiche number 63353 (hereafter RETURN).

82 Viscount Bury, *Exodus of the Western Nations*, 2 vols. (London: Richard Bentley, 1865), 1:v–vi.

83 "Episodes in the Life of Wm. Coutts, Viscount Bury, afterwards 7th Earl," HA67/D2/5, Suffolk Record Office, Ipswich Branch, 204, 213, 231.

84 Barbara J. Messamore, *Canada's Governors General, 1847–1878* (Toronto: University of Toronto Press, 2006), 73, 241n7. Head's essay, *Shall and Will: Two Chapters on Future Auxiliary Verbs*, appeared in 1856.

85 Messamore, *Canada's Governors General*, 75.

86 Lewis Papers, Head to Lewis, 22 January 1850, cited in D.G.G. Kerr, with the assistance of J.A. Gibson, *Sir Edmund Head: A Scholarly Governor* (Toronto: University of Toronto Press, 1954), 57. I thank Jim Taylor for background information on Aeschylus.

87 *The New Brunswick Census of 1851: York County*, compiled by Elizabeth Sewell and Elizabeth Saunders (Fredericton: Provincial Archives of New Brunswick, 1979), 98. Arianna Pennyfather [Pennefather] is listed with her husband, R.F. [T.] Pennyfather. He was 23 and she 21. I thank Twila Buttimer, Provincial Archives of New Brunswick, for this information. Head is quoted in Kerr, *Head*, 57.

88 Alan Rayburn, *Place Names of Ontario* (Toronto: University of Toronto Press, 1997), 46.

89 L.F.S. Upton, *Micmacs and Colonists: Indian-White Relations in the Maritimes, 1713–1867* (Vancouver: UBC Press, 1979), 110.

90 Jeff Gray, "A Fence Separates the Saugeen-owned Part of Sauble Beach, but the First Nation Is Fighting for Another 2.4 Kilometres of Beachfront: It's a Divisive Conflict That's Older Than Canada itself," *Globe and Mail*, 31 August 2015, A6–A7. Laurence Oliphant made the 1854 treaty; see Smith, *Mississauga Portraits*, 121–2.

91 Enemikeese [Conrad Van Dusen], *The Indian Chief: An Account of the Labours, Losses, Sufferings, and Oppression of Ke-Zig-Ko-E-Ne-Ne (David Sawyer): A Chief of the Ojibbeway Indians in Canada West* (London: Sold at 66, Paternoster Row, 1867), 86–7. For an overview of the complicated First Nations political situation in the Bruce Peninsula at this time, see Stephanie McMullen, "Disunity and Dispossession: Nawash Ojibwa and Potawatomi in the Saugeen Territory, 1836–1865" (MA thesis, University of Calgary, 1997).

92 "Copy of a Report of a Committee of the Honorable the Executive Council, approved by His Excellency the Governor General on the 27th September, 1855," in Canada, *Indian Treaties and Surrenders*, 2 vols. (Ottawa: Printed by Brown Chamberlin, 1891), 1:196; Peter S. Schmalz, *The History of the Saugeen Indians* (Ontario: Ontario Historical Society, 1977), 91–2. Lord Bury's name appears on the Ontario historic plaque at Allenford, which recalls the story of "The Allenford Pow-Wow 1855." In northern Bruce and Grey Counties, his family names remain as well, entrenched in legal descriptions of the former townships of Albemarle and Keppel.

93 Lord Bury to Sir Edmund W. Head, Indian Department, Toronto, 5 December 1855, in RETURN, 19.

94 Ibid., 28.

95 Laurence Oliphant to Lord Elgin, dated Indian Department, Quebec, 3 November 1854, in RETURN, 11.

96 Anthony F.C. Wallace, *The Death and Rebirth of the Seneca* (New York: Vintage Books, 1972), 30, see also 31–9.

97 Lord Bury to Sir Edmund W. Head, Indian Department, Toronto, 5 December 1855, in RETURN, 26 and 27.

98 The number of individuals of African background in the province of Canada in the mid-1850s is difficult to estimate. Robin Winks, in *The Blacks in Canada: A History* (Montreal: McGill-Queen's University Press, 1971), 240, suggests "by 1860 the black population alone of Canada West alone may have reached forty thousand."

99 Viscount Bury, M.P., "Notes on Canadian Matters: Third and Concluding Part," *Fraser's Magazine* 56 (July 1857): 98.

100 Ibid., 97.
101 Daniel J. Brock, "Joseph Brant Clench," *DCB*, vol. 8, *1851–1860* (1985), 163.
102 Egerton Ryerson to the Chief Superintendent of Indian Affairs, Quebec, dated 21 November 1854 (copy), RG 2 C 1, Archives of Ontario. I thank Bob Gidney for this reference. For details of the extraordinary friendship of Peter Jones and Egerton Ryerson, see Smith, *Mississauga Portraits*, 8–10, 18–23, 31–2.
103 Jones, *Sacred Feathers*, 249.
104 Jones, *History*, 29.
105 John A. Macdonald to John Langton, Quebec, 6 February 1855, marked "Confidential," in Langton Papers, Archives of Ontario. Reprinted in "The Letters of John Langton about Canadian Politics, 1855–1856," *Canadian Historical Review* 5 (1924): 236–7. For information about Langton, see the sketch by Wendy Cameron in *DCB*, vol. 12, *1891–1900* (1990), 527–9.
106 Lord Bury to F. Talfourd, Indian Department, Quebec, 26 January 1855, Civil Secretary's Office Letterbook, RG 10, vol. 516, microfilm C-13346, Library and Archives Canada; Mrs. Charlotte Vidal Nisbet, "The Talfourd Family," *Western Ontario History Nuggets* 6 (1945): 1–8.
107 The *Montreal Pilot*, for instance, immediately called for his removal from office; see *Quebec Gazette*, 25 August 1855; *Hamilton Spectator*, 29 August 1855. Elsewhere, he was referred to as "a distinguished individual" (*Montreal Transcript*, 15 August 1855).
108 "Where Will It End?" *Brockville Recorder*, 23 August 1855.
109 "Lord Bury: From the Chatham Planet," (St Thomas) *Weekly Dispatch*, 30 August 1855. I thank Janet Forjan for this reference. The article is also reprinted in the *Quebec Gazette*, 8 September 1855.
110 Lord Bury, "To the Editor of the Montreal Gazette," *Montreal Gazette*, 28 August 1855. This same letter appeared in other Canadian newspapers, including the *Quebec Mercury*, 25 August 1855; *The Pilot* (Montreal), 25 August 1855; and *Quebec Chronicle*, 27 August 1855.
111 "Letter from Lord Bury," *Quebec Mercury*, 25 August 1855; *Quebec Chronicle*, 27 August 1855; "Lord Bury," *Montreal Transcript*, 29 August 1855; *Daily Leader* (Toronto), 30 August 1855; "Lord Bury," (St. Thomas) *Weekly Dispatch*, 6 September 1855. The French-language *La Patrie* in Montreal stood up for the viscount, "Lord Bury," 21 August 1855; see also the paper's reference to the incident in their issue of 31 August 1855.
112 Statements of disbelief from numerous Canadian newspapers appear in "Opinions of the Press," *Quebec Gazette*, 8 September 1855.
113 "A Colonial Club in London – Falacious Views of Its Advantages," *Daily Telegraph*, 17 September 1868.

114 E.J.B., "The Great Provincial Fair," *Daily British Whig* (Kingston), 17 October 1855.

115 Ibid. The Cobourg *Star* in its account, "The Governor General's Visit to Cobourg," 17 October 1855, did not mention that Cobourg women refused to attend because Lord Bury was there.

116 "The Governor's Secretary," *Hamilton Spectator*, 24 October 1855.

117 "Canada," *New York Times*, 30 November 1855.

118 "Lord Bury," *Ingersoll Chronicle*, 12 October 1855. The train carrying the viceregal party was briefly detained at Ingersoll on 18 October 1855. See *Hamilton Spectator*, 20 October 1855. Bury was in the party; his presence in London was noted in the *London Free Press*, 25 October 1855. My thanks to George Emery for this reference.

119 "Lord Bury," *Globe*, 30 October 1855. George Brown, the journalist-politician who owned the *Globe*, had a special reason to allow his paper to react so emotionally. According to allegations in the press, Bury used the name of the 37-year-old bachelor as his alias. Allegedly he had entered the names "George Brown and lady" on the St Lawrence steamer's register.

120 "Lord Bury *alias* George Brown," article from the *London Free Press*, cited in the *Quebec Gazette*, 27 October 1855.

121 Peter Jones to David Thorburn, dated Brantford, 22 October 1855, RG 10, vol. 831, pp. 319–20, microfilm C-15110, Library and Archives Canada.

122 Viscount Bury, M.P., "Notes on Canadian Matters. Third and Concluding Part," *Fraser's Magazine*, 56 (July 1857), 97–8.

123 Lord Bury to Sir Edmund W. Head, dated Indian Department, Toronto, 5 December 1855, in RETURN, 22, 33.

124 "Toronto Correspondence of the Montreal Gazette. Toronto, October 26, 1855," *Montreal Gazette*, 30 October 1855.

125 "Bury's" Marriage Settlement, notes on the document included within section "Canada – 1905," by 9th Earl of Albemarle, HA67/D2/1, Suffolk Record Office, Ipswich Branch, 69. "The trustees were John Hillyard Cameron and Thomas G. Ridout – both of Toronto, and George Carr Glyn of London, England. The month was November 1855. The jointure was to be 1,000 pounds sterling, and a lien or charge upon Quidenham, the family seat in Norfolk, England, or his real or personal estate. 300 pounds sterling a year for Sophia and one-third of Sir Allan's Hamilton town land about three-quarters of an acre. Sir Allan allowed his daughter 3,000 [?] pounds sterling a year, and at his death one third of his estate." See also "Lord Bury," *Quebec Gazette*, 3 November 1855.

126 "Canada, Correspondence of the New-York *Daily Times*, Toronto, Saturday, Nov. 24, 1855," *New York Times*, 30 November 1855.

127 John A. Macdonald to Brown Chamberlin, dated Toronto, 21 January 1856, in *The Letters of Sir John A. Macdonald 1836–1857*, ed. J.K. Johnson, vol. 1 (Ottawa: Public Archives of Canada, 1968), 339.
128 "Marriage of the Premier's Daughter," *Hamilton Spectator*, 16 November 1855.
129 MacRae, *MacNab of Dundurn*, 230–1, 234.
130 Lord Bury to Sir Edmund W. Head, dated Indian Department, Toronto, 5 December 1855, in RETURN, 18.
131 Allan MacNab, cited in "Provincial Parliament," *Western Mercury* (Hamilton), 6 March 1834. I thank Reg Good for this reference.
132 One other newspaper article that survives which supplements the details on the wedding is the piece, "Marriage of the Premier's Daughter," *Hamilton Spectator*, 16 November 1855. The clipping from an unidentified source is contained with Lord Bury's 1854 Diary, 73. The quotation is taken from the unidentified article.
133 Albemarle, "Foreword," 4.
134 "Retirement of Lord Bury," *Quebec Gazette*, 5 February 1856.
135 Sir Edmund Head to Sir George Cornewall Lewis, dated Spencer Wood, Quebec, 14 November 1855, Sir Edmund Head Papers, microfilm reel M194, Library and Archives Canada. I thank John Leslie for his assistance in reading this letter.
136 John F. Leslie, *Commissions of Inquiry into Indian Affairs in the Canadas, 1828–1858: Evolving a Corporate Memory for the Indian Department* (Ottawa: Treaties and Historical Research Centre, Research Branch, Corporate Policy, Indian Affairs and Northern Development Canada, 1985), 134–7.
137 Miller, *Skyscrapers*, 140; see also 139–43.
138 David Thorburn, "Transmits Minutes of a Great Council […] with the Six Nations & a deputation of Chiefs from 15 different Bands from the 20th to 29th Sept. 1858," RG 10, volume 245A, Docket #11486–11500, Library and Archives Canada. "Council of Indian Chiefs," *The Grand River Sachem*, 6 October 1858, is one of the few press accounts. My thanks to Anne Unyi, curator of the Heritage and Culture Division, Edinburgh Square Heritage and Cultural Centre, Caledonia, Ontario, for this reference. The Toronto *Globe* allotted the story less than a hundred words on 14 October 1858 and stated that the Council was held "last week," but it actually ended two and a half weeks earlier.
139 "The Troubles on the Manitoulin," *Globe*, 20 July 1863.
140 Joseph Sawyer and Peter Jones, Chiefs, "Statement of the River Credit, claiming certain Tracts of land, which to the best of their knowledge and belief have never been surrendered to the crown, and therefore

remain their property," dated Port Credit, 8 June 1847, No. 5, Letters and Annuities, New Credit Research Office, New Credit. Reg Good located in Library and Archives Canada a copy in RG 10, vol. 182, pp. 105326–7, enclosed under a cover letter (on p. 105334) from Sawyer and Jones to T.G. Anderson dated 8 June 1847. Robert Bruce forwarded this correspondence (p. 135335) to the Commissioner of Crown Lands on 15 May 1850. The Commissioner's response (p. 135336), dated 26 August 1850, rejected the claims.

141 To the Right Honorable the Duke of Newcastle, Her Majesty's Minister for the Colonies, "The Memorial of the Undersigned Chiefs and Warriors of the New Credit Band of Missisauga Indians," Chief Joseph Sawyer, Mess[en]ger James Chechok, George King Interpreter, dated New Credit, 17 September 1860, Witnesses C.A. Jones, David Sawyer, C.O. 42/624, 457–60, Library and Archives Canada.

142 E.E. Rich, *Hudson's Bay Company 1670–1870*, 3 vols. (Toronto: McClelland and Stewart, 1960), 3:823.

143 "The Exodus of the Western Nations," *Times* (London), 14 June 1865, 6.

144 Edward Beasley, *Empire as the Triumph of Theory: Imperialism, Information, and the Colonial Society of 1868* (Abingdon, England: Routledge, 2005), 93–8. Boase, *English Biography*, 5:62.

145 "Episodes in the Life of Wm. Coutts, Viscount Bury, afterwards 7th Earl," HA67/D2/5, Suffolk Record Office, Ipswich Branch, 204–8, 227–35, 247–53; "Accident to Lord Bury," *Times* (London), 10 April 1867.

146 In 1878–80 and 1885–6. See Boase, *English Biography*, 5:62.

147 "Lord Bury at Toronto," *Times* (London), 3 December 1858; "Enthusiastic Reception of Lord Bury," *British Colonist* (Halifax), 9 December 1858. I thank Jan Forjan for this reference.

148 "First Annual Dinner," *Ottawa Citizen*, 25 October 1883.

149 "Lord Bury," *Ottawa Free Press*, 26 October 1883; "Political and Other Notes, *Ottawa Free Press*, 31 October 1883.

150 For further details on John A. Macdonald's "best known personal habit" (p. 420), consult Richard Gwyn, *John A.*, 265–8, 420–1.

151 Sir John Willison, *Reminiscences Political and Personal* (Toronto: McClelland and Stewart, 1919), 180.

152 "Opinions on Canada: By a Distinguished Member of the House of Lords," *Hamilton Spectator*, 13 November 1883.

153 Albemarle, "Foreword," 5.

154 Ibid.

155 Pollard, "Keppel," 373.

156 A.F.P. [A.F. Pollard], "William Coutts Keppel, Seventh Earl of Albemarle and Viscount Bury (1832–1894)," *Dictionary of National Biography*, vol. 9 (London: Smith, Elder, & Co., 1909), 932.

157 "The Dowager Lady Albemarle," *Times* (London), 7 April 1917. Several years after her husband's death, his convent-educated widow had the discomfort to see Alice, the beautiful, vivacious wife of her third son George, become the mistress of the Prince of Wales. After the prince acceded to throne in 1901 as King Edward VII, Mrs. Keppel remained "la favorita," to quote the widely used phrase of the day, throughout the 10 years of his reign. See Theo Aronson, "Alice Frederica Keppel [Née Edmonstone]," *Oxford Dictionary of National Biography*, vol. 31 (Oxford: Oxford University Press, 2004), 359.

"Chief Teller of Tales": John Buchan's Ideas on Indigenous Peoples, the Commonwealth, and an Emerging Idea of Canada, 1935–1940

BRENDAN FREDERICK R. EDWARDS

Canadian attitudes to the British monarchy and the Commonwealth in the twenty-first century range widely from fervent support to stiff opposition to complete indifference. But whatever the attitudes to British royalty may be at present, the monarchy has played a significant, often central, cultural and political role in the Canadian past.[1] And given Canada's geographical distance and relative isolation from the rest of the British Empire, the country's connection to royalty is, and has been, most commonly experienced through the personal representatives of the monarch: that is, the governors general. As Colin Coates has noted, "Governors General wielded significant political, financial, and cultural power into the twentieth century, and in various ways they attempted to ensure Canadians' allegiance to the throne."[2]

The prolific and popular British author John Buchan (1875–1940) was best known to Canadians as Lord Tweedsmuir, thirty-fifth governor general of Canada. He brought to his role as governor general the varied experiences of a writer, administrator, politician, and promoter of literature, all of which left a mark on the country which he served from 1935 to 1940.[3] As the Crown's representative in Canada, Lord Tweedsmuir opened and dissolved Parliament, gave royal assent to acts of Parliament, signed orders-in-council, and was an advisor to Prime Minister Mackenzie King. When King Edward VIII gave up his crown in 1936, Lord Tweedsmuir acknowledged Canada's acceptance of the abdication. In September 1939, he witnessed Canada's declaration of war. As governor general, Tweedsmuir also acted as the nation's host to heads of state and other distinguished visitors, including American president Franklin D. Roosevelt in 1936 and members of the Japanese royal family in 1937. In Lord Tweedsmuir's extensive tours throughout

Canada, he sought personal contact with citizens from all regions and all social conditions – he mixed with rural and urban, spoke in small towns and in the cities of Quebec (in English and French), sailed and fished in the Maritimes, visited First Nations and immigrant communities on the Prairies, and hiked in the mountains in British Columbia and the Northwest Territories.[4]

Tweedsmuir's unique position as a highly literate and public governor general, whose every move and word attracted broad attention, gives the historian an opportunity to draw generalities not only of mid-twentieth-century literary attitudes towards Indigenous peoples but also of the attitudes of governors general to Canada about them. Using Tweedsmuir's correspondence and newspaper reports, recognition of him by various First Nations, and Buchan's writings which feature Aboriginal characters – mainly *Sick Heart River* and *The Long Traverse* – this paper seeks to uncover something of Tweedsmuir's thoughts and feelings towards Indigenous peoples in Canada and also speaks to his precedent-setting views of Canada and the Commonwealth as spaces of celebrated diversity.

Long before his time in Canada, John Buchan was an established and celebrated writer of fiction and history. A film by Alfred Hitchcock, based on his best-known novel, *The Thirty-Nine Steps*, was released in Canada within months of his arrival.[5] His historical contributions included material on Canadian participation in the First World War and a biography of a preceding governor general, Lord Minto. During his time as governor general, Lord Tweedsmuir's energies were devoted mainly to writing speeches and official correspondence, but he nonetheless managed to write an autobiography, *Memory Hold-the-Door*, and his last works of fiction, *Sick Heart River* and *The Long Traverse* (published in Canada and the United States as *Lake of Gold*), between official duties and periods of ill health. Credited with a wide knowledge of Canadian literature, Tweedsmuir was invited to act as honorary president of the Canadian Authors Association in 1935. With the CAA's guidance, Tweedsmuir established the Governor General's Literary Awards in 1936.[6]

Lady Tweedsmuir was likewise active in promoting literature and literacy in Canada during her husband's tenure as governor general. She promoted the Women's Institutes, wrote in their magazine, and encouraged the institutes to record their histories. She also worked to collect and distribute books to people living in remote and economically depressed areas, resulting in the establishment of libraries in the Prairies and New Brunswick.[7] Together with her husband, Lady Tweedsmuir was instrumental in establishing the first library at Rideau Hall, the official residence of the governor general in Ottawa.

Lord Tweedsmuir reminded Canadians of their rich heritage and the future opportunities for the country. He envisioned a strong and united Canada, a mature nation seeking an active role in international affairs. He balanced an enthusiastic admiration for Canada's natural beauty with a practical economic sense of resource development in the North. He reminded Canadians of their varied origins and emphasized a need to reflect a national character in history and literature. Lord Tweedsmuir was a tremendously popular governor general, who reinforced Canada's pride in past achievements and fostered a belief in the country's future.[8] More importantly, perhaps, Tweedsmuir educated the people of Canada about themselves and their role in the British Empire; likewise, he helped to educate the world about Canada. Well known and respected in the United States, having enjoyed a friendly relationship with President Roosevelt, Tweedsmuir was an international spokesman for the Commonwealth and Canada through not only his role as governor general but also his role as a popular and prolific author. *Sick Heart River*, his last completed novel, and *The Long Traverse*, a novel for adolescents, are of particular note from a Canadian perspective, as these provide for the reader an intriguing exploration of Buchan's true feelings about Canada, its people, and its international place. Written outside the confines of his formal duties as viceroy, these works of fiction provide an intriguing look into Tweedsmuir's understandings of and aspirations for Canada.

Furthermore, these last two works of fiction cast Indigenous peoples as central characters. In Tweedsmuir's official duties as governor general, he was honoured no less than five times by various First Nations groups in Canada. While it is certainly not unusual for a governor general of Canada to be honoured or recognized by First Nations peoples,[9] Tweedsmuir's honours are unique in that the people involved usually made a point of recognizing Buchan's previous achievements as an author. The Sweet Grass Band of Cree, for example – at the Indian Diamond Jubilee celebration commemorating the signing of Treaty No. 6 at Fort Carlton, Saskatchewan – honoured Tweedsmuir with the title "Chief Teller of Tales" (or Okemow Otataowkew) in August 1936. This honour by the Cree was noted internationally, with pieces appearing in *Time* magazine in the United States and a striking political cartoon in *Punch* magazine in the United Kingdom.

In the otherwise well-researched biographies of John Buchan, First Baron of Tweedsmuir, there has been almost no discussion in relation to his encounters with Indigenous peoples.[10] Aside from the often reprinted portrait of Tweedsmuir as "Chief Eagle Feather," taken by the highly celebrated photographer Yousuf Karsh, at best a sentence or two outlining the honours bestowed on him by First Nations, and his visit with Grey Owl at Prince Albert National Park in 1936, Indigenous peoples are not of any significance in Buchan's biographies. But Tweedsmuir's own correspondence and the presence of Indigenous characters in his two Canadian-based works of fiction demonstrate that the First Nations of Canada were of some interest to Buchan. Personal photographs included among his papers at Queen's University and the National Library of Scotland also attest to this interest.

Although Tweedsmuir was celebrated in his day as the first "commoner" to be named governor general (the title of baron was conferred on Buchan as a prelude leading up to his appointment) and the first governor general to be chosen by the government in Ottawa, rather than by the monarch, he was nonetheless cut from the same cloth as previous governors general. Like his predecessors, Tweedsmuir was from the British ruling class – his birth, breeding, and background, as well as his values and attitudes, were virtually indistinguishable from the governors general who were chosen by the monarch.[11] But because John Buchan, the author, was widely popular before his appointment, Tweedsmuir was undoubtedly the most widely known and thus, along with the Earl Grey, probably made the widest impact as governor general. In the memory of many Canadians of Buchan's generation, Tweedsmuir was "the pick of the bunch."[12] Of all the governors general, through the 1950s at least, Tweedsmuir was "the most intellectual and articulate of them all,"[13] and was certainly one of the most gifted. His death in office, however, robbed history of a memoir of his time as governor general. But thankfully worthy biographies exist of Tweedsmuir, as his memory and impact were large and long remembered. Further, Tweedsmuir's papers are articulate and accessible, giving historians sufficient fodder to tell his story. And unlike other governors general, we can determine something of the man through his fiction.

We know that Buchan had at least some interest in the Indigenous peoples of North America before his appointment as governor general. In his personal library, now housed at Queen's University in Kingston, Ontario, there are indications of that interest. A few titles, which appear to have been acquired before his stay in Canada, relate to North American

Indigenous peoples. In Buchan's memoir, *Memory Hold-the-Door* (published a year before his death), which discusses his life well before his time as governor general, he says, "I first discovered America through books. Not the tales of Indians and the Wild West which entranced my boyhood; those seemed to belong to no particular quarter of the globe, but to an indefinable land of romance, and I was not cognisant of any nation behind them."[14] And although no further mention of Indigenous peoples is made in his autobiography, Buchan felt it necessary to publish the 1937 Karsh photograph of himself as "Eagle Face … Chief of the Blood Indians" in his chapter on America – appearing chronologically before a photograph of himself with President Roosevelt. Thus, despite his claim that his idea of America came not through books with tales of North American "Indians," Buchan clearly identifies the Indigenous element as a highly recognizable image held in the minds of British readers, and the visual representation of his acceptance by the Blood First Nation is used to prove Tweedsmuir's qualification in expressing his opinions about America.[15]

In Tweedsmuir's day, the governor general was responsible for "setting Canada's social and moral standards."[16] Buchan was a staunch Scottish Presbyterian, with Calvinistic values – believing generally in the predestination of all peoples in the eyes of God, the omnipotence of God, and the powerlessness of man. These beliefs and values are particularly evident in *Sick Heart River*; for Buchan, race appears central in forming a person's characteristics and lot in life. But his Calvinistic values do not limit Buchan's views on diversity, as one might expect.

The main character in *Sick Heart River* is one of Buchan's recurring heroes, Sir Edward Leithen. Leithen here is ailing and, having retired as a high-profile British lawyer and politician, takes on one last challenge in tracking down Francis Galliard, a young displaced Quebecois who has found huge success in New York as a financier. Galliard has disappeared, possibly to Canada, and Leithen imagines this task as his last, allowing him to "die on his feet." We learn that Galliard has indeed returned to Canada and has joined Lew Frizel, a Métis/Scots Cree (or "half-breed") guide in a quest to discover the Sick Heart River, a mythic river in the Nahanni Valley. Leithen tracks Galliard and Frizel with the help of Frizel's brother, the Waskesiu game warden Johnny Frizel.[17] Leiden and Johnny are joined in their search eventually by two Dene, or Hare people, whom Buchan, the writer, describes as "little men compared with the big Plains folk, but stalwart for the small-boned Hares. They had the slanting Mongol eyes of the Mackenzie River tribes, and had picked up some English at the Catholic mission school. Something at the back of Leithen's brain christened them Big Klaus and Little Klaus, but Johnny, who spoke their tongue, had other names for them."[18] We never do learn the true names of "Big Klaus" and "Little Klaus," and throughout the rest of the story, they have little to say. The Dene are thus mainly nameless but necessary figures. It is the Scottish Cree "half-breeds" who provide Buchan with hero-like figures. They (with the noted but largely silent help of the Dene) are the rough-but-ready heroes to Leiden and Gaillard, without whom the North could not be accessed or survived. When the going is good for Leithen and his health and mood reflect the good things in life, the Frizel brothers tend to be described more in terms of their Scottish ancestry. However, when the going is bad and Leithen feels hopeless and lost, the Frizels become mere "Indian half-breeds." In other words, when the Frizels are to be praised, they are Scottish, but when the Frizels are to be criticized or doubted, they are Cree.

Buchan is also somewhat patronizing to the Quebecois, but he is not unlike many others of his age and background in forming his opinions of French Canadians. It has been proposed that Buchan's impressions of the French were influenced by his reading of the poetry of William Henry Drummond (1854–1907), the Irish Canadian doctor, entrepreneur, and folk poet. In Drummond's poetry, the Quebecois speak fractured English, interspersed with hints of colloquial French, "thus giving them a romantically rustic air."[19] But on official occasions, Tweedsmuir's relationship to the Quebecois was cordial and friendly, and Buchan spoke French rather well. Lord and Lady Tweedsmuir, in fact, preferred the governor general's summer residence in Quebec to Rideau Hall, the official residence in Ottawa.[20]

Sick Heart River, published posthumously in 1941, was John Buchan's last completed novel. Buchan scholars consider it his most powerful. Its main setting is the Canadian North, primarily in the South Nahanni River region of the Northwest Territories, an area that Buchan passed close to, but never visited, as governor general of Canada in the summer of 1937. Buchan was fascinated by the much-storied South Nahanni River and intended to visit there himself one day – an intention that unfortunately was never realized. In Buchan's time, the South Nahanni was not yet fully mapped, and it is certainly one of the most rugged terrains in the country.[21] At least one critic has labelled *Sick Heart River* as a seminal work of Canadian writing, despite its virtual non-existence in histories of Canadian literature.[22]

In his time, Tweedsmuir travelled through Canada more than any previous governor general, and he was convinced that the North, in particular, was a region in Canada that needed increased attention and respect. Buchan was of the opinion, as were many Canadian politicians after him, that the North held a considerable storehouse of economic wealth in natural resources, in addition to its natural beauty and charm. His northern and Arctic tour was big news in Canada at the time, and he even published segments of his travel observations in the *Sunday Times* in December 1937 for readers in the United Kingdom.[23]

Galliard, the lost Quebecois, represents what can happen to a man who denies his heritage. Figuratively lost in America, Galliard returns to his homeland to find what he left behind – only to discover what makes him who he is. Galliard is, in this sense, a clear metaphor for Canadians in general, expressing Buchan's opinion that Canadians need to take a closer look at themselves and particularly their ties to Europe, be they French or British – and resist the temptation to become simply another kind of American.

In *Sick Heart River*, the largely voiceless Dene are presented as helpless and without a heritage, in need of Leithen's leadership. Near the end of the novel, ailing in a Dene community, Leithen describes the Dene as "tenuous growths, fungi which had no hold on the soil. They existed in sufferance; the North had only to tighten its grip and they would disappear." Lew and Johnny, the Scottish Cree/Métis, are ranked slightly higher in Leithen's eyes: "They were not mushrooms, for they had roots and they had the power to yield under the strain and spring back again, but were they any better than grassy filaments which swayed in the wind but might any day be pinched out of existence? … They too lived on sufferance." Galliard, the Quebecois, is described as having "deeper roots, but they were not healthy enough to permit transplanting." Then turning to himself, the pure-blood Scot, Leithen says, "Compared to his companions Leithen suddenly saw himself founded solidly like an oak. He was drawing life from deep sources."[24]

The experiences and observations that Buchan made on his trip to the North and the Arctic Circle undoubtedly formed the basis for what was later presented as fiction in *Sick Heart River*. In the published reports of his northern travels, written primarily for a British audience, we see much the same opinion of Indigenous peoples presented as for the characters who later appear in the novel. Although Buchan claims to have met only one "impressive Indian" during his entire northern journey, he goes on at length describing the Indigenous peoples he met and even offers some criticism about their treatment by the Canadian government.[25] With particular note of the poor medical treatment available to the Indigenous peoples of the North – a grievance perpetually noted by the First Nations and Inuit people he met – Buchan wrote, "I feel very strongly that efforts should be made to put the whole medical services on a different basis." Buchan complained that there should be a clear distinction made between Indian agent and doctor, and noted that while some agents and doctors were excellent, "I had a good many complaints of lack of attention, which I believed to be well justified." Further, Tweedsmuir recommended that the North should receive only the very best of the best, when it came to medical and administrative service. In his plea to the British public, he made it clear that "the representative of the Crown feels a special responsibility in this matter, for the original treaties were made in the name of Queen Victoria, and the Indians are in a special degree the wards of the Crown."[26] This last statement is particularly noteworthy. Governors general and representatives of the Crown have famously made such statements only to Indigenous peoples, often as a kind of lip service, but Tweedsmuir made a point of addressing his concerns in the *Sunday Times*, more or less for the whole empire to read.

But while the depictions of non-British characters in *Sick Heart River* are for the most part not very positive, Buchan takes another approach in his novel for young people, *The Long Traverse*, which was also published in 1941, although in an incomplete state. In *The Long Traverse*, French and Cree characters play a significantly positive role in the upbringing of a history-deficient young Scottish boy, Donald. Through time-travelling flights of imagination experienced during trips into the wilderness with Negog, a Cree guide, Donald visits episodes in Canadian history and European-Indigenous contact across Canada. It is Negog, the Cree guide and trapper, who shares the tenet with Donald that "it is right to follow the path of one's ancestors."[27] Furthermore, throughout the story, Buchan allows Indigenous peoples to play a central role in the history and development of Canada – a situation very unlike that in other Canadian history texts of the first part of the twentieth century. Buchan's First Nations characters are featured throughout *The Long Traverse*, and he acknowledges the reality that First Nations peoples "have been here from the beginning," as Negog reminds Donald.[28] And more importantly, there is no evidence in this Buchan text that Indigenous peoples were believed to be disappearing or were somehow less important in his day.

As Corey Coates has observed of Buchan's writing, "knowing one's history is like a secular religion to Buchan."[29] Coates also notes that Buchan's final two works of fiction may be read as an interesting dichotomy of the man. If read as portraying something of his own feelings, his fiction reveals Buchan at the time of his death as, on the one hand, the elder British statesman (Leithen) confident in the superiority and necessity of British imperialism, while on the other he is the Scottish adolescent (Donald) keen to learn about and integrate the traditions of other peoples so that he may become a full-fledged Canadian in the service of the British Empire.[30] In one text, Indigenous peoples are present but without a solid anchor in the past, sure to disappear in the future; in the second text, they are solidly rooted in the Canadian past, and their survival seems secure. This second perception is probably closer to Buchan's own way of thinking, as *The Long Traverse* was intended as an educational tool for Canadian students. As the epilogue makes clear, in this, Buchan's last published work, he "thought that history was too often taught to children in such a way that they found it a dull subject." Although it was never fully completed or widely distributed, *The Long Traverse* was meant to act as an educational tool through which the stories and legends of Canada could be told to students, with the idea of awakening an interest in their ancestors. In *The Long Traverse*, Buchan mixed contemporary times with old times in an effort to show Canadian children that Canadian history was indeed romantic and exciting.

Tweedsmuir was thus a Canadianist at heart. He believed strongly in the British Empire but felt that the history and stories of Canada should come first in Canadian schools. With these ideas, Tweedsmuir was rather ahead of his time, but his efforts opened the door for future statesmen and academics to pursue similar ideas of putting Canada first, within the context of the Commonwealth. Tweedsmuir expressed this sentiment clearly in his speeches. On the Commonwealth, and Canadians' role within it, he observed, "A Canadian's first loyalty is not to the British Commonwealth of Nations, but to Canada and to Canada's King, and those who deny this are doing, in my mind, a great disservice to the Commonwealth. If the Commonwealth, in a crisis, is to speak with one voice it will be only because the component parts have thought out for themselves their own special problems, and made their contribution to the discussion, so that a true common factor of policy can be reached. A sovereign people must, as part of its sovereign duty, take up its own attitude to world problems."[31]

Some contemporary critics have labelled Buchan an anti-Semite and racist who was a reactionary defender of the British Empire, due in large part to generalizations he made about race in his popular works of fiction, including *The Thirty-Nine Steps* and *Prester John*. Other critics have pointed to Buchan as an imperial apologist and a poster boy for the right-wing conception of Canada.[32] But such ideas seem to contradict some of those already noted and Tweedsmuir's comments at a 1936 gathering of Ukrainians in Manitoba when he observed, "The strongest nations are those that are made up of different racial elements."[33] This point was repeated to audiences across Canada. As Buchan scholar and historian Peter Henshaw has noted, it is true that Buchan championed the cause of imperial unity, and above all the unity of the British Isles and the settler dominions of Canada, Australia, New Zealand, and South Africa. It is also true that Buchan believed in a hierarchy of peoples, a hierarchy in which British and other "northern" races were at the top. But he did not believe that it was his role as governor general to promote a homogenous British identity in Canada.[34] As governor general, Lord Tweedsmuir actively promoted an idea of Canadian nationalism and identity that was rooted in Canada's multiplicity of origins – one uniquely distinct that did not merely mirror a British identity. Tweedsmuir encouraged Canadians of all ethnicities and backgrounds to stay true to their individual heritages, promoting a very early idea of Canadian multiculturalism some 30 years before the idea was adopted as official policy. In addition, he promoted an idea of the British Empire that was ahead of its time. While the term "Commonwealth" was not often used in his day, Buchan emphasized the British Commonwealth of Nations as a community which he felt should celebrate its diversity, in part to strengthen its role in fostering international relations; it was not merely a patriarchal institution. Such a view was almost unheard of in the early twentieth century, but it was later adopted by modern supporters and promoters of the Commonwealth through education, literary awards, and sport. Henshaw says Buchan's thinking was directly influenced by his experiences and feelings about his own Scottish heritage. The Scottish identity, in Buchan's mind, was itself a product of ethnic diversity. Scotland had been populated by waves of invaders who pushed out, mixed with, and assimilated existing peoples. Scottish culture, more or less, had coalesced into two identities: Highland and Lowland. By the early twentieth century, each strain of Scottish culture was influencing the other, coming together through literature and a shared attachment to the landscape.

Such ideas were not without controversy. Henshaw explains that Tweedsmuir's notions of a multicultural Canada were out of step with the prevailing notion that British Canadian culture should be privileged and celebrated above all others; that Indigenous peoples and immigrants should be encouraged to conform to this culture; and that French Canadian culture should be tolerated and contained, rather than celebrated. Prime Minister Mackenzie King, in fact, was not comfortable with Tweedsmuir's perspective and made it known to Tweedsmuir that he disapproved of the notion of putting Canada ahead of the empire, if only because King feared the media and some members of the public would hear Tweedsmuir's words as representing government policy. King was already under suspicion by some for holding similar ideas about Canada's role in the empire, and he did not wish further criticism.[35] But Tweedsmuir's ideas of a multicultural Canada were, of course, well received by Canada's minority cultures, a fact which may have contributed to his wide popularity as governor general. And this multicultural view of Canada and the Commonwealth can be read in Buchan's two "Canadian" novels, each emphasizing the existence and persistence of pre-Canadian cultural identities and the possibilities of forging a new identity together. Buchan's multicultural sentiments likely encouraged the warm receptions he received from First Nations in Canada, who had long suffered the federal government's policies of assimilation.

Lord Tweedsmuir was honoured at least five times by different First Nations groups in Canada. The most publicized was his honouring as "Chief Teller of Tales" by a group of Cree at Carlton, Saskatchewan, in August 1936. The act of receiving a name from the Cree meant that Tweedsmuir had been accepted into the Cree brotherhood. The Carlton ceremony was witnessed by more than 5,000 spectators, and the ceremony included traditional gift-giving and dancing. The governor general reportedly spoke to the crowd in both the Cree language and English. The newspapers reported Tweedsmuir as stating, in Cree, "Brother chiefs, I am most happy on this occasion. You have done me great honor in taking me into your Brotherhood."[36] Continuing in English, Tweedsmuir recalled the reasons for the signing of Treaty 6, calling it an honourable treaty which had been honourably observed by both parties. Concluding his speech, Tweedsmuir assured the Cree that he would tell the king of the honour bestowed upon him and of the loyalty to the monarch expressed by the Cree chiefs assembled that day.

The famous author and early environmentalist Grey Owl, who at that time was still considered a North American "Indian" (by non-Indigenous peoples, at least, and by Tweedsmuir for certain), was also present at the Carlton celebration. Tweedsmuir showed interest in Grey Owl and agreed to visit him at his cabin in Prince Albert National Park in the near future.[37] Tweedsmuir did meet with Grey Owl, only a month later, in mid-September, and Grey Owl used that opportunity to secure as much help as he could for the Indigenous peoples of Canada, proposing the idea that they should become official guardians of Canada's wildlife and forests. Tweedsmuir, as governor general, had met with Grey Owl at least one other time, in Ottawa in March 1936. Grey Owl sought an audience with the governor general in his efforts to secure help and recognition for the Indigenous peoples of Canada. One of Grey Owl's biographers, Donald Smith, writes that Grey Owl impressed the governor general and his family at Rideau Hall, playing the role of "Modern Hiawatha." Tweedsmuir is said to have greatly admired Grey Owl's remarkable knowledge of wildlife and the power of his writing. At their later meeting, at his cabin near Waskesiu, Saskatchewan, Grey Owl showed the governor general a beaver dam, trees sawn by beavers, and beaver themselves. Grey Owl's accounts of that meeting indicate that Lord Tweedsmuir was an astute audience; he listened to Grey Owl's pleas for greater Indigenous sovereignty in Canadian life with apparent attention and sympathy.[38] Tweedsmuir's personal correspondence confirms that he was a great fan of Grey Owl, as he repeatedly mentioned in his letters that he was looking forward to spending time with him in Prince Albert National Park. And when the time came, he was disappointed that bad weather cut their visit short.[39]

The Carlton ceremony was not the first instance in which Lord Tweedsmuir was honoured by a First Nations community. Only a week earlier, the governor general was recognized by a group of Huron at Lorette near Quebec City. In his own words, "I was made a Huron Chief, and given the appropriate title of 'The Scribe'!"[40] Lady Tweedsmuir was also impressed by this event, reporting to a friend, "We had a marvellous Indian evening. John was made a chief & wore for a brief moment a coiffure of feathers. He was presented with two addresses written on birch bark."[41]

Tweedsmuir was also honoured by other First Nations in Canada, including the Carrier of British Columbia, who named him "Chetam Squamish," or "Chief of the Big Mountain," only days after the Carlton ceremony in August 1936.[42] That year, August and September were busy months for Lord Tweedsmuir, as he travelled extensively throughout Western Canada. In early September, the Blood people of southern Alberta honoured the governor general as "Chief Eagle Head." In Lord Tweedsmuir's personal correspondence to Lady Tweedsmuir, his friends, and his children, the governor general makes a point of mentioning this honour, and he was most impressed with the feathered headdress presented to him.

The *Prince Albert Daily Herald* featured a photograph and brief caption of Governor General Tweedsmuir as "Chief Morning Light" in September 1936, but failed to say by whom or when the honour was bestowed.[43] However, from Tweedsmuir's personal correspondence, it is likely that this picture and naming was the result of his encounter with the Stoney people of central Alberta that same month. Tweedsmuir wrote to a friend in June 1937, reporting that he was at that time "chief of four Indian tribes." The letter continues, "I send you a photograph of myself in the war paint of the Stoney Indians. Did you ever see a more savage face? It looks as if I were about to burn a few prisoners at stake!"[44] If his honouring as "Chief Morning Light" was indeed by the Stoneys, then Tweedsmuir had miscounted and at that time was in fact an honorary chief of five First Nations. In September 1936, Tweedsmuir was visiting the prairies and since the Stoney Reserve was situated rather close to other points Tweedsmuir was reported to have visited, this honour seems all the more likely.

On his trip to the Western Arctic in July and August 1937, Tweedsmuir reported to a friend that he "had conferences with all the local Indian chiefs, and have learned a good deal about the country."[45] Indeed, he appears to have met with many First Nations, including Chipeweyan chiefs, Cree, and Dogrib. He even attended a Slavey powwow, where he mingled with First Nations children.[46] Magazine and newspaper reports back in the United Kingdom noted that the governor general met northern Indigenous "tribes" but noticed "with sadness their declining numbers and poor physique, discovering the Esquimaux [*sic*] and finding them happy, honest people with a marvellous aptitude for acquiring medical knowledge."[47]

Tweedsmuir met with and was greeted by First Nations around the country. The full extent of these meetings, however, is difficult to determine because newspaper reports of the day tended to report only on the times when Tweedsmuir was presented with an honorary name. Tweedsmuir's own papers and correspondence are a clue, of course, but his meetings with Indigenous peoples were not considered a priority from an official government perspective, so these meetings were rarely noted in official schedules. Worse, the newspaper stories were in almost every case published only when a photo opportunity with Tweedsmuir in a First Nations headdress was available, or when the governor general was with someone dressed in full regalia. Such was the case in June 1938, for example, when Tweedsmuir was greeted in Orillia, Ontario, by John Bigwin, the hundred-year-old chief of the Rama First Nation. Except for a photograph, the *Globe and Mail* mentioned nothing of this meeting, instead focusing on Tweedsmuir's encounter with veterans, foresters, and his officiating over a ribbon-cutting ceremony at a Midland hospital.[48] Tweedsmuir's papers and official schedules relating to his trips west in 1936 and 1937 indicate he also met Indigenous peoples at an unidentified "Indian village" near Calgary, where he judged a tepee, and later watched the First Nations parade at the Calgary Stampede.[49]

First Nations memories of royal visits and meetings, including those with governors general, remain prominent in their understandings and versions of history, and these events have been transmitted across several generations. Viewed as cornerstones to positive future cross-cultural relations, Indigenous memories of royal interaction "reveal an indigenous understanding of a very special relationship between themselves and the monarchy – a relationship that non-Native Canadians have never appreciated."[50] First Nations meetings with royalty and representatives of royalty are, from an Indigenous perspective, reaffirmation and confirmation of earlier promises made on behalf of the Crown.[51] Journalistic coverage of such events (as Keith Carlson demonstrates in the case of the 1906 delegation of Cowichan and Squamish in London to meet King Edward VII) was, however, more along the lines of entertainment than it was news of a political nature. Rather than discussing "Indian" policy in conjunction with royal visits, newspaper reports too often diminished the public's view of Indigenous peoples by portraying them as political caricatures rather than political delegates.[52] This unfortunate trend is certainly evident in the newspaper reporting relating to governor general Lord Tweedsmuir's encounters with First Nations.

Governors general have a lengthy tradition of viceregal visits to First Nations communities, particularly in Western Canada. During such visits, firm assurances of the sanctity of the treaties have always been given, and the special, familial relationship with the British Crown is always reaffirmed. Since the signing of treaties, Indigenous persons have incorporated references to the British monarch into their lore and traditions in terms of kinship, confirming themselves as equals to Europeans and calling on the monarch's representatives to act with honour and integrity.[53] In Western Canada, the treaties signed between First Nations and representatives of the British Crown in the 1870s have been "confirmed and ratified in the years that followed through audiences and ceremonies held with the Queen's representatives, the governors-general of Canada ... First Nations used these visits to restate and recommit the equal parties to the treaties, and to remind their treaty partner of their commitments and obligations."[54] First Nations, according to the historian Sarah Carter, view such visits as ratifying and confirming their special relationship with the Crown, and as tangible recognition of their status as sovereign nations. As such, First Nations' protocol says that these visits should include pipe ceremonies, an exchange of gifts, oratory, and displays of dancing. All such activities were included in the descriptions of Tweedsmuir's visits to First Nations communities, and at the Carlton celebration he was reported to have given a speech noting the lasting power of Treaty No. 6 and the Crown's continued interest in and support of Indigenous peoples.

From the perspective of the governors general, such visits were less about affirmations of equality and treaty rights and more to do with the promotion of settlement in the West (in the late nineteenth and early twentieth centuries, at least) and, more importantly, the establishment of a sense of imperial rule. Speeches by governors general at such events were usually replete with notions of inequality, but "this was not how they were received by First Nations who heard powerful affirmations of their familial relationship."[55] Despite the fact that by the early twentieth century it was clear that the substance of such rhetoric by the Crown's representatives was usually without much intent, First Nations have continued to welcome and honour viceregal and royal visitors, each time confirming their long partnership. Such actions on behalf of Indigenous peoples are not due to oversight or ignorance, but rather because the treaties remain the foundation for their rights and future.[56]

The Earl of Minto, Canada's governor general from 1898 to 1904 – about whom Buchan coincidentally wrote a biography in 1924, and after whom he modelled some of his own actions as governor general – was well known to have a particular interest in First Nations. Before his time as governor general, Minto (then Viscount Melgund) had first-hand experience with First Nations in the West. As governor general, Minto had numerous meetings with First Nations peoples, where he solicited their opinions and complaints on subjects including civil liberties, education, supplies, and the undue interference of the government in their affairs. He objected to Canadian government policies that prohibited Indigenous dances and ceremonies, and he frequently expressed his concerns about First Nations peoples to Prime Minister Wilfrid Laurier and Queen Victoria. Buchan did not shy away from discussing such matters in his 1924 biography of the Earl of Minto – a significant fact considering it was commonplace to ignore or minimize the place of Indigenous peoples in early-twentieth-century political texts and histories.[57]

Although Tweedsmuir never showed the same political courage when it came to Indigenous peoples, perhaps due to an unwillingness to ruffle political feathers or upset his cordial relationship with Prime Minister McKenzie King, it is clear that his interest in Indigenous affairs was greater than that of the average statesman, or mainstream Canadian for that matter. The honouring of governors general by First Nations was not unusual, but the acknowledgment that Tweedsmuir received for his dual role as the Crown's representative and a popular author is significant. Names like "The Scribe" and "Chief Teller of Tales" suggest that at least some Indigenous people considered Buchan's literary successes equal in importance to his role as viceroy. The growing literary awareness of First Nations during this era suggests that members of the Cree and Huron (who gave Tweedsmuir these particular honorary titles) were aware of the power of the written word and, in particular, the power that Tweedsmuir's pen could wield.

Tweedsmuir never made Indigenous peoples his exclusive interest; his varied career of statesmanship, political endeavour, research, and writing indicates that he was interested in a very wide range of topics, peoples, and historical periods. His books range from stories of contemporary Britain to ancient Rome, from South African adventures to fictional accounts of the Canadian North. But it is significant that Tweedsmuir's last two works of fiction were inspired by and related to his time in Canada. The depiction of Indigenous peoples in each is varied but of note because his stories of Canada might have easily avoided any mention of them. A quick survey of Canadian literature of the day demonstrates this point. Indigenous peoples of the early twentieth century were depicted in Canadian literature for the most part in a negative fashion, if at all. Further, Canadians did not read very much of their own literature at this point, so Buchan's stories were quick to get widespread attention. The *Montreal Standard* noted in July 1935, at the beginning of Tweedsmuir's time in office, in an article entitled "The Governor-General and the Great Canadian Novel," that "the people of Canada are keener on him as the author who is our next Governor-General than as the Governor-General who is an author as a side line."[58] Indeed, at the time it was anticipated by Canada's literary public that the "great Canadian novel" had yet to be written, and with a man with Buchan's literary skills and popularity as the Crown's representative, the expectations for Tweedsmuir to produce just such a novel were high.

The similarities in Buchan's two Canadian novels extend most evidently to the following: Scottish, French, and First Nations characters feature prominently, as does the Canadian wilderness (which might be considered a character in itself) and the notion that a uniquely Canadian identity can be forged through the recognition and celebration of each citizen's ethnic origins. Buchan was a proud Scot, so the fact that Scottish characters are evident in his novels should be no surprise. But the prominence of French and Indigenous characters is significant, particularly in an English Canadian novel. Quebecois, Indigenous peoples, and wilderness are for Buchan the three unique features of Canada, and his interest in these was evident not only in his fiction but in his actions as governor general as well. Internationally, these three facets are still perhaps Canada's most widely recognized traits, a testament in some part to the power of Buchan's influence. Lord Tweedsmuir – the writer, statesman, and sportsman – did much to educate the Commonwealth about Canada, Canada about the Commonwealth, and Canadians about themselves.

NOTES

Based on a paper given at the Third Conference of the Association for Commonwealth Studies, 21 May 2007, Cumberland Lodge, Windsor Great Park, England. Thank you to conference participants for their insight and comments, particularly Thomas H.B. Symons, Ian E. Wilson, Alastair Niven, Donald Markwell, Leonard Conolly, and Alamgir Hashmi. The author would also like to acknowledge the assistance and insight provided by Donald B. Smith, Peter Henshaw, Ian Buckingham, William Galbraith, Kate Macdonald, and J.R. Miller. Archivists and librarians at Queen's University Archives, Library and Archives Canada, the Saskatchewan Archives Board, the *Punch* Library, and the National Library of Scotland must also be acknowledged, particularly Megan Kerrigan, Tom Novak, Sally Harrower, and Andre Gailani.

1 Colin M. Coates, "Introduction: Majesty in Canada," in *Majesty in Canada: Essays on the Role of Royalty*, ed. Colin M. Coates (Toronto: Dundurn Group, 2006), 11.
2 Ibid.
3 *Glimpses of John Buchan: His Life in Canada and His Legacy: An Exhibition to Commemorate the 50th Anniversary of His Appointment as Governor General of Canada* (Ottawa: National Library of Canada and Queen's University at Kingston, 1985), 5.
4 Ibid., 8–9.
5 *The Thirty-Nine Steps* still holds considerable appeal. A popular stage production of Buchan's novel played from 2006–15 at the Criterion Theatre at Piccadilly Circus in London, earning glowing reviews and awards. Previously this comedic interpretation, adapted by Patrick Barlow, played a sell-out run at the Tricycle Theatre in London.
6 *Glimpses of John Buchan*, 10–11.
7 Ibid., 12–13.
8 Ibid., 14.
9 See, for example, Sarah Carter, "'Your Great Mother Across the Salt Sea': Prairie First Nations, the British Monarchy and the Vice Regal Connection to 1900," *Manitoba History* 48 (2004/5): 34–48; and Jasper Tough Gilkison, *Visit of the Governor-General and the Countess of Dufferin to the Six Nation Indians: August 25, 1874*, 2nd ed. ([Brantford, Ontario?]: [Indian Office?], 1875); Wade A. Henry, "Imagining the Great White Mother and the Great King: Aboriginal Tradition and Royal Representation at the 'Great Pow-Wow' of 1901," *Journal of the Canadian Historical Association* 11 (2000): 87–108; J.R. Miller, "I Will Take the Queen's Hand: First Nations Leaders and the Image of the Crown in the Prairie Treaties," in *Reflections on Native-Newcomer Relations: Selected Essays* (Toronto: University of Toronto Press, 2004), 217–41; Ian Radforth, "Performance, Politics, and Representation: Aboriginal People and the 1860 Royal Tour of Canada," *Canadian Historical Review* 84/1 (2003): 1–32.
10 Biographies of John Buchan, First Baron of Tweedsmuir, include most notably: William Buchan, *John Buchan: A Memoir* (London: Buchan & Enright, 1982); Andrew Lownie, *John Buchan: The Presbyterian Cavalier* (London: Canongate, 1995); Janet Adam Smith, *John Buchan: A Biography* (London: R. Hart-Davis, 1965); Janet Adam Smith, *John Buchan and His World* (New York: Charles Scribner's Sons, 1979); Arthur C. Turner, *Mr. Buchan, Writer: A Life of the First Lord Tweedsmuir* (London: SCM Press, 1949); and Susan Tweedsmuir, *John Buchan: By His Wife and Friends* (London: Hodder & Stoughton, 1947).

11 Anthony H.M. Kirk-Greene, "The Governors-General of Canada, 1867–1952: A Collective Profile," *Journal of Canadian Studies* 12/4 (1977): 53.
12 See Smith, *John Buchan: A Biography*, 470.
13 Kirk-Greene, "Governors-General of Canada," 36.
14 John Buchan, *Memory Hold-the-Door* (Toronto: Musson Book Company, 1940), 260.
15 The same could be said today. In the theatre performance program of *The 39 Steps*, adapted by Patrick Barlow, the honouring of Buchan as "Chief Teller of Tales" is mentioned in the first paragraph of his biographical sketch. The romantic appeal of recognition by Canadian Indigenous peoples, in the eyes of the British public, still holds considerable weight.
16 Kirk-Greene, "Governors-General of Canada," 40.
17 Waskesiu, also known as Prince Albert National Park, located north of Prince Albert, Saskatchewan, was popular in Buchan's time as the storied home of Grey Owl.
18 John Buchan, *Sick Heart River*, intro. Trevor Royle (1941; repr., Edinburgh: MacDonald, 1981), 77.
19 Corey Coates, "The Governor General's Three Solitudes: The Canadian Geneses of John Buchan's 'Sick Heart River,'" *Canadian Ethnic Studies* 35/1 (2003): 172.
20 Kirk-Greene, "Governors-General of Canada," 41.
21 See William Galbraith, "Sick Heart River," John Buchan Society website, 2005, http://www.johnbuchansociety.co.uk/books/92.htm (accessed 1 June 2017).
22 See David Daniell, "Introduction," in John Buchan, *Sick Heart River* (1941; repr., London: Oxford University Press, 1994), xix.
23 See Buchan, "Down North," *John Buchan Journal* 5 (summer 1985): 3–6, and "Down North," *John Buchan Journal* 6 (autumn 1986): 4–8.
24 Buchan, *Sick Heart River*, 77.
25 See Buchan, "Down North" (1985 and 1986).
26 Buchan, "Down North" (1986): 5–6.
27 John Buchan, *The Long Traverse* (London: Hodder and Stoughton, 1941), 132.
28 Ibid., 69.
29 Coates, "Governor General's Three Solitudes," 172.
30 Ibid.
31 Lord Tweedsmuir (John Buchan), *Canadian Occasions: Addresses by Lord Tweedsmuir* (Toronto: Musson Book Company, 1941), 80–1.
32 See ActiveHistory.ca, "Podcast: Ian McKay on the Right-Wing Reconceptualization of Canada," 15 March 2011, http://activehistory.ca/2011/03/

podcast-ian-mckay-on-the-right-wing-reconceptualization-of-canada/ (accessed 14 July 2015).

33 Buchan's speech to Ukrainians at Fraserwood, Manitoba, 21 September 1936, reprinted in J.M. Gibbon, *Canadian Mosaic: The Making of a Northern Nation* (Toronto: McClelland and Stewart, 1938), 307.

34 Peter Henshaw, "John Buchan and the British Imperial Origins of Canadian Multiculturalism," in *Canadas of the Mind: The Making and Unmaking of Canadian Nationalisms in the Twentieth Century*, ed. N. Hilmer and A. Chapnick (Montreal: McGill-Queen's University Press, 2007), 191–213. See also Henshaw, "John Buchan and the Invention of Canada," *John Buchan Journal* 34 (spring 2006): 18–29, and "John Buchan and the Invention of Post-Colonial Literature," *John Buchan Journal* 32 (2005): 35–40.

35 Henshaw, "John Buchan and the British Imperial Origins of Canadian Multiculturalism." William Galbraith in his research has come to similar conclusions about King's views on Canada and the empire.

36 "Lord Tweedsmuir Now Indian Chief," *Daily Herald* [Prince Albert, Saskatchewan], 13 August 1936, 2.

37 "Grey Owl Lionized," *Daily Herald* [Prince Albert, Saskatchewan], 14 August 1936, 1. It is interesting and significant to note that it was at the Carlton Treaty 6 celebration that the Cree first had serious doubts about Grey Owl's authenticity. Although the Cree honoured Grey Owl as a brother, and showed him much attention, his behaviour and manner at the celebration gave them a clear indication that he did not have the "genre and ethos of an Indian." Euro-Canadians and non-First Nation peoples, like Lord Tweedsmuir, were as yet still utterly convinced of Grey Owl's authentic "Indian" background. For more, see Donald B. Smith's biography, *From the Land of the Shadows: The Making of Grey Owl* (Saskatoon: Western Producer Prairie Books, 1990), 160–1.

38 Smith, *From the Land of Shadows*, 155, 163–4.

39 See Lord Tweedsmuir to Lady Tweedsmuir, 22 September 1936; Lord Tweedsmuir to "Dearest Tim," 16 September 1936; Lord Tweedsmuir to Alastair Buchan, 15 September 1936; Lord Tweedsmuir to W.L. Mackenzie King, 29 September 1936. All in File 1, Box 8, John Buchan Papers (Collection 2110), Series 1 (Correspondence), Queen's University Archives.

40 Lord Tweedsmuir to the Right Honourable W. Mackenzie King, 4 August 1936, in File 11, Box 7, John Buchan Papers (Collection 2110), Series 1 (Correspondence).

41 Lady Tweedsmuir to Mrs Carruthers, 8 Gower Street, London, 4 August 1936, in File 11, Box 7, John Buchan Papers (Collection 2110), Series 1 (Correspondence).

42 Louis Lebourdais, "Governor-General Becomes Chief of the Big Mountain," *Province* [Vancouver], 16 August 1936, pp. 1, 2.
43 "The Newest Chief," *Daily Herald* [Prince Albert, Saskatchewan], 22 September 1936, 7. Photograph and brief caption only, with no explanation as to the band or location of this honour.
44 Lord Tweedsmuir to Stair A. Gillion [Scotland], 19 June 1937, in File 8, Box 8, John Buchan Papers (Collection 2110), Series 1 (Correspondence).
45 Lord Tweedsmuir to Stair A. Gillion [Scotland], 7 September 1937, in File 8, Box 8, John Buchan Papers (Collection 2110), Series 1 (Correspondence).
46 Lord Tweedsmuir's Notes on "Down North" letterhead, dated 23 July 1937, in File 7, Box 8, John Buchan Papers (Collection 2110), Series 1 (Correspondence). For more on Tweedsmuir's northern journey, see William Galbraith, "Lord Tweedsmuir's Visit to the North: Never Be Off the Road," *Canadian Parliamentary Review* 18/1 (1995), http://www.revparl.ca/english/issue.asp?param=152&art=1034 (accessed 1 June 2017).
47 Beverley Baxter, "John Buchan Discovers a New World," *Sunday Graphic and Sunday News*, 19 September 1937, p. 12.
48 "Two Big Chiefs Meet" and "Governor General Cuts First Sod for Hospital," *Globe and Mail* [Toronto], 6 June 1938, p. 4.
49 Tour Programme (1937), File 4, Box 22, John Buchan Papers (Collection 2110), Series 5 (Miscellaneous Materials).
50 Keith Thor Carlson, "The Indians and the Crown: Aboriginal Memories of Royal Promises in Pacific Canada," in Coates, *Majesty in Canada*, 72.
51 J.R. Miller has frequently highlighted the continuing importance of the relationship between the Crown and Indigenous peoples in his work. See, for example, Miller, "I Will Take the Queen's Hand"; J.R. Miller, "Compact, Contract, Covenant: The Evolution of Indian Treaty-Making," in *New Histories for Old: Changing Perspectives in Canada's Native Pasts*, ed. Ted Binnema and Susan Neylan, 66–91 (Vancouver: UBC Press, 2007); "Spirit and Intent: Understanding Aboriginal Treaties," John Borrows and J.R. Miller, co-curators, Library and Archives Canada, 24 September 2007–24 March 2008; J.R. Miller, *Compact, Contract, Covenant: Aboriginal Treaty-Making in Canada* (Toronto: University of Toronto Press, 2009); and J.R. Miller, "The Aboriginal Peoples and the Crown," keynote address to The Crown in Canada: A Diamond Jubilee Assessment, Government House, Regina, SK, 26 October 2012.
52 Carlson, "Indians and the Crown," 78–9.
53 Carter, "Your Great Mother Across the Salt Sea," 34.
54 Ibid.

55 Ibid., 35.

56 Ibid.

57 See John Buchan, *Lord Minto:* A *Memoir* (London: Thomas Nelson & Sons, 1924).

58 H.F. Gadsby, "Governor-General and the Great Canadian Novel," *Standard* [Montreal], 17 July 1935, p. 16.

At the Crossroads of Militarism and Modernization: Inuit-Military Relations in the Cold War Arctic

P. WHITNEY LACKENBAUER

Historians chronically speak of the military opening up the Arctic, as if it had been a kind of locked and mysterious room before some clever army engineers happened by with the keys. Really, the military swept over the Arctic – first during World War II and more so during the Cold War – like an iron cloud, carpet bombing the place with boxes. Their job was the assertion of sovereignty. Every place a box landed became a beach-head for industrialized society. The boxes soon became the foundation for the Canadian government, which the military had given cause to worry about its sovereignty. Boxes were added, and more of our society – with its various virtues and vices, machines and organizations, ideals, morals, values and goals – were shipped north. What adult Inuit recall when they look back, not always in anger, is decade after decade when the skies rained boxes. The skies rain boxes still.

Kevin McMahon, *Arctic Twilight* (1987)

The unfurling of polar projection maps at the end of the Second World War, when the wartime alliance between the Soviet and Western worlds began to unravel, focused unprecedented attention on Canada's Arctic. Geographical isolation no longer would afford Canada the luxury of apathy when it came to its northland. In geostrategic terms, the Cold War Arctic was conceptualized as the front line in a future world war. The United States clambered for access to bolster continental defences, and Canadian decision makers, cognizant of the need to work with their southern superpower neighbour or risk the prospect of the United States acting on its own, proved accommodating allies.[1] Yet "neither the United States nor Canada looked on the North as a *place* to be protected because of some intrinsic value," strategist Kenneth Eyre astutely observed. "It was seen as a *direction*, an exposed flank."[2] Despite framing the Arctic as a vast, empty strategic space, decision makers had to acknowledge that a small population called the region home.

In 1946, geographer Trevor Lloyd recommended that Canadians should "see that none of the contemporary military activity in the Arctic is allowed to touch the lives of the Eskimos."[3] In practice, this wishful thinking proved impossible. The influence of *military modernization* – "a state (or states) working to make a landscape *legible* so as to enrol it more effectively into governmental responsibilities ... through projects backed by the authority of reason and the latest technologies, designed at a distance and implemented without sufficient attention to local nuance"[4] – on Canadian northern peoples has often been noted but seldom explored in detail. Anthropologist John Hughes, in his sweeping 1965 article on cultural change among the "Eskimo," observed that military construction was the key impetus for "the seemingly inexorable gathering of the Eskimo population into more permanent villages and the attrition of outlying settlements." Over the course of a single generation, these "settlement Eskimos" had become "oriented to a fundamentally different way of life."[5]

In their important studies on relocations and game management in the Arctic, Frank Tester and Peter Kulchyski see the state as a totalizing force, its mission underpinned by an ideology of progress. "Totalization of the state involved, for the state, the transmutation of the need away from relations to animals and toward what so-called progress had to offer: wage employment, permanent housing, settlement living, and all that they entail," they argue. "Undermining the hunting regime, as a way of meeting culturally constructed needs, was crucial to attempts to absorb Inuit by the Canadian state into dominant social forms."[6] During the Cold War era, northern military projects were, as documentary filmmaker Kevin McMahon described, beachheads of modernism: sites of wage employment, new housing, and Western technologies, and sources of disruption to northern ecosystems and traditional patterns of life. Although not primarily designed to bring Indigenous peoples under state control, defence initiatives – conceived from afar and implemented locally – had far-reaching impacts. Accordingly, scholars like Frances Abele have argued that "sovereignty and security policy decisions, in their immediate impact, have been and continue to be disproportionately costly to northern indigenous peoples." Inuit spokesperson Mary Simon concurred: "Too often, military projects are centralized undertakings that are unilaterally imposed on indigenous peoples and their territories. Such actions are inconsistent with the basic principles of aboriginal self-government."[7] Militarization appears to fit within the framework of a coercive, totalizing, high modernist[8] state interested in re-engineering Inuit life to conform with modern priorities.

Such critiques, however, conceal aspects of cooperation that have marked the Canadian Forces' interaction with northerners. McMahon, writing in the late 1980s, found that Inuit were really of "two minds" about the military. Although the Inuit Circumpolar Conference (ICC) called for a demilitarization of the Arctic on social and environmental grounds, McMahon noted that Canadian Inuit had "a good deal of respect and goodwill for the military people who worked in the Arctic" and the Canadian Rangers were popular in northern communities.[9] In the wake of earlier military megaprojects, social scientists who visited Inuit communities in the 1950s and 1960s had also been astonished to find that most Inuit "expressed general satisfaction" with settlement life.[10] Concurrently, the federal government's approach to Arctic defence was paradoxical. Although the military was not at the forefront of intentional social engineering nor did its practices represent a well-orchestrated scheme to "civilize" Inuit, its activities created or exacerbated dependencies on wage employment and Western goods, encouraged the sedentarization of Inuit, and set up unsustainable expectations given the "boom-and-bust" cycles associated with defence work. The presence of military installations did circumscribe certain Inuit behaviours, but the coercion implied in recent literature on state-Inuit relations during the Cold War seems strangely absent.[11]

This chapter examines how militarization affected northern Indigenous peoples during the first two decades of the Cold War, reflecting primarily upon three case studies of relationships between the military and northern Indigenous people. "The outlook of the Eskimos ... has been changing since the construction of the northern airfields, the weather and radar stations, and the D.E.W. Line, opened their eyes to the advantages of wage-employment," anthropologist Diamond Jenness observed in *Eskimo Administration* (1964).[12] At Frobisher Bay (now Iqaluit), the military hub of the eastern Arctic, the presence of an airfield, weather station, a Pinetree station, and construction activities related to the DEW Line (Distant Early Warning Line) drew Inuit people into the web of modern urban life. Reports from government officials and oral histories reveal how the expansion of the military's footprint in the 1940s and 1950s, and the concomitant concentration of Inuit migrants from southern Baffin Island, reshaped the boundaries, expectations, and tastes of Frobisher's inhabitants. The young anthropologist Jack Ferguson, who visited the western sections of the DEW Line in 1956, also observed how wage employment associated with military projects "imposed" a "radically different kind of living pattern" upon Inuit. "The description of this type of employment as 'imposed' is not too strong," he argued, even if the actual work was not outright coercive. "The European has created desires for material goods among those people, and these desires can only be resolved by the Eskimos taking every opportunity to earn money." The DEW Line's projection of "modern industrial life on Canada's last frontier" restructured Inuit time, movement, gender roles, and subsistence, Ferguson observed in his final report.[13] Some contact narratives were less formal, and reflected positive Inuit-military relationships based upon accommodation and mutual learning, as seen in the experiences of Canadian Ranger liaison officer Captain Ambrose Shea. His first forays into the Baffin region were a culture shock. Over time, however, he developed a familiarity with the Rangers in the eastern Arctic, visiting them in their remote camps. He ate and fished with them and developed a strong respect for their knowledge and skills. His reflections, like those of the other commentators, also revealed that the consequences of military modernism were readily apparent to federal representatives and social scientists on the ground.[14] They observed changes at the local level and reported their findings to Ottawa, emphasizing the need for constructive action. They also retreated to the modernist language of "inevitability" when the forces of change seemed to fundamentally alter Inuit society.

The Military Transformation of Frobisher Bay (Iqaluit)

The Second World War had a transformative impact on Canada and on Indigenous peoples in particular, (re)shaping social discourses and the physical and cultural geographies of interaction.[15] This process was particularly evident in the Canadian Northwest, where military development projects brought a flood of outsiders (predominantly Americans) into the region. Their presence incited a sovereignty panic in Ottawa, prompting Vincent Massey's famous claim that a US "army of occupation" had "apparently walked in and taken possession [of the North], in many cases as if Canada were unclaimed territory by a docile race of aborigines."[16] Massey's colourful commentary on the broad Canadian-American relationship also played upon a stereotypical image of Indigenous peoples. In reality, Inuit and First Nations were marginalized, their land rights ignored, and a distant federal government both regulated and protected them from outside threats.

In other areas, the effects of the war were less acute but initiated a process of "military modernization" that culminated during the 1950s.[17] Frobisher Bay (Iqaluit) was a temporary fishing spot for Inuit of southern Baffin Island but had never hosted a settlement or trading post. Its first permanent incarnation was Crystal Two, an airbase and weather station at the head of the bay and a stop on the Crimson Staging Route, the series of bases and depots established by the United States (with Canadian approval) to facilitate the transfer of planes and other materiel from North America to Europe during the Second World War. By the time the Crystal Two station became operational in 1943, the installation was "virtually obsolete" for wartime purposes.[18] Nevertheless, the Crimson Route airfields were heralded as modern miracles. In the words of Malcolm MacDonald, the British High Commissioner to Canada, the Americans "treated ... with indifference the obstacles which Nature – whose sovereignty in the Arctic is even more supreme than that of the Canadian Government – put in their way." Crystal Two was effectively "a small town" with every imaginable amenity: "the latest feature films from Hollywood can be seen in the Arctic wastes before they are seen in New York or Chicago."[19]

The imprint of the Western military was particularly obvious to Inuit drawn to the new settlement. Tomassie Naglingniq encountered the Americans in 1941, when they first arrived in Frobisher Bay to find a location to build houses and an airfield. "The *qallunaat* [non-Inuit] started giving us biscuits, sugar, tea, chocolate and Coca-Cola. They started opening pop and handing them to us," he remembered. "I took a sip when [one man with a long beard] told me to, and my tongue felt like it burned, but it was just Coca-Cola. When my tongue burned, I threw the pop inside our tent and it exploded. The next day the Americans gave out so many things, including cigarettes, to my family and everyone else." The Americans hired Inuit for $5/day:

> On a Saturday or a Sunday, when the Americans were not working, they took us to the ship and we watched a movie. We had never seen anything like that. Neither my grandparents nor my mother had ever seen anything like that before ... Once inside the theatre on the ship we saw a big white screen. It was really big. Niaquq, the man that spoke Inuktitut, told us to

> look at the screen … because we were going to watch a war movie. My mother and her family and a lot of other Inuit were watching. When the movie started, everybody started yelling "*ajait ajai*" ["I'm scared"] because we never saw anything like that before. It was like the people in the movie were coming and shooting at us, and we were crying, us children anyway. We were even scared to look at the screen. My mother and my grandparents were yelling *ajait* when the people in the movies were shooting. The sound of the shooting sounded like "tuk tuk tuk tuk tuk tuk." The Inuit were ducking and taking cover, because they thought they were being shot at.

The arrival of the Americans marked a turning point in the history of the region. Food, cigarettes, and movies (usually Westerns) are common elements in Inuit narratives of their encounters with armed service personnel. Before the war, the only *qallunaat* (non-Inuit or "White" people) that Naglingniq's family had seen were the Hudson's Bay Company (HBC) employees at the local trading posts. They had never seen mechanized vehicles like bulldozers. "When they started unloading the ship, their vehicles just started moving on the ground even though they were made of metal," Naglingniq recounted. "Looking back, we must have thought they were from the moon."[20]

Historian Mélanie Gagnon's collection of Iqaluit elders' memories provides poignant insight into how the military presence at Frobisher transformed lives of Baffin Island Inuit. Elijah Pudlu was about nine years old when he arrived in Frobisher to find "lots of houses by the airport hangar where the Americans were." The Indigenous people he encountered living at the site seemed "very wealthy" compared to those living on the land:

> They had all kinds of things such as candies. The Americans were here then. All the people that lived here were helped by the Americans very much. The Americans used to give us fuel for free. We used to get 45 gallons of fuel. Those fuel tanks weren't there when we came here. All the fuel tanks were by the church. There were a lot of barrels. They were refilled from a ship. Inuit didn't use fuel in their stoves back then. There were lots of American ships coming here. Whenever they arrived during the summer, they used to bring lots of supplies. It was like the ship was making babies. We used to watch them when the barges landed. It was like on a movie when they had their combat vehicles. There were a lot of ships that would arrive at once. They were all American. Whenever the

> combat vehicles were on the land, it used to be very noisy. They were the kind that could drive onto the land. Some of them were small. I heard that there was a war when the Americans were here. They even had a cannon on top of the hill because they were keeping watch. Also over by the airport where there was a military base for the Americans, I heard that they had a big cannon ... They were protecting the Inuit. This town probably wouldn't exist if the Americans hadn't come here to protect us.[21]

The comparison to a "movie" is telling, given the language of protection and how surreal the resupply operations must have appeared to Inuit living in a comparatively depauperate environment. This was not an invasion force. Indeed, elders recall disappointment when US Army Air Force personnel were replaced by a token Canadian staff in 1944. More Inuit worked, but while the Americans tended to give out things like food for free, the Canadians insisted that they pay. The jump in the price of a carton of cigarettes from $1 to $5 was a source of particular unhappiness.[22]

As relations cooled between the West and the Soviet Union at the end of the Second World War, the threat of a transpolar attack on North America became more real. The bilateral military bond between Canada and its southern neighbour tightened, and basic agreements for shared continental defence took shape. In 1947, the Canadian Cabinet Defence Committee authorized American authorities to perform maintenance at certain airfields and weather stations, allowing the US military to return to the Canadian North. Frobisher Bay re-emerged as a strategically significant site.

Andrew Thomson, controller of the meteorological division at the Department of Transport, visited Frobisher Bay in early April 1948. "The Eskimos run tractors and trucks, pump out oil daily from drums and distribute it to station personnel by truck," he reported to External Affairs. "The local laundry is operated by 3 Eskimos; one runs the dry cleaning section and the other two the washing and ironing section." The American officer in charge at Frobisher said that without Inuit help it would be "a real problem" distributing the 15,000 barrels of oil taken ashore annually.[23] About 185 Inuit lived in a village about half a mile from the weather station, an area that was strictly off-limits to military personnel – except "between 2:00 and 4:00 p.m. Sunday afternoon for taking pictures." Tourists who expected a romantic image of Inuit life were disappointed. Thomson found the living conditions deplorable, which he documented to convey "the extremely difficult problem that is created by bringing in Eskimos to work at a weather station." Inuit inhabited extremely dirty, small frame huts, much less satisfactory than their snow igloos. "The Eskimo natives employed attempt to follow the white man's customs," he noted. They had replaced their traditional clothing with "woolen underwear and a fur parka; the woolen underwear is left on until, the RCMP told me, it fairly rots off. Normally, in the native state, the Eskimo would take off the clothing and hang it up outside in the cold and sleep in a sleeping bag; in the morning the Eskimo would beat out their fur clothing and get rid of the dirt." Fortunately, in Thomson's view, better access to medical care at Frobisher helped Inuit to overcome "the health problems created by the change from their native habits and customs."[24]

While the Royal Canadian Air Force was officially in charge of the Frobisher Bay airfield, US military personnel and contractors returned to the community "in several waves" during the 1950s. Frobisher served as a transshipment point during the construction of the massive American airbase at Thule, Greenland, and a radar station (the terminus of the Pinetree Line which spanned southern Canada and ran up the Newfoundland-Labrador coast) was built near the Frobisher airfield.[25] In 1953, the American 926th Aircraft Control and Warning Squadron arrived to maintain the radar site. With the arrival of more armed forces personnel came more restrictions on local mobility. Tomassie Naglingniq recalled walking too close to the "Upper Base" as a teenager hunting with some friends. They were arrested.

> It was scary when the Americans came with their guns. We were not supposed to be in that area with guns. We had caught a lot of ptarmigans. They took the ptarmigans from us. I guess they called the RCMP officer because he came. He was the only policeman at that time. When he took us, we thought we had been arrested, but he just took us home. The next day they did not return the ptarmigans, but they gave us pop and chocolate in return. That was a scary experience. We were scared. The next day they just told us not to go up there again.[26]

Similarly, Akisu Joamie recalled that "Inuit were not allowed to go beyond where the breakwater is today." At that location, they would hand over goods and carvings they were trying to sell to the RCMP officer, who would act as a liaison and offer them to the *qallunaat* working at the base. Although Inuit-*qallunaat* interaction was prohibited, this did not mean that service personnel were uninterested in the plight of their neighbours. Joamie and others remembered how service personnel "would pile up food, such as a hundred pounds of flour, or a hundred pounds of sugar," at a place where they knew Inuit visited.[27]

For their part, Ottawa officials lamented the growing dependency of the locals on the military, and the concomitant loss of traditional land skills. Although defence projects attracted Indigenous people from the surrounding areas, it would be erroneous to presuppose that government planners sought Inuit sedentarization. Geoffrey Bruce, a member of the Defence Liaison Division at External Affairs, visited Frobisher in 1953. At that point, the site consisted of an Inuit settlement, RCAF and USAF buildings, a radio and meteorological building belonging to the Department of Transport, and a radar station. "The Eskimo community is a pitiful, pathetic site and one of the most perplexing and infectious problems facing the Northern Administration of the Department of Resources and Development," Bruce lamented. "I understand that these Eskimos are almost completely dependent on the white settlement." Many of the local inhabitants had worked at the station since 1942 and consequently had forgotten many of their old ways of life: hunting, fishing, and trapping. Living in permanent, ramshackle houses made out of old scraps of material, they no longer migrated seasonally "but continue to live in increasing filth." Wage employment was not an equalizer. "Although a couple of Eskimos drove trucks, the great majority worked in the kitchens and around the buildings," Bruce observed. "It was pitiful and tragic in that the Eskimos have given up their own culture and have accepted, or are accepting, many of the material advantages but few of the non-material benefits of the 'Western World.'"[28]

In Bruce's eyes, the convergence of militarism and modernism had created an unavoidable storm. "Since it is quite clear that now it is too late to turn back, Canada has inherited an obligation to provide these people with something more than Family Allowances, a shovel, cigarettes, Coca-Cola, clothing, fuel and a healthy credit account at the Hudson's Bay Company," he insisted. The military had surpassed the fur traders and whalers as "the greatest employers" of Inuit, and their clustering around defence installations had fundamentally disrupted their traditional patterns. "Before this development, there was probably some chance that these people could continue living their own life; now this is impossible," Bruce asserted. "Perhaps because there are only several thousand Eskimos in the entire Canadian Arctic the transition will be easy and painless. Possibly, it may be tragic."[29] This language of inevitable demise, which was inextricably linked to a sense of modern progress, was commonplace in the 1950s.

As Frobisher increased in importance as a communication and construction hub for the eastern section of the DEW Line system, the tempo of activity accelerated once again. In April 1955, Pierre Berton found the Frobisher base to be "a confused mosaic of men and machinery." He described huge planes on the runways, a great host of noisy vehicles and machines, and a list of southern food: "Coca-Cola, T-bone steaks, Irish stew, dumplings, grapefruit, pickles, ham and eggs, apple pie, and ketchup, ketchup, ketchup."[30] Alootook Ipellie recalled, as a child, going to the base "to wait outside their kitchen in hopes of being offered something to eat. We often succeeded and the smell of their food was like nothing that we had ever smelled before." Eventually, the tastes of Western society infiltrated Inuit dreams. "There came a time when at least once a day I would start to dream of having tons and tons of Quallunaaq food right in our little hut," Ipellie remembered. "Even if all of the food could not go in, I would think of becoming a genius at storing food and somehow get it all in there."[31]

The growth of the town was explosive, fed largely by an influx of Inuit from Lake Harbour (Kimmirut) on southern Baffin Island,[32] prompting bold visions about its future. Anthropologist Toshio Yatsushiro counted 258 Inuit in 1956 and 624 by 1958. By that point, 59 per cent of Inuit residents lived in tents in summer and "wooden huts" in winter – mostly "'shacks' or hovels of the worst imaginable type," with poor insulation and overcrowding.[33] The US Strategic Air Command was building a base at Frobisher, and the site assumed a second identity as an administrative centre, prompting various interdepartmental meetings in Ottawa on its future. A 1957 Department of Transport press release, echoing a familiar Cold War theme, located Frobisher in the heart of a new "Polar Mediterranean" around which "the three big powers of the world – Canada as a member of the Commonwealth, U.S.A. and U.S.S.R – [faced] each other over this ice- and island-filled ocean." Frobisher could be the Alexandria of the North, located at a new "crossroad of the world."[34] Expectations were high: *The Canadian Architect*, which laid out a plan for a huge geodesic bubble to protect the townsite from harsh weather, anticipated that "Frobisher Bay promises to be a town which will make all Canada – all the world, probably – think again about living and working in the north."[35] *Time* magazine described it as a "new dream town [that] may prove the prototype for next-century towns across the North," complete with all the amenities of southern life. Inhabitants would travel in special buggies, which would provide "a means to make today's muskeg wastelands bloom with oil derricks, grainfields, mines and forests."[36] Of course, this imagined "model" community at the centre of a booming Arctic economy, reminiscent of Stefansson's visions of a northern empire during the interwar years, never materialized. Jet technology meant that commercial and military flights could bypass Frobisher without refuelling. When the United States withdrew its personnel from the air base in 1963, many southern Canadians followed.[37] The military was a transient actor in the North, fulfilling the adage that southerners go north "to make a killing, not a living."

Frobisher did not become the "cross roads of the world," but it did reveal how defence installations served as catalysts for cultural change. Anthropologist John Honigmann held up the settlement as an example of the "radical situational transformation" approach to modernization. There was no "formal and explicit program" akin to community development schemes in South Asia, and "broad and very vague goals for Canada's northern people ... periodically enunciated by political figures" visualized the North as a partnership between Inuit and southern Canadians. "Developing a new life for town-dwelling Eskimo has an *ad hoc* character when viewed in historical perspective," Honigmann observed, "but it has nevertheless rapidly transformed Eskimo culture at practically every observable point."[38] After the military departed, the growth rate in Frobisher continued through the 1960s, propelled by even more migration from neighbouring communities. Quinn Duffy noted that "by 1969 only 5 percent of the area's population was entirely dependent on the traditional way of life based on the fur trade."[39] The military had played the formative role in transforming Frobisher from a fishing spot to the largest community in the eastern Arctic.

J.D. Ferguson and the DEW Line in the Western Arctic

To say that the Eskimos located at the various D.E.W. line sites stand at a cross-roads is to state the obvious. One might add that it is a cross roads at which there are sign-posts with meaningless words written on them.

J.D. Ferguson, *A Study of the Effects of the Distant Early Warning Line Upon the Eskimo of the Western Arctic of Canada* (1957)

During the 1950s, defence planners sought high-tech solutions that conceptualized the Arctic as part of a broader continental space or grid,[40] and yet decisions made in southern laboratories, boardrooms, and government offices had socio-economic and political impacts on northern peoples. The geodesic domes of the DEW Line not only reshaped the physical face of the Arctic from Alaska to Greenland,[41] but also affected what anthropologist Charles Hughes called the "behavioural environment" – the environment *as it is* and *as it is conceived to be*. He noted that the effects of the flood of southern workers to the Inuit homeland during the construction phase "in underscoring outside reference images and standards will be irreversible."[42] The Inuvialuit and Inuinaktuit of the western and central Canadian Arctic had already dealt with whalers, fur traders, and missionaries. The accoutrements of the modern world – from outboard-powered canoes to rifles – had been introduced to the Inuit world over the previous half century, but their migratory hunting life and customs had not been fundamentally disrupted. The DEW Line's impacts were of a higher magnitude. Journalists played on the theme of a dramatic transition from the Stone Age to the Atomic Age overnight. While this was a stretch, given previous relationships with *qallunaat*, the rapidity with which the military megaproject began to reshape the structure of Inuit life was unprecedented.

During the early negotiations that culminated in the bilateral agreement to build the DEW Line, Canadian officials expressed concerns about the effects that the project would have on Inuit. At the request of the Department of Northern Affairs and National Resources (DNANR), the conditions for the building of the radar system included provisions to protect Inuit, "in a primitive state of social development," from the fundamental disruption to their way of life and health (see appendix 1 at the end of this chapter). Commentators took note. The government "insisted that no activity in any form should interfere with the Eskimos' normal way of life, or of making a living," Richard Morenus wrote in his epic 1957 book on the DEW Line. "Eskimos could be used as guides or as workers in certain types of jobs, but only after the Department agents had given their okay." He painted a positive portrait of "very intelligent" government support:

> These people, they explained firmly, were Canadian Eskimos, and Canada planned to have them stay that way. Eskimos, living as Eskimos have always lived, will remain a proud and valiant race with intelligent co-operative help. Canada will never allow her natives to become serfs or charges through assimilation if she can possibly prevent it ... They are not menials or servants. They are a proud people in their own land. The

> result is a splendid sense of equality among all the men working on the Line. There is no segregation, favoritism, or sense of superiority in one human over another. Up there in the Arctic there is a common bond in one world.[43]

The Canadian government was succeeding in insulating its Inuit from changes to traditional life, Morenus suggested, and they were flourishing in a broader world. Others were less certain that transformation of Inuit life could be avoided. "The question whether the DEW Line will serve any useful military purpose has still to be answered, but there is no doubt that it will have a profound and lasting effect on the Arctic," C.J. Marshall, the director of the Northern Co-ordination and Research Centre of the DNANR,[44] anticipated the same year. "Inevitably, the lives of most of the Eskimos in the region will be drastically altered." Material prosperity brought benefits and temptations that would usher in a "new pattern of life" for Inuit, but Marshall ended with optimism: "The adjustment will not be easy but with reasonable controls and guidance there is no reason why the DEW Line should not be a boon to the Arctic even if it does not prove to be a shield for the rest of North America."[45]

The phrase "reasonable controls and guidance" was predicated on an assumed knowledge of anticipated socio-economic, cultural, and political impacts in the Arctic. Alongside the comprehensive data generated to determine the feasibility of and appropriate sites for the DEW Line stations, Northern Affairs and National Resources initiated a series of research programs and studies to evaluate changes in the northern economy. In the summer of 1956, the Northern Research Co-ordination Centre sent a graduate student in anthropology at the University of Toronto, John Duncan "Jack" Ferguson, "to describe the changing way of life in the western Canadian Arctic, and the way in which its Eskimo residents are adjusting to the new opportunities of wage employment" during the DEW Line construction phase.[46] His report, submitted the following year, retained in a locked cabinet at Northern Affairs and never circulated beyond the department and select parliamentarians, offers a perceptive commentary on the social changes associated with the construction of the Line. His first-hand perspectives on these sites of military modernization reveal discernible changes that were transpiring to reshape Inuit life.

Cambridge Bay (Ikaluktutiak – "the fair fishing place"), a settlement on the southwest coast of Victoria Island, had been an important Inuit site for millennia owing to abundant caribou, seal, fish, and waterfowl.

Although British explorers had visited the area in the mid-nineteenth century and ethnographers such as Vilhjalmur Stefansson and Diamond Jenness followed in the early twentieth, sustained contact with *qallunaat* began with the establishment of an HBC depot in 1920 and a trading post in 1923. At the end of the Second World War, Cambridge Bay was chosen as the site of a low-frequency Loran (long-range navigation) station. The Inuit population jumped from three or four families to more than 100 residents, who used scrap lumber and plywood from the site to build about twenty cabins.[47] In the end, the Loran system "proved unsatisfactory and was discontinued, but the 625-ft. tower at Cambridge Bay remain[ed] as a prominent land mark." The RCAF continued to return to the settlement each winter to train air crews in Arctic survival, and the Department of Transport established a weather and radio station at the old Loran site.[48] The construction of CAM-MAIN – one of six main DEW Line stations, which served as the command, communications, maintenance, and supply headquarters for auxiliary and intermediate radar stations in its sector – was the primary impetus for the town's growth. In the second half of the 1950s, the settlement became the key transport and supply centre for the central Arctic and Inuit families immigrated from nearby camps in search of employment.[49]

When Ferguson arrived, three groups of Inuit resided in the community. The hunters, who lived in tents during the spring to trade fur before heading off to fish, hunt, and trap for the remainder of the year, were now a minority. The settlement was only "a stopping point in their year-round migration." The second group of residents worked for the Department of Transport, the RCAF, and the RCMP. Most lived in surplus Quonset hunts "under very primitive conditions," their living quarters embodying "a series of anachronisms." European bedstands, electricity, radios, phonographs, oil-burning space heaters, and discarded Transport or RCAF furniture adorned houses where "sanitation is rudimentary." The third group was families supported by DEW Line employment, who had to provide their own shelter and thus lived more like hunter-trappers than the government employees. They moved their tents close to the DEW Line site in the spring when the ice on the bay was unsafe for travel.[50] In an old shack, which the Northern Construction Company loaned to Ferguson and dragged to the edge of the main Inuit camp, the young anthropologist was able to closely observe dynamics therein.[51]

Although the number of Inuit men employed on the DEW Line was relatively small (never more than 200 along the entire line), the impact was significant. Ferguson estimated that one-quarter of the Western Arctic population depended directly or indirectly on DEW Line employment.[52] "Eleven married and four unmarried men were employed [at CAM-MAIN] during June, 1956, but the figure fluctuated almost weekly," Ferguson noted. He asked every Inuk working there if he liked his job. "Almost all replied in the affirmative," the young sociologist reported. "However when the older men were asked whether they would rather remain at wage employment or go back to their former occupation, doubt immediately was apparent, and most of them finally said that they would prefer to return to hunting and trapping." He saw this indecision as reflective of the conflict between the "opportunity for high wages coupled with an occupation which made little apparent sense to the average Eskimo" and "the traditional, highly valued life of the hunter with its low income. For the same reason that a white farmer regrets going to work in a factory, the Eskimo hunter regrets going to work on the D.E.W. line." Inuit culture and tradition encouraged a hunting lifestyle, but Ferguson found it

> easily understandable that the young men aged 16 to 20 at Cambridge Bay are much more willing to work for the white employer than to embark on a career as a hunter. They have been raised in the old tradition but most of them have not experienced the rewards associated with it. It is rarely that a young man can accumulate the necessary equipment or skill to make hunting and trapping fully productive, much in the same way that a member of European society rarely is able to reach his maximum income before the age of 35. The rewards offered these young men by the D.E.W. line employment are not only financial – they include more subtle kinds, such as the chance to handle impressive machines and to associate with the prestige-laden Europeans. These latter rewards do not have the same value attached to them by the successful hunter and trapper who has already made a more or less successful adjustment to his economic and cultural milieu.[53]

The young men "enjoyed an almost unbelievably high income for their age and experience," and through their ample savings, could afford "many items such as watches, guitars, violins, and a wide variety of clothes." None of them bought hunting equipment, however, and none intended to return to "traditional life."[54]

DEW Line employment, which offered larger cash rewards than trapping, changed the local socio-economic hierarchy. The net income of a skilled Inuit trapper had averaged $1,400; the average $2,250 that a DEW Line worker earned represented a 50 per cent increase. For an average trapper, a DEW Line salary would represent an increase of several hundred per cent. Ferguson observed that this wage employment was undermining traditional social organization based upon "the attributes of materialism and individuality," particularly in terms of the status enjoyed by hunters and trappers:

> In the traditional community this meant that the man who had a large store of material goods was a person of high status in the community. In order to acquire these material goods he was necessarily a good hunter and, latterly, a skilled trapper. It has been suggested that only one trapper in ten was able to achieve this distinction. Now, at least fifty percent of those men working for the D.E.W. line have been able to accumulate the capital needed to obtain these material goods.
>
> Although there was certainly no formal government in the traditional Eskimo community ... there were certain channels of authority which tended to make for common action. The authority of the skilled trapper was unquestioned in the community. His less skilled companions tended to emulate him not because he ever suggested or ordered them to do anything, but because he held status and excited admiration ...
>
> Not only have incomes been leveled to a certain extent between the three types of trappers, but uniformity of D.E.W. line work has tended to upset the formal social order. Casual, average, and skilled trappers often worked side by side on a labour gang performing the same tasks and receiving the same pay. Some of this certainly appeals to the Eskimos [*sic*] individualism but it has come into conflict with the formal social order in the sense that the "leaders" of the community no longer have their status conferred through their superior performance of occupation.[55]

These observations fit with those of other anthropologists, such as Diamond Jenness, who noted that "men whose force of character or superior skill and prowess in hunting gained them acknowledged influence over their fellows." Instead, southern "strangers, ignorant of the language and thoughts of the Eskimos," assumed leadership positions.[56] Inuit now looked to the construction company building the DEW Line station – which distributed water to residents, delivered mail and bulky items free of charge, offered employment, and used its construction equipment to help everyone from the missionary to the Northern Service Officer – as the new "seat of authority," even though the general superintendent in Cambridge Bay did not want to get "mixed up" in local politics.[57]

Wage employment also changed the pattern and structure of family life. DEW Line work at Cambridge Bay separated the men from their families for most of the day and throughout the week, "and their work is in no direct way related to the subsistence of the family – at least not in the traditional terms." Rather than primarily hunting for food, he now provided it "indirectly through employment, money and a commercial source of food." As a consequence of wage employment reliant upon a fixed daily schedule, Ferguson observed that Inuit women's work was "sharply curtailed and divorced from that of the men. The children no longer spend a good part of the day in the joint activity with the mother and father." None of the twenty-eight school-age children in families supported by DEW Line employment was in school. Instead, the typical daily routine in the DEW Line worker encampment at Cambridge Bay was very different from that on the land. Men got up between 6:00 and 6:30; drank some tea; ate some pilot biscuit, bannock, fresh fish, seal meat, or a chocolate bar; then left for work. Three hours later, the women prepared a light meal of tea and bannock with any or all of the above items added. Between 10:00 a.m. and 6:00 p.m., the women and children did little "except attend to each other," Ferguson observed.

> Some do a little sewing, while others may spend the time by jigging for cod on the ice, or casually fishing in one of the nearby lakes or in the large river. In the main, the women spend this period visiting each other. The children wander further afield playing the traditional group games such as "wolf and caribou," "blind man's buff" ... or walking along the shores in groups of two to four. A few of them go to the R.C.A.F., D.O.T., and D.E.W. line sites where they attempt to invade the cookhouse, or cadge a ride with one of the truck-drivers. The characteristics of all this activity is that it is without any direction and that while it is a highly social kind of day, it could not be described as purposeful. Because the men have not been hunting or trapping there is little game or fur to be processed and few repairs to be made to equipment or clothing. Store clothes are more durable and require less repair than traditional clothing.
>
> The women at Cambridge Bay do not hunt or fish without their husbands, except in a desultory manner, and they therefore find little work except the tending of children ... This is not a full-time task in an Eskimo community since the children form into "gangs" at about the age of six or seven and start to look after themselves.

When the men returned from work at 6:00, the women prepared "a more substantial but nevertheless simple meal of the same basic foodstuffs." Then the couple would spend the evenings either visiting other families or entertaining in their own tent. "The men tend to go to bed about 11.00 p.m., while the women and children frequently stay up another hour or more," Ferguson noted. "Indeed the women often go visiting in the evening and leave the men at home to sleep."[58] Anthropologist Robert G. Williamson later confirmed that wage employment on the DEW Line led to "the diminution of the technical significance of the women as busy and vital elements in the family economic team."[59]

"Cambridge Bay is just one of twenty-four locations in the Western Arctic where the D.E.W. line sites are beginning to change the landscape, the black skyline, and the way of life of the indigenous people," Ferguson noted.[60] Nearly all of the auxiliary and intermediate DEW Line stations that extended east and west of CAM-MAIN had not been settlements before, and it was at these "smaller sites where the Eskimo have not been in contact with white men for any long period" that he felt he got his "best information." Although at Cambridge Bay he assessed that "they have all drawn into their shells, or, have thrown aside as much as possible their Eskimo way of life,"[61] the "Mackenzie River Eskimo" had used DEW Line work only as "another means of casual income" and did not allow it to disrupt their way of life. The situation was different in the Coronation and Queen Maud Gulfs, where wage employment was "a totally new thing and the Eskimos have had to make some radical readjustments. The routine work, the long hours and the baffling demands made upon them have turned many away and confused others." The money was the only "universal reward." While the economic effects were "startling and obvious" to Ferguson, the cultural effects were "less extreme. Because the majority of Eskimos in this eastern area have continued to live in the same tents and shacks as before, eat the same food and have the same families as neighbours, this wage employment has merely been a new occupation which makes different demands than trapping." Wholesale changes to traditional life had not yet occurred:

> The future is another matter. These communities will be drawn fully into a wage economy and probably into the European culture which accompanies it. This will be accompanied by a decline of the original Eskimo culture. It would be quite satisfactory if the new filled the gap left by the disappearance of the old, but the plain fact is that the Eskimos are offered

> only a fraction of the incredible volume of European civilization. At the moment they seem to get only such incidentals as comic books, cow-boy music and "junk" jewellery. While the economics of these D.E.W. line communities may be quite healthy, the basic culture may be impoverished. This is the way that "hill billies" are created.[62]

The accommodations in which Inuit employees resided reflected how the economy was being materially shaped by the DEW Line. The system was built on a "cost-plus" basis, which gave construction companies little incentive to carefully ration or reuse materials. The tremendous resources at their disposal flowed to the local community directly and indirectly, and facilitated the transition from snowhouses to shacks. "They gave them such things as fuel oil and scrap lumber; showed them how to use scrap insulating paper, and how to attach fuel oil regulators or 'carburetors' to their oil-drum stoves," Ferguson explained. "They repaired outboard and marine engines in their workshops and generally made the superior technology of the European available for the first time. This was the one aspect of European culture which the Eskimos did not get from their previous contacts."[63] His report, like most Inuit recollections of the period, also emphasized the value of the detritus and waste from the DEW Line.[64] By mid-1956, Ferguson noted that every DEW Line station already had an Inuit camp within two and a half miles consisting of winter quarters "of the packing-box and canvas variety" and canvas tents with an oil-drum stove and plank bed during the summer.[65] Dumps provided supplies to build houses and sleds, as well as food for dogs and people. The garbage flowing from the DEW Line fed the modernization of Inuit in the central Arctic.

The conditions of Inuit employment on the DEW Line in mid-1956 did not provide shelter or food for families; they "were expected to maintain themselves by their own resources supplemented by the limited amount of food available from the trading post at Cambridge Bay."[66] Thus, most Inuit employees had to spend between 20 and 25 per cent of each month hunting and fishing – except in the spring, when ice conditions made country foods particularly difficult to procure, thus creating a dependency on store food flown in from the Hudson's Bay Company post at Cambridge Bay. Ferguson learned that few sites offered enough country food for year-round living. After all, the DEW Line stations had been positioned at particular sites for technical reasons related to radar coverage and logistics; most were not in traditional hunting areas, and none offered "the two essentials (seal and fish) consistently and easily." Naturally, food shortages resulted at certain camps in 1956. Inuit workers, fed in the dining halls of the stations, neglected hunting, and the food supplies through the Cambridge Bay post arrived irregularly. The head cook at Site 16 received an impassioned letter from a woman at a nearby camp pleading, "Would you please let us have a piece of meat to cook even thou its small. We got nothing to eat. My children will be starving while there Dad working and getting good meat everyday while we got hungry having nothing to eat." Kitchen staff "surreptitiously" gave food to Inuit families such as this one.[67] Recognizing the incompatible expectations between the rigid DEW Line work schedule and the flexibility inherently required in a hunting economy, regulations were amended the following year so that Inuit employees received a standard ration for up to three family members.[68] Despite the initial government faith in their ability to ensure that Inuit did not become dependent upon the stations, the employees and their families were indeed adopting the food, clothing, habits, and language of the *qallunaat*.

J.D. Ferguson had anticipated that military-related employment would be transformative for Indigenous people:

> For the Eskimos who have worked on the D.E.W. line and who will remain at this employment, the end of the frontier period in the Arctic will become a reality. The attributes of the frontier such as economic laissez-faire, emphasis upon individual enterprise at the expense of community solidarity, the abandonment of former customs and the creation of new ones; all of this will disappear with the settling effect of D.E.W. line operation. The economy will be stable, as long as the D.E.W. line is in operation, and will certainly provide a basis for a stable social order.[69]

The stability never came. "The employment opportunities for local labour, created by the construction of the Distant Early Warning line, the move of Aklavik, and other government construction programs have provided some much needed additional income for a number of those who were formerly dependent upon fur trapping for a livelihood," the DNANR Annual Report for 1955–6 noted. "These and similar opportunities will occur for several years, but only a relatively small proportion can be counted upon to continue for longer than that. They therefore cannot be regarded as a cure for the problem of economic distress in these communities but merely as a short-term palliative."[70] In the end, the DEW Line caused the same "temporary boom and bust" conditions as other military and federal development projects, but with more sweeping effects. Less than one hundred Inuit were employed in maintenance work across the Canadian Arctic after the DEW Line went operational in 1957, and the unskilled labour which most Inuit had provided during the construction phase did not translate into readily transferrable skills.[71]

When the DEW Line intermediate stations were closed in the mid-1960s and strategic requirements indicated that additional closures were forthcoming, a military report gauged the local effects of decreasing military interest in northern Canada. "The loss of about 80 [Eskimo] jobs might not appear very serious in absolute terms," the report noted, "but it came at a time when employment was badly needed." More Inuit had received technical training than ever before, but they no longer possessed the equipment or skills to trap and hunt. They sought suitable employment, but resource development prospects were modest and labour supply far exceeded demand.[72] Inuit had followed the path towards wage employment and static communities, which had been encouraged by the DEW Line, and there was no turning back. Anthropologist Charles C. Hughes observed that the most profound effect of the military megaproject "was not so much in the actual jobs it gave as in the illustration it provided of the scope and capabilities of the technological culture of the outside world, and the measure of its control over the environment demonstrated by weather-indifferent housing, military facilities, and defense activities." DEW Line dumps had grown into shanty towns "that now spot the Arctic," exacerbating the public health problems that Inuit endured "living in a harsh environment."[73]

In his 1964 study *Eskimo Administration*, anthropologist Diamond Jenness depicted Inuit as caught in a transitional state between their traditional life and the modern world. Police posts, mines, radar lines, and northern weather stations had "given our natives no training except on unskilled jobs," he argued. "They have left the racial problem exactly as they found it, and hastened the entrances of the Eskimos into the world of civilization only to the extent that they familiarized a small number of families with some peripheral features of our daily life."[74] To accelerate what Jenness saw as an overly "academic and leisurely" educational strategy, he suggested that the military – the catalyst of so much of the change – assume a direct leadership role in preparing them for modern life. "Eskimos recruited into our army and brought south would probably learn more English in six months than their brothers and cousins in the Arctic are learning in six years," Jenness suggested. Accordingly, he proposed a program wherein Eskimo boys would volunteer for two years' service defending and developing the Far North. He saw roles for the army, air force, and navy in training these young men, "whom our schools are now casting adrift," so that they could more quickly take up "the administrative posts in the Arctic, and the skilled and semi-skilled jobs, now being filled by whites from southern Canada, thus substantially reducing the unemployment that prevails in the north today and the government's mounting expenses for straight relief." Even though "Canadians are not a military-minded people," Jenness justified assigning the lead role to National Defence because urgency dictated it. "The emergency is already pressing, and the Department of National Defence seems to be the only branch of the federal government possessing the readymade organization and the means to implement the program without delay," he wrote.[75] Appearances can be deceiving, as the military faltered with its own special force designed to accommodate Inuit and the northern First Nations. The boom-and-bust mentality associated with defence development projects was also obvious in its commitment to the Canadian Rangers.

Captain Ambrose Shea and the Canadian Rangers

In the immediate post-war years, the Canadian Army sought to integrate northern residents into a unique Reserve force, the Canadian Rangers. The concept, introduced in 1947, held that civilians, pursuing their everyday work as loggers, trappers, or fishermen, could serve as the military's "eyes and ears" in remote regions where demographics and geography precluded a more traditional military presence. With little training and equipment, the Rangers could act as guides and scouts, report suspicious activities, and – if the unthinkable came to pass – delay enemies using guerrilla tactics. The only equipment issued to Rangers was an obsolete .303 Lee Enfield, 200 rounds of ammunition annually, and an armband. From the onset, the force structure was decentralized and each Ranger platoon was operated and administered on a local basis.[76]

The question of Indigenous participation in the Rangers generated some initial apprehension. Brigadier S.F. Clark, the deputy chief of the General Staff, cautioned that "folk-lore attribute many qualities to outdoor people and especially to natives (such as Indians and Eskimos) which, in fact, they do not possess." Their innate "sense of direction" that might allow them to serve as military guides, for example, had been questioned by the explorer Vilhjalmur Stefansson, who "invariably … found that Indians and Eskimos were reasonably good guides in country with which they were familiar but that as soon as they were taken into unfamiliar country, they displayed no 'sixth sense of direction' but were, in fact, less able to find their way about than an experienced Anglo Saxon."[77]

Some regional commanders were more encouraging. Major General R.O.G. Morton of Quebec Command felt that Indigenous traits and lifestyles were appropriate for the force. After all, "the Eskimos and Indians living in isolated communities were excellent marksmen and probably would use the annual 100-round allotment of ammunition (the only remuneration they received) for hunting seal and reindeer."[78] As Ranger platoons expanded through northern Quebec, the western and central Arctic, and Baffin Island from 1948 to 1951, senior officials in Ottawa responsible for Eskimo affairs stressed that Inuit were "reliable, honest and intelligent and would make good Rangers." A rifle was "a major asset to an Eskimo and something he had to earn by hard work," and bullets for hunting cost significant money in the Arctic,[79] so Ranger service had material benefits. "Nobody has ever attempted to calculate, or could if one wanted to, the number of caribou, moose, and seal that fell to Ranger marksmen," Kenneth Eyre noted in hindsight.[80] The .303 Lee Enfield was a reliable weapon, even in Arctic conditions, and the number was undoubtedly substantial.

The few popular articles about the Rangers were laudatory. Larry Dignum told readers of the *Beaver* magazine that this "Shadow Army of the North," functioning as civilians and carrying out their duties in conjunction with their "regular jobs," quietly defended Canada and maintained law and order in isolated areas. "They have no uniforms, receive no pay, seek no glory," he observed, "but these men of known loyalty, Indian, Eskimo and white, take pride in standing on guard in the empty and remote parts of Canada with vigilance and integrity, and in silence."[81] Dignum's article, and another by Robert Taylor in *Star Weekly Magazine*, highlighted the vital importance of First Nations and Inuit cooperation. "Some of [the Rangers] can't read their own names but they are the real scholars of this country when it comes to reading signs on the trails of the north," Taylor's article stated. "Eskimos, Indians, whites and all the mixtures of these races, they are united in one task: Guarding a country that doesn't even know of their existence."[82]

While the Rangers watched remote regions through the 1950s, they received little institutional support. Their only contact with the larger army came through Ranger liaison officers (RLOs). Captain Ambrose J. Shea in Eastern Command was responsible for keeping in touch with Ranger company commanders along the Atlantic and eastern Arctic coasts, helping them with planning and training "the boys for action in their areas."[83] It was no easy feat. "One of the greatest difficulties facing this Headquarters, as far as the Rangers are concerned, is keeping in personal touch by means of liaison visits," Shea wrote in his first liaison letter in January 1953. "The very nature and scope of the Ranger Organization demands that it should exist in the more inaccessible parts of the Canadian seaboard. And in Eastern Command, it certainly does!" The entire responsibility for liaison fell on one man, in his case a "latter-day version of the 'Flying Dutchman' covering the island of Newfoundland, Labrador from the Quebec border to Hebron, and Baffin Island (which was about the size of Newfoundland and Labrador in itself."[84] Fortunately, Shea was keen to serve, approached the job with an open mind, and proved remarkably adaptable and effective.

In January 1955, Shea embarked for Baffin Island on board the Eastern Arctic Patrol vessel the *C. D. Howe*. He referred to it as his "Arctic Indoctrination Course" and was prepared to learn from his hosts. First he met with the Ranger officer at Frobisher Bay, HBC post manager Bob Griffiths, over a card table with local RCMP officers. Then he ventured out on dog-team patrols with Constable Deer to visit camps along the bay. He carefully observed Inuit dress, travel techniques, and the setup of their camps, and he compared the Reverend F.W. Peacock's Labrador Eskimo vocabulary to the local dialect. At Eethaloopia's camp, 30 miles from the base, Shea discerned a difference between Inuit living in settlements such as Frobisher and those living in outpost camps:

> We were accompanied on this trip by a relative of Eethaloopia's, who is an Eskimo version of a "Zoot-Suiter" or City Slicker. He parrots a few English phrases with a pseudo-Brooklyn accent and has an air of sleazy sophistication most unusual amongst Eskimoes, who generally have a simple dignity which is both impressive and appealing. Eethaloopia, on the other hand, is the exact opposite of his cousin and looks like something left over from the Paleolithic Age. I am certain that if he ever fell into the hands of an anthropologist he would be stuffed and mounted in no time![85]

In town, he had met with the local Ranger sergeant, Sageakdok, "a short, thick-set man of about thirty," who also surprised him. Not only did he have "an energetic, almost aggressive manner, rather unusual in an Eskimo," but Sageakdok had become remarkably proficient in English for a person who had known little to none of the language a year earlier. "He takes an obvious pride in his efficiency both as a truck-driver and Ranger-Sergeant," Shea noted. "Well he might. These things represent a tremendous and rapid change in outlook."[86]

When Shea returned to Frobisher in April 1956, he witnessed even more changes in the community. "Because of work connected with the D.E.W. Line and the setting-up of an 'Eskimo Centre' by the Dept. of Northern Affairs," Shea wrote, "there is much activity here just now and a good deal of coming and going." He also witnessed the ironies and contradictions that abounded as southerners tried to impose the amenities of modern life on northern landscapes. The Foundation Company of Canada building in which he stayed was about 80 degrees Fahrenheit, while the outside temperature was below zero. He was particularly struck by the film shown at the schoolhouse for a large, very enthusiastic Inuit audience. "Rather more shooting took place in this film than during the last World War," Shea observed, "and when the actors were not shooting they were hitting one another on the jaw with loud reports by with little effect." Alongside the "Western-type smooching" in the film and thirteen rounds of the Marciano-Walcott boxing match, the officer noted how surreal their impressions of North American society must have been. "If the Eskimos regard these films as representative of our normal way of life on the Outside, which seems quite possible," Shea reflected, "then I can easily understand why they prefer to remain in the Arctic."[87]

A few days later, Shea prepared the local Rangers for a VIP visit, which included US Secretary of Defense Charles Wilson, Canadian Minister of National Defence Ralph Campney, and Minister of Trade and Commerce C.D. Howe. Shea had little time to prepare them, but with the assistance of Northern Service Officer Doug Wilkinson, Bob Griffiths, and Sergeant Sageakdok, fourteen Rangers assembled in the townsite garage. Working with section Sergeant Simonee as interpreter, Shea explained basic drill to them, "sized them," and taught them to stand at ease and come to attention. It would be a "purely Eskimo show," with Sageakdok as honour guard commander and Simonee as sergeant. When the first plane-load of dignitaries arrived and the Rangers performed this novel duty, Shea watched with fascination – a sentiment shared by the VIPs themselves:

> None of the men concerned had ever heard of a Guard of Honour or done any drill until last night. They were dressed in their best clothes and

> for the sake of uniformity wore the hoods of their parkas up. Normally, Eskimos tend to slouch, but I had told them that soldiers were important people and that they should hold their heads high and not move a muscle while they were being inspected. They did this and were amazingly steady. As long as they didn't move anyone would have thought they had had months of training.[88]

They performed admirably. Sageakdok carried himself "with all the aplomb of a veteran NCO, and I was both amused and amazed to see him stop and adjust one man's arm-band as he walked behind the inspecting party, looking each man over from head to foot as though he had been doing it for years!" Shea was amazed until he remembered the powerful observation and imitation skills of Inuit: Sageakdok was simply mimicking his own demonstration from the previous evening. Simonee, the section sergeant, had been similarly indispensable. "A young man, tall for an Eskimo, good looking, and very intelligent," Simonee worked for Northern Affairs at the townsite and was an interpreter, carpenter, and mechanic. Shea thought he would "almost certainly" become mayor of Frobisher in due course.[89]

Shea's respect for Indigenous residents, and for the Rangers in particular, was based upon a belief that "civilizing" was not his role. Instead, he attempted to learn what he could of Inuktitut and Inuit culture, testing his knowledge in correspondence with Moravian missionary F.W. Peacock (who had lived among Inuit of Labrador for decades) and in liaison letters with the Rangers. He was humbled by his travels and harboured no delusions that his army training or sporadic visits gave him special "authority" on Arctic matters. "If you ever again refer to me as 'an expert,'" Shea replied to his counterpart in Quebec, Major Peter Templeton, "I shall definitely shoot to kill! In my opinion, there are far too many alleged experts around as it is, especially 'Arctic Experts,' and I have no intention of joining their ranks!" Shea recognized that "the only real Arctic experts are the Eskimoes, who have forgotten more about living in the North than most white men ever learn. That is why I am so anxious to hang on to them and encourage them where the Rangers are concerned, but it is not easy to make people see this point and take them seriously."[90]

Captain Ambrose Shea took Inuit in the Rangers seriously, but their world was changing before his eyes. The journal of his voyage on the 1958 Eastern Arctic Patrol – his seventh such patrol – provides an intimate perspective on the state of the Rangers and on the changes transpiring during that era. He departed from Montreal on the *C. D. Howe* in late June, hitching a ride with the northern administrators and medical personnel who annually braved the ice, storms, and fog to visit isolated settlements across the eastern Arctic. He approached his liaison trip with his usual enthusiasm, checking his Inuktitut phrases with the ship's interpreter and finding two Rangers on board returning from hospital in the south (a common occurrence given the high rates of tuberculosis in the Arctic and the high percentage of Inuit in southern sanitoria).[91]

At each port, Shea met with the Rangers and other members of the community. This required adapting to local realities and maintaining a flexible approach to doing "Ranger business," rather than applying the rigid military mind common in regimental life down south. When Shea tracked down the platoon commander at Lake Harbour, he learned that half of the platoon had left or were leaving for Frobisher. "The rapid growth of Frobisher is sucking the life out of the nearby posts," Shea noted, "and [HBC post manager Don] Baird thinks that Lake [Harbour] may cease to exist in a few years." The RLO offloaded the ammunition and met some local Rangers, but there was no formal inspection because they were all working. At Pangnirtung, a chickenpox epidemic curtailed onshore excursions, but he managed to meet with the local sergeants and provide them with their ammunition. Along the northern Quebec coast he met more Rangers, some sporting old army battledress with sundry flashes and badges. At Resolute, founded in 1947 as the site of a military airfield and weather station and six years later populated with Inuit relocated from Port Harrison (Inukjuak) and Pond Inlet, three Rangers met Shea aboard the ship. The officer had few concerns about the platoon: he found most of the local Inuit to be prosperous, with adequate game and employment at the local weather station.[92]

Shea brought a down-to-earth demeanour when he visited local communities and camps. He visited the Inuit camp near Resolute to meet with the Rangers and played "polar-bears" with a young boy, all the while learning about who had moved where, assessing the state of the Ranger rifles, and handing out military identification cards. On 12 August, for example, he visited the Ranger Sudlavinek in his tent. "To say that he is 'well-fixed' for an Eskimo would be putting it mildly," Shea wrote. He had an old military chesterfield (minus one cushion which he used in his outboard canoe), an expensive radio, and a telephone to the RCMP constable. The modern world was colliding with the traditional life of Inuit, and Shea witnessed the impacts first-hand. He brought photographs of Rangers he had taken the previous year and handed them out to the individuals he met. Given the small population of Baffin Island and the Inuit habit of visiting other camps, "many of the Rangers are known over a wide area" and they got "a big kick" out of recognizing one another. Shea also showed pictures of Rangers in Labrador, army photographs of troops serving with the United Nations in the Middle East, and winter training at Churchill. "Labrador they had heard of as a legendary Eskimo country in the far South," he noted, "and Churchill they knew as 'Kokjuak' (Big River), but I don't know what they made of soldiers in an armoured car, stripped to the waist under a hot desert sun." Through this informal process, Shea connected the Rangers to other members of the force and to their military comrades around the world.[93]

Each annual trip was a voyage of intense cross-cultural contact. Relationships were forged over the years between officers like Shea and the Rangers in remote communities and camps across the breadth of the North. Grise Fiord on Ellesmere Island had only one Ranger, relocated from Pond Inlet, but he obviously appreciated Shea and his annual allotment of ammunition:

> When I met Const Bob Pilot, RCMP, who handles Ranger affairs, such as they are, in this lonely place, he told me that Ranger Akpaliapik had made a carving for me during the year which he proposed to give me on the grounds that I was "his boss." Later when I was issuing Akpaliapik with his ammunition he produced the carving from under his parka and with characteristic Eskimo detachment offered it to me "piumavit" – "if I wanted it?" Naturally, I did want it, gave him a clasp-knife in exchange and with the help of Alec Spalding [the interpreter], praised it and thanked him. It is a small ivory carving of a walking polar-bear, carefully carved and highly polished ... He said then that he was giving it to me because I was "always giving him things." When I pointed out that it was the Canadian Army that gave him the ammunition, not me, he said, "Well, anyway, I was easy to get along with." Although Eskimoes are intelligent they are often lacking good judgement.

Given Shea's demeanour and obvious respect for the Rangers, this sarcasm was directed more at himself than at Inuit.

The annual allotment of ammunition was the only "remuneration" that the Rangers received for their service, and it was welcomed. Shea called around Inuit camps in the Pond Inlet area, issuing forty-eight rounds of ammunition to each Ranger that he met and informing them that they could pick up the remainder from the Ranger officer in the community. At Eglinton Fiord, Ranger Ashevak collected ninety-six rounds and explained that "something" had fallen off the side of his rifle, but that it still worked. Functionality, not aesthetics, was all that mattered to Shea. Other equipment did need replacing, such as Clyde River Ranger Peeyameenee's rifle. He and his wife had been travelling by dog team that spring when he spotted a seal on the ice. Running ahead of the team, he asked his wife to bring his rifle. She did, but dipped the muzzle in a snowdrift along the way. Without taking his eyes off the seal, he simply aimed and fired. "How the seal fared I don't know," Shea reported, "but I should think that Peeymeenee must have got an awful jolt, and the muzzle of the rifle opened up like a piece of wet card-board." Shea took the damaged rifle back and let the Ranger retain another left by a deceased member of the patrol. There were no reprimands and no hassle.

Shea's trip ended at Frobisher Bay, the burgeoning administrative centre of the eastern Arctic and hotbed of military and government activity. The rapid growth of the community and the influx of Inuit (including Rangers) into the settlement from the outlying posts had "rather confused" the local situation over the last few years. Originally, there were thirty Rangers at Frobisher, but twenty more were recruited in 1955 for a home defence role which did not materialize. The Hudson's Bay Company, which had always provided the platoon commanders on Baffin Island, were forced to convert their one-man trading post into a retail store with a manager and four clerks. Consequently, it became very difficult for Captain G.M. Rennie (the officer commanding 28 Company and the local platoon commander) to juggle Ranger affairs alongside his burgeoning responsibilities, particularly when he knew that in addition to the fifty Rangers known to be at Frobisher, an unspecified number of others had arrived from the outlying posts.

Typically, Shea used his time in Frobisher not just to meet with the officer commanding but to meet with as many Rangers as he could and to strengthen strategic alliances for the local unit. In particular, he reconnected with Sageakdok, adding that he "looks like an Eskimo gangster" but was demonstrably "military minded." The front of Sageakdok's parka bore a large Ranger badge, handsomely embroidered out of beads, he saluted correctly, and he startled Shea "by springing smartly to attention when I entered a room in which he was seated." This salute was all the more surprising because RCMP superintendent Henry Larsen, the venerable Arctic navigator who was Shea's "senior in rank, years, and experience," was also in the room. Shea was particularly pleased that the RCMP was taking a greater interest in the Rangers. "They feel that in a place like Frobisher an organized and trained body of men, as the Rangers here might be, would be a source of moral and social strength in the Eskimo community," Shea reported, "and would give direction to the efforts being made to turn the Eskimo into a responsible Canadian citizen." Locally, at least, Shea had done all that he could to generate interest in the Rangers. If there were failures on the part of the military establishment to support the force, they were not at the grassroots level.

Two years later, Captain Shea became disillusioned with the military's disregard for the Rangers. After expanding into communities across the North, he lamented,

> the Army seemed to stand aghast at its own temerity and from then on, and in an increasing degree, the attitude of Higher Command towards the Rangers can be best summed up in the words of the old ballad:
>
> "Mother, may I go out to swim?"
> "Yes; my darling daughter,
> Hang your clothes on a hickory limb
> But don't go near the water."

Shea had received one simple message repeatedly from Ottawa: "The Rangers may exist but under no circumstances must they do anything."[94]

Shea recognized that the Ranger organization in his area was too unwieldy to be effective. He was the only liaison officer in Eastern Command, responsible for organizing and maintaining eleven Ranger companies scattered over 8,000 miles of coastline. Liaising with the Baffin Island Rangers alone consumed three months of his year. Itineraries that looked fine on paper became impractical in the field, and he had learned that "constant liaison" was essential. As matters stood, the Rangers could not report anything more quickly than an ordinary telegraph and the postal system, and their paltry combat training and scattered presence were inadequate. Shea explained,

> It is doubtful if some of the Rangers really understand what the whole business is about and for various reasons it is difficult to explain it to them.

> The Eskimoes, in particular, have no real word for "soldier" ("Unataktik," that is, "one who fights," is as near as they get) and look upon warfare as a species of insanity peculiar to the white man. "I hear that the white men are fighting like dogs again," was one man's comment on the Suez affair. Furthermore, it is the RLOs belief that some of the Eskimoes think that he is the entire Canadian Army and that, as such, he is an eccentric but benevolent dispenser of free rifles and ammunition. The name given the RLO in certain localities "Kokiutit angayak'ok," "Rifle Chief" or "Boss of the Rifles," is sufficient indication of this.

Only sustained contact could bridge the cultural divide, coupled with greater clarification of what the Rangers were supposed to actually do.[95] This arrangement required resources, of course, which the military was unprepared to invest in a community-based, part-time force.

Shea still envisioned a place for the Rangers. "The idea of arming a local population and asking them to take a hand in defending their own locality is an ancient one and eminently sensible," he argued. "It does not become out-dated, even in this atomic age." Their contributions were modest but significant. The Rangers had amassed considerable military intelligence over the previous decade, including topographical detail, submarine and ship sightings, and reports of suspicious individuals. They had reported unexplained bomb drops on northern Baffin Island, producing bits of the bombs to verify their reports, and provided evidence of guided missile activity.[96] Perhaps most importantly, the Rangers were keenly interested in service. Even if Baffin Island's Eskimo Rangers had a "distorted" idea of their role, Captain Shea explained, they identified themselves as soldiers:

> An extreme example of this occurred three years ago when a Ranger in North Baffin Island began, but fortunately did not complete, a single-handed attempt to capture the US Coast Guard Cutter "Staten Island." He realized that she was not a Canadian ship, jumped to the conclusion that she was a Russian, and felt that it was his duty as a soldier to take some action. This man's enthusiasm may have been misdirected but there is no doubt that he took his position as a Ranger seriously and realistically.

Although these people were "so cut off from the world in many respects," Shea observed that they were "vividly aware of the Russian threat; so much so that the RLO has sometimes wondered whether they may not have had some personal contact with the Russians with which they are afraid to reveal." He found them "intelligent, adaptable and intensely practical" and noted that they naturally took to military training. Indeed, few white men could navigate the Arctic without their assistance, making them "good people to have on *our* side." Shea's final flourish reminded the military this was a relationship that needed to be respected:

> A small quantity of obsolescent equipment is issued to them in the same spirit that an engagement ring is issued to a prospective bride: as a token of engagement.
>
> Their main virtues are that they are willing to serve the Army voluntarily in the capacity of "friends on the ground" to the best of their ability, which is often considerable, and to the best of their local knowledge which is likewise. Their cost is negligible.
>
> These are virtues which are becoming increasingly rare and which deserve encouragement.[97]

Encouragement was not forthcoming. In the 1960s, the military's attention turned away from the North and the Rangers were left to "wither on the vine," with little direction, sporadic resupply, and no training.[98] When Shea was replaced as RLO, the Rangers on Baffin Island were seldom visited. Their "cheapness," not their Indigenous knowledge and contributions, ensured the force's survival through the 1960s. Just as Inuit stood at a crossroads during this era, so too did the Rangers. The collapse of the fur market, unskilled wage labour, and Inuit migration from camps to permanent settlements conspired to further undermine traditional community leadership. The influence of family groups weakened as employment became more centralized around settlements, which offered improved medical and educational facilities, and northern Indigenous peoples became caught in the vortex of welfare colonialism.[99] By 1970, Major Bill Stirling, asked to report on the future viability of the Rangers, concluded that northern Canadian society was no longer a place where the organization would find solid ground:

> Perhaps the most important piece of general advice I received was that southern Canadians should rid themselves of their romantic concept of the North. The Arctic has become a rather sophisticated social environment. Hunting and trapping, although still carried on are not the main pursuits of the indigenous people. Eskimos are being collected into permanent

> settlements such as Frobisher, Cambridge Bay and Tuktoyaktuk where they are provided with houses and to a large extent live on welfare. The young Indian and Eskimo is being well educated in modern schools at Inuvik, Yellowknife and Frobisher. When they complete their education they will be trained to take their place in modern society and not on the Arctic ice or the trap line.

Investing resources in a disappearing way of life seemed misguided to Stirling. "Certainly there are still people in the North who hunt, trap, fish and prospect and one hopes there always will be," Stirling opined, but these people were now the exception, not the rule. "The people who know the North best are the RCMP, bush pilots, certain members of the Territorial Government, some prospectors and the missionaries." Unfortunately, these were not categories of people upon which to base a Ranger organization. "The type of people envisaged by the [defence] planners in 1946 on which to develop the Canadian Ranger concept simply no longer exist in sufficient numbers," he concluded.[100] In his view, the crossroads had been passed.

Reflections

As soon as the Mid-Canada and DEW Lines, designed to deal with the manned bomber threat, were completed in 1957, the Soviets launched the *Sputnik* satellite, demonstrating that they could hurl missiles at the North American heartland over the polar ice cap. "It is the way with weapons systems to become obsolete on becoming operational," political scientist James Eayrs noted. "In this respect the DEW Line ran true to form."[101] Existing detection and communication systems, from the technological marvel of the DEW Line to human assets like the Rangers, could not counter the new challenge posed by intercontinental ballistic missiles. *Sputnik* showed that "the northern defence structure could not only be outflanked but could be literally hopped over," strategic analysts noted. "For all intents and purposes the Canadian north, in terms of a remote and safe battlefield, was obsolete in the defence of the continent."[102]

Kenneth Eyre observed in the late 1980s that "while the military has had a considerable impact on the North, the northern fact has had surprisingly little impact upon the Canadian military."[103] The military swept into the region in response to perceived sovereignty and security crises and, like other actors with transitory interests in the Arctic, departed once its interest had passed. A military report in the late 1960s noted that defence facilities were often built as "'crash' programs," offering significant but short-term local employment during the construction phase before being "staffed predominantly by technically trained personnel brought in from the south" once they became operational. When strategic or political changes rendered facilities obsolete, the military "ceased operations abruptly, with little or no warning."[104]

These boom-and-bust cycles led to dramatic changes for Inuit. The prospect of wage employment led families to concentrate around military installations, and this sedentarization persisted after the jobs dried up. The impacts of militarism, however, did not disappear with the withdrawal of the armed forces. Anthropologist John Honigmann observed that "the truly remarkable feature in Frobisher Bay is the way Eskimo at almost every turn are able to gear their behaviour to a modern culture into which, well within a single generation, they have transformed their lives. New jobs, new housing and house furnishings, new patterns of organization, new forms of recreation, new problems and temptations, new agents of social control, new models – all appeared simultaneously and invited a wholesale cultural upheaval which, as has been indicated, still goes on."[105] The same could be said of the DEW Line stations and the Inuit communities with Ranger units that spanned the Cold War Canadian Arctic.

In the early twenty-first century, Canadians found themselves immersed in another round of Arctic intrigue, this time predicated on an alleged "polar race" precipitated by climate change and competition for Arctic resources. The Harper government committed to a spate of investments in Arctic military capabilities, including new port facilities at Nanisivik and a training centre at Resolute. Yet for all the rhetoric surrounding the need to defend Canadian sovereignty, the Harper government's early "use it or lose it" message inherently treated the Arctic as a there rather than a here.[106] All too often in the southern imagination, the Arctic continues to be a resource-rich frontier and a potential military front more than a homeland. Inuit commentators emphasize that their voices must be central as Canadians chart their future course in the region. "Use it or lose it" might be rephrased as "use us," suggests Paul Kaludjak, the former president of Nunavut Tunngavik Inc. "People confuse this military symbolism of ships with guns and ownership," he explains, "but ownership means a lot more than that."[107] The Canadian Rangers now flourish across the North, but apprehensions about militarism – particularly in the form of defence development projects – remain. Inuit are still of "two minds" about the military's presence,[108] a reflection of the government's poor track record in delivering on its promises and the unintended consequences of past southern-directed developments, as well as the material benefits that flow when the military's "boxes" land in town.

Appendix 1: Statement of Conditions to Govern the Establishment of a Distant Early Warning System in Canadian Territory, 1955[109]

13. Matters Affecting Canadian Eskimos

The Eskimos of Canada are in a primitive state of social development. It is important that these people be not subjected unduly to disruption of their hunting economy, exposure to diseases against which their immunity is often low, or other effects of the presence of white men which might be injurious to them. It is therefore necessary to have certain regulations to govern contact with and matters affecting Canadian Eskimos. The following conditions are set forth for this purpose:

(a) Any matters affecting the Eskimos, including the possibility of their employment in any area and the terms and arrangements for their employment, if approved, will be subject to the concurrence of the Department of Northern Affairs and National Resources.
(b) All contact with Eskimos, other than those whose employment on any aspect of the project is approved, is to be avoided except in cases of emergency. If, in the opinion of the Department of Northern Affairs and National Resources, more specific provision in this connection is necessary in any particular area, the Department may, after consultation with the United States, prescribe geographical limits surrounding a station beyond which personnel associated with the project other than those locally engaged, may not go or may prohibit the entry of such personnel into any defined area.
(c) Persons other than those locally engaged shall not be given leave or facilities for travel in the Canadian Arctic (other than in the

course of their duties in operation of the project) without the approval of the Department of Northern Affairs and National Resources, or the Royal Canadian Mounted Police acting on its behalf.

(d) There shall be no local disposal in the north of supplies or materials of any kind except with the concurrence of the Department of Northern Affairs and National Resources, or the Royal Canadian Mounted Police acting on its behalf.

(e) Local disposal of waste shall be carried out in a manner acceptable to the Department of Northern Affairs and National Resources, or the Royal Canadian Mounted Police acting on its behalf.

(f) In the event that any facilities required for the system have to encroach on or disturb past or present Eskimo settlements, burial places, hunting grounds, etc., the United States shall be responsible for the removal of the settlement, burial ground, etc., to a location acceptable to the Department of Northern Affairs and National Resources.

NOTES

1 Canada did not issue the United States a blank cheque, however. For example, see David Bercuson, "Continental Defence and Arctic Sovereignty, 1945–1950: Solving the Canadian Dilemma," in *The Cold War and Defence*, ed. Keith Neilson and Ronald Haycock (New York: Praeger, 1990), 153–70; Peter Kikkert, "The Polaris Incident: 'Going to the Mat' with the Americans," *Journal of Military and Strategic Studies* 11/3 (2009): 1–29; and Gordon W. Smith, "Weather Stations in the Canadian North and Sovereignty," *Journal of Military and Strategic Studies* 11/3 (2009): 1–63.

2 Kenneth C. Eyre, "Forty Years of Military Activity in the Canadian North, 1947–87," *Arctic* 40/4 (Dec. 1987): 294.

3 Trevor Lloyd, "Frontier of Destiny – The Canadian Arctic," *Behind the Headlines* 6/7 (1946): 8.

4 Matthew Farish and Whitney Lackenbauer, "Modular Modernization: The DEW Line and the Construction of the Cold War Arctic," paper presented to the Canadian Association of Geographers annual meeting, Saskatoon, 31 May 2007.

5 John Hughes, "Under Four Flags: Recent Culture Change Among the Eskimos," *Current Anthropology* 6/1 (Feb. 1965): 14–15.

6 Peter Kulchyski and Frank James Tester, *Kiumajut (Talking Back): Game Management and Inuit Rights, 1900–70* (Vancouver: UBC Press, 2007), 7.

7 Frances Abele, "Confronting 'Harsh and Inescapable Facts,'" in *Sovereignty and Security in the Arctic*, ed. Edgar Dosman (London: Routledge, 1989), 189; Mary Simon, "Militarization and the Aboriginal Peoples," in *Arctic Alternatives: Civility or Militarism in the Circumpolar North*, ed. Franklyn Griffiths (Toronto: Samuel Stevens, 1992), 60.

8 High modernism, to borrow James C. Scott's framework, sought "a sweeping, rational engineering of all aspects of social life in order to improve the human condition." Scott, *Seeing Like a State: How Certain Schemes to Improve the Human Condition Have Failed* (New Haven, CT: Yale University Press, 1988), 88. See also M. Farish and P.W. Lackenbauer, "High Modernism in the Arctic: Planning Frobisher Bay and Inuvik," *Journal of Historical Geography* 35/3 (2009): 517–44.

9 Kevin McMahon, "Strangers in the Land ... Again," *Peace and Security* (Canadian Institute for International Peace and Security) 3/1 (spring 1988): 3.

10 Yatsushiro, quoted in and supported by John J. Honigmann's response to Hughes's "Under Four Flags," *Current Anthropology* 6/1 (Feb. 1965): 60.

11 In this sense, my findings support those of David Damas in *Arctic Migrants/Arctic Villagers: The Transformation of Inuit Settlement in the Central Arctic* (Montreal: McGill-Queen's University Press, 2002).

12 Diamond Jenness, *Eskimo Administration*, vol. 2, *Canada* (Montreal: Arctic Institute of North America, 1964), 97.

13 J.D. Ferguson, *A Study of the Effects of the Distant Early Warning Line Upon the Eskimo of the Western Arctic of Canada* (Ottawa: Northern Research Co-ordination Centre, Department of Northern Affairs and National Resources, April 1957), 3.

14 This observation resonates with J.R. Miller's comments on Indian agents in his groundbreaking article "Owen Glendower, Hotspur, and Canadian Indian Policy," *Ethnohistory* 37/4 (autumn 1990): 386–415.

15 R.S. Sheffield, *The Red Man's on the Warpath* (Vancouver: UBC Press, 204); Ken Coates and William R. Morrison, *The Alaska Highway in WWII: The U.S. Army of Occupation in Canada's Northwest* (Norman: University of Oklahoma Press, 1992) and *Working the North: Labor and the Northwest Defense Projects 1942–1946* (Anchorage: University of Alaska Press, 1994).

16 Vincent Massey, *What's Past Is Prologue* (Toronto: Macmillan, 1963), 371.

17 On this theme, see Farish and Lackenbauer, "High Modernism in the Arctic."

18 See Robert V. Eno, "Crystal Two: The Origin of Iqaluit," *Arctic* 56/1 (2003): 72.

19 Quoted in Shelagh Grant, *Sovereignty or Security? Government Policy in the Canadian North, 1936–1950* (Vancouver: UBC Press, 1988), 275.

20 Mélanie Gagnon and Iqaluit Elders, *Inuit Recollections on the Military Presence in Iqaluit* (Iqaluit: Nunavut Arctic College, 2002), 10–12.

21 Ibid., 37–8.
22 Ibid., 44.
23 Andrew Thomson to Under Secretary of State for External Affairs, "Notes Taken On Visit to the Arctic – April 5–15, 1948," May 13, 1948, File 9061-A-40, Part 3 FP, vol. 6298, RG 25, Library and Archives Canada [LAC].
24 Ibid.
25 Eno, "Crystal Two," 73; Sheila MacBain Meldrum, "Frobisher Bay: An Area Economic Survey, 1966–1969" (Ottawa: DIAND, 1975), 34.
26 Gagnon et al., *Inuit Recollections*, 55.
27 Ibid., 72.
28 "Arctic Province," ca. August/September 1953, file 9061-J-1–40, pt. 1, vol. 3842, RG 25, LAC.
29 Ibid.
30 Pierre Berton, *The Mysterious North* (New York: Knopf, 1956), 235–6.
31 Alootook Ipellie, "Frobisher Bay Childhood," *Beaver* (spring 1980): 4–8.
32 See Nelson H. Graburn, *Lake Harbour, Baffin Island* (Ottawa: Northern Co-ordination and Research Centre, Department of Northern Affairs and National Resources, 1963), and Damas, *Arctic Migrants*.
33 Toshio Yatsushiro, *Frobisher Bay 1958* (Ottawa: Northern Co-ordination and Research Centre, 1963). See also Yatsushiro, "The Changing Eskimo: A Study of Wage Employment and Its Consequences Among the Eskimos of Frobisher Bay, Baffin Island," *Beaver* 42/1, Outfit 293 (1962): 19–26.
34 Department of Transport press release 823, 1 September 1957, in "An Introduction to Frobisher Bay," File 83/15, Department of National Defence, Directorate of History and Heritage (DHH).
35 "The North," *Canadian Architect* 3/11 (1958): 39.
36 "Reveille," *Time* (Canadian edition), 29 December 1958, 6–7, quoted in Jeffrey D. Noakes, "Under the Radar: Defence Construction (1951) Limited and Military Infrastructure in Canada, 1950–1965" (PhD diss., Carleton University, 2005), 436.
37 See "Unveil High Arctic Town Plans," *Globe and Mail*, 26 July 1961, 3.
38 John J. Honigmann, "Transforming the Arena of Action: Two Paths to Cultural Modernization Compared," *Dalhousie Review* 47/3 (1967): 388.
39 R. Quinn Duffy, *The Road to Nunavut: The Progress of the Eastern Arctic Inuit since the Second World War* (Montreal: McGill-Queen's University Press, 1988), 163.
40 See, for example, Fred Kaplan, *The Wizards of Armageddon* (New York: Simon and Schuster, 1983), and Farish, "Frontier Engineering."
41 On the origins of the DEW Line, see Joseph Jockel, *No Boundaries Upstairs: Canada, the United States, and the Origins of North American Air Defence, 1945–1958* (Vancouver: UBC Press, 1987).

42 Charles Hughes, quoted in John Nicholas Harris, "National Defence and Northern Development: The Establishment of the Dewline in the Canadian North" (MA thesis, Simon Fraser University, 1980), 210.

43 Richard Morenus, *The DEW Line: Distant Early Warning, The Miracle of America's First Line of Defense* (New York: Rand McNally, 1957), 82.

44 The NCRC was created in 1954 to report through the Secretary of the Advisory Committee on Northern Development. It functions included collecting and disseminating scientific and technical data, as well as coordinating, sponsoring, and conducting scientific research. Harris, "National Defence and Northern Development," 195.

45 C.J. Marshall, "North America's Distant Early Warning Line," *Geographical Magazine* 29/12 (April 1957): 616–28.

46 R.G. Robertson, Deputy Minister of DNANR, to Vincent W. Farley, Legal and Patent Division, Western Electric Co., New York, 14 May 1956, file NR2/3–3 pt. 1, vol. 1654, RG 85, LAC.

47 Doug Stern, "Community of Cambridge Bay," historical notes provided to the author, August 2008; CAM-MAIN, "Dewline Information Brochure," n.d., file KHP 120–1-3, Kiyikmroy Heritage Society (KHS).

48 Federal Electric Corporation, "The DEW System," c. 1958, p. 8–6, KHS file KHP 120–1-3.

49 Peter Kikkert and P. Whitney Lackenbauer, "A History of Ikaluktuuttiaq," in *A Guidebook for Research with Nunavut Communities*, Iqaluktuuttiaq (Cambridge Bay) ed. (Cambridge Bay, NU: Polar Knowledge Canada/ Pitquhirnikkut Ilihautiniq, 2016), 14–31.

50 J.D. Ferguson, *A Study of the Effects of the Distant Early Warning Line upon the Eskimo of the Western Arctic of Canada* (Ottawa: Northern Co-ordination and Research Centre, April 1957), 13–18. Although the copy at the Indian and Northern Affairs Canada Library (INAC) was lost, I obtained copies of this document from Dr Bob Williamson, Ottawa, and David Neufeld, Whitehorse, and have provided INAC with an electronic version. For a breakdown on DEW Line housing in the Cam sector the following year, see Jameson Bond to R.A.J. Phillips, Chief of the Arctic Division, 12 September 1957, file A207–2 pt. 2, vol. 674, RG 85, LAC.

51 Ferguson, "CAM" (Cambridge Bay), to G.W. Rowley, DNANR, Ottawa, 2 July 1956, file NR2/3–3 pt. 1, vol. 1654, RG 85, LAC.

52 J.D. Ferguson, "Field-Work in the Western Arctic," file NR2/3–3 pt. 1, vol. 1654, RG 85, LAC.

53 Ferguson, *Study of the Effects of the DEW Line*, 22–3.

54 Ibid., 36. In an interim report, Ferguson observed that "at two sites, young married men are living in bunkhouses. These few persons have

certainly adopted the trappings and habits of their white companions and, moreover, they don't want to go back to the Eskimo way. This small group of 'changelings' is an exception to my single, broad generalization. It may prove to be the crucial exception in the next few years. Though since this generation, if given the opportunities of steady employment, will undoubtedly reject their traditional life." Ferguson, "CAM," to C.J. Marshall, DNANR, Ottawa, 9 July 1956, file NR2/3–3 pt. 1, vol. 1654, RG 85, LAC.

55 Ferguson, *Study of the Effects of the DEW Line*, 37–9.

56 Jenness, *Eskimo Administration*, 162. This dynamic was not limited to Inuit at Cambridge Bay. See newspaper reporter Lauchie Chisholm's observations about Great Whale River in the *Montreal Gazette*, 22 December 1959.

57 Ferguson, *Study of the Effects of the DEW Line*, 26–7.

58 Ibid., 19–20.

59 R.G. Williamson, "The Canadian Arctic, Socio-Cultural Change," *Archives of Environmental Health* 17 (Oct. 1968): 487, quoted in Harris, "National Defence and Northern Development," 211.

60 Ferguson, *Study of the Effects of the DEW Line*, 28.

61 Ferguson, "CAM," to "Chuck" (C.J. Marshall), DNANR, 9 July 1956, file NR2/3–3 pt. 1, vol. 1654, RG 85, LAC.

62 Ferguson, "Field-Work in the Western Arctic."

63 Ferguson, *Study of the Effects of the DEW Line*, 42.

64 See, for example, Maxime Steve Bégin, "Des radars et des hommes: mémoires inuit de la station Fox Main de la DEW Line (Hall Beach, Nunavut)" (MA thesis, Laval University, 2004); Gagnon et al., *Inuit Recollections on the Military Presence in Iqalui*; and Eric Robitaille, "Militaires et Inuit dans l'Est de l'Arctique canadien, 1942–1965" (MA thesis, Laval University, 1987).

65 Ferguson, *Study of the Effects of the DEW Line*, 34.

66 Ibid., 34–5.

67 Ibid., 34–6.

68 R.H. Cruzen, Vice President, Federal Electric Corporation, to Commander, 4601st Support Group (DEW), Air Defense Command, 23 April 1958, LAC, file 851-1-10 pt. 1, vol. 2873, RG 29, LAC.

69 Ferguson, *Study of the Effects of the DEW Line*, 43.

70 Department of Northern Affairs and National Resources Annual Report, 1955–6, 101–2.

71 Jenness, *Eskimo Administration*, 114.

72 "The Local Effects of Decreasing Military Interest in Northern Canada," c. 1966, file 27-14-8 pt. 1, vol. 10364, RG 25, LAC.

73 Hughes, "Under Four Flags," 19. See also Hughes, "Observations on Community Change in the North: An Attempt at Summary," *Anthropologica* 5/1 (1963): 69–79.

74 Jenness, *Eskimo Administration*, 95.

75 Ibid., 175, 183. In time, Jenness hoped that this program "would be superseded by a more mature and far-reaching one, drawn up by civilian authorities and administered by a purely civilian staff."

76 For a detailed history of the Rangers, from which parts of this section of the chapter were drawn, see P. Whitney Lackenbauer, *The Canadian Rangers: A Living History* (Vancouver: UBC Press, 2013).

77 DCGS(B) to DMO&P, 1 November 1946, file 2001–1999/0 pt. 1, vol. 321, RG 24, LAC.

78 Morton to CGS, 17 December 1948, file 2001–1999/0 pt. 1, vol. 321, RG 24, LAC.

79 Major F.B. Perrott to DMO&P, 11 July 1951, accession 83–84/215, file 2001–1999/0 pt. 2, Box 321, RG 24, LAC.

80 Kenneth Charles Eyre, "Custos Borealis: The Military in the Canadian North" (PhD thesis, University of London, 1981), 178.

81 Larry Dignum, "Shadow Army of the North," *Beaver* (autumn 1959): 22–4.

82 Robert Taylor, "Eyes and Ears of the North," *Star Weekly Magazine*, 22 December 1956, 2–3.

83 *The Canadian Militia Rangers Liaison Letter No 6* (2 September 1953), Acc. 1983–84/215, F. S-2001–1999/0 pt. 6, Box 322, RG 24, LAC.

84 Canadian Ranger Liaison Letter, HQ Newfoundland Area, 3 January 1953, file 323.009 (D 144), DHH.

85 Captain A.J. Shea, "The Two Camps: Extract from the Journal of a Ranger Liaison Officer," *Canadian Army Journal* 10/2 (April 1956): 65.

86 Shea, "Two Camps," 59.

87 Ambrose Shea, "Rangers of Frobisher," *Beaver* 287 (winter 1956): 42.

88 Ibid., 43. The editor of the *Beaver* could not help but note that "Eskimos get used to this sort of thing when they stand motionless for hours over a seal's breathing hole."

89 Shea, "Rangers of Frobisher," 42–3.

90 Shea to Templeton, 16 May 1955, DHH file 323.009 (D 150).

91 This detailed discussion of Shea's 1958 tour is based upon "Canadian Rangers: Journal of Eastern Arctic Patrol 1958 by Capt AJ Shea, Ranger Liaison Officer, Eastern Command," 22 September 1958, acc. 1983–84/215, file S-9105–21/0, box 399, RG 24, LAC. On the Eastern Arctic Patrol, see Pat Sandiford Grygier, *A Long Way from Home: The Tuberculosis Epidemic Among the Inuit* (Montreal: McGill-Queen's University Press, 1997), 86–102.

92 The relocation of Inuit from Port Harrison (Inukjuak) to Resolute and Grise Fiord in 1953 has generated significant political and scholarly debate, particularly over the motivations behind the move. While government officials insisted that humanitarian reasons lay behind the decision, some Inuit residents and scholars have asserted that the primary motive was sovereignty: that Inuit were used as "human flags" to bolster Canada's presence in the archipelago. See, for example, Frank Tester and Peter Kulchyski, *Tammarniit (Mistakes): Inuit Relocation in the Eastern Arctic, 1939–63* (Vancouver: UBC Press, 1994), and Alan Marcus, *Relocating Eden: The Image and Politics of Inuit Exile in the Canadian Arctic* (Hanover, NH: University Press of New England, 1998). For a contrary perspective, see Gerard Kenney, *Arctic Smoke & Mirrors* (Prescott, ON: Voyageur Publishing, 1994).

93 Shea was also sensitive of not creating divisions within communities. At Pangnirtung, he explained that he "was able to distribute the snapshots which I took last year and to take a few more, including one of quite a large group of the Rangers and another larger group of non-Rangers, just so they wouldn't feel left out of things."

94 Captain A.J. Shea, "An Appreciation of the Situation of the Canadian Rangers in Eastern Command," 23 February 1960, DHH file 323.009 (D 261).

95 Ibid.

96 Ibid.

97 Ibid.

98 On this period, see Eyre, "Forty Years of Military Activity," 292–9.

99 For a superb overview of these developments, see Duffy, *Road to Nunavut*.

100 Stirling Report, 16.

101 James Eayrs, *In Defence of Canada*, vol. 3, *Peacemaking and Deterrence* (Toronto: University of Toronto Press, 1972), 372.

102 R.J. Diubaldo and S.J. Scheinberg, *A Study of Canadian-American Defence Policy (1945–1975) – Northern Issues and Strategic Resources* (Ottawa: Department of National Defence, 1978), 36–7.

103 Eyre, "Forty Years of Military Activity," 292.

104 "Local Effects of Decreasing Military Interest in Northern Canada."

105 Honigmann, "Transforming the Arena of Action," 389.

106 On these developments, see Franklyn Griffiths, Rob Huebert, and P. Whitney Lackenbauer, *Canada and the Changing Arctic: Sovereignty, Security and Stewardship* (Waterloo: Wilfrid Laurier University Press, 2011); P. Whitney Lackenbauer and Adam Lajeunesse, "The Canadian Armed Forces in the Arctic: Building Appropriate Capabilities," *Journal of Military*

and Strategic Studies 16/4 (March 2016): 7–66; and P. Whitney Lackenbauer and Ryan Dean, *Canada's Northern Strategy under the Harper Conservatives: Key Speeches and Documents on Sovereignty, Security, and Governance, 2006–15* (Calgary: Centre for Military, Strategic and Security Studies/Centre on Foreign Policy and Federalism/Arctic Institute of North America, 2016).

107 Paul Kaludjak, "The Inuit Are Here, Use Us," *Ottawa Citizen*, 18 July 2007.

108 See, for example, the interview with Mary Simon, "Sovereignty and the Arctic," *Globe and Mail*, 22 October 2007 (http://www.theglobeandmail.com/globe-debate/sovereignty-and-the-arctic/article1085192); Charlie Evalik, "Canadian Sovereignty, the Military and Infrastructure Development in the Inuit Homeland," Kitikmeot Inuit Association submission to the Senate Standing Committee on National Security and Defence, December 2010 (http://www.nunavutrc.com/assets/Uploads/Senate-Defence-Committee-Dec-2010-Final.pdf); Whit Fraser, "Inuit View on Canada's Arctic Sovereignty," *Above & Beyond: Canada's Arctic Journal* (May/June 2012): 25–31, http://arcticjournal.ca/inuit-view-on-canadas-arctic-sovereignty/; and Inuit Tapiriit Kanatami, *Nilliajut: Inuit Perspectives on Security, Patriotism and Sovereignty* (Ottawa: Inuit Qaujisarvingat Knowledge Centre, 2013).

109 Source: Annex to Exchange of Notes (5 May 1955) between Canada and the United States of America Governing the Establishment of a Distant Early Warning System in Canadian Territory, Canada, Treaty Series 1955, No. 8.

Alaska Highway Nurses and DEW Line Doctors: Medical Encounters in Northern Canadian Indigenous Communities

MYRA RUTHERDALE

In the years following the Second World War, the Canadian government began the process of building a Westernized medical infrastructure in the North. When a Ministry of National Health and Welfare was created in 1945, it included a special branch to attend to "Indian" and northern health care needs.[1] An increasing number of complaints had been reaching the ears of Ottawa bureaucrats, and pressure had been rising on humanitarian and political grounds. In particular, American military personnel, on patrol during the war, had sounded the alarm over the poor health of the local population, notably the rising levels of tuberculosis among Inuit populations. And so the Indian and Northern Health Services (INHS) Branch opened its doors, began hiring nurses and doctors for the work, and made plans for the ways in which their services could be offered and administered. Nursing stations were to be established in communities that had populations of over 200. If nurses needed help or advice, the branch planned to contact doctors who would be located in larger northern centres. In dire circumstances, doctors could be flown in to smaller communities; more often patients would be flown out. Evacuation increasingly became the norm for patients with tuberculosis in the late 1940s and throughout the 1950s. By 1963, the Indian and Northern Health Services Branch had a staff of 2,500, including nurses, doctors, dentists, and administrative officials.[2]

This new federal medical program, like the earlier church-sponsored health care initiatives, has been criticized by scholars who have seen the work as either being colonialist in approach or a failure because it did not offer as much as it could. In his study of Inuit reactions to incoming nurses, John O'Neil argues that "northern medical dialogue is a discourse on colonialism, influenced heavily by the medical and nursing ideologies of control and surveillance."[3] Walter J. Vanast argues in his history of medical care for Inuit of Ungava that the federal government "lacked motives for providing help and humanitarian agencies were busy elsewhere."[4] According to these authors, a combination of neglect, parsimony, and colonizing discourse characterized northern health services. Perhaps the most critical is an article by sociologists Frank Tester and Paule McNicoll, who examined the diaries and correspondence of Dr Jon Bildfell, a doctor who worked in Panniqtuuq (Pangnirtung) on Baffin Island during the 1930s. Tester and McNicoll concluded that Bildfell's contributions were essentially negative and that Western medicine in general had been destructive to Inuit cosmology:

> The result of confronting Inuit with western scientific medicine contributed to a fragmentation and to cultural contradictions that underpin many contemporary Inuit problems, including that of youthful suicide. The state, augmented by Bildfell's plethora of measures, attempted the totalisation of Inuit culture. Evidence from a survey of contemporary problems – suicide, alcoholism, depression – designated by O'Neil as the stresses of definition, isolation, transition, timing and consolidation, suggest that if such problems are taken as indicators of a successful integration with the colonizing culture, the attempt has, in some considerable measure, failed.[5]

This interpretation places a disproportionate historical burden upon the shoulders of one doctor who laboured in the North in the 1930s, if not on an entire system of medical care.

There is little doubt that the programs headquartered in Ottawa, conceived of in a southern framework by many bureaucrats who possibly never travelled to the North, were often questionable and problematic and were products of internal colonization. This chapter observes that at the micro-historical level of everyday experience, some of the nurses and doctors hired for northern service felt and expressed a degree of professional vulnerability, that they often relied heavily upon Native guides and interpreters, and that they frequently expressed admiration for local Native medicine. Taken together, these three aspects of the introduction of Westernized medicine in the North suggest that the power dynamics between patients, community members, and outside doctors and nurses sometimes shifted and are therefore difficult to categorize consistently or accurately. At the same time, however, the voices of the patients must also be heard. Those voices sometimes speak of accommodation, but more frequently of fear and misunderstanding.

A balance of perspectives leads us to understand that northern health care as offered by southerners would have benefited greatly by the promotion of cross-cultural education – something that was never seen as a priority by its founders.

The Context

While embarrassment over American complaints about the state of health among Canada's northern peoples was one motivator for government action, politicians and bureaucrats were also undoubtedly compelled by a shift in focus away from international affairs and towards internal domestic development that was promoted by Department of External Affairs mandarins like Escott Reid and Lester B. Pearson. Even before the war ended, Reid recognized that the North could fill a void at the end of the current quagmire, an emptiness that he predicted would accompany the cessation of battle. The attention of Canadians, he argued, might be captured by a national focus on the North:

> The opening of a new frontier in the Canadian North, can I think, become a national objective of some importance to the Canadian people. Even if, from the point of view of securing the highest possible national income, the Canadian north is not worth a large expenditure of national energy and capital, a very large expenditure might nevertheless be justified in an effort to realize an inspiring and somewhat romantic national objective.[6]

The North was being framed by the south as a "romantic national objective": a place that Canadians could imagine but probably never visit.[7]

Pearson reinforced this imaginative framing of the North in an article that he wrote for *Foreign Affairs* in 1946. As Canada's ambassador to the United States, he wanted to alert his readers that the "Go West" imperative had been replaced with advice to "Go North." Adventure was the appeal, and economic opportunity the rational impetus. According to Pearson, this "new" region "had been brought out of the blurred and shadowy realm of northern folklore and shown to be an important and accessible part of our modern world." Pearson asserted that the Arctic was "no country for weaklings and its economic development will test the finest qualities of the men of the North." Canada's ambassador portrayed the North as a modern land of opportunity ready to be exploited and best suited to strong men, not "weaklings." While economic opportunity beckoned, there was also an awareness that southern Canada should begin to demonstrate moral responsibility for northern Natives.[8]

The creation of the Ministry of Northern Affairs and National Resources was meant, to some extent, to recognize this responsibility. When Prime Minister Louis St Laurent opened the department in 1953, he admitted that heretofore the government had approached the North "in an almost continuing state of absence of mind."[9] Jean Lesage, its first minister, proposed a new direction to help the "Eskimo" to "climb the ladder of civilization." For Lesage, this new direction had a straightforward objective: "It is to give the Eskimos the same rights, privileges, opportunities, and responsibilities as all other Canadians; in short to enable them to share fully in the national life of Canada."[10] He believed that southern relations with the northern Canadians should be based on more than just "sentimentalism," that in fact it was the moral responsibility of Canadians to embrace this "primitive group." Lesage's ideas were premised on the fact of a historical relationship between Natives and newcomers: "The moral responsibility is the greater because, for so long, men were content to change the ways of the north without stopping to reckon, let alone pay, the price of their influence."[11] The minister thought that the contemporary problems Inuit faced were the result of contact with newcomers who had relentlessly exploited the North's natural resources, especially the white fox, without recognition of the long-term consequences. Lesage's solutions were a vague mixture of education, health care, and economic development. And to realize these goals, direction and control would be taken from the hands of the Christian churches who had been active in the Arctic since the early twentieth century.

Professional Vulnerability

On his way home to London, Ontario, after his interview at the offices of the Indian and Northern Health Services Branch in Ottawa, Dr Joseph Moody began to feel some doubt about the contract he had just signed which specified that he would be the new officer of health for the eastern Arctic. What had he done? What did that "impersonal wall covering in the director's office" representing the Arctic actually mean? And how would his young wife and two-year-old daughter cope with northern life? "By the time I reached home," he recalled, "to face Viola and little Gloria-May I felt more like a culprit than a medical health officer of the Canadian government."[12] It has become customary to associate doctors with knowledge, power, and overwhelming confidence, not self-doubt and insecurity. For Moody, it would take time before he could shake his feeling that perhaps he had made a mistake. Moody's arrival at Chesterfield Inlet did little to ease his anxiety:

> Here I would practice my profession among people, some of whom doubtless had more faith in their own witch doctors than in the Kabloona medicine man. I'd have to make many "little patrols" into the barren stretches, leaving Viola to run a household without modern conveniences, each of us constantly meeting situations not in the books. As my thoughts ran on, I felt terribly inadequate. What did I know about medicine up here?[13]

Moody was not alone in expressing his feeling of inadequacy when arriving in the North. So too did nurse Betty Woods, who arrived in Aklavik in 1954 and later worked in Pangnirtung. In an interview conducted after her tenure in the North, she was asked where her sense of strength or support came from. She recalled that she felt supported by her colleagues but also that she had to overcome feelings of inadequacy:

> The doctors in Frobisher Bay, the time I was there anyway, we felt were absolutely just waiting to do everything they could to help or give us certain advice and just standing right behind us, you know the medical services doctors down there in the hospital down there you know you felt that. And, then there was this sort of feeling that you were the person that was there and you would have to get on and do what needed to be done which I found quite calming. I just found it a calming fact that it had to be done and you were there and very often there was another nurse to consult. I think there were a lot of times when I sort of felt well you know God give me some wisdom in this because really I don't know what to do next, and you would sort of think that, and then you would go on with what you had to do, sort of think well I absolutely feel inadequate about this and then you went on.[14]

Woods and Moody shared the same sense of inadequacy, but each seemed to realize the necessity to move on with the work.

Northern nurses and doctors found that, in time, their experiences sharpened their confidence and their anxieties dissipated. Certainly, they all faced new working conditions. Diagnosing, for example, could present problems. Joseph Moody felt out of his league when it came to giving a diagnosis for something that seemed familiar in terms of symptoms but odd in other ways. His first case of midwinter polio surprised him greatly. Furthermore, Moody had never tried to make a diagnosis by ham radio, something at first he found particularly challenging. Dr Gareth Howerd, a DEW Line doctor who worked on Baffin Base near Frobisher Bay in 1957–8, also discussed in his memoir his anxiety about diagnosis:

> I knew how difficult it was to sometimes make a diagnosis in a city surgery or hospital ward where there was usually time to examine a patient again and again, and if necessary to call in a specialist. I had known too the agony of being upset when things went wrong, and had often felt a sense of loss when a patient died. But at least I had known in these cases that I had made the right decisions and had done all I could for the patients.
>
> Now I was faced with making a diagnosis and prescribing treatment from a short message on a Marconigram form, words probably written by a layman who thought the stomach was located in the paunchy part of the body that fat old men rub after a good meal, and that every ache in the right side of the abdomen was appendicitis.
>
> How difficult it would be to work under these conditions I did not know.[15]

Attempting to diagnose could also unsettle nurses. Carol Soper, one of the early nurses hired by the Anglican Diocese of the Arctic, was perplexed by an outbreak of illness which happened just after their ship dropped her and her family off in Lake Harbour in the summer of 1930. Soper quickly figured out the common symptoms of "soar throat and difficult swallowing, with very little rise in temperature." "I tried hard to diagnose and treat it," she recalled, "but soon felt utterly helpless."[16] Soper learned in the spring of the following year that it had likely been a lethal outbreak of respiratory polio. More often than not, nurses were simply unaccustomed to diagnosing. They had to adjust to this new duty quickly.

Nurses and doctors felt cautious when they first encountered Inuit patients. They did not want to frighten them away. While Gareth Howerd was hired to look after DEW Line workers, the Department of National Defence had an arrangement with the Department of Health and Welfare such that if local Inuit needed urgent care they could go to the DEW Line stations. He felt quite pleased when he noted his first patient making a recovery at the base hospital: "This was a great relief to me, for I did not want anything to go wrong with my first Eskimo case lest it should destroy the Eskimos' confidence in me right at the start and undermine the Government scheme for helping them."[17]

The need to assuage the feelings of their patients and the community members is a central motif in the life writing and correspondence of both nurses and doctors. They recognized that it was important to gain the respect of elders, medicine makers, and Native midwives, and in so doing they could gain a new cultural sensitivity. The notion that they would actually be creating a pluralistic medical system was not part of what they had anticipated, nor was Native medicine well understood by the INHS bureaucrats. Nonetheless, the new northern medical professionals learned as they went along.

In his three years in the Arctic, Joseph Moody repeatedly found himself caught between carrying on his work and the ire of the local medicine man, but he learned to solve the difficulties that arose. At one point, Moody started to immunize a group of Inuit against polio. His first patient was a woman whom he "picked at random." Suddenly, as the doctor recorded, "commotion rippled through the group around me, turning into a show of excitement that I didn't like."[18] He quickly learned from the interpreter that he had managed to offend the "witch doctor" or *angakok* by not offering him the first needle. Moody perceived the situation as vulnerable:

> Now, changing tactics, I gave the chief the first injection with all the ceremony I could muster for the occasion. The instant I finished with him he marshaled everyone in line and, directing the vaccinations that followed, turned the whole thing into a social affair. The Eskimos thought it was great fun. So, for once did I.[19]

In the same way that Moody was forced to come to terms with the tradition of deferring to the *angakok* in matters medicinal, nurse Amy Wilson, hired to work along the Alaska Highway in 1949, realized that she too had to rely on elders to introduce her medical program. Her goal was to administer vaccinations against diphtheria to Aboriginal community members in her jurisdiction. In the winter and spring of 1949 she sought to vaccinate as many people as she could, but she found herself first trying to convince the elders to support her. In one case, she claimed to have the support of an old chief who himself was badly scarred from smallpox. He remembered how his people had died during a smallpox outbreak during his childhood. Wilson appealed to him to encourage the others to line up for the vaccine to avoid what he called the "white man sickness." "And tell them he did," Wilson recalled in her memoir *No Man Stands Alone*; "no parents refused the injections, either for themselves or for their children."[20]

In this case, the elder encountered by Wilson was quite clear that the cause of disease was the white man or at least that the diseases were new since white men had arrived. Anthropologist Julie Cruikshank discusses the extent to which projects like the Alaska Highway, and no doubt too the DEW Line, caused tremendous disruption. "Among the most immediate and horrifying results of the coming of the highway were the epidemics brought to settlements along the route," she observed. "Any discussion of genealogies or old family photographs leads to commentary on people who 'died in '42' or people who became ill during or after the construction."[21] To relieve, if not stop, these new illnesses, Alaska Highway nurses and DEW Line doctors worked with Aboriginal people.

Gareth Howerd realized that it was important not to frighten his patients away and that in order to have patients evacuated, he had to rely on one woman who was able to convince them that they had to go because they would not recover at home. Howerd tried to converse with Ouha, the woman he relied on, but she did not speak much English, so most of their conversation was in sign language. Nevertheless, she never failed to convince her people that they had to go outside of their communities to be cured. In his memoir, Howerd recollected,

> I also went down to the Old Settlement from time to time and sought out Ouha, an old woman who seemed to rule the Eskimo community – even among the men her word was obeyed, so she was a useful ally for me.
>
> Whenever a young Eskimo refused to go to southern Canada for hospital treatment I would send for Ouha and she would come and sit before the patient in her usual posture, legs thrust straight out before her. Ouha's arms would slice the air as she emphasized each point, and she would talk on and on, never raising her voice in anger. At last her brown, weather-beaten face would crinkle into a smile and she would turn to me and say, "O.K., doc, he go."
>
> Ouha's persuasion never failed and I often sent for her to come to the nursing station or the base hospital to help me.[22]

Elders and healers held the power to persuade their community members, and the doctors and nurses of the North recognized that to be successful in their work they had to rely on them. Nurses and doctors did not have all the power. In fact, they openly discussed how they were in positions of vulnerability in their new environments, in communities that already had hierarchies and traditions associated with health and healing.

Aboriginal Interpreters, Guides, and Workers

Reliance on *angakoks* and women like Ouha, people who were local leaders and elders, was one informal aspect of how doctors and nurses operated in northern communities. They also relied heavily on paid interpreters and workers to help them communicate with their patients and to operate the nursing stations and hospitals. An assessment of these relationships reveals just how dependent northern medical professionals became on local community members and how close the ties became between newcomers and Natives. It also reinforces the dynamic nature of this medical encounter.

Central to fur trade society as well as to the treaty-making process in the nineteenth century, interpreters have occupied a central place in Native-newcomer relations. In *Translation and Power*, Maria Tymoczko and Edwin Gentzler recognize the powerful position occupied by translators in the colonial process, especially in the making of knowledge and the creation of colonial citizenship: "Translation has been a key tool in the production of such knowledge and representations," they argue.[23] Yet it was not always the colonizers who had the power and knowledge. On both sides of the colonial divide, the role of the interpreter was vested with power. Sometimes, in fact, Aboriginal interpreters determined the parameters of the working relationship.

Nurse Andrea Houseman recalled just how challenging it could be to communicate with her patients and the critical role played by her interpreter in an interview about 10 years after her Arctic sojourn in both Frobisher Bay and Arctic Bay:

> It was difficult to understand them and for them to understand me because our languages were different and whenever I spoke to them it was through an interpreter … and the interpreter was only about eighteen and you kind of wondered what impression she made on older people because she was your voice and if you said things which you ought not to have said she would not say anything you know and you could tell by her actions.[24]

This young interpreter could choose whether or not to repeat what the nurse had said. There were times if she deemed what the nurse said to be inappropriate then she would not repeat it to the patients.

Similarly, the extent to which his interpreter made the rules may have come as a surprise to Dr Otto Schaefer. Schaefer was hired by the INHS in 1953 to work at the hospital at Aklavik, where he stayed for two years before going to Pangnirtung. When he arrived at Pangnirtung in 1955 as the medical officer for the eastern Arctic, he was introduced to Etuangat Aksayook. Etuangat was a man in his 50s who from a young age had interpreted for newcomers. He had worked for one of the first northern doctors (Dr Leslie Livingston) and had become familiar with the medical histories of many eastern Arctic families, so familiar in fact that Schaefer's biographer was prompted to comment that Schaefer "trusted his knowledge of patients, their families, and their medical histories more than any hospital or resident doctor's files."[25] Etuanguat's many years of experience served both men and many patients well.

His knowledge was not the only way Etuanguat was able to convince Dr Schaefer that he would determine how the doctor/interpreter relationship would proceed. Etuanguat had certain expectations from the beginning. One of them was that he planned to speak mainly Inuktitut. He made his position quite clear: "I'll speak English when I go to your country; you speak Inuktitut when you come to mine."[26] Each evening Etuangat offered both Otto and his wife Didi lessons in Inuktitut, a language in which they would both become conversant. Etuangat also made it clear that he did want to hear the term "Eskimo" to refer to his people. Instead he preferred the word "Inuit."

When Schaefer and Etuangat were out on the land making their medical rounds, their relationship became particularly poignant. Etuangat was in control of arranging all the supplies for their trips, of managing the dog teams, and of leading the expeditions. He also planned for their sleeping arrangements, which usually involved bunking in with Inuit families in their tents. Etuangat did the cooking when they were on medical rounds, usually preparing a combination of what he called "white man's food" and "proper food." "Proper food" consisted of seal meat, raw caribou meat, and muktuk.

The young interpreter who worked for Andrea Houseman and Etuangat, the interpreter who helped Otto Schaefer, were each portrayed as individuals who had the power to determine the nature of the relationship between themselves and the doctor or nurse for whom they were working. In each case, the medical worker was appreciative of their interpretative work and Schaefer developed a close intimate bond with his guide.

Certainly not all of these cross-cultural relations went smoothly from start to finish. When Joseph Moody first met his interpreter Sheeniktook, he felt a bit unsure of how the relationship would work out, or, as he said, "It took adjustment on both sides before we managed to get along together."[27] Unfortunately, he does not reveal the difficulties Sheeniktook had adjusting to Moody, but he does discuss his great admiration for his interpreter's dog driving skills and the fact that he was an "excellent guide" and an "expert igloo builder," claiming that Sheeniktook knew "more than any Eskimo I had ever met" on matters related to ice formation, animals, and sea currents.[28] Moody's annoyance towards Sheeniktook arose out of the interpreter's hesitation (if not sometimes refusal) to embrace household labour:

> But menial tasks around the house were below his dignity. These he performed with reluctance, bordering on the comic. When he came to us he knew little English, but he loved to learn, and particularly to teach. He and Viola spent hours, each teaching his language to the other.
>
> Overhearing Sheeniktook shoveling snow one day, I turned to Viola: "Where does he get all those 'damns' and 'hells'?" "They just come naturally," she laughed, "whenever he does something that he thinks beneath him."[29]

Sheeniktook, it seems, enjoyed being an interpreter but did not see his job as that of a handyman or housemaid. He wanted to teach his language, learn English, and work as a guide. Not unlike Etuangat, Sheeniktook sought to define the terms of his employment and delineate the work he considered appropriate.

Dependency on Aboriginal interpreters, guides, and workers was central to the establishment of a Westernized medical infrastructure in the North. Not only did interpreters translate and teach Inuktitut, but they also provided much needed transportation to camps so that doctors and nurses could visit patients. On these expeditions, they made the travel arrangements and usually did all of the cooking. In the settlements, housemaids and interpreters too maintained the houses and did onerous tasks like shovelling, moving blocks of ice, preparing for baths, unpacking ships, and of course most of the upkeep in nursing stations and hospitals. These relationships were not of equal power, but clearly, without Aboriginal helpers, the medical staff could not have done their work. And the interpreters were not utterly powerless in determining their position within the relationship. They made demands that had to be followed.

Indigenous Medicine

If the role of Aboriginal people in the creation of a northern health care system has often been ignored by those who insist on describing northern doctors and nurses as "totalizing" and "colonizing," then it is equally true to say that the Westernized medical staff's acknowledgment of the value of Indigenous medicine has also been overlooked. The usual narrative is that doctors and nurses who came from the south sought to undermine if not eradicate the work of Indigenous medicine makers and midwives. While some medical professionals felt challenged by traditional medicine, it certainly was not universally the case that they worked to undermine it. In fact, several of the nurses and doctors who worked in the North after the Second World War looked favourably upon Aboriginal medicine and attempted to learn more about it. This is not necessarily to say that they used it, but they observed and often admired what they saw.

In an interview, nurse Andrea Houseman was asked to describe her experiences with maternity cases in the late 1960s when she worked at Arctic Bay. She sometimes sent patients to Frobisher Bay (now Iqaluit) so they could deliver their babies in the hospital, but this was not always the case. When Houseman delivered children, she often did so with Inuit midwives in attendance. Midwives were allowed to stay at the nursing station with the mothers-to-be, and as she later recalled this arrangement was beneficial to everyone:

> But the local midwives came in and stayed with the mothers because really it was a teaching thing for them and also it was surprising how much you could learn from them too. I saw one resuscitate a baby doing the knee-chest form of artificial respiration. They are quite good in lots of ways.[30]

Houseman appreciated the efforts of the local midwives and did not seem to feel challenged by their attendance or their help in birthing cases. Certainly during the late 1960s and throughout the 1970s in particular, some mothers were jarringly airlifted out of their communities and sent to regional or southern hospitals for delivery. However, the purpose here is to highlight the fact that other patterns emerged. Dorothy Knight, working in Lake Harbour in the late 1950s, remembered how pleased she was to be invited to a local birth which was controlled by the community midwives. Knight had asked her hospital interpreter and helper, a man named Ishawakta, if he could arrange it for her. Tagalik, an expectant mother, and two midwives, Oola and Pitsulala, agreed to have her in attendance. During the birth, she watched Tagalik squat on a sealskin with two wooden crates supporting her elbows. Each time she had a contraction, the midwives on either side of her massaged her abdomen, or as Knight's biographer put it, "the midwives kneaded and pushed at the woman's swollen belly."[31] The Inuk woman took occasional sips of tea and became increasingly "shiny with sweat" and weary, until finally the baby boy was born. The midwives cut the umbilical cord, wrapped the afterbirth in seal skin, and arranged to have it taken outside. The mother sipped tea and relaxed with her newborn son Nootoosha, named after a well-respected hunter from the community. In this instance, Knight served as an observer. She did not attend the birth as a participant or necessarily with reform as her goal, nor was she overly judgmental in her responses.

However, sometimes during their early encounters, nurses and doctors could be judgmental. As Otto Schaefer recalled, he had to recover from what he labelled his "haughty disregard" for "folk medicine."[32] In his Arctic travels, he witnessed some of the results of local medicine. One woman he met had sewn her daughter's head wound with a long sheath of the little girl's hair and her fur-sewing needle. Schaefer was amazed at what he saw as sophisticated "plastic surgery." He also met an *angakok* who successfully performed surgery on his nephew's distended bladder and a midwife who had a reputation as a "skillful remover of placentas."[33]

In her autobiography, Alaska Highway nurse Amy Wilson provided detailed descriptions of local plants and Indigenous remedies which she saw applied in her travels throughout British Columbia and the Yukon. One woman she befriended had gathered the fluff from the heads of bulrushes. These contained seeds which when mixed with "lard and pitch" proved to be an effective rubefacient ointment used to reduce swelling in her husband's rheumatic knee. Wilson also noted an evergreen shrub that produced what was called locally "kinnikinnick." This plant was dried with tobacco, but it also was mixed with water to produce a kidney and bladder diuretic.[34] Wilson encountered several midwives in her travels and claimed to have been on rather friendly terms with them. She was impressed with their abilities and commented on the high rate of infant survival. Wilson also boasted about never having seen diaper rash because of the efficacy of dried muskeg moss diapers.[35] The Aboriginal midwives and healers whom she met in her travels did not seem overcome by colonization. Instead they were described as self-sufficient and capable.

While Aboriginal medicine unquestionably endured and was often appreciated by outsiders, there was also a certain level of accommodation shown towards the practitioners of Western medicine from northern Aboriginal people. Of course, it is impossible to say that this was always the case since circumstances and experiences varied considerably, but for some northern Aboriginal people, doctors and nurses from the south sometimes represented relief.

In an oral history compilation consisting of interviews with Dene elders from Fort Resolution, community members were asked by younger-generation Dene investigators if they remembered when "white man's medicine" first arrived in the community.[36] Isidore Edjericon recalled being sent to the local hospital: "I stayed in the hospital for over a year when I had TB. My lung healed so I went home. It wouldn't be good for people if there were no hospitals or doctors. The people would have died without the doctors."[37] Another community member, George Sanderson, born in 1910, remembered the first "white" doctor and his medicine:

> The first white medicine that we had was Painkiller. We would put three or four drops on a sugar cube and take it for a cold. When we were tired we would put a little bit in water and drink it. It was really good. Dr. Rymer was the first doctor here. He was old when he came here. He stayed here quite a while but I don't remember how long. He was a good doctor. When people were sick he would take them and look after them really good.[38]

Judith Giroux, another community elder, reminisced about another early medication, commonly called rubbing medicine or Capsoline. "That was the best medicine in those days. When you rubbed it on your skin it burned. Some people didn't want to use Indian Medicine after the doctor brought medicines here, but my dad made medicine for the people and he cured a lot of people."[39] The elders of Fort Resolution recalled a positive relationship with the first doctor, as well as the continuation of the production of their own medicine, a pluralistic system of medicine which offered help but sometimes struggled to fight against the worst ravages of TB or other debilitating illnesses.

Not everyone had such positive memories. In 1986, Martha Flaherty, granddaughter of the filmmaker Robert Flaherty and a trained nurse originally from Inukjuak in northern Quebec, wrote about her experience with a southern doctor and nurse. In the article entitled "I Fought to Keep My Hair," Flaherty recalled being on board the ship the *C. D. Howe* when her family was being relocated from Inukjuak to Grise Fiord. Martha had been told while growing up that white people were friendly, but this was not confirmed in her early contact with them. As she put it,

> For as long as I can remember, Inuit believed that the white people were very helpful. Because these sayings were driven into my soft mind, I really believed we were going to get some help. Instead I went through hell with doctors and nurses.
>
> Not to name any of them, they wore white clothes, carried needles, stethoscopes, tongue depressors, cotton balls and scissors. Of course, that is not to mention what they smelled like. That is scary enough for any kid. It is the scissors, I remember the most. With needles and other equipment, I wasn't going to lose anything. But with scissors I found out they wanted something from me. They wanted my hair – to give me a brush cut.[40]

Flaherty went on to say that on this particular ship, a doctor had witnessed an Inuk mother looking for lice in her child's hair and had decided that all the children on board should have their heads shaved, boy or girl, with no regard for the opinions of the parents. Flaherty ran away and managed to elude capture.

Often the removal of lice or the removal of hair features as Indigenous peoples' first encounter with medical newcomers in the North. Children dodging health care workers was obviously just as apparent to the caregivers or parents as it was to the medical professionals themselves. One Dene community health representative, Regina Pastion from Assumption, Alberta (in the northwest corner of the province), recalled that when she made her home visits it was very common to see children scattering "heading for the bushes, or down the creek or sometimes to see little feet sticking out from under a bed."[41]

Conclusion

It would be incorrect to conclude that all doctors and nurses shared the same motivations and objectives when they signed on for work in the North or when they departed for their new communities. Some signed up for this work because they saw it as an opportunity to see the North, or as Dorothy Knight bluntly put it when asked why she wanted the job by the government interviewer, "Because I'm curious!" She went on to admit that she "felt a flush of guilt. Well, it was true. It wasn't some missionary zeal to improve the health of the northern people or save them from diseases that had prompted her to answer the advertisement."[42] Inquisitiveness had inspired her. Others were keen for adventure, while some such as Otto Schaeffer saw moving to northern Canada as an opportunity for a change in circumstance; in his case it was escape from post-war Germany.

Their motivations for moving to the North varied, as did their approaches. But there are certain discernible patterns suggestive of the fact that as professionals, they were well aware that they were crossing cultural boundaries and they did not have all the answers or hold all the power in their day-to-day encounters with patients and community members. Many especially felt when they first arrived that they had overestimated the ease with which they would make the transition from south to north. They certainly did not predict the extent to which they would come to rely on local community members as helpers around their houses and hospitals and as interpreters. Nor did they seem to imagine the close bonds that would sometimes be forged between themselves and their local aids and assistants. Joseph Moody described Sheeniktook as being like a member of his family, and Otto Schaeffer went back to Pangnirtung to visit Etuangat several times after he finished his work there.

Of equal importance, these doctors and nurses gained an education about the people they worked with in the North, something they would later share with their southern colleagues, either through preparing their autobiographies or biographies or in their subsequent medical practices. For example, after his work at Pangnirtung, Schaeffer set up his base at Edmonton's Charles Camsell Hospital from where he wrote and researched northern medical conditions. His first contribution towards a better understanding of Inuit, however, came not through his many *Canadian Medical Association Journal* articles but rather on the operating floor at the hospital. A nurse at the Camsell remembered how he taught them that Inuit felt pain just like any other people. The commonly held belief that since Inuit did not call out in pain they must have a higher pain threshold was discarded at Schaeffer's insistence. As nurse Emmi Nemetz recalled, "After Otto came back from the North patients got the drugs for pain after surgery without having to ask or wait."[43]

Taken collectively, the experiences of these doctors and nurses reveal that in order to gain a full understanding of the creation of Westernized health care in northern Canada, it is necessary to interrogate individual encounters. These allow for insight into doctors' and nurses' sense of professional vulnerability, their reliance upon local helpers, and the new understandings about northern Indigenous medicine gained by southerners. At the same time, however, it is apparent that the patients who received health care were not always aware of these factors. Instead, they often felt disempowered and demeaned by a system which generally failed to acknowledge their traditional practices and their sense of fear.

NOTES

1 The legacy of disease and ill health that followed contact has been well documented by historians. See especially Kathryn McPherson, "Nursing and Colonization: The Work of Indian Health Services Nurses in Manitoba, 1945–1970," in *Women, Health and Nation: Canada and the United States since 1945*, ed. Georgina Feldberg, Molly Ladd-Taylor, Alison Li, and Kathryn McPherson (Montreal: McGill-Queen's University Press, 2003), 223–46; Maureen K. Lux, *Medicine That Walks: Disease, Medicine and Canadian Plains Native People, 1880–1940* (Toronto: University of Toronto Press, 2001); and Mary-Ellen Kelm, *Colonizing Bodies: Aboriginal Health and Healing in British Columbia 1900–50* (Vancouver: UBC Press, 1998). For the Arctic, see Pat Sandiford Brygier, *A Long Way from Home: The Tuberculosis Epidemic Among the Inuit* (Montreal: McGill-Queen's University Press, 1994). This paper builds on the work of historians who have started to probe the history of outpost nursing, including Jayne Elliott, "Blurring the Boundaries of Space: Shaping Nursing Lives at the Red Cross Outposts in Ontario, 1922–1945," *Canadian Bulletin of Medical History/Bulletin canadien d'histoire de la médecine* 21 (2004): 303–25; Nicole Rousseau and Johanne Daigle, "Medical Service to Settlers: The Gestation and Establishment of a Nursing Service in Quebec, 1932–1943," *Nursing History Review* 8 (2000): 95–116; Laurie Meijer Drees and Lesley McBain, "Nursing and Native Peoples in Northern Saskatchewan: 1930s–1950s," *Canadian Bulletin of Medical History/Bulletin canadien d'histoire de la médecine* 18 (2001): 43–65. See also Dianne Dodd, Jayne Elliott, and Nicole Rousseau, "Outpost Nursing in Canada," in *On All Frontiers: Four Centuries of Canadian Nursing*, ed. Christina Bates, Dianne Dodd, and Nicole Rousseau, 139–52 (Ottawa: University of Ottawa Press, 2005).

2 Alice K. Smith, "Nursing with Indian and Northern Health Services," *Canadian Nurse* 59/2 (February 1963): 130.
3 John D. O'Neil, "Self-Determination, Medical Ideology and Health Services in Inuit Communities," in *Northern Communities: The Prospects for Empowerment*, ed. Gurston Dacks and Kenneth C. Coates (Edmonton: University of Alberta Press, 1988), 34.
4 Walter J. Vanast, "Hastening the Day of Extinction: Canada, Quebec, and the Medical Care of Ungava's Inuit, 1867–1967," *Etudes/Inuit Studies* 15/2 (1991): 76.
5 Frank James Tester and Paule McNicoll, "'Why Don't They Get It?': Talk of Medicine as Science, St. Luke's Hospital, Panniqtuuq, Baffin Island," *Social History of Medicine* 19/1 (February 2006): 104.
6 Cited in Richard Diubaldo, "The North in Canadian History: An Outline," *Fram: The Journal of Polar Studies* (winter 1984): 195.
7 On the history of southern representations of the North see Sherill E. Grace, *Canada and the Idea of North* (Montreal: McGill-Queen's University Press, 2001).
8 Lester Pearson, "Canada Looks 'Down North,'" *Foreign Affairs* 24/4 (July 1946): 642, 647.
9 Jean Lesage, "Enter the European: Among the Eskimos (Part II)," *Beaver* (Outfit 285, spring 1955): 7.
10 Ibid., 4.
11 Ibid.
12 Joseph P. Moody, *Arctic Doctor* (New York: Dodd, Mead, 1955), 6.
13 Ibid., 18.
14 Betty Woods, interview [probably with Myra Rutherdale].
15 Gareth Howerd, *DEW Line Doctor* (London: Robert Hale, 1960), 49.
16 Carolyn K. Soper, "A Nurse Goes to Baffin Island," *Beaver* (Outfit 295, winter 1964): 33.
17 Howerd, *DEW Line Doctor*, 68.
18 Moody, *Arctic Doctor*, 119.
19 Ibid., 120.
20 Amy V. Wilson, *No Man Stands Alone* (Sidney, BC: Gray's Publishing, 1965), 61.
21 Julie Cruikshank, "The Gravel Magnet: Some Social Impacts of the Alaska Highway on Yukon Indians," in *The Alaska Highway: Papers of the 40th Anniversary Symposium*, ed. Kenneth S. Coates (Vancouver: UBC Press, 1985), 182.
22 Howerd, *DEW Line Doctor*, 123.
23 Maria Tymoczko and Edwin Gentzler, *Translation and Power* (Amherst: University of Massachusetts Press, 2002), xxi.
24 Andrea Houseman, interview, February 6, 1977, Joy Duncan Pioneer Nursing Collection, Glenbow Archives. For purposes of anonymity, this is a pseudonym.

25 Gerald W. Hankins, *Sunrise Over Pangnirtung: The Story of Otto Schaefer, M.D.* (Calgary: Arctic Institute of North America, 2000), 75–6.
26 Ibid., 3.
27 Moody, *Arctic Doctor*, 38–9.
28 Ibid., 39.
29 Ibid.
30 Houseman, interview. Two particularly useful articles on childbirth in the North are Patricia Jasen, "Race, Culture, and the Colonization of Childbirth in Northern Canada," in *Rethinking Canada: The Promise of Women's History*, ed. Veronica Strong-Boag, Mona Gleason, and Adele Perry, 353–66 (Toronto: Oxford University Press, 2002); and Judith Bender Zelmanovits, "'Midwife Preferred': Maternity Care in Outpost Nursing Stations in Northern Canada 1945–1988," in Feldberg et al., *Women, Health and Nation*, 161–88.
31 Betty Lee, *Lutiapik: The Story of a Young Woman's Year of Isolation and Service in the Arctic* (Toronto: McClelland and Stewart, 1975), 102–3.
32 Hankins, *Sunrise Over Pangnirtung*, 87.
33 Ibid., 88.
34 Wilson, *No Man Stands Alone*, 120.
35 Ibid., 49.
36 Interview conducted 1984/85 for the Deninoo Community Council. Recordings held at the Northwest Territories Archives, Fort Resolution Community Education Council Fonds, N-1993-016. One fine example of a team of scholars who attempted to learn how Natives responded to public health nurses can be found in Emily Abel with Nancy Reifel, "Interactions Between Public Health Nurses and Clients on American Indian Reservations During the 1930s," *Social History of Medicine* 9/1 (1996): 89–108.
37 Interview, FR, conducted 1984/85 for the Deninoo Community Council.
38 Ibid.
39 Ibid.
40 Martha Flaherty, "I Fought to Keep My Hair," in *Northern Voices: Inuit Writing in English*, ed. Penny Petrone (Toronto: University of Toronto Press, 1988), 274.
41 J. Karen Scott and Joan E. Kieser, *Northern Nurses: True Nursing Adventures from Canada's North* (Oakville, Ontario: Kokum, 2002), 141.
42 Lee, *Lutiapik*, 17–18.
43 Hankins, *Sunrise Over Pangnirtung*, 127.

PART THREE

Interraciality and Education

Negotiating Aboriginal Interraciality in Three Early British Columbian Indian Residential Schools

JEAN BARMAN

In *Shingwauk's Vision* published in 1996, J.R. Miller transformed our understanding of residential schools.[1] He detailed their inner workings and probed their role in the larger society. Miller's meticulous scholarship and brave findings turned Canadians' attention in this direction as never before. A consequence of his and others' efforts is governmental acknowledgment that generations have had their lives turned upside down by an upbringing separate from family and community. On 11 June 2008, a dozen years after the publication of *Shingwauk's Vision*, the Canadian prime minister stated in the House of Commons, "On behalf of the government of Canada and all Canadians, I stand before you, in this chamber so central to our life as a country, to apologize to the aboriginal peoples for Canada's role in the Indian residential school system."[2] The subsequent Truth and Reconciliation Commission (TRC), which engaged residential school survivors across the country and reported in 2015, has alerted all Canadians to residential schools' legacies.[3]

For all of their breathtaking significance, the apology's language and the TRC's focus obscure an important dimension of the residential school system. The common use of the adjective "Indian" to describe schools and the TRC's goal of "reconciliation between Aboriginal and non-Aboriginal peoples" encourages the assumption that the children attending them were all from what the apology terms "aboriginal cultures." As for the reason, both the apology and the TRC build on a generation of scholarship, including my own, which largely took for granted the public claims of school administrators, religious denominations running the schools, and the federal government sustaining and overseeing them that they were wholly "Indian" residential schools.

The historical reality is that Indian residential schools also negotiated Aboriginal interraciality. Although funded by the federal government to educate status Indian children, some schools for various reasons accommodated mixed-race children as part of their pupil bodies. The ways in which they did so are often not immediately visible, given the loss or obscuring of pupils' records as well as the contemporary rhetoric. I realized I got it wrong some time after publishing an article on All Hallows, an Anglican residential school begun in 1884 that intrigued me for enrolling "Indian" and "white" girls in the same institution.[4] This focus distracted me from attending to pupils embodying both inheritances.

That was then, this is now. My ongoing research around Aboriginal interraciality in British Columbia has alerted me that All Hallows' acceptance of interracial pupils, who were depicted as "Indians" for public consumption, was not an anomaly in the west coast province. It was rather a repeat occurrence boosting schools' numbers and conveniently facilitating their claims of pupil transformation under their aegis. Some of the Indians so remarkably made white-like may have been quite white-like prior to their enrolment. Schools' willingness to negotiate Aboriginal interraciality also corresponded, at least to some extent, with parents' literacy hopes for their offspring.

Here I focus on three early British Columbian Indian residential schools, two of which came to my attention through side doors. Roman Catholic St Mary's was founded at Mission in the Fraser Valley in 1863, Anglican All Hallows at Yale at the entrance to the Fraser Canyon in 1884, and Methodist Coqualeetza at Sardis also in the Fraser Valley in 1894.[5] With each school I integrate extant school, government, and other records with family profiles for their insights respecting the negotiation of Aboriginal interraciality.

Context

The negotiation of Aboriginal interraciality in these three early British Columbian Indian residential schools may or may not be unique in Canada. Certainly, the province's history has distinctive aspects. Aboriginal interraciality had two points of origin. The first was, as in much of the rest of Canada, the fur trade, which resulted in Vancouver Island being made a British colony in 1849. Men employed for any length of time tended to have families with local Indian women. The second point of origin was unique to British Columbia. A gold rush beginning in 1858 in what was still a fur trade enclave brought many thousands of men to the British Columbian mainland, which was within the year proclaimed a second British colony. While most men soon departed, some of those who remained also had families with local women.

The two circumstances were so significant that at the time British Columbia entered the Canadian Confederation in 1871, the majority of non-Indian children in the areas of the fur trade and gold rush embodied Aboriginal interraciality. As reported by the first superintendent of education, "There are 402 children, of all ages [of which] 287 are of school age, that is between 5 to 16; and 115 under five years. Dividing them into whites and half-castes, there are 105 of the former of school age, and 61 under; of the latter, there are 182 of school age, and 54 under."[6] The total numbers were not great, nor could they have been in a province whose entire non-Aboriginal population did not much exceed 10,000.[7]

The other distinctive aspect of British Columbia was its large size and difficult terrain. The fur trade and then the gold rush had taken men to parts of the province that otherwise might not have become sites of non-Aboriginal settlement. To raise a family and make a living there was quite different from having access to schooling. The new provincial government did work hard to provide what was one of the few public services of the day in the form of free non-denominational primary schooling. It even opened a public boarding school aimed at the sons and daughters of one-time miners become farmers, ranchers, or businessmen. The Cache Creek boarding school in the southern interior operated from 1874 to 1890. Of the eighty pupils attending in 1874, 1875, and 1877, the three years for which names survive, just over half had Indian mothers.[8]

At this time religious denominations considered the education of their parishioners' children to be in their purview. Unlike in other parts of Canada, where the Roman Catholic Church operated its own schools within provincial systems, no such option existed in British Columbia. The Catholics as well as other denominations had to scramble to initiate private alternatives. British Columbia's colonial status gave the Anglicans, the establishment church in Britain, the advantage,[9] but the Roman Catholics were not far behind. While some schools restricted themselves to white pupils, others, as with the Catholic boarding school founded in the heart of the gold rush at the end of 1873, did not do so. Intended to compete head on with Cache Creek, St Joseph's operated until 1888 with a similarly mixed white and interracial enrolment.[10]

The daughters of an American entrepreneur and Lillooet woman who attended St Joseph's in 1876–83 recalled only three pupils being white girls, all the rest like themselves having white fathers and Indian mothers.[11]

Other mixed-race children attended local public schools, although not necessarily on an equal basis with other pupils. The superintendent of education noted in his second annual report how "considerable difficulty has been experienced during the year in keeping some of the small rudimentary schools supplied with teachers" and gave the reasons: "Salaries in those districts are necessarily small; and as the pupils are few and merely beginning, and in many cases a majority of half-breeds, duly qualified teachers are not obtainable."[12] The teacher at Yale grumbled how "the presence of halfbreeds, so many of them," was keeping other children away.[13] Whether or not pupils and their families were so aware, their racial circumstances set them apart.

All the same, Aboriginal interracial children attending public boarding or day schools or religiously based private schools were perceived as more able to become white-like than not, or they would not have been permitted to be there. The prejudices of the day were alive and well, thanks to what came to be seen as scientifically determined differences between persons based in physical appearance and skin colour. Yet hope was held out, at least to some extent, through appropriate schooling.

The situation with Aboriginal interracial children who had been slipped into Indian residential schools was the reverse. At the core of racism was the assumption that persons who were non-white would perform less well, whatever the measure, be it in or out of school. Such persons were, as notions of survival of the fittest growing out of social Darwinism seemed to attest, inferior by virtue of their genetic inheritance. The prophecy became self-fulfilling. As discrimination intensified, so generations of persons who did not physically mirror members of the dominant society ended up as adults almost entirely at the bottom ranks of Canadian society. The assumption made by those Indian residential schools that admitted interracial children appears to have been that to be part Aboriginal was to be Aboriginal. The quantity mattered far less than did the presence of any quantity at all.

Over time, questions began to be raised about the presence of Aboriginal interracial children in Indian residential schools. The reason lay in the Indian policy put in place by the federal government, to whom "the charge of the Indians" in British Columbia passed by the terms of union whereby it joined Canada in 1871.[14] Five years later, the Indian Act, 1876, imposed a fundamental divide on Aboriginal peoples across Canada. The act restricted federal oversight by the Department of Indian Affairs to status Indians, defined in a patrilineal fashion in line with the assumption in the dominant white society that women were not persons in their own right but rather the property first of their fathers and then of their husbands. As spelled out in Article 3 of the Indian Act, 1876,

> The term "Indian" means –
> *First*. Any male person of Indian blood reputed to belong to a particular band;
> *Secondly*. Any child of such person;
> *Thirdly*. Any women who is or was lawfully married to such person.[15]

Aboriginal interracial children, all of whom in British Columbia had non-Aboriginal fathers just as they did generally across Canada, were placed outside the purview of the Department of Indian Affairs, which increasingly exercised oversight of Indian residential schools through financial support and other means.

St Mary's at Mission

The earliest of the three Indian residential schools considered here is the Roman Catholic St Mary's which opened at Mission in the Fraser Valley in 1863 for boys and 1868 for girls in similar circumstances as St Joseph's in the Cariboo. However, unlike St Joseph's, which three years after closing as a school for white and mixed-race pupils restarted in 1891 as an Indian residential school with federal funding, St Mary's operated as such in a seemingly unbroken line.[16] A St Mary's history published in 2002 terms it "the oldest permanent Indian residential school in British Columbia."[17]

The Department of Indian Affairs appears to have accepted the composition of St Mary's and its thirty-five or so pupils at face value, lauding the school for its "training of the poor children of the forest."[18] From 1874 onward, St Mary's received an annual federal grant of $350, raised in 1883 to $500.[19] The only other British Columbian institution to receive such favourable financial treatment was the Anglican Metlatkatla on the north coast.

The Roman Catholic religious orders of the Oblates of Mary Immaculate and Sisters of St Ann, who jointly ran St Mary's, emphasized the pupils' Indian inheritance, which from the church's perspective marked them. The historian of the girls' school, basing herself on a contemporary journal, described how St Mary's "was to be a purely Indian school – including, by right, blood relations."[20] A summary account referred to "Indian parents," the "out-door Indian life," and the "Indian nature" in reference to pupils, while also noting, almost in passing, how in 1871–2, "ten were half-breeds and five full blooded Indians," and in 1879–80 there were "thirty six Indian and semi-Indian girls."[21] The boys' school, as of 1875–6, enrolled a mix of "native and half breed boys," but in almost the same breath the account referenced "the camps, or lodges of absolutely uncivilized natives, ignorant, uncouth," from which they came.[22] Another account described all of the school's pupils as "Indian girls" and "Indian school boys."[23]

A more complex story lay beneath the veneer. Federal officials appear to have tacitly accepted a mix of pupils. The provincial superintendent of Indian Affairs signalled in 1882 to his federal superior how "about twenty pupils attend there, but I believe they are half-breeds."[24] Six years later he reported privately that "at present most of the attendees are half breeds."[25] No pupil register appears to have survived, but two early lists verify this circumstance. The first was compiled by a former pupil, the second is in the 1881 manuscript census.

It was in the course of research on the early settlement history of the Fraser Valley that I encountered Josephine Humphreys. Her English-born father was a member of the British Columbia colonial legislative assembly and executive council and later of the provincial legislative and a cabinet minister, her mother a Chehalis chief's daughter, by whom he had three children before marrying a Welsh woman well positioned to further his career. Then aged four, Josephine lived with her reconstituted family in Victoria for two years in what remained for her "a grief stricken memory." All her life protective of her father, she explained her arrival at St Mary's in 1874, where she would remain for the next ten years: "They had two little girls who were in Victoria with them, and I was put in St. Mary's. [My father wanted] to place his small daughter where she would be cared for. We had to have a boarding school so I came to St. Mary's."[26]

In old age, Josephine Humphreys compiled a list of her remembered classmates from 1874 to 1884, during which time St Mary's was receiving federal funding as an Indian industrial school, meaning it was intended for older students. The list contains fifty-nine names including her own. Of these, seven are almost certainly wholly Indian, the other fifty-two interracial like herself. She omitted six names of other interracial girls who turn up in the 1881 manuscript census.[27] All but two of the forty families from which these fifty-eight girls came consisted of a white father, likely arrived with the gold rush but possibly with the fur trade, and an Indian mother. In the two exceptions, the girls' mothers each had a white father and Indian mother, making their daughters only one-quarter Indian by descent.

Half of the forty families had undergone dislocation through a father either dying or disappearing or a biological mother no longer being present, as with Josephine Humphreys. The other half were intact, settled down in the Fraser Valley, in other areas of the gold rush, or around Burrard Inlet, the future Greater Vancouver. Some sent their daughters, and likely also their sons, due to the desire for a Catholic education, others because no public school was nearby.

Sometimes, as with the Perrault, Lacroix, and Merrifield families, these reasons intersected, both with each other and with St Mary's need for pupils. François Perrault, his Thompson wife Lucy Kesaltsa, and their five children were well settled on a remote ranch west of Kamloops when the mother became ill and died. The two sons and the oldest daughter were already enrolled at the Cache Creek public boarding school, but either Perrault or others considered him unsuitable or unable to care for his three daughters on his own. The head of Cache Creek recorded that "on the death of the mother, she & two younger sisters [were] taken entirely off the father's hands by the sisters" and deposited at St Mary's.[28] Long-time French Canadian fur trade employee Michel Lacroix and his Babine wife Catherine Pookrvietak left central British Columbia for the Fraser Valley in 1869 precisely in order to give their children access to schooling. Good Catholics, they settled almost within sight of St Mary's Mission, which their daughters Helen and Mary attended, certainly after and perhaps also before his death in 1873. Alex Merrifield – an Englishman who took up land in the future North Vancouver shortly after the opening of the large Moodyville sawmill there in 1863, where he worked as a sawyer – had two children with a Squamish woman when the Catholic church intervened. As recalled in old age by a nearby white child,

> When the Roman Catholics came, the priests wanted the whitemen to marry their squaws, but they would not. Alex Merryfield wouldn't anyway. He and she had two little girls. So Mary left Alex, and went to the

[North Vancouver Catholic] Mission, and Alex sent the two girls up to [St Mary's] school ..., and he kept them there until they were quite an age. They were very well educated; understood music and all that, and used to play the organ.[29]

Theotiste, Elodie, and Melina Perrault, Helen and Mary Lacroix, and Annie and Mary Merryfield were among Josephine Humphreys's friends at St Mary's.

Roman Catholic attitudes towards Aboriginal interraciality are particularly evident in the case of Humphreys's fellow pupil Elizabeth Willing, described by the school's historian as "the daughter of a [French] Canadian father and a Fraser Valley native woman."[30] Her father was a long-time employee at the fur trade post of Fort Langley in the Fraser Valley who had Elizabeth baptized Roman Catholic shortly after her birth in 1858.[31] "Orphaned in babyhood, she was received in the home and arms of her uncle a chief ... When the Mission was opened she and her cousin were among the first enrolled." The sisters soon discovered that ten-year-old Elizabeth "had gentle qualities and an inclination for all things pertaining to religion."[32] She sought her First Communion at the usual age of twelve or thirteen, only to be refused. The reason reveals much about the way in which residential schools positioned their interracial charges:

The Oblates had a ruling of their own, founded on their experience of the fickleness of the Indian character ... so prone to be superstitious, to polygamy ... Rather than expose the Holy Eucharist to desecration by too readily admitting their semi-savage followers to the Holy Table, they had established the custom in these B.C. tribes of making their first communion only after marriage.

St Mary's historian, using the contemporary journal, elaborated on the situation:

Elizabeth knew this. But she had determined never to marry, never to leave the convent. Was she for this to be forever deprived of Holy Communion? Did she cherish the hope that her mixture of white blood would incline to her being classified with the first communicants of her father's race? Missionaries have learned not to be easily influenced by the spirituality of the Indian temperament. If, in consequence, a favored soul is denied the religious aliment for which she hungers, it is for the general good.[33]

By the time "this half-breed girl" had reached the age of 16, the head of the girls' school was so convinced that Elizabeth's spirituality overcame her race that she successfully interceded for an exception to the rule. It was fortunately so, the story continues, since Elizabeth died shortly thereafter of a form of tuberculosis: to quote the school's historian, of "scrofulu, that implacable disease of half breeds."[34]

St Mary's encouragement of interracial pupils was well known to Fraser Valley contemporaries, as indicated by a dispute in 1884 over the location of a new public school. The location selected at a public meeting was denounced for there being few nearby families with children, "except 2 frenchmen who has halfbreeds and lives on the river bank at the north end of the school district and in my opinion was only used as stools for those voters [childless speculators wanting to improve property values for resale] as I don't think there spiritual advisors would allow them to go if they were willing to send them [to public school] as they are so near St. Mary's Mission and belongs to that faith."[35] In the view of this losing parent, Roman Catholic interracial children belonged there rather than in public school.

All Hallows at Yale

The second school in time is All Hallows, whose pupil body I oversimplified in a previous publication.[36] The school owed its impetus to an activist bishop who in 1884 enticed out to the gold rush town of Yale several members of an English order of Anglican nuns, the Sisters of All Hallows, for the purpose of establishing an Indian girls' school.

The catch was that, by the time the sisters arrived, finances were in disarray due to the bishop's enthusiasm for new projects. In line with an earlier initiative that had faltered, the bishop persuaded the sisters also to accept some fee-paying white students, principally the daughters of Anglican ministers in remote areas of the province. Consequently, over time, two boarding schools operated side-by-side in the same buildings.

Much as with St Mary's, families embodying Aboriginal interraciality from early on made the running at All Hallows. The motherhouse in England reported in January 1885, three months after the sisters' arrival, that they had "started a day school for 'the Yale Indians'" but numbers dwindled as winter set in. Then something else happened:

> In the meantime a few half-breed girls showed a desire to receive instruction from us, and we admitted them gladly. They speak English, and,

> having attended the Free [public] School, are fairly advanced, but as religious teaching and influence are greatly needed by this particular class of children, who are often placed in circumstances of peculiar temptation, we are making a special effort for them.[37]

The public school teacher at Yale confirmed the situation in his complaint to the superintendent of education in April 1885: "There has been a school started here by the Episcopalians, and as a consequence mine has become somewhat smaller. I have not lost any Whites but all my half-breeds excepting one have gone ... In losing the half-breeds I lost two of my best pupils."[38]

One of the two pupils transferring to the new school was Rosie Oppenheim, whose Polish Jewish father was so committed to his children's education that he had been a Yale school trustee and was serving as board chairman about the time the sisters appeared.[39] According to Rosie, who had by now spent two or three years in the local public school, "My father was just then thinking of sending my two older sisters and myself to California to be educated there. He was quite a scholar. I've seen his books. Shakespeare, Roman History, his small Hebrew Testament and many others." A "trader in dry goods 'clothing,'" Louis Oppenheim was so taken by the new arrivals that he changed his mind.[40] "We went to day school at the Sisters school as we lived just across from the church and the parsonage, where the Sisters had residence."[41] Rosie's mother was the local chief's daughter.[42]

The Anglican bishop sought to capitalize on the situation by requesting provincial funding as if All Hallows were a public institution:

> In my school at Yale, under the Sisters of All Hallows, are about ten half-breed girls being boarded and educated. Certain payments in *partial* defrayment of costs are being made in respect to some of them, others are entirely dependent upon the institution. Will you have the kindness to inform me whether the Provincial Government would entertain an application for State aid in respect of these children, or any of them.[43]

The negative response reflected provincial education policy: "Application for State aid to private schools cannot, I fear, be entertained."[44]

The bishop thereupon requested a per-pupil subsidy in line with the federal Department of Indian Affairs' declared goals for Indian residential schools. Unsurprisingly, his portrayal of All Hallows' student body was now wholly different. "The boarding school dissociates the Indian child from the deleterious home influences to which he would be otherwise subjected. It reclaims him from the uncivilized state in which he has been brought up."[45] Following a fact-finding visit to All Hallows, the Indian Superintendent for British Columbia supported the application on the grounds that the interracial pupils were de facto Indians:

> There are seventeen girls at this Mission, seven of whom are full blooded Indians and ten are half-breeds. These half-breeds are children of white men and Indian women who have been deserted by their white fathers, and have always lived on Indian Reserves until taken into the Mission house by the Sisters, and are in habits and customs as much Indians as the full blood girls are.[46]

An agreement was concluded in June 1888 whereby this "School of Indian Girls," to use the language of all concerned, received partial assistance to construct a new dormitory and an annual grant of $60 per pupil up to a maximum of twenty-five pupils, an upper limit later rising to thirty-five.[47]

The Department of Indian Affairs repeatedly expressed satisfaction with All Hallows. In 1890, the local Indian agent described the three "Indian schools" in his jurisdiction as the "Yale school for girls," the "school for boys and girls at St. Mary's Mission," and a small "school for boys and girls" which would shortly be transformed into Coqualeetza, the third school considered here.[48] Five years later the Indian agent detailed how they "have each been well attended, and are doing an excellent work for the Indian youth of this district."[49]

As a matter of practical necessity, All Hallows carefully cultivated its image as tending to Indians. The official examiner in 1890 considered pupils' academic progress especially impressive since, he was informed, "to most of the pupils English is more or less a foreign tongue."[50] A visitor of 1891 came away impressed with "the subject and manner of their recitations, music, range of information, (surprised as I was at this, for I had no idea the Indian was capable of such speedy development)."[51]

Other accounts make clear interracial girls were part of the mix. Christmas 1889 was celebrated, to quote a young participant as published in the school magazine, by "twenty of us Indians and Half-breeds, and only two young ladies," those being the white girls.[52] A visiting bishop in 1892 observed "about 30 children 15 of whom are half breeds."[53] Although no register survives and very few names appear in extant issues of the school magazine, a dozen interracial families can be identified as sending daughters to the All Hallows Indian School. Others remain enigmas, as with the passing reference to a pupil aged "about 11, named Maggie, a 'quarter-breed,'" meaning she had a white father and a mother of mixed white and Indian descent.[54]

One of the most vivid accounts has to do with Rosie Oppenheim, who was encouraged to take, and passed, Royal Academy of Music examinations alongside eight white pupils.[55] A teacher lauded her in a letter home to England:

> I think you would be surprised at some of the Indian girls' music. Rosie has a very pretty touch and a good deal of taste, and it generally surprises people to see this nice looking neatly dressed girl of seventeen sit down to the piano and play Mendelssohn or Beethoven. She plays for all the school songs and drill, and lately she has been teaching the singing class all by herself.[56]

At no time in the various accounts was consideration given to the idea of any of the interracial girls, however talented, transferring to the white school. Their Aboriginal descent made it impossible. Indeed, the separation between the two schools in the same set of buildings became so complete that many white girls never realized that the others were also being educated. A former white pupil explained how All Hallows "was run by the Anglican Sisters assisted by young Indian girls working in the school."[57] As put to me by another, "they were the servants; they did the work."[58]

Coqualeetza Industrial School at Sardis

The third school to come to my attention did so precisely because of its admission of Aboriginal interracial pupils.[59] A determined Methodist minister spearheaded the formation of Coqualeetza Industrial School at Sardis in the Fraser Valley only to discover he did not have enough children to fill the hundred spaces for which it had been allocated per capita federal financial assistance. The numbers had to be got by the time of the school's opening in February 1894. So the head returned to his old haunts on Burrard Inlet, now the young city of Vancouver, where he had earlier served as a missionary. In the course of my research on the families who lived in Stanley Park before and after it became a park and at nearby Kanaka Ranch at the foot of Denman Street, now downtown Vancouver, I tracked most members of the second generation to

Coqualeetza. The second Kanaka Ranch's name combined the general term for native Hawaiians, *Kanaka*, meaning a person in the Hawaiian language, with the commonly used "ranch" or "rancherie" to describe an Aboriginal settlement. Not only does Coqualeetza's original admissions register survive, but so does the diary of an early head along with other records. The primary sources make it possible to interrogate with some specificity how the school negotiated its interracial pupils, whose numbers included not only those I encountered in my related research but others as well.

Fourteen children from Stanley Park and six whose families originated at Kanaka Ranch filled spaces at Coqualeetza during its first decade as an industrial school. All had non-Aboriginal fathers, which meant that, despite having Aboriginal mothers, none had status. The reasons they attended exemplify the interplay between an Indian residential school's priorities and families' survival strategies.

A parent's death was the critical factor to the Burns, Smith, Cole, and Cummings families contributing their offspring to make up Coqualeetza's numbers. A Squamish chief's daughter who had grown up in the future Stanley Park had her world turned upside down by her white husband's death. According to her brother,

> Burns was a whiteman married to my sister Louisa, and, after he die, they "kick" her out; he had a six acre orchard there [in the Point Grey area of today's Vancouver]. But that's the way they do with Indian woman who married whiteman; when their husbands die, they kick the womans out – because she's "just a squaw."[60]

Louisa had few options. Twelve-year-old Addie and her half-brother Dave were among the children enrolled at Coqualeetza at its official opening February 1894. Clearly conscious that the school was being monitored by the Department of Indian Affairs, its official ledger recording "Admission and Discharges" manicured the records. In the column for "tribal origin," they were described, based only on their mother, as "Squamish."[61] Four weeks later 14-year-old Maggie Burns joined her siblings at Coqualeetza.

The death of Peter Smith's Squamish wife Kenick left this Portuguese-born fisherman, whose English surname likely reflected his having earlier jumped ship, with the care of his three youngest children. By whatever means this Roman Catholic father was induced to give up his children to Methodist Coqualeetza, he must have, as had Louisa

Burns, considered he had little choice. The school matron sympathetically described the children's arrival at the new school's opening: "The Smith family – Johnnie, nine; Maria, five; and Rita, three, – were accompanied by their father, who seemed almost heart-broken to part with his children, but the mother was dead, and he had to be from home most of the time, for he was a fisherman."[62] The school register described the young Smiths as "Squamish" with a father named only as "Peter" and an "unknown" mother. School officials must have had a word with Peter Smith as to the advantages of his two older sons also getting an education, for Thomas (aged seventeen) arrived a week later and Peter (aged eighteen) in November 1894. Unlike their young brother John, who had earlier attended public school in Vancouver, neither of them had done so, according to the register. The admission of the much older Smith boys exemplifies Coqualeetza's mad scramble to make up the numbers, which reached fifty-two by March and eighty-six by the end of the year. As a contemporary explained, "a large proportion of the new boys are pretty well grown."[63]

With thirteen-year-old Tommy Cole, it was his Scots-born father, a longshoreman, who died, whereupon his Squamish mother remarried. According to family memory, provincial authorities decreed her to be an unfit parent and whipped him off to Coqualeetza. Once again the official record was made to read as if the new entrant was wholly Indian, Tommy being, like the young Smiths, described as Squamish.

A year later, the Cummings family, also from Stanley Park, contributed to Coqualeetza's well-being. Scots fisherman James Cummings became so ill at the beginning of 1897 that, seeking to secure his family's future, he made out his will. He left his money in trust for "for the education of my children."[64] Whether or not the school got a financial advantage as a consequence, just two weeks after his death in March 1897, Timothy (aged sixteen), Agnes (thirteen), and William (nine) joined their neighbours at Coqualeetza. Annie (aged twelve) followed in August, Maggie (just seven) in November. Their Bella Coola mother Spukh-pu-ka-num was left on her own in their Stanley Park home. The children's niece explained the reasons, as the story came down through the family:

> They were all taken from the mother to Coqualeetza, an Indian residential school. She had no way of supporting them, there was no welfare, she had berries in her garden and she went fishing in the inlet, caught the odd fish but that's all the income she had, and she had those five kids. So

> the government came along and said, "Well, we'd better take them to the residential school," and that's what they did. They all went.[65]

The identity of the Cummings children was even more obscured in the Coqualeetza records than were those of the others. They were recorded in the ledger without a surname and with "father's name unknown" and no information as to whether he was living or dead. Their tribal origin was, not surprisingly, given as Bella Coola. While Tim, William, and Maggie were described as without previous schooling, Agnes had attended "Vancouver Public School, 2 years & 3 months," Annie for three years. As with the others, the Cummings children in no way conformed to the stereotypes that Coqualeetza and the other residential schools were evoking to justify their existence.

Nearby Kanaka Ranch was home to a number of families composed of the first generation of native Hawaiian men employed in nearby lumber mills and mostly Squamish women. Religious affinity may have been the impetus to thirteen-year-old Seraphine McCord's enrolment. Her father had come as a gold miner; her mother Maggie was the daughter of one of the Hawaiians and of a Squamish woman. Seraphine had already attended public school for four years, but Coqualeetza gave an opportunity for her to be exposed to her father's Protestantism and perhaps also for her mother to steady a new relationship with a second husband. The Coqualeetza ledger conveniently described Seraphine, who was just one-quarter Indian by descent, as Musqueam.

Maggie did not just send her daughter to Coqualeetza; she acted as intermediary to three of her nephews and nieces enrolling a few months later in November 1894. Emma Smith (aged eleven), Bertha (nine), and Richard (five) were the three oldest children of Maggie's younger half-sister Lucy, whose father James Nahanee was another of the Hawaiians living at Kanaka Ranch. Maggie wrote to Coqualeetza's head concerning their possible admission even though they were, like her daughter Seraphine, only one-quarter Indian by descent, their father having been born in Germany. None of the three had attended school previously, perhaps because their father's occupation of steamboat engineer caused them to travel.

Convenience likely played a role in the decision by a part-Hawaiian woman to dispatch her two children by passing white men to Coqualeetza upon her marriage to another second-generation Hawaiian. The records for Frederick Halliday West and Joe Harmon, each also only one-quarter Indian by descent, were skilfully written. Ten-year-old

Freddy, who had already attended public school for several years, and his seven-year-old half-brother Joseph, both Protestant, were described by tribal origin as "Tswassen." They each stayed only a year before going home to live with their mother and stepfather, whose father had earlier lived at Kanaka Ranch.

Nor did sparse Aboriginal descent prevent two children of yet another Hawaiian, James Keamo, who had also briefly lived at Kanaka Ranch, from attending Coqualeetza. Not only were Emma (aged fourteen) and Josephine (twelve) just one-eighth Aboriginal by descent, they were Roman Catholic by religious affiliation. Young Emma had already completed the third grade and Josephine the second in public school at the time they were enrolled in Coqualeetza, making it even more puzzling as to why they were recruited and how their presence was justified. The head of Coqualeetza acted as facilitator, so he recorded in his diary,

> Thurs. 9 [June 1896]: Got off [boat] at Hammond [a small Fraser Valley community] & ... had a long talk with Keamo & his wife & got agreement signed for their two daughters Emma & Josie to come to school. The father is a Kanaka [Hawaiian].
>
> Sat. 13 [June]: We left at 8 a.m. ... Took on Emma & Josie Keamo.[66]

Stanley Park and Kanaka Ranch offspring were not the only children embodying Aboriginal interraciality at Coqualeetza. In total, 40 or more such families sent offspring there between 1894 and 1911, when the final entry was made in the school register. Some, like the Canessa and Newton offspring, were only one-quarter Indian by descent. Sons of an Italian fisherman, John and Amengo Canessa (aged fourteen and fifteen), arrived in October 1894 following their mixed-race mother's death. The register noted their religion as Catholic, their tribal identity as Kamloops. The Newtons' interracial mother, Mary Louise Lacroix, had been an early pupil at St Mary's, their father a sapper with the Royal Engineers arrived from England to build infrastructure during the gold rush. His Methodism may explain the generational shift between schools, but it was Coqualeetza's head who took the lead in getting him to move his children out of the public schools they were attending:

> April 25, 1895. Went on [river steamer] *Gladys* to Dewdney & walked to Geo. Newton (2 1/2 miles) where I had a talk with him & his wife re the five boys. Agreed to take 4 of them on condition that he would pay what

> he could toward their xpenses & we can return them home one or all at any time as we choose. Had agreement signed.[67]
>
> April 30, 1896. Came home in *Transfer* bringing ... George & Samuel Newton from Dewdney with me as pupils for the Institute.[68]
>
> June 13, 1896. It was my painful duty to inform Geo. & Sam. Newton of the death of their poor father at his home, Dewdney, yesterday morning ... Poor man! He was one of the old timer sappers & had been ill for years. He leaves a wife & 7 children the eldest only 17. George & Sam felt very bad & cried for a long while refusing to be comforted.[69]

George was aged twelve, Samuel eleven, Isaac eight, and Rosina five when they arrived at Coqualeetza in 1896; Edward was eleven and Fred five when they joined them there in 1897. By 1899 their mother had remarried and moved them out of Coqualeetza into the local public school.

The question as to whether parents of interracial children were indeed permitted to remove them came to the fore with the sons of a Fraser Valley farmer, Mexico-born Santos Gomes, by a Fraser Valley Indian woman, who were listed in the school register as Louis and Frank Saunders and Tsoweallie by tribal origin. In September 1894 Santos Gomes made his will, appointing Coqualeetza's founding head to see "that my boys Louis and Frank are properly cared for, trained and educated" and to look after his property on their behalf until they came of age.[70] A year and a half later Coqualeetza's second head recorded in his journal,

> May 9, 1896. Old Santos Gomez [*sic*] called ... and wanted to take his boys – Louis & Frank away from school. I ... told him plainly, he could not have the boys away as he had placed them here & signed an agreement to allow them to remain till the Indian department should see fit that they shall go away. He left threatening to come & a forceful removal of the lads.[71]

It is interesting to speculate whether such agreements did in fact cover non-status children or if knowledge of the will's contents played a role in the school's refusal to permit their departure.

Whatever the circumstances by which it got and kept its pupils, Coqualeetza acted as if they all were wholly Indian, thus the report at the end of 1896 noting that "one hundred and seven Indian children have been enrolled."[72] The school repeatedly lauded pupils' progress, patting itself on the back:

> We have had several visitors who are interested in the education of Indian children. They are surprised to find these children speaking fluently in English, as in many Indian schools, one of the hardest things the teachers have to contend with in training children, is their persistence in using their own language.[73]

The staff pointed to the "squalor and filth unutterable" of the homes whence pupils came, their task being to "teach them some of the refinements of life from which they are so far removed in their own homes."[74] A visitor in 1894 came away overwhelmed, based on conversations with staff, by the "stress and trial" they endured due to "the native Indian character impregnated, as it necessarily is, with heathenism."[75] For Coqualeetza to fulfil its mandate, interracial children as well as the others had to be constructed as "wild and wandering," to quote from a Methodist promotional pamphlet, prior to their being taught the white ways with which at least some of them entered the school in the first place.[76] That duplicity was involved does not appear to have mattered.

In January 1895, federal officials were made explicitly aware of the presence of Aboriginal interraciality when a "half-breed Simsean [Tsimshian]" and three others from the British Columbian north coast were turfed out by Coqualeetza. These boys' misdeeds on their way home hit the press, to embarrassment all around.[77] Responding to federal queries "relative to half-breed children attending the Coqualeetza home," the Methodist church asserted, somewhat disingenuously, that "application [of the federal regulation] will be very embarrassing, as in many of the tribes the number of children who are of pure Indian blood is very limited."[78] Possibly as an object lesson to other institutions, the Department of Indian Affair's annual published report of 1896–7 quite unusually distinguished Coqualeetza's "Indian boys and girls" from the school's "half-breeds."[79]

Coqualeetza thereafter took even greater pains to treat all its pupils as if they were wholly Indian and thereby inherently inferior.[80] As it noted in its annual report for 1897, "We are helping them to break their 'birth's invidious bar,' and to rise in the scale of being to a position religiously, socially and educationally nearer to that of our own more favoured race."[81] Lest the meaning be lost, the school's head reiterated the same point rhetorically a year later: "How much training is required to take the crookedness out of the very twigs and to make them grow straight?"[82] It was invidious, misleading, self-serving rhetoric almost certainly not limited to these three residential schools.

Consequences

The negotiation of Aboriginal interraciality in these three early British Columbian residential schools was not without consequence. Schools benefited from the presence of such pupils, whereas they lived as adults in the shadow of their experiences. The federal government was eventually compelled to effect policy changes.

St Mary's, All Hallows, and Coqualeetza needed interracial students to maintain their numbers and so fulfil their mandates. It was only in 1897 that All Hallows could report the "present difficulty is, not to secure children for the school, as in former years, when we had to go to the Indian Reservations to coax the parents into sending their children to school and the children into coming, but to find room for those who are desirous of admission."[83] The fourteen members of the second generation from Stanley Park contributed seventy-seven years of their lives to Coqualeetza, the ten Hawaiian descendants with family ties to Kanaka Ranch thirty-five years. Their 112 pupil-years of federal funding permitted Coqualeetza to maintain its public face as the largest Indian residential school in British Columbia.

Consequences for individuals mirrored those for all Indian residential school pupils. Some, like Elizabeth Willing at St Mary's, died while at school or shortly thereafter on being sent home very ill. Among others doing so were three of the fourteen Stanley Park children – two Smiths and a Cummings.

Girls in particular, but all pupils in general, might find themselves married off on leaving an Indian residential school, if not to each other then to someone else considered worthy of them. For girls, the imperative was particularly urgent, those in charge considering that it was the destiny of female pupils to become the mothers to the next "improved" generation of Aboriginal people and, more immediately, that wives had to be delivered sexually "pure" to their husbands. Josephine Humphreys had been ten years at St Mary's when she was told, in her own words written when she was eighty-five, that she "was to marry a young school boy age about 21 or so, I married June 16. my 16th birthday had not talked to the man the day I was married was the most terrible time of my life. however here I am after many changes."[84]

Another course favoured by residential schools was to train their very best pupils to teach in Indian day schools. In July 1904, Annie Cummings from Stanley Park gained high school admission and attended a nearby public high school for a couple of years while still living at Coqualeetza. The matron made a special request that, after taking "a sort of Practical Normal Course under our teachers here for three or four months," Annie "be permitted to teach an Indian school under the Methodist Missionary society." As to the reason, "she is very virtuous and though timid has a strong will and impresses every one with a sense of dignity which defies undue familiarity."[85] Coqualeetza's annual reports to the government repeatedly put Annie front and centre:

> 1906: One of our pupils has been in the high school all the year with the object of preparing herself to be a teacher. She hopes to secure a position where she may help her own people as mission teacher.
>
> 1907: One of the pupils from the school left last November to take charge of an Indian school, and is doing excellent work. She has obtained a teacher's certificate. This gives one an idea of the possibilities of the Indian children.[86]

Annie Cummings was sent to teach at a Methodist Indian day school on Vancouver Island, but her heart was not in it. For all of the rhetoric to the contrary, she was not an Indian, nor were the pupils "her own people." Annie Cummings returned home after a year to marry the brother of two of her Coqualeetza classmates.

A linked option was to apprentice departing students, boys into farming and girls into domestic service, to teach them white people's ways and also to inculcate deference to their supposed betters. Rosie Oppenheim, on leaving All Hallows, was dispatched to Vancouver to work as a nursemaid and while there met and married a young Englishman employed as a teamster.[87]

While it is difficult to assess life-course consequences for residential schools' interracial students as compared to how their lives might otherwise have unfolded, Rosie Oppenheim for one "cherished her years at All Hallows." The sisters' cultivation of her musical ability gave her a skill she shared all her life that cut across the usual divides. Very importantly, as recalled by a granddaughter who grew up in her care, Rosie determinedly "lived all her life in a manner of which the nuns of All Hallows would have been proud."[88] It was in this sense not so much the distinctive setting that mattered as it was the commitment and dedication of those in whose care pupils were put to treat them as the fellow human beings they were, as it was with the Merrifield children from North Vancouver at St Mary's.

The inclusion of interracial pupils in Indian residential schools rebounded not only on individual students but also on the Department of Indian Affairs and hence back to the schools themselves. It became increasingly clear that the large and exemplary Coqualeetza had crossed too many lines for the Department of Indian Affairs to continue to look the other way. By early 1897 the school was being scrutinized, not just for the presence of interracial pupils but also for its willingness, indeed eagerness, to accept Roman Catholic children in the face of nearby St Mary's repeated demands that they be enrolled there. In the spring of 1899, after three years at Coqualeetza, the Keamo daughters were "discharged as Roman Catholics by order of the Department" of Indian Affairs. With others, it was their sparse Indian credentials that caught them up. In 1901, the three Kanaka Ranch Smiths, just one-quarter Indian by descent, were "returned" home. The notation at the end of their entries read simply, "Non-Indian." In 1907, Coqualeetza's situation was resolved for the moment by the Department of Indian Affairs adopting a dual policy whereby the school acknowledged eight "halfbreed children for whom the Government allows no Grant."[89] This list did not, however, include all the Stanley Park and other interracial children attending the school, but likely only those whose parentage had become obvious.

The 1910 annual report of the Department of Indian Affairs attempted to justify a dual role for Indian residential schools:

> The British North America Act gave to the Dominion government the burden of the Indian; and, aided materially by missionary effort, the work of education ... Not only are our schools every day removing intelligent Indian children from evil surroundings, but they are very often ministering to a class which would be outcasts without such aid; I refer to the illegitimate offspring of white men and Indian women who are thrown upon their mothers for support, and who have no legal status as Indians. This great charitable work, which parallels the efforts put forth by white communities, aided by provincial, municipal or private endowment, must be carried on by the Dominion government, aided by Christian missionaries and missionary societies.[90]

The argument that interracial offspring in attendance were almost by definition illegitimate, without paternal support, and thereby able to be considered Indians by default did not reflect the reality in the three British Columbian schools. It was, however, a perspective on human relationships in line with the racism endemic at this time.

A year later the federal government did tighten its regulations. The management of Indian boarding schools had to agree, in the contracts they signed with the Department of Indian Affairs, that

> No Half-breed child shall be admitted to the said school unless Indian children cannot be obtained to complete the number authorized ... in which event the Superintendent General may in his discretion permit the admission of any Half-breed child; but the Superintendent General will not pay any grant for any such Half-breed pupil ... nor any part of the cost of its maintenance or education whatever.[91]

In line with this new policy came the acknowledgment two years later, in 1913, that at All Hallows, "there is one quarter-breed child at the [Indian] school; her parents pay for her."[92]

Coqualeetza long continued to slip in interracial pupils. The school carefully monitored past pupils through correspondence and periodic visits, so it is not surprising that some former pupils felt obliged to send their offspring there. The two oldest Stanley Park Smiths, who had themselves been at Coqualeetza, acquiesced. In 1909–10, they handed over five offspring, some of whom had already spent several years in Vancouver public schools. There were no pedagogical reasons, yet they were surrendered until the age of eighteen, indicating the tremendous hold that the residential school maintained over men and women subject to its precepts during their childhoods and youths. One of the families was firmly Roman Catholic, at a time when Coqualeetza was being monitored to ensure it did not enrol such children, and perhaps for that reason the children had "Methodist" put after their names in the school register.

Once again, Coqualeetza played a double hand, but this time more deliberately so than earlier. In the hopes of obtaining federal funding, the head attempted to portray these children as status Indians. Government officials were not impressed, particularly with the addition of two more Smith family members in 1914. The government memo makes clear the full extent to which, while missionaries may have been operating residential schools, the Department of Indian Affairs by now maintained very close oversight of them:

> Adelaide Smith's parents are both half-breeds living in Stanley Park near Vancouver; they never lived on an Indian reserve nor are they following the Indian mode of life. Josepha Long's father was a white man and her mother [Mary Smith] a half-breed. She has lived at Stanley Park all her

> life … Mr. Raley [principal of Coqualeetza] was informed … they could not be considered as grant earning pupils.[93]

Times had changed since the earlier negotiation of Aboriginal interraciality in British Columbia. Some educational initiatives had treated offspring as inferior whites, as with public day and board schools and the early Roman Catholic school in the Cariboo. Indian residential schools had done precisely the opposite. In their scrambles for sufficient numbers of bodies and perhaps also due to their general attitudes towards racial difference, they were content to consider Aboriginal interraciality as akin, if not identical, to Indian identity. Likely part of the reason, the boundary constructed in the mind of the dominant society between races left no room for persons in between. To be of Indian descent was to be on the other side of an abyss that could not be bridged.

The cases of St Mary's, All Hallows, and Coqualeetza demonstrate that early Indian residential schools in British Columbia, and almost certainly across Canada, were more complex institutions than they are usually considered to have been. The federal limitation of status, and thereby of federal oversight, to persons with paternally based Indian descent created an outsider category of interracial persons who did not fit neatly into a white/Indian dichotomy. These three schools operated as they did for reasons that had to do with their own priorities but also with those of interracial families. There is still much to learn about the history of Indian residential schools so powerfully laid out in J.R. Miller's *Shingwauk's Vision*.

NOTES

1 J.R. Miller, *Shingwauk's Vision: A History of Native Residential Schools* (Toronto: University of Toronto Press, 1996).
2 Stephen Harper in "The Apology Decoded," *Vancouver Sun*, 12 June 2008.
3 The multivolume reports of the Truth and Reconciliation Commission of Canada are available online.
4 Jean Barman, "Separate and Unequal: Indian and White Girls at All Hallows School, 1884–1920," in *Indian Education in Canada*, vol. 1, ed. Jean Barman, Yvonne Hébert and Don McCaskill (Vancouver: UBC Press, 1985), 110–31; reprinted in *Children, Teachers and Schools in the History of British Columbia*, ed. Jean Barman and Mona Gleason (Calgary: Detselig, 2003), 283–302.

5 A related phenomenon engaging my colleague Jan Hare and myself is the Indian girls' home which we interrogate in *Good Intentions Gone Awry: Emma Crosby and the Methodist Mission on the Northwest Coast* (Vancouver: UBC Press, 2006), showing that, as in the case of the residential schools considered here, it did not discriminate between wholly Indian and interracial girls.
6 "Supplementary Report" to British Columbia, Department of Education, *First Annual Report*, 38.
7 For details on this and other aspects of British Columbian history, see Jean Barman, *The West Beyond the West: A History of British Columbia*, 3rd. ed. (Toronto: University of Toronto Press, 2007).
8 See records of the Superintendent of Education, GR 1445, British Columbia Archives [BCA].
9 This topic is explored in Jean Barman, *Growing Up British in British Columbia: Boys in Private School* (Vancouver: UBC Press, 1984).
10 See Margaret Whitehead, *The Cariboo Mission: A History of the Oblates* (Victoria: Sono Nis, 1981), esp. 71–3, 78.
11 Vera Baker Curie, "Cariboo Pioneers: Elmores and Bakers 1858–1973," unpublished manuscript (1992), 27. Manuscript courtesy of family historian Vera Baker Curie, to whom I am very grateful.
12 British Columbia, Department of Education, *Second Annual Report on the Public Schools in the Province of British Columbia*, 1873, 8. The first superintendent of education's attitude is explored at length in Jean Barman, "Families vs. Schools: Children of Aboriginal Descent in British Columbia Classrooms of the Late Nineteenth Century," in *Family Matters: Papers in Post-Confederation Canadian Family History*, ed. Edgar-André Montigny and Lori Chambers (Toronto: Canadian Scholars' Press, 1998), 73–89.
13 John Please, teacher at Yale, to John Jessop, Superintendent of Education, Yale, 12 October 1872, in BC Superintendent of Education, Inward Correspondence, GR 1445, BCA.
14 See Terms of Union, clause 13, reproduced in Robin Fisher, *Contact and Conflict: Indian-European Relations in British Columbia, 1774–1890*, 2nd ed. (Vancouver: UBC Press, 1992), 176–7.
15 *An Act to Amend and Consolidate the Laws Respecting Indians*, assented to 12 April 1876, paragraph 3.
16 The history of St Joseph's is elaborated in Whitehead, *Cariboo Mission*, and as an Indian residential school in Elizabeth Furniss, *Victims of Benevolence: The Dark Legacy of the Williams Lake Residential School* (Vancouver: Arsenal Pulp Press, 1995).
17 Terry Glavin and Former Students at St Mary's, *Amongst God's Own: The Enduring Legacy of St. Mary's Mission* (Mission: Mission Friendship Centre

and Longhouse Publishing, 2002), 11. For another example of this claim, see Whitehead, *Cariboo Mission*, 111.

18 Department of Indian Affairs [DIA], *Annual Report*, 1875, pt. 1, 55–6.

19 Ibid., 1874, pt. 2, 9; 1875, pt. 1, 48; 1877, 141, 171; 1879, 245; 1880, 220; 1881, pt. 2, 103; 1882, 252; 1883, pt. 2, 111; 1884, 121; 1885, 123. The grant for 1880–1 was for only nine months, probably due to a shortage of students.

20 Sister Mary Theodore, "St. Mary's Mission Matsqui," [1943] typescript in Archives, Sisters of St Ann, Victoria. The archives were subsequently transferred as a discrete entity to the British Columbia Archives, Victoria.

21 Sister Mary Theodore, "Sister Mary Lumena #42," typescript in Sisters of St Ann, Victoria, Archives, RG 1, S.24, pp. 8, 10, 11, 15, 25, 42.

22 Ibid., pp. 31, 32.

23 Sister Mary Theodore, "St. Mary's Mission Matsqui," no number.

24 Report of I.W. Powell, British Columbia Superintendent of Indian Affairs, 22 November 1882, in DIA, *Annual Report*, 1882, 167.

25 I. Powell to Superintendent of Indian Affairs, Victoria, 3 March 1885, in RG 10, vol. 3694, file 14676, reel C-10121.

26 Interview with Josephine Edwards by Guy Symons, ca. 1953, Mission Community Archives; "One of Earliest Pioneers Recalls Past Pleasures," *Fraser Valley Record*, 20 February 1952. In this quotation, I have reordered her comments for coherence.

27 Census of Canada, 1881, British Columbia, 187 NWN, household 305.

28 Joseph Jones to John Jessop, Superintendent of Education, Cache Creek, 24 January 1876, Superintendent of Education, Inward Correspondence, GR 1445, BCA.

29 Alice and Muriel Crakanthorp, conversation with Major J.S. Matthews, Vancouver, 8 January 1944, in City of Vancouver Archives.

30 Sister Mary Theodore, "St. Mary's Mission Matsqui."

31 Church records, St Andrew's Catholic Church, Victoria, 1849–1934, in BCA, Add. Ms. 1. The baptismal record gives Elizabeth Willing's mother as a Cowichan woman named Julie rather than, as in the school history, a Fraser Valley woman.

32 Sister Mary Theodore, "St. Mary's Mission Matsqui."

33 Ibid.

34 Ibid.

35 M. Nicholson to S.D. Pope, Superintendent of Education, Mount Lehman, 13 July 1884, in Superintendent of Education, Inward Correspondence, BCA, GR 1445.

36 Barman, "Separate and Unequal."

37 *New Westminster Quarterly Paper*, no. 4, 1885, 24.

38 Joseph Irwin, teacher at Yale, to S.D. Pope, Superintendent of Education, Yale, 13 April 1885, in Superintendent of Education, Inward Correspondence, BCA, GR 1445.
39 See, for instance, James Fraser, secretary of Yale school board, to S.D. Pope, Superintendent of Education, Yale, 24 September 1886, in Superintendent of Education, Inward Correspondence, BCA, GR 1445.
40 British Columbia, Division of Vital Statistics, Death Registration, 1890–69758, BCA, GR 2951.
41 Rose Oppenheim Christopherson, "Just a Few Memories of Fort Yale," unpublished manuscript. Manuscript courtesy of her granddaughter Bonnie Campbell.
42 British Columbia, Division of Vital Statistics, Death Registration, 1890–69758, BCA, GR 2951.
43 A.W., New Westminster, to C.C. McKenzie, Superintendent of Education [*sic*], New Westminster, 26 January 1886, in Superintendent of Education, Inward Correspondence, BCA, GR 1445 (emphasis in the original).
44 S.D. Pope, Superintendent of Education, New Westminster, to Bishop Sillitoe, Victoria, 10 February 1886, in Superintendent of Education, Inward Correspondence, BCA, GR 1445.
45 DIA, *Annual Report*, 1888–9, xi.
46 I.W. Vowell, Indian Superintendent, to Superintendent General of Indian Affairs, Victoria, 18 April 1888, in DIA, RG 10, vol. 6042, file 165–1-1, part 1.
47 Bishop of New Westminster to E. Dewdney, Superintendent General of Indian Affairs, New Westminster, 26 September 1888, and response, 14 October 1888, in DIA, RG 10, vol. 6042, file 165–1-1, part 1.
48 P. McTiernan, Indian Agent, 12 October 1890, in DIA, *Annual Report*, 1889–90, 129.
49 Frank Devline, Indian Agent, 22 July 1895, in DIA, *Annual Report*, 1894–5, 164.
50 *East and West* (published by the Order of All Hallows in England), Ascension 1890, 32.
51 *New Westminster Diocesan Chronicle*, 1891, 858.
52 *Monthly Record* (published in England), no. 11, 1890, 6.
53 8 July 1892, entry in Bishop George Hills, diary, Anglican Provincial Synod of British Columbia and Yukon Archives, University of British Columbia.
54 *Work for the Far West*, no month, 1898, 18.
55 *All Hallows in the West* (published in British Columbia) 2, no. 3 (Christmas 1900), 64.
56 *Work for the Far West*, no month, 1896, 13.

57 Interview with May Armstrong Clayton by Marie Logan, ADD MS 151 F7, Nicola Valley Archives.

58 Interview with Mrs Mary Hickman, Chilliwack, 17 December 1983.

59 The consequence was Jean Barman, *Stanley Park's Secret* (Madeira Park, BC: Harbour, 2005), which provides more detail on the families introduced here.

60 August Jack, conversation with J.S. Matthews, 31 October 1938, in J.S. Matthews, *Conversations with Khahtsahlano* (Vancouver: City of Vancouver Archives, 1955), 107.

61 "Coqualeetza Industrial School, Admissions and Discharges," United Church Archives, Vancouver School of Theology. Where clear from the text, information taken from the register is not subsequently footnoted.

62 Lavinia Clarke in Women's Missionary Society of the Methodist Church, Canada, *Monthly Letter* 10, no. 4 (April 1894): 4.

63 Ibid., 2.

64 Adapted from exhibit 10, in Canada (Attorney General) v. Cummings, Supreme Court of Canada, Case on Appeal, RG 125, v. 123, Library and Archives Canada.

65 Olive Keamo O'Connor, conversation, 10 April 2000. I am tremendously grateful to Olive for her initiation and support of the Stanley Park project.

66 9 and 13 June 1896, entries, Ebenezer Robson, diary, BCA, R/D/R57.

67 Ibid., 26 April 1896, entry.

68 Ibid., 30 April 1896, entry.

69 Ibid., 13 June 1896, entry.

70 J.R. Bowser, barrister, to J. Sutherland, Chilliwack, 20 February 1908, and Joseph Hall to A. Sutherland, Los Angeles, 10 March 1908, in Sutherland Papers, Foreign Department, Methodist Church Society, accession no. 78.092C, box 5, file 90, in United Church Archives, Toronto.

71 9 May 1896, entry, Ebenezer Robson, diary.

72 Women's Missionary Society of the Methodist Church, Canada, *Annual Report*, 1897, lxxv.

73 Ibid., lxiii.

74 "Review of Year's Work," Women's Missionary Society of the Methodist Church, Canada, *Monthly Letter* 12, no. 5 (May 1895): 5.

75 "A Random Visit to the Coqualeetza (Indian) Institute," *Missionary Outlook* 15, no. 9 (September 1894): 135.

76 "Prayer Card Leaflet," Women's Missionary Society of the Methodist Church, Canada, *Missionary Leaflet* 8, no. 3 (March 1892): 7.

77 19 January 1895, entry, Ebenezer Robson, diary; *Colonist*, 1 March 1895; E. Robson to F. Devlin, Indian Agent, Chilliwack, 19 February 1895, in DIA, RG10, vol. 6422, file 869-1, reel C-8754.

78 Alexander Sutherland, General Secretary of Methodist Church of Canada, to Deputy Superintendent General of Indian Affairs, Toronto, 23 January 1897, in DIA, RG10, vol. 6422, file 869-1, reel C-8754.
79 Report for Fraser River Agency in DIA, *Annual Report*, 1897, 80.
80 Ibid.
81 Missionary Society of the Methodist Church of Canada, *Annual Report*, 1897, xci.
82 Ibid., 1898, xcvii.
83 *East and West*, Ascension 1897, 516.
84 Josephine Humphreys, unpublished manuscript. Courtesy of her granddaughter Rosemary George.
85 Sarah Sprott to Alexander Sutherland, 26 February 1906, file 88, box 25, accession number 78.092c, Alexander Sutherland Papers.
86 Report of principal of Coqualeetza in DIA, *Annual Report* 1906, 449; 1907, 414.
87 British Columbia, Division of Vital Statistics, Marriage Registration, 03–09–049264, BCA, GR 2962.
88 Bonnie Campbell, personal exchange, 8 July 2015. I am very grateful to Bonnie for her insights.
89 R.H. Cairns, Principal, Report of Coqualeetza School, 25 July 1907, in fonds 14, series 2, 78.083, box 25, Alexander Sutherland Papers.
90 Annual Report on Indian Education, 1 June 1910, in DIA, *Annual Report*, 1910, 273–4.
91 Copy of Contract between Department of Indian Affairs and the Management of Indian Boarding Schools, in DIA, *Annual Report*, 1911, 440.
92 Report of school inspector in DIA, *Annual Report*, 1913, 532.
93 Memo, Department of Indian Affairs, Ottawa, 30 December 1914, in DIA, RG10, v. 6422, file 869-1, reel C-8754.

Language, Place, and Kinship Ties: Past and Present Necessities for Métis Education

JONATHAN ANUIK

Mi'kmaw educational scholar Marie Battiste observes that contemporary educational research concentrates on academic performance.[1] Historians of education traditionally have studied the evolution of formal schools or those institutions with grade-promotion standards and their curricula, and have raised questions about how teachers past and present have dealt with questions of citizenship, instruction in basic academic skills, and pedagogy devised for honing interpersonal communication abilities. And while these scholars examine the effects of formal classroom instruction on Aboriginal[2] and non-Aboriginal students' success in learning,[3] this essay argues that educators must do more and must pay attention to proficiency in traditional languages, knowledge of kinship ties, and connection to place or the land, all of which inform Aboriginal identity. Such knowledge must be understood as part of Indigenous lifelong learning journeys.[4] Both scholars of education and historians have largely failed to consider how identity, self-esteem, motivation, and life aspirations shape students' lives at school. Twenty-first-century education and literacy scholars challenge us to rethink or broaden this narrow trajectory of scholarly work on Aboriginal students.[5] An exclusive focus on formal education diminishes the significant contribution of three major factors in Indigenous learning: first, ecological teachings and traditional knowledge; second, skills learned outside of the formal institutions; and third, those teachings that nourish lifelong learning in communities.

The life histories of four Métis children and youth illustrate the value of non-formal or non-standardized teachings based on narratives told in traditional languages that are rooted in place and shared by families. These life histories are a result of interviews conducted by the author, a non-Aboriginal historian interested in Métis family history and Métis understandings of childhood and lifelong learning. For two of these youth, language, place, and kinship ties boosted their self-esteem and helped them negotiate the academic and social pressures of secondary and post-secondary education. Two other individuals spent their childhoods and young adult years in families who survived removal from their homelands and whose ancestors chose, for the next three generations, to conceal their Métis heritage. These decisions, made by their parents or grandparents, resulted in identity crises for these two youth on their lifelong learning journeys. Those individuals who came from families who shared traditional teachings and language as well as information about their family history perceived that they faced less conflict with students and community members than did those whose families concealed their Métis past. Consequently, life circumstances affected these youths' lifelong learning journeys.

Language Leads to Tradition and Makes You Strong

Postcolonial scholars of education such as Battiste and S'ak'ej Henderson know that language is the gateway to the traditions and heritages shared by Indigenous peoples around the world. Proficiency in the languages of one's ancestors gives children and youth and their families access to (among other things) Indigenous educational epistemologies. One of the most authoritative commentators on Indigenous education, Tewa scholar Gregory Cajete, likens learning in Indigenous contexts to finding one's face. Cajete writes that "there is a shared body of understanding among many Indigenous peoples that education is really about helping an individual find his or her face, which means finding out who you are, where you come from, and your unique character ... That education should help you to find a foundation on which you may most completely develop and express both your heart and your face. That foundation is your vocation ... This ... is the intent of Indigenous education."[6]

However, Cajete warns that formal education which is, for the most part, designed by non-Indigenous people, does not nourish Indigenous learners' learning spirit or lifelong learning journeys.[7] Students must be able to identify with the curriculum and the teaching styles of educators. Cajete compares this identification to looking in the mirror, and he observes that when formal education neglects Indigenous knowledge, heritage, and history, students see nothing.[8] Similarly, educational psychologist Kristen Muis finds that children and youth take their own epistemological beliefs with them into classes. She states that as learners receive feedback on their journeys, their epistemological beliefs change, or they fuse comments they receive with their ways of knowing.[9] Therefore, teachers and instructors who facilitate opportunities for learners to engage with traditional languages, teachings, and lands nourish the epistemologies that directly feed into their learning spirits.

Comprehension and nourishment of the learning spirit represents the foundational work of Aboriginal lifelong learning. Four pillars support the learning spirit: respect for Indigenous teachings, comprehension of our place in creation, knowledge of our purposes in this world, and recognition of how our thoughts and actions affect everyone. Indigenous teachings emphasize that we are spirit, heart, mind, and body. We are a part of creation and we do not control it nor are we separate from it. Everyone has a purpose in this world, and all learning is tailored towards the discovery of our gifts that drive what we wish to accomplish. Finally, our thoughts and actions are propelled by energy, so learners must be considerate of how their thoughts and actions affect those around them. Although these principles emerge from reviews of literature on Aboriginal lifelong learning and are always seen by elders, old people, and traditional teachers and healers as crucial to healthy learning environments, their application in contemporary schools is inconsistent.[10] Public schools have ignored Indigenous spiritualities, and in denominational schools, teachings influenced by Christianity often replace Indigenous understandings of competency, success, and lifelong learning. Non-Indigenous teachers have assessed mental competencies, promoted rote learning, and devised standards for measurement of student success. Under the pressure to conform to these standards, conceived without input from Aboriginal leaders, students' spirits hibernated. Unfortunately, as their spirits have slept, their attention to the teachings in the schools waned.

Teaching Canadian History

Western scholars concede that the writing of Canadian history and its instruction in the classrooms of the country's schools has for some time presented a dominant grand narrative. Timothy Stanley defines grand narrative as "the stuff of the most widely circulated, 'commonsense' representations,"[11] and he identifies the Canadian Broadcasting Corporation's *Canada: A People's History*, school textbooks, and speeches from politicians as examples of this type of narrative. According to Stanley, the grand narrative of Canadian history

> begins with the arrival of Europeans[,] ... almost completely disregards non-Europeans and focuses on the progress of European resettlement, emphasizing "nation building" by far-seeing "great men" and even today, the occasional "great woman." The Confederation of four British North American colonies in 1867 is taken as its major starting point, and non-Europeans, such as Louis Riel or Elijah Harper, seem only to intrude when they block European progress ... Despite its narrative form that moves forward in time from the moment of European arrival ... grand narrative imposes an organization on the past that starts with the present and works backwards ... The narrative makes the present dominance of Europeans seem inevitable and natural ... [and] is premised on a series of exclusions, the marginalization of Aboriginal people, the infantilization of people from Quebec, and the exclusion of Africans and Asians ... because it is always told from the point of view of English Canadians.[12]

If we consider Stanley's thoughts in terms of Cajete's arguments, then these textual and audiovisual depictions of Canadian history in the classrooms contribute to the nothingness Aboriginal students see in the mirrors. Recent initiatives by Canadian educators are attempts to remedy these shortcomings in the Canadian historical narrative. For example, the Nunavut Sivuniksavut program from Algonquin College in Ottawa, Ontario, provides Nunavut high school graduates with the chance to see the history of Canada from the perspective of Inuit through their land claims history and the history of the territory in Canada.[13] However, for the most part, the predominance of the grand narrative in Canadian history erodes or damages Aboriginal learners' interest in Canadian and world history.

J.R. Miller has attempted to counter these exclusions in a number of ways, including the use of oral history. He argues that Indigenous perspectives remain absent from Indian residential schools' history because historians have privileged the official educational record of church and state. In his study of residential schools, not only has Miller supplemented that history with voices of the First Nations, Métis, and Inuit survivors, he has adopted a life story approach to reframe the narrative of education from Indigenous points of reference.[14]

Engagement with oral teachings of elders and knowledgeable Indigenous teachers can bring nuanced interpretations to bear on the history of Indigenous education in Canada. We can learn lessons such as Battiste's that all learners have, inside of them, a spirit or energy that directs the learning path they undertake. Her conception of the learning journey may be likened to Cajete's idea of finding one's face. These spirits or energies are individual entities that gravitate towards particular occupations, roles, and responsibilities in life.[15] However, Battiste and psychologists M. Chandler and C. Lalonde argue that the contemporary policy climate prescribes antidotes to the "monolithic Indigene" through top-down knowledge transfer. These solutions negate diversity in aspirations and desires on the part of learners and their diverse communities, revolve around a deficit paradigm, and seek to drag Indigenous peoples into the modern body politic.[16] In terms of education, policymakers narrowly interpret critical policy advances such as the National Indian Brotherhood's 1973 policy statement, "Indian Control of Indian Education," to mean delegation instead of autonomy.[17]

The outcome, according to Battiste, is the silencing or suppression of Aboriginal children and youth's learning spirits and energies or the catapulting of the spirit into hibernation, where it remains dormant until the conditions are ripe for its revival. Donald Taylor finds that without a strong collective identity expressed through the consensus of community leaders, learners are unable to formulate a strong personal identity or to power their self-esteem.[18] It is through the aforementioned policy interventions – founded on language, kinship ties, and place – and recognition of the learning spirit's role in lifelong learning that Aboriginal children and youth can be lifelong learners in Canada.

Policy Context

The period dealt with in this chapter is the post–Second World War era. In these years, the Government of Saskatchewan concerned itself with the integration of First Nations and Métis children and youth into the public school system. Saskatchewan was the only one of ten provinces to accept a proposition from the federal government of Louis St Laurent in 1948 to assume authority over the administration of status Indian education in lieu of church- or state-operated residential schools.[19] Saskatchewan was the only province to embrace the devolution of responsibility for First Nations education to provincial authorities; the plan was in line with the goal of the provincial government, led by Premier Tommy Douglas of the Co-operative Commonwealth Federation, to modernize northern Saskatchewan, where the majority of the province's Aboriginal population resided.[20]

A Task Force on Indian Opportunity was established, with one committee delegated to study education issues. Among its recommendations was one that supported twelve bursaries and grants for Métis youth unable to afford post-secondary education. For the students in Division IV or the high school grades, this same commitment would allow northern students who resided outside of La Ronge to obtain full financial assistance to go to school in Prince Albert, Nipawin, and other towns in north-central Saskatchewan. It also directed the provincial Department of Education to review the grants policy for northern education.[21]

For its part, the federal government attempted to assist status Indian youth transitioning to off-reserve high schools. The Indian Affairs Branch, in concert with the Anglican Church of Canada, discussed recommendations in 1967 that "where children need to leave home to continue their education a number of resources be developed including … transition centres where special emphasis will be placed on assisting the child to adapt from the Indian to the white culture … [and] hostels to provide for group care for Indian children in the urban setting."[22] Unfortunately, federal policy initiatives for Métis youth who left their communities to pursue secondary or higher learning did not exist until the 1970s. However, the Government of Saskatchewan attempted to conceive strategies designed to retain and support Métis youth in formal schooling.[23]

By the 1970s, educational administrators, curriculum planners, and teachers started to recognize the challenges that the public school system imposed on First Nations and Métis children and youth. In 1973, senior Saskatchewan Department of Education administrator D.M. McLeod wrote that "a committee of Northern Areas teachers is working on a program designed to assist Indian and Métis children [aged five to seven] in their orientation to school and to develop a language arts program that will enable them to make the transition from native language to English."[24] As well, an Early Childhood Readiness Committee for Northern Areas was formed in the early 1970s. The committee operated from the belief that children of the North were culturally different rather than deprived or disadvantaged.[25]

However, administrators and scholars never considered the impact of family ties on the success of students; instead they linked the intimacy of families and the use of traditional language and its ties to pursuits such as trapping, hunting, and fishing, which they considered outdated, unprofitable, and backwards systems of social and economic organization.[26] Historian Laurie Barron found that one of the postwar Saskatchewan government's success indicators was "the extent to which Métis children were leaving the rural areas for employment in the cities."[27] Although the provincial government recognized the obstacles Métis and First Nations students faced (i.e., racism, unemployment and underemployment, and homesickness), the proposed remedies operated under the umbrella of "progress": acquisition of English and Euro-Canadian world views concerning education, household organization, and profit accumulation. Indigenous languages were seen only as transition languages. Extended families were unnecessary holds on children and youth, and the communities represented relics of a declining northern economy.[28]

The Participants

In order to illustrate how these ideas have played out in people's lives, this paper profiles four Métis youth educated in the public school system in the post-war years: Anna, David,[29] Beverley, and Mary-Rose. All four were born between 1940 and 1961. All four students attended school in western Canada.

Anna originates in northern Manitoba, in a community "where people stayed … [and the] population was never more than 300 and could have been less."[30] The residents of the village relied on the fur trade, muskrat, and stretched-out beaver for sustenance. Family ties bound most of the residents of the community as many had migrated from the Red River Settlement in the years following the 1870 resistance. Many were pushed off their land at Red River and forced to establish communities removed from the burgeoning agrarian west. In her village, the Roman Catholic and Anglican churches ministered to the people, but the children attended public school. The village was truly isolated, as running water, electricity, and store-bought meat, fruit, and vegetables were unknown to the residents until the last decades of the twentieth century. One could leave town only once every three days when the train passed through the village bound for either Churchill or Winnipeg. Isolation and removal after the resistance allowed the residents to establish a safe community.

Anna's family did not originate in northern Manitoba. Her father was born in 1897 not far from Red River and in 1912 met her mother. The two then moved north, where Anna and her siblings were born. Anna's father spent his formative years in a family traumatized by removal and dispersion after the annexation of the Red River Settlement to Canada. Anna's mother attended residential school and suffered abuse from teachers angered by her inability to speak English.

The North promised a reprieve from prejudice; the majority of the village's residents were of Métis ancestry.

Neither the teachers at school nor Anna's family provided her and her siblings with information about her racial background or the history of the Métis. Anna's father provided her with a few shreds of knowledge. However, most of her childhood conversations with her father obscured her understanding of the past more than they informed her. She describes her father as a man who "retreated into the bush" in an attempt to cope with adversities that plagued the society outside of "the bush."[31] To her father, the village was a bush, and he was hiding out. Anna worked on the trap line with her father for weeks at a time and all he would say was "*motootoofee*, if there ever is a war in Winnipeg, come back."[32] Although the two formed a close bond facilitated by a traditional Métis occupation, she would not learn of her ancestry and heritage from her father, and the teachers were not trained in Métis history nor had they any desire to instil in the children the self-confidence and motivation to learn of their heritages. When it was time to go to high school, prejudice overpowered her fond memories of church, family, and nature.

There was no high school in Anna's village. Therefore, she had to choose from one of two high schools in nearby towns. She chose the community closest to her father and left her family's home after completing grade eight. In town, she attended a public high school and resided in a boarding home.

David's roots are in northern Saskatchewan. He is of French and First Nations backgrounds, but his mother never spoke of their First Nations side. David remembers, "I asked my cousin about my aunt; did Auntie ever speak of her Native side? No, she was ashamed. My mother never spoke of her Native side."[33] David suffered a bout of polio the summer of the year of his seventh birthday; after he recuperated, his parents sent him to a convent, where he resided for five years and attended school. When he completed grade eight, his parents sent him to a Francophone town in Saskatchewan to receive his secondary and post-secondary education from an elite private Roman Catholic college. David admits his parents were one of a privileged Métis few – persons with enough money to ensure their children had access to the best forms of formal education.[34]

Beverley and Mary-Rose grew up in the southeastern Saskatchewan towns of Sintaluta and Macoun, respectively. Beverley's grandmother cared for her. Beverley remembers that her grandmother "believed nothing was a secret ... [which she] think[s] ... kept ... [her] family very special. [And] we were told about our relations and discussed relationship matters."[35] Mary-Rose described herself as the daughter of "a Native American and a Métis woman."[36] Mary-Rose's parents separated before she started grade one, and she lived with her maternal grandfather for the majority of her formative years. However, Mary-Rose stated that her home life was stable and that she grew up comfortably.

The Difference Between Knowing and Not Knowing

Anna and David said they did not know of the rich heritage that preceded them. They came from families who attempted to pass into the newcomer society of the post-1870 or post–Red River Resistance years,[37] the era that western Canadians believed was a time of newcomer or immigrant settlement and expansion.[38] Their experiences in denominational and public education resulted in trauma.

David and Anna recall that teachers dedicated no class time to the discussion of ethnicity and current events, and both understood that their classrooms were not environments in which they could be comfortable disclosing their racial backgrounds. David believed the convent school and, later, his private Roman Catholic high school served to protect him from the "savagery" associated with "pagan" spirituality.[39] Anna remembers learning that she had to conceal her First Nations ancestry when she faced what she believed was an opportunity to become closer to her brother.

Anna had two brothers to whom she was close in age and in affinity. Brian and Chris[40] were born in the two years preceding Anna's birth, and she shared a crib with Brian. Anna, Brian, and Chris also started elementary school together at the respective ages of six, seven, and eight. When Brian informed Anna of troubles at the high school he attended, she offered him the chance to stay at her boarding home. The home manager agreed to have Brian as a boarder, but there would be one profound consequence that would permanently affect their relationship; Brian had darker skin and, very soon, Anna would learn about prejudice and racism.

In the town where Anna resided during her high school years, residents knew only "Native" and "white." "White" residents considered First Nations to be "Dirty Squaws," and the First Nations considered the "whites" to be "white trash." "Trash" and "Squaw" were the only terms the people knew to use when they distinguished each other. People judged both First Nations and whites by their skin tone, and for Anna and Brian this guide destroyed their relationship and adversely affected their family. Anna was a fair-skinned teenager in a town where the majority of persons were "white."[41]

After her brother arrived, the "whites" who welcomed her now considered her a "Dirty Squaw." She feared for her personal safety; she did not leave her boarding home after dark for fear of violence and rode her bike to school long before the other students arrived. She never joined any extracurricular activities, as she felt unaccepted by her peers once her classmates saw her with her brother and concluded she had First Nations blood. Despite her best efforts to shield herself from harm, First Nations girls from the reserve outside of the town accosted her at school and burnt her winter jacket.[42]

For his part, David knew the convent elementary school contained many students with mixed heritage, but shame led to silence and denial. David also understood the prejudice towards non-"whites" in his home hamlet but recalled many of the individuals who were victims of systemic and, at times, blatant discrimination overcame the comments and barriers and grew up to be highly successful professionals. Unfortunately, David's family heaped enormous amounts of pressure on him to be successful as a student. He suffered a nervous breakdown in his last two years of undergraduate study.[43]

David and Anna each learned that in their new homes, their mixed ancestry was not a part of themselves that they could reveal to classmates, teachers, community members, or boarding home operators. Furthermore, they found out that residents had a limited understanding of Aboriginal peoples and their heritages and histories. It was hard for Anna to figure out where she belonged because she faced the rejection by both the First Nations and the "whites" in her town; for David, suppression of an Aboriginal past was the reality of his family situation. Racism in her high school and around town adversely affected Anna's relationship with her brother Brian. Despite the closeness of their relationship, forged by play in the crib and attendance at primary school, the two grew distant. Brian fell in love with a First Nations girl from the reserve. The girl's parents disliked "whites" so Brian learned to hide his "white" (French) background from his girlfriend. When Brian left the boarding home to go to school or to see his girlfriend, he disassociated himself from his sister, a situation Anna considered painful and heartbreaking. Brian inevitably crumbled and, when he was 17, he died by suicide. In his suicide note, he reported the world was "too mean."[44] Anna said she could not discuss the circumstances of Brian's death for seven years afterward.

Anna's high school career abruptly ended. Although she was a first-rate student and maintained high marks throughout secondary school, an incident in grade 10 soured her to public education. Anna held a B in social studies, but she had a doctor's appointment that conflicted with the last class of the school year. She explained the conflict to an unreasonable teacher who threatened her with a D final grade should she not show up at class. She missed the class and returned for grade 11 to a D. Unable to rectify an unfair situation, she left the high school and the community. Therefore, Anna coped with the conflicts she faced by leaving both school and town and entering the workforce.[45]

Both Anna and David believed the pressure placed upon them by their families, teachers, and community members to conceal their heritage adversely affected their academic performance and, inevitably, their self-esteem, identity, and motivations. Anna stressed in all of my communications with her that no one knew what a Métis person was and, therefore, she knew nothing of the language, traditions, and history of the Métis Nation. Although the adults spoke Michif among themselves, they usually communicated with the children in English. In David's family, French was the dominant language of communication. Anna's family had to resettle after they were forced out of Red River, and David's family passed into the pioneer and immigrant society; their lives both became part of the larger history of progress and immigrant resettlement. Anna's family did not retain strong ties to their extended family, and David's parents forgot their Aboriginal ancestry. Both believe these gaps in their personal histories negatively affected their experiences as students of Christian and public schools. The lessons in the schools and their teachers provided no opportunity for them to see themselves in the mirror or to find their faces in formal learning.

Beverley's grandmother served as the gateway into the history of her family and its ties to the Qu'Appelle Valley of southeastern Saskatchewan. Her grandmother's honesty and openness with her when she was a child and, later, when she went to school gave her the confidence to defend the integrity of her ancestry in at least two situations: when she registered for public school and in her relationships with her teachers and her classmates.

Beverley remembers a registration form from one of the first days of her elementary school years. A question asked the students to identify the ethnic background of their families. She replied that she "couldn't fill out [the] form because she was not French but French and Cree. The teacher insisted … [I] choose one option or another. And … [I] replied 'no,' and [the] teacher replied, 'you had better fill out the form.' [I] wouldn't, and that was in grade 6, and [I] refused to sign something that was not myself."[46] Despite the pressure from the teacher to fit in to a prescribed ethnic category, Beverley refused to register for school under an ancestry to which she did not belong.

Beverley was aware of the attitudes people held towards the Métis population of her community. She remembers that although the Métis and non-Métis children grew up together and played together, some white families did not allow their children to play with the children of Aboriginal ancestry. One of Beverley's friends stated that she "did not understand why she was not allowed to play with … [me]. She would say, 'My parents think you are a dirty half-breed, but your house is always cleaner than ours.' … We did get to play together because she told her parents she was going to run away and that I had talked her out of it."[47] Beverley knew that residents of her town considered her "and several of the families to be poor. People considered us [the Métis in the community] to be poor. We didn't have a lot of things, but I didn't consider ourselves poor. We didn't have a lot of material things. We had things but we made them."[48] Beverley observes that many of the Métis children and youth lived between acceptance and contempt, inclusion and isolation. When the students in a class misbehaved, many teachers singled out the Métis children and youth in the classroom. Beverley remembered students running out of the window of the classroom once to avoid punishment from a teacher so that she was the one who faced the wrath of the teacher. However, Beverley attributed her resilience to her grandmother's love, care, and the wealth of history that she shared with her granddaughter.

Mary-Rose, too, knew that community members in her hometown of Macoun harboured animosity towards the Aboriginal families. She mentioned that people thought of all of the local Aboriginals as alcoholics or as predisposed to unemployment. However, Mary-Rose understood that her family members did not fit into such arbitrary designations:

> I knew that people were talking about other First Nations and Métis people in the community as being Souris Valley Half-Breed River Rats or something like that and, in a way, that was quite negative, of course, but

> I would say that I don't like Indian people being talked about as being shiftless and lazy, and I just said maybe there are people who are Métis who are lazy, but my family is not like that because my grandfather and all of my uncles were hard workers and they had good and decent jobs in the community. Everybody had drinking problems, every family, so it wasn't a big deal, especially in this community [she laughs]. You know when I was growing up, it wasn't just my father. He would come home with drinking partners, and there was this one guy who was Norwegian, and I know that not only Indian people got drunk [she laughs]. And then the other thing was that I had uncles, and my uncle and my grandfather were veterans, and I think that had another affect on how the community treated me because there was a great deal of respect for the veterans.[49]

Mary-Rose believes a critical point in her schooling experience came in 1955, when she was a fourth-grade student in a social studies class at a public school in Estevan, Saskatchewan, a town near her home community of Macoun. Mary-Rose and her classmates had to prepare a family tree for homework:

> I was going to school in Estevan, in a public school, where I was the only Métis child as far as I knew. The teacher asked us to do this ethnic background check. Everybody reported back on the next day. They told who they were [i.e., I am English or French]. Then it came to my turn, and I replied, "My grandmother was a Chippewa from Turtle Mountain." Then I noticed a little bit of a silence in the classroom, kind of a break in the rhythm. The teacher said to the class "well," she said, "there's really only one person in this classroom that we can say is Canadian," and of course, that was me … and because she saw it as a positive thing the students, too, thought it was a positive thing. No one bothered me, and life continued as before. I had a lot of friends and fun.[50]

This teacher satisfied two of Cajete's requirements for successful learning: Mary-Rose looked in the mirror, saw her family's history, and conveyed it to the class; she saw herself in the mirror when she looked at Canadian history and by doing this she was also able to see Canadian history from her own point of view. And the teacher reinforced her understanding of the history of Aboriginal peoples in western Canadian history by informing the students that she was indigenous to Canada and one of the First Peoples of the country. Acceptance, celebration, and nurturing by the teacher helped build Mary-Rose's confidence in her abilities as a student and positively affected her learning journey. Role models in her family aided her in combating the racial sentiments expressed by other members of her home community.

Beverley and Mary-Rose grew up in families whose members spoke Cree and Michif and shared the stories of their family's history in southeastern Saskatchewan with the children. Although Beverley's schoolteachers did not appreciate or know of her Métis heritage, her grandmother's teachings gave her the strength to endure prejudicial remarks, attitudes, and forced isolation imposed by the white majority. Mary-Rose's family shared their history with her and instilled in her feelings of pride in her family's ties to the region. Both women's families stressed the importance of formal education and were able to reinforce and sustain them throughout their learning journeys.

For Anna and David, the shame, unpleasant silences, and family conflicts drove their learning spirits into hibernation. As had Beverley and Mary-Rose, the two faced pressure in school to conform to a preconceived curriculum but unlike those two, Anna and David lacked the supports at home necessary for them to affirm their Métis ancestries. The use of Michif and Cree to share family histories compounded with the ties of their families to southeastern Saskatchewan and the presence of extended family permeated all of Beverley's and Mary-Rose's stories, but Anna's parents fled racial strife and deliberately chose not to share their language with the next generation. Even though David's parents spoke French and worshipped at the Roman Catholic Church,[51] they opted to ignore their family's Aboriginal ancestry. Anna's and David's educational paths faced disruption not because of any inability to perform in the classroom but because of the trauma they faced struggling to conform to the expectations of a dominant non-Aboriginal society. Beverley's and Mary-Rose's families nurtured their family history and thereby boosted their self-confidence and self-esteem and motivated them as they progressed through formal education; choices made by their parents helped them excel in their learning journeys and, when necessary, combat negative impressions shared by teachers, classmates, and settler townspeople.

"Strong like Two People"[52]

Contemporary educational scholars argue that Aboriginal students who succeed in formal schooling come from homes where traditional languages, ties to the land, and kinship bonds are reinforced and celebrated.[53] Their parents value formal learning and encourage their children to attend school; they provide constructive solutions to encounters their children may experience with racism. Therefore, not only do these children emerge with the skills needed to persevere in formal learning and to find their faces and their vocations, they and their families develop resilience.[54]

Beverley's and Mary-Rose's families taught their history and language to the children and ensured that they went to public schools. In 1932, Beverley's recently widowed grandmother moved her children out of the Qu'Appelle Valley and into Sintaluta, Saskatchewan. Her grandmother later recalled that the move was to enable her children to be educated.[55] In Mary-Rose's family, her maternal grandfather ensured Mary-Rose went to school:

> I lived with him the most after I started school. He made sure I got to school. It was quite a struggle for him because we lived two-and-a-half miles at the end of a prairie trail. Therefore, the school bus couldn't even come to our place. He would have to get me to the school bus stop by himself. He had a variety of ways to get there. He had an old Model T car. I remember helping him start it in the mornings. I would hold something by the steering wheel, and he would crank, and away we would go, and he would drive me to the bus stop [she laughs]. The other way was the sleigh. He would have to get up pretty early, in the dark, and get out there and hitch up the horses and get me over to the school bus stop. Later, they had to pay someone for me to live in town, for a while, when I was in grade two and grade three.[56]

Beverley's and Mary-Rose's grandparents stressed the value of formal education for their children. Conversely, David's and Anna's families stressed formal learning but ignored the rich Métis and First Nations heritages that preceded them; instead, their parents emphasized learning in the English and French languages, did not discuss their family ties, and provided minimal opportunities for them to build ties to the land and a sense of place. Consequently, David and Anna perceive they did not have the opportunity, in their homes, to build the same personal strength and self-esteem that Beverley and Mary-Rose were able to in the atmosphere of their homes.

Ties to traditional languages, the land, and knowledge of kinship bonds energize students and inspire them to gravitate towards the training and occupations that attract their learning spirits. Students then graduate able to walk in both their traditional Indigenous communities and in the postcolonial and largely white or immigrant Canadian society. The four life histories in this paper illustrate how two students were able to perform well and grow in the classroom and, when necessary, defend the integrity of their ancestry. The stories here also show how children dealt with racism and the ignorance of community members, teachers, and clergy. Subsequent studies into the history of Indigenous education must consider how family and community, self-esteem, identity, motivation, and life aspirations affect student achievement in formal learning. These five dimensions add considerable texture to policy discussions concerning Aboriginal student achievement in formal schooling and, more specifically, animate the history of education of Indigenous peoples in Canada.

NOTES

The literature review for this paper was supported by the Canadian Council on Learning as part of the Aboriginal Learning Knowledge Centre's work on Animation Theme Bundle 2, "Comprehending and Nourishing the Learning Spirit." Data collection for this paper was supported by the Canada Research Chair in Native-Newcomer Relations doctoral scholarship with supplements from the Messer Fund for Research in Canadian History. I thank Marie Battiste, Mi'kmaw professor of Educational Foundations at the University of Saskatchewan in Saskatoon, Saskatchewan, Canada, for her critiques of this essay. As well, I gratefully acknowledge comments from participants at the Writing New Histories of Indigeneity and Imperialism Workshop, Winnipeg, Manitoba, 21–23 May 2008. I also thank my dissertation supervisor, J.R. Miller, and committee members Keith Thor Carlson, Valerie Korinek, Bill Waiser, Margaret Kennedy, and Jean Barman for their critiques on my doctoral dissertation "Métis Families and Schools: The Decline and Reclamation of Métis Identities in Saskatchewan, 1885–1980" in 2009. Parts of this chapter come from this dissertation. I am most grateful to the participants in this study and in particular to Beverley Worsley for her assistance with recruitment of participants.

1 Marie Battiste, personal communication, 26 August 2007. A broader approach to measuring, monitoring, and reporting on the state of learning in Canada can be found from Canadian Council on Learning (CCL), a non-profit agency funded through agreement with Human Resources and Skills Development Canada. It identified four "pillars": "Learning to Know"

("the development of skills and knowledge needed to function in the world ... [including] literacy, numeracy, critical thinking and general knowledge"); "Learning to Do" ("the acquisition of applied skills often linked to occupational success, such as computer training, managerial training and apprenticeships"); "Learning to Live Together" ("developing values of respect and concern for others, fostering social and inter-personal skills, and an appreciation of the diversity of Canadians"); and "Learning to Be" ("learning that contributes to the development of a person's body, mind and spirit. Skills in this area include personal discovery and creativity, acquired through reading, use of the internet and activities such as sports and the arts"). However, this index does not report on learners in the Yukon, the Northwest Territories, Nunavut, or status Indians living on reserves. See Canadian Council on Learning, *The 2008 Composite Learning Index* (Ottawa: Canadian Council on Learning, 2008).

2 This chapter defines Aboriginals as individuals who are of First Nations, Métis, or Inuit ancestry. I use the term "Indigenous" when I refer to colonized peoples throughout the world.

3 See Bruce Curtis, *Building the Educational State: Canada West, 1836–1871* (London: Althouse Press, 1988); J.R. Miller, *Shingwauk's Vision: A History of Native Residential Schools* (Toronto: University of Toronto Press, 1996); and Jonathan Anuik, "Forming Civilization at Red River: 19th-Century Missionary Education of Métis and First Nations Children," in *The Early Northwest*, vol. 1 of *History of the Prairie West*, ed. G.P. Marchildon (Regina, SK: University of Regina, Canadian Plains Research Center), 249–69.

4 S'ak'ej Henderson, "Insights on First Nations Humanities," *Australian Journal of Indigenous Education* 34 (2005): 143–5, 150; Nathalie Kermoal, *Un passé métis au feminin* (Quebec: Les Editions GID, 2006), 60; and Jacqueline Margaret Pelletier, "The First of All Things: The Significance of Place in Métis Histories and Communities in the Qu'Appelle Valley, Saskatchewan" (MA thesis, University of Alberta, 2006), 64, 110.

5 See Marie Battiste and S'ak'ej Henderson, *Protecting Indigenous Knowledge and Heritage: A Global Challenge* (Saskatoon: Purich Publishing Limited, 2000); S'ak'ej Henderson, "Ayukpachi: Empowering Aboriginal Thought," in *Reclaiming Indigenous Voice and Vision*, ed. Marie Battiste (Vancouver: UBC Press, 2000), 248–78; Gregory Cajete, "Indigenous Knowledge: The Pueblo Metaphor of Indigenous Education," in Battiste, *Reclaiming Indigenous Voice and Vision*, 181–91; Linda Curwen Doige, "A Missing Link: Between Traditional Aboriginal Education and the Western System of Education," *Canadian Journal of Native Education* 27/2 (2003): 144–60; and Ningwakwe George, "Aboriginal Adult Literacy: Nourishing the Learning Spirits"

(Saskatoon: University of Saskatchewan, Aboriginal Education Research Centre; First Nations and Adult Higher Education Consortium, 2008), http://www.ccl-cca.ca/pdfs/ablkc/NourishingSpirits_LitReview_en.pdf (accessed 14 July 2015).

6 Cajete, "Indigenous Knowledge," 183.

7 For a discussion of the nourishing the learning spirit concept, see Jonathan Anuik, Marie Battiste, and Ningwakwe George, "Learning from Promising Programs and Applications in Nourishing the Learning Spirit," *Canadian Journal of Native Education* 33/1 (2010): 63–82.

8 Cajete, "Indigenous Knowledge," 186.

9 Kristen R. Muis, "The Role of Epistemic Beliefs in Self-Regulated Learning," *Educational Psychologist* 42/3 (2007): 184–5.

10 Anuik, Battiste, and George, "Learning from Promising Programs."

11 Timothy Stanley, "Whose Public? Whose Memory? Racisms, Grand Narratives, and Canadian History," in *To the Past: History Education, Public Memory, & Citizenship in Canada*, ed. Ruth W. Sandwell (Toronto: University of Toronto Press, 2006), 34.

12 Ibid.

13 Nunavut Sivuniksavut, *Nunavut Sivuniksavut: A Pedagogical Profile of the Nunavut Sivuniksavut Training Program: A Successful Transition Year Program for Inuit Youth from Nunavut* (Ottawa: Nunavut Sivuniksavut, 2001), 13, 26–7.

14 Miller, *Shingwauk's Vision*; and Miller, *Reflections on Native-Newcomer Relations: Selected Essays* (Toronto: University of Toronto Press, 2004), especially the essay titled "Aboriginal Peoples and the Academy," 279–95, which uses the life history narrative approach.

15 See Marie Battiste, *Decolonizing Education: Nourishing the Learning Spirit* (Saskatoon: Purich Publishing, 2013).

16 M. Chandler and C. Lalonde, "Transferring Whose Knowledge? Exchanging Whose Best Practices? On Knowing about Indigenous Knowledge and Aboriginal Suicide," in *Aboriginal Policy Research: Setting the Agenda for Change*, vol. 2, ed. J. White et al. (Toronto: Thompson Educational Publishing, 2004), 111–23; and M. Chandler and C. Lalonde, "Suicide and the Persistence of Identity in the Face of Radical Cultural Change," presentation to the Assembly of First Nations National Policy Forum, 2005. Terese Fayden challenges the objectivity and neutrality of the 2001 US No Child Left Behind Act and finds that children learn through collaboration and copying, learning styles that contradict the perceived objectivity of standardized tests mandated in the American government policy. See Terese Fayden, *How Children Learn: Getting Beyond the Deficit Myth*

(Boulder, CO: Paradigm, 2005), especially chapter 3. Also see K. Absolon and C. Willett, "Putting Ourselves Forward: Location in Aboriginal Research," in *Research as Resistance: Critical, Indigenous, and Anti-oppressive Approaches*, ed. L. Brown and S. Strega (Toronto: Canadian Scholars' Press, 2005), 97, 106–10; C. Kapasalis, "Aboriginal Occupational Gap: Causes and Consequences," in *Aboriginal Policy Research: Moving Forward, Making a Difference*, ed. J.P. White et al. (Toronto: Thompson Educational Publishing, 2006), 87–99; Canadian Council on Learning, *Redefining How Success Is Measured* (Ottawa: Canadian Council on Learning, 2007); and National Council of Welfare, "First Nations, Métis, and Inuit Children and Youth: Time to Act," vol. 127 (Ottawa: National Council of Welfare, 2007), for arguments that Indigenous learning in modern formal schooling must grow organically, be regionally specific, and account for differences among Indigenous peoples.

17 Sheila Carr-Stewart, "A Treaty Right to Education," *Canadian Journal of Education* 26/2 (2001): 128.

18 Donald M. Taylor, *The Quest for Identity: From Minority Groups to Generation Xers* (Westport, CT: Praeger, 2002), 11–12.

19 Byron K. Plant, "'The Indian Administration Problem': Aboriginal Urbanization and Federal-Provincial Relations, 1945–1969," paper prepared for the 85th Annual Meeting of the Canadian Historical Association, York University, 29–31 May 2006.

20 David Quiring, "'The Ultimate Solution': CCF Programs of Assimilation and the Indians and Métis of Northern Saskatchewan," *Prairie Forum* 28/2 (2003): 145–60.

21 SAB, Department of Education, 87–361, R1234, 2.5, "Interprovincial Conference Instructional Materials for Children – Indian Ancestry," and "Recommendations of Education Committee Saskatchewan Task Force on Indian Opportunity and Comments by Department of Education and Northern School Board."

22 ADS, Indian Affairs Dept. – Bishop's Correspondence – 1960–1969 (I)1(f).

23 Jonathan Anuik, "'In From the Margins': Government of Saskatchewan Policies to Support Métis Learning, 1969–1979," *Canadian Journal of Native Education* 32, Supplement (2010): 83–99.

24 SAB, Department of Education, 87–361, R1234, 4.9, "Curriculum Committees, 1950–1976, Early Childhood Readiness Committee for Northern Areas, 1972–1973," D.M. McLeod to E.H. Fowlie, 9 January 1973.

25 SAB, Department of Education, 87–361, R1234, 4.9, "Curriculum Committees, 1950–1976," "Minutes of Early Childhood Readiness Committee for Northern Areas Meeting, Buffalo Narrows School, Buffalo Narrows,

Saskatchewan," Thursday, 9 November 1972, and Friday, 10 November 1972, 4; and Anuik, "In From the Margins."

26 Anuik, "In From the Margins."

27 F. Laurie Barron, *Walking in Indian Moccasins: The Native Policies of Tommy Douglas and the CCF* (Vancouver: UBC Press, 1997), 57.

28 W.D. Knill and A.K. Davis, "Provincial Education in Northern Saskatchewan: Progress and Bog-down," in *A Northern Dilemma: Reference Papers*, vol. 1, ed. A.K. Davis et al. (Bellingham: Western Washington State College, 1967), 275, 278; also Anuik, "In From the Margins."

29 Pseudonyms assigned for these two participants.

30 Anna, personal interview, 2 September 2005.

31 Ibid.

32 Ibid. *Motootoofee* translated from Michif into English means "my baby girl."

33 David, personal interview, 9 January 2006.

34 Ibid.

35 Beverley Worsley, personal interview, 24 October 2005.

36 Mary-Rose Boyer, personal interview, 26 May 2006.

37 African American scholars also identify incidents of part-time or complete passing in their family histories. For Arthe A. Anthony, passing is "a metaphor for masking the real – and most often marginalized – self" and it is accomplished through a severance of family ties. Arthe A. Anthony, "'Lost Boundaries': Racial Passing and Poverty in Segregated New Orleans," in *Creole: The History and Legacy of Louisiana's Free People of Color*, ed. Sybil Kein (Baton Rouge: Louisiana State University Press, 2000), 296–7.

38 Gerald Friesen, *The Canadian Prairies: A History* (Toronto: University of Toronto Press, 2002), 221.

39 David, interview.

40 Pseudonyms assigned for the two brothers.

41 A First Nations reserve existed across the river from the town and interactions between the First Nations people on reserve and the non–First Nations in the town were violent.

42 Anna, interview.

43 David, interview.

44 Anna, interview.

45 Ibid.

46 Beverley, interview.

47 Ibid.

48 Ibid.

49 Mary-Rose, interview.

50 Ibid.

51 I emphasize French and Roman Catholicism here because the Métis Nation and Métis identity considered the French language and Roman Catholicism to be integral to their history in the West. See Diane P. Payment, *"The Free People – Otipemisiwak": Batoche, Saskatchewan, 1870–1930* (Ottawa: Environment Canada, 1990), 21. However, in David's Francophone family, the French language and the Catholic faith were split from their Aboriginal past. Payment observes that this practice was common in northern Saskatchewan Métis families and may be seen in the 1911 Census (79). I am grateful to Brian Gettler and Sherry Farrell-Racette for these observations and the discussions concerning language, religion, and splitting.

52 Chuck Tolley, "Chief Jimmy Bruneau School," in *Sharing Our Success: More Case Studies in Aboriginal Schooling*, ed. George Fulford (Kelowna, BC: Society for the Advancement of Excellence in Education, 2007), 96.

53 See David Bell, ed., *Sharing Our Success: Ten Case Studies in Aboriginal Schooling* (Kelowna, BC: Society for the Advancement of Excellence in Education, 2004); and Fulford, *Sharing Our Success*.

54 Jacqueline Ottoman, "Princess Alexandra Community School," in Bell, *Sharing Our Success*, 225.

55 Beverley, interview.

56 Mary-Rose, interview.

PART FOUR

Law, Legislation, and History

They Have Suffered the Most: First Nations and the Aftermath of the 1885 North-West Rebellion

BILL WAISER

On 30 April 1885, Charles Tupper, the Canadian high commissioner to the United Kingdom, frantically cabled Prime Minister John A. Macdonald about a London news story claiming there had been an "indian rising" in western Canada.[1] The report was a gross exaggeration. In fact, in the weeks immediately following Métis leader Louis Riel's declaration of a provisional government at Batoche on 19 March 1885, several First Nations leaders across the west came forward and solemnly affirmed their allegiance to Queen Victoria and to the spirit of the treaties they had signed in the 1870s. Canadian officials, however, chose to ignore these declarations of loyalty in favour of portraying the 1885 North-West Rebellion as a concerted, yet futile, attempt by the First Nations and Métis to wrest control of the region away from the Canadian state. They were all traitors, united in an evil cause, and political figures like Tupper and Macdonald had good reason to worry about their seditious behaviour.

This idea of a First Nations–Métis uprising in 1885 has evolved into one of the most enduring myths in western Canadian history. And it has been expressed in many forms. In his 1910 history of the force, *Riders of the Plains*, mounted police historian A.L. Haydon observed that "both half-breeds and Indians [had been] taught a severe lesson" in 1885. "There had been war – red war, with its opportunities for fighting, for revenge, and for many other outlets of energy so dear to the primitive mind. These instincts are hard to eradicate."[2] The idea also spilled over into fiction. In *The Patrol of the Sun Dance Trail*, minister-turned-novelist Charles Gordon (Ralph Connor) had a handful of resolute Mounties facing the prospect of a First Nations' war in 1885. It was a prospect "so serious, so terrible, that the oldest officer of the force spoke of it with face growing grave and voice growing lowered."[3]

The most influential expression of the First Nations–Métis conspiracy theory has been historian George Stanley's 1936 book, *The Birth of Western Canada*. In trying to make sense of the 1885 rebellion, Stanley attributed the outbreak to a clash of cultures between primitive and more advanced peoples. "The gravest problem presented to the Dominion of Canada by the acquisition and settlement of Rupert's Land and the North-West," he observed, "was the impact of a superior civilization upon the native Indian tribes." He went on to explain how the First Nations were bewildered and frustrated by the momentous changes occurring around them and, not knowing how to respond, fell under the influence of Louis Riel and the Métis. The "Indians," according to Stanley, were "rebels" in 1885, and the only reason things did not turn out worse was because "the demands of savage democracy rendered them incapable of rapid decision." In the end, though, despite their treasonous acts, the First Nations suffered less than the Métis for their involvement; they were "punished," and rightly so, "but not with vindictive severity."[4]

Seductive in its simplicity, *The Birth of Western Canada* is generally regarded as the classic work on the rebellion – one that continues to be consulted by university students even today, more than 80 years after it was published.[5] It has also cast a long shadow over writing on the topic. Several recent books that deal with Riel and the rebellion continue to insist that Plains Cree leaders, driven by broken promises and incredible hardship, joined Louis Riel in armed struggle against the Canadian government in the spring of 1885.[6] Not only is this argument misleading, but it has prevented any sympathetic understanding and appreciation of the First Nations' role in the 1885 troubles, especially the motivations underlying their behaviour. First Nations are reduced to helpless, confused victims who saw the rebellion as their "last chance to 'rage against the dying of the light.'"[7]

This popular image is confirmed by the official record, which suggests that First Nations were anything but innocent. Twenty-eight reserves were identified as disloyal in 1885, while over 50 Indians were convicted of rebellion-related crimes.[8] Those sentenced included chiefs Big Bear and Poundmaker (two prominent Cree leaders) and eight warriors who dropped to their deaths simultaneously at Battleford on 27 November 1885 in Canada's largest mass hanging. The notion of an Indian uprising has also become ingrained in the western Canadian conscience – thanks, in no small part, to how the events have been interpreted. The original commemorative bronze plaques at rebellion sites such as Battleford and Frenchman Butte created the distinct impression that First Nations were full and willing participants.[9] This apparent involvement in the rebellion was also one of several factors that delayed the resolution of long-standing Indigenous grievances. It was not until the mid-1970s, for example, that the question of treaty land entitlement went forwards in Saskatchewan.[10]

Running counter to the idea of a grand First Nations–Métis alliance in 1885 is the information that has been forthcoming from First Nations elders over the last few decades, especially since the centenary of the rebellion. Overcoming a fear of continued retribution, they have quietly, though resolutely, asserted that their ancestors were not rebels and that the First Nations' role in the troubles has been sadly misrepresented or grossly misunderstood.[11] This alternative interpretation has been supported by a growing body of scholarly literature over the last quarter century – largely based, ironically, on the records of the Department of Indian Affairs and the papers of federal politicians and government officials. Its genesis, though, at least in the scholarly community, was a 1983 article in the *Canadian Historical Review*, in which John Tobias refuted the Stanley interpretation by demonstrating that the Canadian government deliberately interpreted the isolated incidents of First Nations violence as acts of rebellion in order to derail a growing Indigenous movement for renegotiation of the treaties and to make the government's policy of coercion more effective.[12] Tobias's subjugation argument generated considerable scholarly interest. It was even picked up by the *Globe and Mail*, no small achievement for an academic article. But more importantly, his findings were supported, if not enlarged upon, by a number of related studies.

Hugh Dempsey, Big Bear's biographer, described how the powerful Cree chief was interested in a peaceful resolution of First Nations' grievances and that the spontaneous action of younger frustrated warriors in early April 1885 effectively ended his political career. Along similar lines, Gerry Friesen, author of the award-winning *The Canadian Prairies*, observed that there was no Cree military movement in 1885 – let alone a First Nations and Métis uprising – and that Big Bear and Poundmaker remained "aloof" from Louis Riel. That same year, Bob Beal and Rod Macleod argued in *Prairie Fire: The 1885 North-West Rebellion*, now the standard text on the rebellion, that Ottawa was determined to punish the First Nations even though the Métis had started the agitation. A few years later, Sarah Carter, in her examination of Indian agricultural policy in western Canada, *Lost Harvests*, not only noted that most First

Nations honoured their treaty pledge not to take up arms, but also drew attention to the "often overlooked" fact that they were "equally uneasy and apprehensive" in 1885. Finally, Blair Stonechild and Bill Waiser in *Loyal till Death*, an account of the rebellion from the First Nations' point of view, insisted that the First Nations had their own strategies for dealing with their situation in 1885 and that these strategies did not involve open rebellion with the Métis. The book, according to a 2003 study of Riel in Canadian culture, "amply demonstrated how difficult it will be to continue to portray him [Riel] as an unproblematic promoter of the First Nations."[13]

Perhaps the strongest rebuttal of Stanley was made by J.R. Miller in *Skyscrapers Hide the Heavens*, one of the first comprehensive histories of Native-newcomer relations in Canada. In a chapter devoted entirely to the North-West Rebellion, Miller maintained that First Nations interests should not be confused with those of the Métis and that "a proper understanding" of the event required a careful understanding of three distinct players: the First Nations, the Métis, and Riel. He then went on to explain that even though First Nations were the one group who "had reason to rebel," their leaders sought a peaceful resolution to their grievances by pursuing a diplomatic offensive intended to force the federal government to honour its treaty pledges. It was only "a matter of coincidence," Miller continued, that a few limited and localized acts of First Nations' violence happened around the same time as the Métis resistance. But the Macdonald government responded to the apparent First Nations involvement with a number of restrictive and repressive measures. "It is almost as though a great amnesia descended on Canadians as a result of the crushing of the Indian leadership after the rising of 1885," Miller emphatically concluded. "The Indians did not rebel. Yet they have suffered the most."[14]

But exactly how the First Nations "suffered the most" in the weeks and months after the rebellion was never fully explained by Miller. He devoted only a paragraph to the First Nations' trials and even then did not mention the execution of eight warriors at Fort Battleford in late November 1885, the largest mass hanging in Canadian history.[15] Nor did John Tobias deal with the topic in any detail. He provided only a brief summary of the actions taken by federal Indian Commissioner Edgar Dewdney to complete the subjugation of the Cree by the end of 1885 and then directed the reader in a footnote to "a very good account" by Jean Larmour.[16] That account, "Edgar Dewdney and the Aftermath of the Rebellion," appeared in *Saskatchewan History* in 1980 and was based on a chapter from Larmour's 1969 MA thesis at the University of Saskatchewan (Regina campus). Larmour suggested in her article that Dewdney was faced with the challenge of restoring peace and order in the region after the rebellion and took whatever steps were necessary "to eliminate trouble" in order to "restore the confidence of the settlers." That was Dewdney's priority – ensuring that Macdonald's western settlement and development policies were realized – and his decisive action, according to Larmour, led to "the return to more normal conditions."[17] Curiously, though, the cost of these actions to the First Nations was never mentioned nor considered – simply forgotten as Miller had argued. Dewdney, it seems, was honourable, fair-minded, even just – ironically, the exact opposite of what Tobias had argued in his *Canadian Historical Review* article.

Other authors who have examined how First Nations were treated in the aftermath of the rebellion have concentrated on the trials in Regina and Battleford in the late summer and early fall of 1885.[18] This focus is understandable, given the large number of First Nations charged with rebellion crimes. Prominent among them were Poundmaker and Big Bear, who were both found guilty of treason-felony even though their trials clearly demonstrated that they had acted as peacekeepers during the rebellion. Several others received ridiculously long sentences for such offences as stealing a horse or burning a building. These convictions were part of the Macdonald administration's strategy to divert attention from its mishandling of western affairs. Primitive Native peoples, not government mismanagement, had allegedly spawned the recent unrest, and they deserved to feel the full sting of British justice.[19]

But the First Nations trials were only the *public* part of a concerted, at time vicious, campaign by the Indian Affairs Department against the Plains Cree and other western First Nations. While the Macdonald government was seen to be punishing through the courts those who had played a leading role in the troubles, Indian Affairs officials were quietly putting in place a number of repressive measures that went well beyond retribution for their part, real or imagined, in the rebellion. In order to bring the First Nations under its absolute control and supposedly prevent another uprising, the Indian Affairs Department adopted a program of coercion and interference that negated the spirit and purpose of the treaties. Centuries-old traditions and practices were to be stamped out in the interests of forced assimilation and civilization. The department also took deliberate steps to ensure its objectives by instituting a policy of rewards and punishments: those bands and individuals considered loyal were recognized, while those who supposedly had been unfaithful to the Crown were denied annuity payments (in violation of the Treaty No. 6 agreement) and, in a few cases, even their reserves. Tragically, these government measures – and the great suffering that accompanied them – were unjustified. Indeed, the story of Ottawa's private war on the First Nations substantiates Miller's claim that it was they "who lost the most by the North-West Rebellion."[20]

The Rebellion[21]

In the summer of 1884, exiled Métis leader Louis Riel had returned to Canada at the invitation of the mixed-blood and white settlers of the Saskatchewan country to secure redress for a number of grievances. At first, Riel sent petitions and letters to Ottawa, but by the late winter of 1885 he increasingly began to advocate more provocative measures in the naive belief that he could repeat the success of the Red River resistance 15 years earlier – only this time with the collective might of a grand First Nations–Métis alliance. Riel made his move on 19 March 1885, when he declared the formation of a provisional government at his Batoche headquarters and demanded the surrender of Forts Carlton and Battleford. One week later, a small Métis party under Riel's general Gabriel Dumont intercepted a combined force of North-West Mounted Police (NWMP) and civilian volunteers on its way from Carlton to confiscate guns and ammunition at a nearby Duck Lake store. From the beginning of the troubles, Riel's strategy was to take hostages, make threats, and force the Canadian government to negotiate. But the Carlton force suspected a trap that early spring morning, and the tense standoff quickly dissolved into shooting. By the time NWMP superintendent Leif Crozier ordered a retreat, he left behind twelve dead; the Métis lost four men. The police subsequently abandoned Fort Carlton and fled north to Prince Albert, where they hunkered down for the remainder of the troubles.

The battle of Duck Lake is often cited as the opening salvo in Canada's first and only civil war. The clash was significant for a number of reasons. First, it made a negotiated settlement impossible and effectively forced Riel and his Métis followers to fight a rebellion they could not win. And the reason they could not win is that the Conservative government, upon learning of Crozier's defeat, quickly mobilized a large militia force to put down the insurrection; Prime Minister Macdonald may have ignored western grievances, but war was another matter. The situation was also fundamentally different from that at Red River in 1869–70. Now, not only did Riel enjoy limited support, but more importantly, the territories were also not as isolated, thanks to the nearly completed Canadian Pacific Railway. Ottawa could consequently get thousands of men in the field in a matter of weeks. The swiftness of the government response was also motivated in part by its misguided belief that the Métis could count on First Nations' support. The Duck Lake battle had taken place on that part of the Carlton trail that ran through Beardy's reserve; First Nations men were also spotted in Métis ranks. It was easy for Canadian officials to conclude, then, that the Cree had joined forces with Riel and that they were actually dealing with a combined First Nations–Métis insurgency that could sweep across the western interior. Little did they realize that the majority of the region's First Nations wanted nothing to do with the rebellion and that most of those at Batoche had been taken there against their will. Michel Dumas, the farm instructor at the nearby One Arrow reserve and future secretary of Riel's governing council, for example, ordered the Willow Cree to slaughter their cattle and join the Métis.

This fear that the North-West Rebellion, like a prairie fire, might not be contained was fuelled by events elsewhere. Upon hearing of the Duck Lake battle, chiefs Little Pine and Poundmaker decided to lead a delegation to Fort Battleford, at the junction of the Battle and North Saskatchewan Rivers, to confirm their allegiance to the Crown and secure rations for their hungry bands. But by the time the delegation reached Battleford on 30 March 1885, all of the town's 500 residents had taken refuge in the small police stockade in the belief that incoming Cree had war-like intentions. Little Pine and Poundmaker patiently waited all day for the local Indian agent to meet with them; only when it became apparent that their mission to Battleford had been in vain did some of the delegation help themselves to provisions and other items in the abandoned stores and homes before heading back home late that night. From the vantage of the stockade, it appeared to the frightened residents that they were under siege – how else would one explain the looting if Cree intentions were peaceful? The Cree had done nothing, however, to harass the townspeople; the telegraph line, for example, was not cut. Yet this same telegraph line would be used by the beleaguered residents of the stockade to plead with Canadian authorities to send someone to rescue them before it was too late.

Three days later, the horrifying news of a massacre at the tiny hamlet of Frog Lake, along the North Saskatchewan River near the present-day

Alberta-Saskatchewan border, made things seem even worse. Chafing at the hands of a mean-spirited Indian agent, several of the more aggressive members of Big Bear's band decided to take advantage of the police defeat at Duck Lake by taking the residents of Frog Lake prisoner and helping themselves to much-needed rations. But the plan turned into a murderous rampage on the morning of 2 April 1885, when Wandering Spirit and his warriors found alcohol during their looting spree and turned their guns on their hostages. By the time Big Bear, who had been away at the start of the trouble and pushed aside by the warrior society, could stop the carnage, nine men lay dead, including the Indian agent, the farm instructor, and two Roman Catholic priests. Although the killings at Frog Lake had not been orchestrated by Riel, the link between the two *seemed* obvious; it was as if the rebellion virus had infected the entire North Saskatchewan country. The other victim that tragic morning was Big Bear's diplomatic initiative. Even though he exercised only limited authority over his followers, as chief, he was held personally responsible for the murders.

Such was the situation that faced Major General Frederick Middleton, the 60-year-old commander of the Canadian militia who was handed the task of organizing and leading the 8,000-strong punitive force against Riel. Old Fred, as he was mockingly called by his men, decided from the outset to concentrate his army's energies on the Métis stronghold at Batoche, believing that a quick knockout blow there would effectively end the rebellion. He consequently started north from Fort Qu'Appelle on 6 April with the first of the troops in the field, confident that any resistance would melt away like the spring snow once his force arrived in rebel territory. The events in the Battleford and Pitt areas, however, forced Middleton to amend his plan. On 11 April, he instructed Lieutenant Colonel W.D. Otter and his 500 men to proceed directly from Swift Current to North Battleford, instead of descending the South Saskatchewan River to Batoche as originally arranged. Another assault force would march north from Calgary to Edmonton and then eastward along the North Saskatchewan River. Middleton largely regarded these secondary columns as a security measure; his sights remained firmly fixed on Batoche.

The Métis, in the meantime, made no attempt to draw on their familiarity with the countryside and conduct a guerrilla campaign, but calmly prepared to meet the Canadian response by building an elaborate system of trenches at Batoche. This decision to lie in wait on Métis home ground was made at the urging of Riel; as a prophet with a divine mission, he believed that God was on his side and that there was nothing to fear from the approaching army. Indeed, the only action that Riel approved in the first few weeks of the campaign was the dispatch of messengers to outlying First Nations reserves with an invitation to join him. This search for First Nations recruits – by force in the case of the Whitecap Sioux at Moose Woods – was made necessary because too many of the local Métis refused to take part in the troubles. Only an estimated 250 of a total regional Métis population of some 1,500 were prepared to defend Batoche. How much military support the First Nations actually offered Riel is debatable. Not only were many aged and even more poorly armed than the Métis, but most were there reluctantly.

Middleton captured Métis headquarters on 12 May 1885 after a four-day battle that amounted to little more than a series of skirmishes. In fact, the final assault in the battle of Batoche was over in minutes, largely because the remaining defenders had all but exhausted their ammunition and were unable to offer any resistance. Many paid with their lives. Whereas Middleton lost only eight men during the four-day battle, the Batoche dead may have numbered as high as two dozen. Riel was much luckier. He had prayed for a miracle throughout the siege and had initially escaped with Gabriel Dumont, but he decided to surrender three days later in a bid to take his cause to the courts.

The fall of Batoche was the first Canadian victory of the North-West campaign. The troubles were far from over though – there was still the matter of Poundmaker and Big Bear. Following their unsuccessful pilgrimage to Battleford, the Cree had anxiously gathered on the Poundmaker reserve in early April along a creek not far from the base of Cut Knife Hill. Instead of joining the rebel cause, as events in late March had implied, the local bands were just as frightened and confused by events as the townspeople cowering in the fort. Like their white counterparts, they had essentially come together for defensive reasons. This uneasy calm was shattered following the arrival of Colonel Otter's relief column at Battleford on 24 April. Disappointed that he had not seen any action on his march north from Swift Current and determined to punish the "Indians" for their apparent siege of Battleford, Otter assembled an attack force of about 325 men, complete with two cannons and a Gatling gun, and planned to storm the sleeping Cut Knife camp in the early hours of 2 May. But people in the camp were alerted to the coming of the troops and mounted a counter-attack, which proved so effective that Otter's retreating force might have been wiped out if not for Poundmaker's restraint of the warriors.

Two days after the surprise Otter attack, the Cut Knife camp was visited again – this time by a group of Métis emissaries sent by Riel to bring the First Nations to Batoche in preparation for the showdown with Middleton. Poundmaker had steadfastly avoided such a commitment since the Métis leader's return to Canada the previous summer, but he was effectively taken prisoner and forced to go along. The Cut Knife party, however, was soon abandoned at the east end of the Eagle Hills, just south of Battleford, when the Métis agents learned of the fall of Batoche and Riel's surrender. It now fell to Poundmaker, the diplomat, to reach a settlement with Canadian authorities, and on the morning of 26 May, exactly two months after the Duck Lake skirmish, he proudly led his people into Battleford to submit to a waiting General Middleton.

That left Big Bear, who had been busy adding to his list of supposed rebellion crimes. On 15 April, less than two weeks after the brutal Frog Lake slayings, Wandering Spirit and his warriors moved against Fort Pitt in order to secure the area and gain access to much-needed food and provisions. Yet instead of attacking the defenceless post, the Cree, at Big Bear's urging, allowed the mounted police detachment to escape aboard a scow down the ice-choked North Saskatchewan River to Battleford. The remaining occupants of the post, including several families, were taken hostage and joined a growing camp, eventually numbering around 1,000 people, back at Frog Lake. Nothing more was done. The Cree made no attempt either to move eastward to Batoche or prepare for an eventual Canadian response. As in the case of the Cut Knife camp, they waited peacefully in the region to see how the rebellion would unfold.

The answer was forthcoming in the form of the Alberta Field Force headed by Major General T.B. Strange. On 20 April 1885, the 1,000-man column had left Calgary for the North Saskatchewan country and, despite encountering not a hint of resistance along the trail, marched into Fort Edmonton like liberating heroes. Not until 26 May, however, did the force finally arrive in the Fort Pitt district – just in time to interrupt a thirst dance which the Cree were holding for spiritual guidance at the base of Frenchman Butte. The arrival of the troops threw the camp into turmoil, and under Wandering Spirit's guidance, the Cree moved a few miles north to a more defensible position along the valley of Red Deer Creek. The battle of Frenchman Butte, as it was incorrectly named at the time, started on the morning of 28 May, when Strange shelled the Cree pits on the north side of the creek valley and then ordered his men forwards into the ravine. But Wandering Spirit had chosen his position well and Strange had to abandon the frontal assault in favour of using his cannon to inflict whatever damage he could; both sides eventually withdrew after a few hours of skirmishing.

The Cree were thoroughly shaken by the intensity of the assault and decided to flee north through the muskeg-riddled forest rather than face the troops again. They eventually reached the southwest corner of Loon or Makwa Lake on 2 June. But any hope of safe haven was dashed the next morning when an advance of party of about sixty men under NWMP inspector Sam Steele swooped down on the unsuspecting group and their prisoners who were camped at the lake narrows. The fight at Steele's Narrows, the final battle of the rebellion, lasted little more than half an hour, but it seemed to break any remaining resistance. The camp divided into smaller groups, which went their separate ways, while the last of the prisoners were released.

The flight of the First Nations kept the Canadian troops busy for most of June. With the capture of Riel and the surrender of Poundmaker, General Middleton was determined to apprehend Big Bear and bring the campaign to a successful conclusion, even if it meant tying up his troops for several weeks in a seemingly futile chase. He consequently moved to Fort Pitt with a large force and ordered three other columns north: Commissioner A.G. Irvine of the NWMP would march from Prince Albert to Green Lake; Colonel Otter from Battleford to Turtle Lake; and General Strange from Frog Lake to Cold Lake. But the largest manhunt in Canadian history came up empty-handed. In fact, it was only because the fugitive Cree decided that they could not wander in the northern wilderness for much longer that they either gave themselves up at the nearest community or sought asylum in the United States. These defections meant that Big Bear was effectively abandoned by the time he surrendered to authorities near Fort Carlton on 4 July; by that point, the old chief had been reduced to a shell of his former self, while his strategy for dealing with the Canadian government lay in total ruin.

Canada Responds

The Cree had never been more vulnerable in their relations with Ottawa as they were in the weeks and months after the North-West Rebellion. Canadian authorities keenly appreciated the club that Riel's activities had handed them and were determined to beat into the ground – once and forever – all remaining vestiges of "Indian" autonomy. These actions, culminating in the mass execution of eight warriors in late November 1885, went beyond punishing First Nations for their crimes and restoring the peaceful image of the western Canadian settlement frontier. Indian officials had been desperately searching for a way to destroy the treaty rights movement, which had gained unprecedented momentum during the summer and fall of 1884, and used the First Nations' apparent involvement in the rebellion to pursue a public and private campaign against them. Over fifty First Nations men were sentenced for various offences, more than twice the number of Métis convictions. As well, the Indian Affairs Department, with Prime Minister Macdonald's active compliance, privately contemplated a number of restrictive measures that amounted to an abrogation of Canada's treaty obligations. It was as if the First Nations, and not Riel and his followers, were the culprits. And Ottawa was determined to see that they were never led astray again.

Once the hostilities had ended, the bands who had been displaced for one reason or another during the rebellion wandered into the nearest community, hungry and exhausted, but relieved that the troubles had passed. They were anxious to return to some semblance of normalcy, and many gladly returned to their reserves and immediately started to work their fields and gardens.[22] Dewdney, for his part, was well aware that the majority had remained aloof from the Métis during the rebellion. In a long, reflective letter to Prime Minister Macdonald in early June 1885, with Big Bear still on the run, Canada's most senior official in the west laid the blame for much of the death and destruction over the past few weeks on the pernicious activities of Riel and his emissaries. He also severely criticized the behaviour of those settlers who had abandoned their homes in panic and confusion and, in doing so, created the false impression that the insurgents were carrying the day. "That they [the Cree] ever thought, intended or wished that the uprising should have reached the proportion it has," he emphatically told Sir John, "I do not believe."[23]

But Dewdney's understanding of the situation had its limits. In the same letter, he advised the prime minister that the "break[ing] loose" of a few bands had turned "a Half-breed revolt of small magnitude into an uprising of large dimensions." According to the commissioner, the country had come perilously close to "an Indian war from one end of the Territories to the other."[24] Dewdney realized that this assessment of the gravity of the situation was totally unrealistic and dangerously misleading. Nor was he sympathetic to the bands that had been tampered with and were innocent of any misconduct. Why should he be? Watching the conflict unfold from the territorial capital in Regina, Dewdney saw in the rebellion an unprecedented opportunity to rid himself and the Canadian government of troublesome First Nations leaders and their nagging call for revision of the treaties. Though privately he knew better, it was to his advantage to portray them as reckless allies of Riel who would cause trouble in the future unless reined in.

Dewdney's campaign against the First Nations began to take shape in mid-June. He sent three letters to the prime minister in the space of seven days. In them, he reported that Indian Agent Ansdell Macrae had found several incriminating notes that Riel had sent the Cree in the Battleford district, including the one calling on them to destroy the fort.[25] He also urged Lawrence Vankoughnet, the deputy superintendent general of Indian Affairs, to withhold annuity payments until he could determine who had "participated in anyway whatever in the late rebellion."[26] He even went so far as to suggest the breaking up of several reserves. "Some bands have violated the terms of the treaty made with them," Dewdney concluded, "and ... it will be for the govt to say what will be done with them and their reserves."

This tough talk found a receptive audience in Ottawa, and on July 3, the day before the surrender of Big Bear, Dewdney was instructed to "quietly collect evidence" against all First Nations suspected of any wrongdoing, no matter how trivial.[27] Local agents and farm instructors had already been doing this, for they looked upon the troubles as a chance to strengthen their own hands over their charges, as well as to extract a measure of revenge against recalcitrant chiefs and individuals. In the Battleford district, for example, Macrae had been visiting the outlying reserves since late May, collecting evidence and lining up witnesses for the expected trials of those who had been at Cut Knife.[28] To the south, meanwhile, in the Qu'Appelle district, Treaty No. 4 Agent Allan McDonald was demanding that the File Hills chiefs and headmen be deposed for allowing the slaughter of twenty head of cattle on the four reserves. His earlier concern for the bands' welfare, especially when the Canadian troops had first arrived in the region, had given way to intense anger and suspicion, and he wanted General Middleton to deal with them as he had with the disloyal Cree in the Saskatchewan country. There was no room in his heart for leniency. The guilty parties had to be harshly punished. "Action of this kind will settle all difficulties in the future," McDonald implored, "an example ... must be made."[29] Dewdney agreed, and at a Regina hearing in early July, two of the File Hills chiefs, Peepeekisis and Starblanket, were reprimanded for being off their reserve.[30]

Hayter Reed, Dewdney's ambitious assistant and the former Indian agent for the Battleford reserves, was given the job of determining the loyalty of the bands. Reed had been in the field since late March, spending almost two months hunkered down in Prince Albert with Mounted Police commissioner Irvine before proceeding westward to Battleford and then on to Pitt with Middleton's entourage. This experience hardened Reed's resolve – if that was possible – and he returned to Regina convinced that only a program of repression against the First Nations would set things right.[31] He was personally offended by their conduct. How dare they cast off the government hand that fed them? He also believed that they enjoyed far too much freedom and that drastic measures were necessary in order to squeeze every last savage ounce out of them. As a result, Reed tackled the task of determining who had been unfaithful with a vicious enthusiasm; all agents were called upon to submit a summary report for each band, emphasizing any transgressions.[32] He also started work on a list of recommendations for future management of the First Nations that would ultimately shape and inform his career as Dewdney's successor. The Canadian military had had their crack at subduing the Cree; now it was Reed's turn.

The Macdonald administration's plan to subdue the Plains Cree, and in the process, crush the treaty rights movement, was first given expression in early July 1885. While camped at Fort Pitt, awaiting the surrender of the Plains and Woods Cree, General Middleton issued a set of instructions to his soldiers regarding the treatment of incoming First Nations.[33] Although Middleton had signed the orders, they were clearly the handiwork of Assistant Indian Commissioner Hayter Reed.[34] Their intent was brutally clear – abject subordination. All guns, ammunition, horses, cattle, carts, wagons, harnesses, and even treaty medals were to be taken from the Cree. Shotguns, once branded on the stock, would be returned to the owners on the understanding that the guns were now the Queen's property and could be confiscated at any time; meanwhile, those who were found with a rifle or handgun in the future were "liable to be shot on sight."[35] All males, including chiefs and councillors, were also required to register and their future movements made fully known. Finally, no rations were to be distributed, except to those willing to work for them. "Having revolted," Reed coolly reasoned, "no doubt they have seen their way clear to earning a livelihood without aid from the Queen."[36]

Reed expanded upon these directives once he returned to Regina in anticipation of the upcoming trials. On 13 July, he submitted a draft memo to Commissioner Edgar Dewdney, in which he set forth eighteen hard-hitting recommendations for the "future management of Indians" – not just those implicated in the rebellion. Dewdney evidently endorsed the document in principle, for he was given a longer, more palatable version one week later. No amount of editorial refining, however, could blunt the thrust of the proposals. Reed first zeroed in on the pending trials and suggested that all who could be charged with a particular crime should "be dealt with in as severe a manner as the law will allow."[37] No one, especially prominent leaders, was to be exempt. He then recommended abolishing the existing tribal system and ousting rebel chiefs and councillors so that Indian Affairs employees could deal with band members on an individual basis. He also urged – on the grounds that the treaties had been "entirely abrogated by the rebellion"[38] – that annuity payments to rebel groups be suspended and that any future payments be seen as a gift, not a right. There would also be no more handouts. If Reed had his way, all "Indians" would have to work for any food and provisions not specified in the treaties. Nor would the disloyal be able to leave their reserves without first securing a permit from the local Indian Affairs Department official; in fact, to ensure that they stayed put, horses were to be confiscated and sold for cattle and other necessities. "This action," in Reed's words, "would cripple them for future rebellious movements."[39]

Most of the other recommendations in the memo dealt with particular bands. Reed suggested, for example, that the One Arrow band be stripped of its reserve and amalgamated with Beardy's, while Big Bear's followers be broken up and scattered. He also encouraged the Macdonald government to recognize loyal bands, such as Ahtahkakoop and Mistawasis, by providing them with presents. His most bizarre and shocking proposal was recommendation eight: "The leaders of the Teton Sioux who fought against the troops should be hanged, and the rest sent out of the country."[40] Reed had confused Whitecap's band, who were Santee or Eastern Sioux, with the Teton Sioux from the Upper Missouri. It was an outstanding gaffe for someone in Reed's position and underscored his profound ignorance of the situation. It also revealed how nasty Reed could be, especially since Whitecap's band had wanted no part in the rebellion and had been forced to Batoche against its will.

Reed's recommendations constituted one of the most far-reaching initiatives in the history of Indian-government relations in Canada.

They advocated an entirely new relationship with First Nations – on the government's terms. Most disturbing, though, is that the proposals became, in effect, the working policy of the Indian Affairs Department and its senior officers. Commissioner Dewdney found the measures "very desirable,"[41] and though he believed that some of the recommendations were unworkable or unrealistic, he was entirely sympathetic with the document's intent and was eager to see the ideas pursued. Nor was he alone in his thinking. There was no shortage of advice on how to handle the First Nations. John Rae, the Battleford Indian agent, regarded leniency as a sign of weakness and proposed that any chief or headman who had been involved in the fighting be shot. Otherwise, the government would be asking for more trouble in the future.[42] T.G. Jackson, a settler in the Fort Qu'Appelle district, warned that farmers would leave the region unless the military completely disarmed the First Nations. Only then, Jackson predicted, would there be a lasting peace.[43] Even the local clergy had suggestions. Drawing upon over 30 years' experience in the Northwest, mostly spent in present-day Alberta, Oblate priest Albert Lacombe put forward his own list of recommendations that were remarkably similar to the sentiments expressed in Reed's memo. He proposed that First Nations be deprived of their arms and horses and be forced to stay on their reserves and work on their farms. "Consider the Indians in all and everywhere at least for many years as real minors," Lacombe remarked at one point, sounding much like Reed. "Consequently they are not at liberty and are under the tutelage of the Government."[44]

Dewdney submitted Reed's recommendations, along with his own brief, marginal comments, to the prime minister on 1 August, the day after Riel was sentenced to death. He told Macdonald, in a matter-of-fact style, that "considerable changes would seem necessary"[45] in light of the recent unrest. It was not until some three weeks later, however, that Ottawa came to appreciate the apparent magnitude of First Nations involvement, when Dewdney provided a table listing the behaviour of nearly eighty bands during the rebellion.[46] It was an extraordinary document – in terms not only of the number of bands considered disloyal but also of how Reed had determined the classification. The assessment was more a reflection of the author's attitude and agenda than of reality. He identified twenty-eight bands as rebellious – not surprisingly, the bulk of them in the Carlton, Battleford, and Pitt agencies. Curiously, he described Beardy's band as "all disloyal," yet the chief had not been arraigned on charges as had his Willow Cree neighbour, One Arrow. On the other hand, Reed designated the Dakota band at Moose Woods as loyal, even though Chief Whitecap was awaiting trial in the Regina gaol for treason-felony. Several other bands accused of disloyalty, moreover, had been reported absent during the fighting and hence in violation of Dewdney's order of 6 May that required all First Nations to remain quietly on their reserves or be treated as rebels. That many of these people had fled their homes in fear of the Canadian troops or come together in the Frog Lake and File Hills areas did not enter into Reed's thinking. He was also prone to sweeping conclusions. Thunderchild and Sweetgrass, for example, were included simply because they were part of the Battleford agency and likely participants in the siege of the fort and the battle at Cut Knife. That their designation as disloyal was later reversed only confirmed the hastily contrived nature of the list.[47]

Reed, in the meantime, had returned to the North Saskatchewan country to restore order at the agency offices, as well as to investigate which individuals should be singled out for some kind of reward. It was evident from two letters he sent to Dewdney at the end of August that he could not resist implementing some of his measures, even though they were still under consideration in Ottawa. On 29 August, Reed reported from Battleford that he had taken away all the First Nations' ponies and branded them department property and that the police were chasing away anyone in town without a pass. Two days later, he bragged that he had cut the ration list down to forty souls. Reed justified these steps as the department's only alternative in the wake of the troubles. "Now is the time to strain every nerve and be constantly on the jump," he wrote Dewdney, "so as to prevent these Indians reverting back into their old state."[48]

"Managing" the First Nations

While this private campaign against the First Nations took shape, preparations were also under way for a series of rebellion trials in Regina and later Battleford. The first and most famous trial – both then and now – was that of Louis Riel, who was found guilty of high treason. But what is overlooked or simply ignored is the fact that eleven First Nations men had also been condemned to death by the end of the Battleford trials. Dewdney was initially worried about the handling of the executions and wired Macdonald that "any Indians sentenced to be hanged should be executed where tried. Object to hanging on reserves. Might lead to desertion of reserves. Indians very superstitious."[49] Reed, meanwhile, pushed for a public execution, even more so if the condemned could be hanged at the same time. The assistant Indian commissioner insisted that "the punishment be public as I am desirous of having the Indians witness it – no sound thrashing having been given them I think a sight of this sort will cause them to meditate for many a day and besides have ocular demonstration of the fact."[50] Reed's suggestion won out and on 27 November 1885, eight warriors went to their death on a massive gallows erected inside the walls of Fort Battleford, while dozens of people from outlying reserves were forced to witness the event. One week before the largest mass hanging in post-confederation history, Prime Minister Macdonald mused in a confidential letter to the Indian commissioner, "The executions ... ought to convince the Red Man that the White Man governs."[51]

This statement did not represent an isolated sentiment. The attitude also coloured Macdonald's reaction to Reed's "management of Indians" recommendations. His response was overwhelmingly positive, as seen by the prime minister's repeated notation – "approved," followed by his initials – on an earlier briefing document that Vankoughnet had prepared for his consideration.[52] Macdonald agreed that the tribal system should be abolished where possible, that annuity payments to rebel bands be suspended, that able-bodied Indians be required to work for any provisions, and that guns and horses be turned in on a voluntary basis. He also sanctioned the abolition of Big Bear's band, one of the largest Plains Cree groups at one time. What was particularly revealing, however, were those instances where Macdonald, at Vankoughnet's urging, took Reed's suggestions one step further. For example, Macdonald directed Dewdney to treat any "Indian" who had been implicated in the troubles as a rebel, even if the courts had found otherwise. He also ordered, despite qualms about its legality, that the proposed pass system be applied as soon as possible to all First Nations, including those who had been loyal.[53]

This heavy-handed response would perhaps be understandable, if not forgivable, had Macdonald been depending upon Dewdney and Reed for information and advice. But the prime minister knew better. In an earlier exchange with Lansdowne, he had referred to the uprising as a form of domestic trouble that did not deserve to be elevated to the rank of rebellion. The governor general bristled at the comment and chastised Macdonald, "We cannot now reduce it to the rank of a common riot. If the movement had been at once stamped out by the NWM Police the case would have been different, but we were within a breath of an Indian war."[54] A somewhat unrepentant Sir John replied in his defence, "We have certainly made it assume large proportions in the public eye. This has been done however for our own purposes, and I think wisely done."[55]

The trials and executions initiated an exodus of First Nations to the relative safety of the United States. At first, only about one hundred Cree fled to Montana in the early summer with Imasees, Lucky Man, and Little Poplar from the Frog Lake area. But once it became apparent that the Canadian government was determined to punish anyone suspected of being involved in the rebellion, the urge to leave the Northwest grew stronger. The implementation of Hayter Reed's recommendations made things even worse. In a sense, the people were pushed into exile – a phenomenon that Reed discovered in late August, when a survey of five Cree bands in the Battleford district found that close to seventy families were gone; thirty families alone were missing from the rolls of the Sweetgrass reserve, one of the bands that had originally been charged with disloyalty but subsequently exonerated.[56] Less than two months later, Grizzly Bear's Head abandoned his reserve and headed south with about one hundred Assiniboine, including many from the Lean Man and Mosquito bands.[57] Dewdney tried to stem this flow by announcing in early November that there would be a general amnesty for all First Nations, except those still wanted for the Frog Lake murders. But by the time the governor general formally approved the pardon the following summer, several hundred members of Canadian First Nations bands had sought asylum in Montana.[58]

For those bands that remained in Canada after the rebellion, the situation was equally bleak, especially if the reserve had been designated disloyal. Chiefs and councillors of so-called rebel bands were deposed, and the positions left vacant to undermine First Nations' autonomy. Many of these groups also suffered through five years without annuity payments.[59] The Chacastapasin and Young Chipewyan bands, on the other hand, were eventually stripped of their reserves in 1897 on the grounds that they had joined the rebels and then fled to the United States. They had never occupied the land before the rebellion, but officials ignored this in favour of portraying them as rebels who had been off their reserves and thereby in violation of Dewdney's May 1885 edict.[60]

One of the most tragic stories was that of the One Arrow band. In mid-January 1886, a mounted police inspector sent to investigate rumours of starvation in the Duck Lake area found instances of acute deprivation in the Métis communities, but nothing prepared him for the horrifying scene on the One Arrow reserve. When the band refused to move to Beardy's, as recommended in Reed's report, and give up their land, they were left to cope on their own – with bows and arrows and little else. "Their state ... would be impossible to exaggerate," the policeman wrote his supervisor. "They are miserable beyond description ... poorly clothed and huddled in their huts like sheep in a pen ... Last summer they lived on gophers and this winter on rabbits ... They can't go far because they have no clothes because of the severe weather."[61] He went on to describe how the wife of the imprisoned chief would often have to walk the 10 miles to Duck Lake in severe weather to get a few pounds of flour for her sick daughter. He also reported that the local agent and farm instructor had not visited the reserve in almost a year and how a few old horse blankets had been welcomed like priceless gifts. This act of kindness elicited a stern reprimand from Dewdney, who resented the interference and bluntly told the mounted police commissioner that rebel "Indians" were to be treated as such.[62]

Commissioner Dewdney was anxious to limit and regulate access to provisions and supplies in the aftermath of the rebellion, whether it be tobacco, sugar, or old horse blankets, because he saw it as an effective way to control the western First Nations. Much as a person would train a dog, loyal and obedient chiefs and bands would receive gifts and other recognition, while the uncooperative received the equivalent of a good cuff. After a few years, this system of rewards and punishments would convince the recalcitrant to behave or bring them to their knees. Either way, Dewdney won, and he was determined to push ahead with this plan once the executions were over. He consequently opposed a suggestion from General Middleton, in response to rumours that winter of another First Nations uprising, that a flying column be sent through the Saskatchewan country in the spring of 1886. He was convinced that a show of force was not the way to proceed – it would simply demoralize the Cree or, worse, cause panic and encourage more to flee. The only way to get the "Indians" to work, in Dewdney's mind, was through his subtle, though more insidious, plan.[63]

In late January 1886, the Regina office finally provided Macdonald with a detailed, itemized list of rewards for loyal chiefs and bands that amounted to over $11,000. Chiefs Mistawasis and Ahtahkakoop, for example, were each to receive $50, one gun, twenty sheep, and two oxen, while their bands were to be given an additional twenty sheep and five cows. Piapot, on the other hand, was singled out for remaining aloof from the troubles and setting an example for his band; it earned him two oxen. In the covering letter that accompanied the list, Reed justified the cost of the rewards by arguing that many of the agricultural items had been held back from the bands at the time of the treaties and that the people could now be trusted with the care of cattle and other livestock. He also indicated – in complete contradiction to what had been said publicly – that so many "Indians" had remained loyal during the troubles that only those "worthy of some marked recognition"[64] could be rewarded. The Indian department's most symbolic gesture was a proposed tour of eastern Canada by a handful of representative Cree and Blackfoot leaders that would include a meeting with the prime minister and governor general. Dewdney hoped this event would strengthen the bonds between loyal chiefs and the government and act as a deterrent to future unrest.[65]

Suffered the Most

Dewdney and Reed were able to act with such impunity after the rebellion because they had the blessing of Macdonald and his hard-line assistant, Vankoughnet. The Canadian west had failed to attract the great number of immigrants that had been enthusiastically predicted only a decade earlier, and in laying the blame for this stalled settlement, it was easy to point to the "Indians" as an obstacle. This did not mean that the Macdonald administration escaped criticism for its handling of Western affairs, and in particular its Indian policy. In the House of Commons in April 1886, Liberal Malcolm Cameron provided a devastating critique of the department, its officers, and its methods that was subsequently printed and distributed in pamphlet form. He charged that a deliberate policy of neglect, dishonesty, and starvation had driven the "Indians" to revolt. An annoyed Macdonald countered that it was Riel who had roused the First Nations and that they had no legitimate reason to revolt. Then, in what would become a standard defence of federal Indian policy over the next few decades, the prime minister laid the blame squarely on the "Indians" themselves and their slovenly ways – an argument that the government put forward in its own publication on the topic.[66] "It is a peculiarity of their race," Dewdney observed in his annual report for 1886, "to be extremely susceptible to influence, to care little for the morrow if the day satisfies their wants."[67] This kind of subterfuge suggested that Ottawa had not only been just but had met its commitments to the First Nations and then some. It also conveniently implied that the "Indians" were the problem, not the policy, and that the coercion and interference being advocated by Dewdney and Reed were necessary to bring about meaningful change.

By the first anniversary of the rebellion's end, then, Ottawa had completely transformed its relationship with the First Nations of western Canada. Choosing to ignore the limited and isolated First Nations involvement, the Macdonald government deliberately portrayed the trouble as the work of the Métis traitor Riel and his brutal Indian henchmen. They were common allies in an evil cause, rebels who had to be punished – not only for bringing the Saskatchewan country to the brink of a full-scale war but for breaking their treaty promises and turning against the very government that sustained them. Ottawa's response was swift and methodical. Indeed, the repressive measures that the Indian department introduced were unprecedented in their scope and severity. The First Nations may not have rebelled in 1885, but as Jim Miller rightly observed, they "suffered the most."

NOTES

1 C. Tupper to J.A. Macdonald, 30 April 1885, J.A. Macdonald papers, vol. 283, 129919, Library and Archives Canada [LAC].
2 A.L. Haydon, *Riders of the Plains* (1905; repr., Edmonton: Hurtig, 1971), 155–6.
3 Ralph Connor, *The Patrol of the Sun Dance Trail* (Toronto: Westminster, 1914), 12.
4 G.F.G. Stanley, *The Birth of Western Canada: A History of the Riel Rebellions* (London: Longmans, Green, 1936), 364, 378.
5 As recently as 1992, *The Birth of Western Canada* was reissued by University of Toronto Press in the Reprints in Canadian History series with a new laudatory introduction by Thomas Flanagan.
6 See, for example, Maggie Siggins, *Riel: A Life of Revolution* (Toronto: HarperCollins, 1994); and the more recent G.E. Tolton, *Prairie Warships: River Navigation in the Northwest Rebellion* (Vancouver: Heritage House, 2007).
7 J. Jennings, "The Plains Indian and the Law," in H. Dempsey, ed., *Men in Scarlet* (Calgary: Historical Society of Alberta, 1974), 65.
8 On 8 March 1885, Justice Minister John Thompson told the House of Commons that forty-four "Indians" were convicted of various rebellion-related crimes. The annual report of the North-West Mounted Police for 1885, however, indicates that fifty-five were sentenced to six months or longer for so-called rebellion crimes. Canada, House of Commons, *Debates*, 8 March 1886, 61; *Sessional Papers*, n. 8, 1886, "Report of the Commissioner of the North-West Mounted Police, 1885," appendix O.

9 Parks Canada officials are equally concerned with correcting past, one-sided accounts of the events of 1885 and have updated site interpretation, including the commemorative signage, and involved First Nations communities.

10 *Regina Leader-Post*, 28 June 1977 and 25 August 1977.

11 Interviews began to be collected in 1984–5 by Wilfred Tootoosis of the Poundmaker reserve for the Saskatchewan Indian Federated College. The results of this oral-history research program was first published in B. Stonechild, "Saskatchewan Indians and the Resistance of 1885: Two Case Studies," Saskatchewan Education curriculum resource book, 1986; and B. Stonechild, "The Indian View of the 1885 Uprising," in *1885 and After: Native Society in Transition*, ed. F.L. Barron and J.B. Waldram (Regina: University of Regina, Canadian Plains Research Center, 1986).

12 J.L. Tobias, "Canada's Subjugation of the Plains Cree, 1879–1885," *Canadian Historical Review* 64/4 (1983): 519–48.

13 H.A. Dempsey, *Big Bear: The End of Freedom* (Vancouver: Douglas & McIntyre, 1984); G. Friesen, *The Canadian Prairies: A History* (Toronto: University of Toronto Press, 1984); B. Beal and R. Macleod, *Prairie Fire: The 1885 North-West Rebellion* (Edmonton: Hurtig, 1984); S. Carter, *Lost Harvests: Prairie Indian Reserve Farmers and Government Policy* (Montreal: McGill-Queen's University Press, 1990); B. Stonechild and B. Waiser, *Loyal till Death: Indians and the North-West Rebellion* (Calgary: Fifth House, 1997); A. Braz, *The False Traitor: Louis Riel in Canadian Culture* (Toronto: University of Toronto Press, 2003), 202.

14 J.R. Miller, *Skyscrapers Hide the Heavens: A History of Indian-White Relations in Canada* (Toronto: University of Toronto Press, 1989), 170–1, 180, 188.

15 Miller did, however, write about the "coerced assimilation" of First Nations in a subsequent chapter ("The policy of the Bible and the plough"), which examined the ban of traditional religious practices, the introduction of residential schools, and the implementation of a peasant farming policy. Ibid., 189.

16 Tobias, "Canada's Subjugation," 548n101.

17 J. Larmour, "Edgar Dewdney and the Aftermath of the Rebellion," *Saskatchewan History* 23/3 (autumn 1970): 105, 117.

18 Beal and Macleod in *Prairie Fire*, for example, devote two chapters (16–17) to the trials in a section entitled "Stamping Out the Embers." D'Arcy Jenish in *Indian Fall: The Last Great Days of the Plains Cree and the Blackfoot Confederacy* (Toronto: Viking, 1999) is also largely concerned with the rebellion trials. See also Bill Waiser, "The White Man Governs: The 1885 Indian Trials," in *Canadian State Trials*, vol. 3, *Political Trials and Security Measures*,

1840–1914, ed. B. Wright and S. Binnie (Toronto: Osgoode Society for Canadian Legal History, 2009), 451–82.

19 S.E. Bingaman, "The North-West Rebellion Trials" (MA thesis, University of Regina, 1971), 3.

20 Miller, *Skyscrapers Hide the Heavens*, 188.

21 This section on the North-West Rebellion is largely taken from the author's contribution to *Canada: Confederation to Present*, CD-ROM, Chinook Multimedia, June 2001.

22 See, for example, Ansdell Macrae's report on the situation on the Battleford reserves in late May. J.A. Macrae to E. Dewdney, 10 June 1885, pt. 1A, file 1130, vol. 3584, RG 10, Indian Affairs, Government Archives Division, LAC.

23 E. Dewdney to J.A. Macdonald, 3 June 1885, 43110–18, vol. 107, Macdonald papers, LAC.

24 Tobias, "Canada's Subjugation," 538–9.

25 E. Dewdney to J.A. Macdonald, 16 June 1885, 566–67, file 38, box 2, E. Dewdney papers, Glenbow Archives [GA]; Dewdney to Macdonald, 22 June 1885, 43166, vol. 107, Macdonald papers, LAC; Dewdney to Macdonald, 23 June 1885, 43171, vol. 107, Macdonald papers, LAC.

26 E. Dewdney to L. Vankoughnet, 19 June 1885, file 1130, vol. 3584, RG 10, Indian Affairs, Government Archives Division, LAC.

27 L. Vankoughnet to E. Dewdney, 3 July 1885, ibid.

28 J.A. Macrae to E. Dewdney, 10 June 1885, pt. 1A, file 1130, vol. 3584, ibid.

29 A. McDonald to E. Dewdney, 29 May 1885, file 19550–53, vol. 3710, ibid.

30 D. Light, *Footprints in the Dust* (North Battleford, SK: Turner-Warwick, 1987), 506.

31 Carter, *Lost Harvests*, 145.

32 See, for example, the list that Agent McDonald provided for his agency, in file 19,350–51, vol. 3710, RG 10, LAC.

33 F. Middleton, "Memo Relative to Indians who may surrender at Pitt," 3 July 1885, vol. 14, Hayter Reed papers, Manuscript Division, LAC.

34 H. Reed to E. Dewdney, 23 June 1885, 43180–83, vol. 107, Macdonald papers, LAC.

35 Middleton memo, 3 July 1885, Reed papers, LAC.

36 Ibid.

37 H. Reed, "Memorandum for the Honble the Indian Commissioner relative to the future management of Indians," 20 July 1885, Dewdney papers, GA.

38 Ibid.

39 Ibid.

40 Ibid.

41 Ibid., marginal comments by Edgar Dewdney.
42 J. Rae to E. Dewdney, 18 May 1885, file 1130–1A, vol. 3584, RG 10, LAC.
43 T.G. Jackson to J.A. Macdonald, 18 May 1885, 201253–60, vol. 415, Macdonald papers, LAC.
44 A. Lacombe memorandum, n.d. (July 1885), 43240–42, vol. 107, LAC.
45 E. Dewdney to J.A. Macdonald, 1 August 1885, file 19550–53, vol. 3710, RG 10, LAC.
46 E. Dewdney to J.A. Macdonald, 21 August 1885, in ibid. (Twenty-seven-page list of band behaviour during rebellion attached.)
47 Reed also accused the Flying Dust band of disloyalty, even though James Sinclair, the HBC agent at Green Lake, reported that they had been loyal. J. Sinclair to J. Fortesque, 1 October 1888, file 1130, vol. 3585, ibid.
48 H. Reed to E. Dewdney, 29 August 1885, 1232–39, file 57, box 4, Dewdney papers, GA.
49 E. Dewdney to J.A. Macdonald, 3 September 1885, 90330, vol. 212, Macdonald papers, LAC. The prime minister immediately relayed this information to the governor general, Lord Lansdowne, who was somewhat intrigued by Dewdney's explanation but supported the recommendation. Lansdowne to J.A. Macdonald, 4 September 1885, 71811–14, vol. 174, Macdonald papers, LAC.
50 H. Reed to E. Dewdney, 6 September 1885, file 57, box 4, Dewdney papers, GA.
51 Macdonald to E. Dewdney, 20 November 1885, file 38, box 2, Dewdney papers, GA.
52 L. Vankoughnet to J.A. Macdonald, 17 August 1885, file 19,550–53, vol. 3710, RG 10, LAC. Macdonald's comments are found in the margin along with his initials.
53 L. Vankoughnet to H. Reed, 28 October 1885, in ibid. This letter was written on behalf of Macdonald.
54 Lansdowne to J.A. Macdonald, 31 August 1885, 42559–62, vol. 106, Macdonald papers, LAC.
55 J.A. Macdonald to Lansdowne, 3 September 1885, 271–72, vol. 23, Macdonald papers, LAC.
56 H. Reed to E. Dewdney, 31 August 1885, 90322–26, vol. 212, Macdonald papers, LAC.
57 K. Tyler, "The History of the Mosquito, Grizzly Bear's Head, and Lean Man Bands, 1878–1920," unpublished interim report, 5.
58 Light, *Footprints*, 532; *The Canada Gazette* 20/3 (17 July 1886): 68.
59 L. Legoff to A.A.C. La Rivière, 31 March 1889, file "Treaty Payments to Rebel Indians," vol. 18, Reed papers, LAC. A May 2015 ruling by the

Specific Claims Tribunal found that the Crown breached its lawful obligation to pay annuities to the Beardy's and Okemasis bands. Other bands are contemplating legal action.

60 See, for example, T. Pyrch, "The Chacastapasin Surrender," unpublished interim report, 1973.

61 Cuthbert to A.B. Perry, 20 January 1886, pt. 8, file 1130, vol. 3585, RG 10, LAC.

62 Ibid., Government Archives Division, Royal Canadian Mounted Police.

63 E. Dewdney to J.A. Macdonald, 26 January 1886, 90430–33, vol. 231, LAC.

64 Hayter Reed to J.A. Macdonald, 25 January 1886, 550–55, file 19, vol. 3710, RG 10, LAC.

65 E. Dewdney to J.A. Macdonald, 26 January 1886, 90430–33, vol. 213, Macdonald papers, LAC.

66 Carter, *Lost Harvests*, 130–6.

67 Canada, *Sessional Papers*, 1186, n. 4, "Annual Report of the Department of Indian Affairs," 141.

"Powerless to Protect": Ontario Game Protection Legislation, Unreported and Indetermined Case Law, and the Criminalization of Indian Hunting in the Robinson Treaty Territories, 1892–1931

FRANK J. TOUGH

Introduction: An Encounter with Justice

In July 1914, an incident occurred which captured many of the legal problems facing the Indians[1] of the Robinson Treaty territory. Moses and Barnaby Commanda (Nipissing Reserve) were charged under the Ontario Game and Fisheries Act. The events of this incident, as derived from archival evidence, make for an insightful introduction to a concealed legal history. Apparently, they were guilty of possessing twelve beaver skins and were therefore sentenced to twelve months in jail. They were also charged with assaulting game wardens in the discharge of their duties. This more serious charge was heard by Judge F.R. Latchford of the Supreme Court of Ontario (High Court Division). The Commandas were acquitted; the judge noted, "The shooting was begun by one of the game wardens, and the only wounding that took place resulted from the fact that when one of the wardens had his revolver pointed at the younger Commanda, the father struck down the revolver with a birch stick slightly injuring the game warden's hand."[2]

Latchford, who was not only a Supreme Court justice but also a former attorney general and the first Ontario Commissioner of Fisheries, was very concerned about the prior conviction for possessing beaver pelts and the severe prison sentence imposed by the magistrate. By the time Latchford heard the assault charges, the Commandas had already spent several months in jail. He pressed for their release, arguing that "a gross injustice has been done to these Indians, and they should not only be discharged from custody at once – if they have not already been discharged – , but compensation should be made [to] them for the unlawful imprisonment which they have suffered."[3] The judge's reasoning was not simply a matter of pity; in his correspondence to the attorney general he stated, "Under the Robinson Treaty, the Indians in the district in which the beaver were taken appear to have the right to hunt as their forefathers hunted prior to the making of the treaty" and "there is no doubt that the rights of these Indians under this Treaty made with her late Majesty should be sacredly regarded ... and the Robinson Huron Treaty should not, in my judgment, be regarded as *un chiffon de papier*."[4] Latchford also pressed the attorney general to have the matter of treaty hunting rights settled definitely, but he was probably unaware that in a case before the Ontario Court of Appeal, on this very question, confidential communication between the attorney general and the chief justice had resulted in delaying the proceedings.[5]

Eventually, an order-in-council released the Commandas. Latchford's correspondence to the attorney general, followed by letters from the Department of Indian Affairs and the federal Justice Department, had an effect. The Commandas were fortunate, largely because a very persuasive individual, who understood how the system worked, respected their treaty rights. While their immediate problem was resolved, provincial and federal officials were extremely reluctant to consider legally the larger issue of hunting and trapping rights. We begin with the story of the criminal prosecution of Commandas and Judge Latchford's advocacy because this encounter illustrates the resilience of the legal system at consciously dispensing with the legal rights of the Robinson Treaty First Nations. Convictions for violations of the Ontario Game and Fisheries Act, especially in the Robinson Treaty territories, had constitutional implications and the Supreme Court of Ontario twice refused to render judgment on the authority of provincial game protection legislation with respect to treaty rights. For several decades, a legal standoff existed.

Defining the Central Jurisdictional Problem

As Judge Latchford's urgent correspondence highlighted, a conflict between the solemn promises of a treaty and the enforcement of provincial laws had resulted in the unlawful imprisonment, in the judge's view, of two Robinson-Huron Treaty men. Because the 1850 Robinson Treaties protected an Aboriginal right to harvest resources by allowing "the said Chiefs and their Tribes the full and free privilege to hunt over the territory now ceded by them and to fish in the waters thereof, as they have heretofore been in the habit of doing," the imposition of provincial regulations obviously conflicted with the written version of the treaty.[6] The geographical focus of this paper on the Robinson Treaties is justified because the Province of Ontario's early success at derogating treaty hunting rights had de facto precedential effects. By the time of the Commanda convictions, the dispute between treaty rights and provincial regulations had been further exasperated by the failure of the federal government to defend its jurisdiction over Indians as provided by the British North America Act, 1867.[7] Earlier, in 1896, Indian Affairs Deputy Superintendent General Hayter Reed had lent support to treaty rights, stating, "The necessity for certain well defined limits under which such rights may be exercised is evident to the Department, in view of the possibility of the extermination of the game, yet the claims of the Indians would appear to call for very liberal treatment."[8] Later, however, Indian Affairs officials simply acquiesced to the Province of Ontario's view that its laws were not subordinate to Indian treaties. Dispensing with treaty obligations by the Crown was rationalized because Indians in particular "benefited" from game protection.

The clash between treaty hunting rights and Ontario statute law was not a matter of cultural misunderstanding or ignorance concerning the treaties.[9] As will be demonstrated, the initial development of provincial game protection legislation began with a mindful recognition of its limited authority over First Nations' hunting. However, over several decades, statutes and regulations progressively, and with cumulative effect, changed the legal framework for Indian hunting. As provincial game protection laws evolved, both in terms of the technical ability to manage wildlife harvesting and the provisions that affected First Nations, the readiness of the federal government to protect treaty rights faded.[10]

This chapter will trace the legal history of a drawn-out conflict between treaty rights and game protection, or more generally "conservation."[11] With respect to the regulation of Indian hunting, provincial control over lands and resources seemingly conflicted with the federal responsibility for "Indians," which included upholding the solemn promises of treaties negotiated with First Nations. Unlike the Department of Indian Affairs, First Nations people did not yield to the mischievous constitutional mandate claimed by Ontario; their actions slowed down the province's ability to regulate their hunting.[12] Although the authority of Game Protection Acts was challenged in court on two occasions, Ontario superior courts refused to render judgments.[13] Documentation on these unreported cases forms part of a legal history of treaty rights.

This study will survey the process by which Ontario's initial recognition of a treaty hunting right was negated by a series of prosecutions. In effect, the natural or customary activities of First Nations' livelihood was criminalized.

As the government archival records aptly demonstrate, the demise of protection for Indian hunting rights was not a case of authorities being misinformed about the ambit of treaty rights, or even a divergence between written and oral versions of the treaty. As a consequence of Ontario's opposition to hunting rights, a well-informed and profound, if somewhat hidden, debate about the legal standing of Indian treaties unfolded. The reconciliation of the need for conservation regulations with the recognition of Aboriginal and treaty rights is an old and troubling problem, and the resulting complexities are certainly not understood by merely focusing on the reported case law.[14] In this era, the federal government's responsibility for Indians conflicted with the provincial government's control over lands and resources. In point of fact, and perhaps to the surprise of today's practitioners, the substantive questions dealt with by *R. v. Sparrow* – Aboriginal resource rights, allocation of resources, and the justification requirement for infringement on Aboriginal resource harvesting – were not new legal conflicts. The measure of justice secured by this 1990 judgment was long overdue.[15]

Federal and Provincial Recognition of Indian Hunting, ca. 1892–1900

Both Ontario and the Dominion governments had greater appreciation for the validity of Aboriginal treaty rights in the late nineteenth century than in the first few decades of or perhaps the entire twentieth century. Initially, both governments tended to agree that Indians had to have access to game for subsistence purposes and that they should not have to pay for licenses.[16]

The pre-1892 legislation had been limited in scope and effect; some restrictions were placed on hunting gear and some closed seasons were designated.[17] The provisions for enforcement were very limited and there were no special statutes designed to constrain Indian hunting. Then, in the early 1890s, long-forgotten provincial legislation for the protection of game and fur-bearing animals represented a major development in the conservation of wildlife; however, despite the perceived need for protection, Indian hunting rights were recognized. With the Game Commission of 1892, major changes resulted in the institutionalization of game protection and conservation: a system of enforcement using wardens was created; more species were placed under protection through closed seasons; hunting big game now required a license; a bag limit was set for deer; hunting elk, moose, and caribou was banned; the closed season for deer was shortened; and the procedures for conviction and punishment were strengthened. Throughout the 1890s, a ban existed on trapping beaver and otter. The social force behind the legislation of the 1890s and the Game Commission of 1892 was the sportsmen. In this era, the subsistence needs of settlers and Indians were given some consideration; however, the overall accomplishment of this game protection initiative was to legitimize sport hunting.[18]

The act to amend the Act for the Protection of Game and Fur-bearing Animals, 1892, made three particular provisions for Indians.[19] Section 12 read, "The provisions of the game laws of this Province shall not apply to Indians or to settlers in the unorganized districts of this Province with regard to any game killed for their own immediate use for food only and for the reasonable necessities of the person killing the same, and his family, and not for the purposes of sale or traffic." Both Indian Affairs and the province agreed that Indians should be able to provide for their immediate needs but that hunting for the market would weaken game protection. The wording of this provision became controversial, but it might be understood as an exemption applicable to Indians throughout Ontario and for settlers in the unorganized districts only, but if narrowly construed, Indians in unorganized districts were exempted, as were settlers. Section 12 continued, "And nothing herein contained shall be construed to affect any rights specially reserved to or conferred upon Indians by any treaty or regulations in that behalf made by the government of the Dominion of Canada, with reference to hunting on their reserves or hunting grounds or in any territory specially set apart for the purpose." Hunting grounds can be understood to mean the territory ceded by treaty. This provision clearly indicates a mindful concern by the province of federal jurisdiction, and it limits the potential for any conflict between provincial regulations and treaty hunting rights. If anything, it might anticipate federal and not provincial regulations. The final concern raised by Section 12 read, "nor shall anything in this Act contained apply to Indians hunting in any portion of the Provincial territory as to which their claims have not been surrendered or extinguished."[20] This last provision demonstrates recognition of Indian title; Ontario did not claim any authority over Indian hunting in unceded territory. It limited the geographical scope of the legislation and the act was inapplicable in the non-treaty regions of the province.

As a provincial statute, Section 12 of the Ontario Game Protection Act made three important provisions: (1) restrictive regulations concerning hunting did not apply to Indians, provided they were hunting for subsistence purposes; (2) regulations could not interfere or conflict with rights reserved to Indians; and (3) the act did not apply to Indians hunting on unceded lands. In 1893, the provincial secretary explained to the Department of Indian Affairs, "I beg to state that it has been the desire of this Government to interfere as little as possible with the Indians ... in the northern portions of the Province."[21] In several respects, Ontario's process for protecting game began with a mindful respect for First Nations' interests, although the legislation understood "Indian" rights in terms of subsistence or domestic hunting.

Nonetheless, the perceived necessity for a legal division between commercial and subsistence hunting, an explicit assumption of both federal and provincial officials, was not a practical way of understanding the traditional economy; for instance, beaver meat was eaten and the pelt was sold. For centuries, Aboriginal peoples had sold game and furs to traders in order to obtain the necessities for a livelihood. The commercial and subsistence sectors of the economy were intertwined. Because of a long engagement with the fur trade, the Robinson Treaty First Nations would have understood commercially oriented hunting protected by the treaty as activities "they have heretofore been in the habit of doing." During the treaty talks, the chiefs-in-council were advised by W.B. Robinson that settler "establishments among the Indians, instead of being prejudicial, would prove of great benefit as they would afford a market for any things they have to sell."[22]

In the mid-1890s, charges involving selling moose meat and possession of furs revealed the ambiguity of provincial policies and the difficulty of regulating multipurpose use. One consequence of these prosecutions was that John M. Gibson, the commissioner of Crown lands for Ontario, adopted the position that treaty hunting rights merely secured to "Indians" access to lands and released them of the need for licenses, but that "a treaty of this nature could not bind Parliament [Ontario Legislature] so as to prevent the making of laws with reference to hunting and fishing intended for the benefit of Indians as well as for that of other persons."[23] Such an assertion appears inconsistent with the expressed statutory intention to respect treaty rights (construed to affect any rights specially reserved to or conferred upon Indians by any treaty) in the Ontario Game Protection Act, 1892.

In 1896, the Department of Indian Affairs opposed the view that Indian treaties could be subordinated to provincial legislation. Deputy Superintendent General Hayter Reed recognized a need for well-defined limits for the exercising of treaty rights but rejected categorically the argument that Indian treaty rights were subject to the Ontario Legislature. He stated that "it has always been held by this Department that a Treaty solemnly entered into between the Crown and its Indian wards and in which the national honour is pledged can not be limited, altered or annulled by an Act of the Provincial or any other legislature. It has, the Department contends, *all the force of and is as binding as any law on the Statute book*."[24] Significantly, treaties not only involved the honour of the Crown but were also legal authorities in their own right. The terms of a treaty could not be unilaterally altered. Not surprisingly, the Dominion's position on the legal force of treaty rights was not acknowledged by Ontario, and similarly, clarification sought by Indian Affairs officials on the general applicability of Indian subsistence hunting rights provided by Section 12 of the 1892 legislation remained largely unanswered. While Indian Affairs officials agreed that year-round hunting for the market would result in the extinction of game, which would adversely affect Indians,[25] in the mid-1890s they advanced a clear legal position on the treaties, affirming the political importance of treaties. They also offered to work with provincial officials towards a practical understanding of the limits of treaty rights with respect to conservation needs.

Subsequently, in the late 1890s, Ontario was able to prosecute and convict Indian hunters because Indian Affairs was unwilling to actively defend rights to protect that hunting. The central problem remained: "the right of the Indians to hunt and fish over territory ceded to them by the Crown, and as to how far the restrictions imposed by the Ontario Game Laws apply to them."[26] The conviction of Whiteduck (Golden Lake Band) represented a setback for the prospect that the Ontario Game Protection Act permitted First Nations people throughout the province to hunt for domestic purposes. A Justice Department opinion on this case stated that any conviction would be quashed by a higher court but that the legislation could easily be amended to suit the provincial policymakers.[27] In the late 1890s, charges against Commanda and the Ottawaski (Nipissing Band) raised the issue of hunting for the market. An Indian Affairs law clerk developed a forcible argument, pointing to particular irregularities in prosecution and punishment, as well as the larger issue of treaty hunting rights.[28] At this point, Indian Affairs officials understood, based on a Justice Department opinion, that treaty nations could hunt for domestic purposes and then sell hides or portions of the meat.[29] However, in this particular case it seems that the hunters had entered into a contract with surveyors to provide moose meat. Officials found such situations indefensible.[30]

The discrepancy between the legislative recognition of Aboriginal rights and treaties and the prosecutions in the late 1890s may indicate a desire not only to protect but also to reallocate resources. In 1899, Crown Lands Commissioner Gibson stated,

> I have always endeavoured to avoid taking any course that could be considered antagonistic to the true interests of the Indians, but I fear there is a sort of feeling on the part of some of the Indians that our laws do not really affect them and that in any case they will be protected against the Province by the "big Government" at Ottawa. It will never do to allow Indians to kill moose for sale … What is wanted is co-operation between your Department and our Government in the matter of having the Indians taught that their true and permanent interests are to protect the deer and moose. Bye and bye they will get good wages as licensed guides if they will only turn in and respect the law and help to protect these game animals. It is necessary that we should make an example of some of them who really know better than to openly violate the law as they do.[31]

The professed leniency, the claim to know the real interests of Indians, and threats of punitive actions remained tenets of provincial policy for decades. Moreover, Gibson expected Indians to trade off hunting for wages, thereby enhancing the prospective supply of big game to sportsmen. Regrettably, Dominion authorities were reluctant to pursue a protection of the treaty right. Not surprisingly, an Indian Affairs law clerk noted that "the divergent views of the Department of Justice and the Department of the Attorney General of Ontario in regard to the construction of the Act" had resulted in injury to Indians.[32]

Misappropriating Indian Hunting Rights, ca. 1900–14

In the first two decades of the twentieth century, Ontario asserted de facto control over Indian hunting. The Department of Indian Affairs, especially when matters were left to department secretary James Douglas McLean, abandoned any defence of treaty rights. In 1906, when an Indian requested assistance after being fined for killing a moose, McLean responded, "In reply I beg to inform you that the Department entirely fails to see that it can do anything for you in the matter since Indians who break the game or other laws do so at their own risk and the Department is *powerless to protect* them from the consequence even if it thought right to do so."[33] In the same reply, the reason for concurring with conservation laws was asserted: "As to the game laws you must remember that there is no class of the community who will ultimately benefit more from proper protection of the game than Indians."[34] Throughout the next decade, the expression "powerless to protect" was very much a mantra for McLean when Indians needed assistance. Ontario's authority over their hunting became an accepted fact; McLean asserted that "the provincial game laws apply to white men and Indians alike, and only exemption in the province of Ontario in favour of Indians is such as may be conferred by … the Game Protection Act."[35] This approach conceded a broad authority to the province. If Indians were anticipating protection from the Crown for their Aboriginal and treaty livelihood rights, it was not forthcoming from senior officials such as Secretary McLean.

Nor would Indians necessarily receive a sympathetic hearing from the Department of Indian Affairs. When Peter Stock (Wahta Band) notified the department that he had been fined for shooting a deer, contrary to his treaty rights (and the exemptions provided in provincial statutes), McLean doubted that Stock had told the whole story since "it seems hardly credible that the Magistrate … can have been in ignorance of the law."[36] McLean's correspondence indicates a major shift away from Hayter Reed's 1896 unequivocal support for treaty rights. In the department's language, treaty rights became mere "claims" and "stipulations." With respect to Indian hunting rights, McLean stated,

> This is a claim that has frequently been advanced, but, so far as the Department is aware, never successfully in Ontario, the Courts always having taken the view that the Province has sole and all the right governing game and that only exception in favour of Indians is such as may be provided by the Provincial Ordinances. It may be added that it has been held that each Province has constitutionally the rights to legislate with regard to the game, even if such legislation should clash with what may be thought by the Indians to be their Treaty rights.[37]

This position, seemingly based on a misapprehension of Justice Department legal opinions, was frequently advanced to misdirect local Indian agents and to discourage First Nations' efforts to defend their treaty rights. Ontario's constitutional authority over "Indian" hunting, that is the right of a province to change a treaty, had not in fact been determined in court. Ontario magistrates had merely enforced summary convictions.

Partly as a consequence of Indian Affairs' timid position on treaty rights, First Nations' political activism ensued. While petitions often dealt with the particulars of prosecutions, the protests were well grounded in a sense of Aboriginal and treaty rights. Typical of this era was a 1911 petition from the General Council of Indians from Robinson-Huron and Manitoulin Island bands.

> Whereas all the Chiefs residing under the Robinson-Huron Treaty and the Chiefs on the Manitoulin Island together with their respective people do claim with One Voice as being deprived of their privileges of fishing, hunting and trapping rights, according to the understanding under the Robinson-Huron Treaty and the Treaties of earlier dates, thus taking away the means of their livelihood.
>
> As the consequence of the prohibition law many of our people have suffered the penalty there of not only in fines but also in imprisonments ...
>
> We therefore, humbly submit our grievances to your Government as Guardians and trustees of the Indians for redress.[38]

Arrests, convictions, fines, confiscations, prison sentences, and requests for support for appeals produced a stream of correspondence to Ottawa. Department officials had to deal with pressure from individual members of First Nations, their lawyers, chiefs and band councils, and tribal political organizations. Many prosecutions seemed to be inconsistent with a literal interpretation of the exemptions remaining in the act.

Understandably, First Nations could no longer rely on Indian Affairs. At a meeting in September 1909 the General Council of the Rama, Georgian, and Christian Islands Indians agreed,

> Upon the discussion with the interference with our hunting, fishing and trapping rights Preserved to us and our people by our treaties it was moved ... that we in councill [*sic*] appoint Mr. J. Hugh Hammond ... Solicitor to act for us and in our name to Protect and have restored to us and our people the hunting, fishing and trapping rights that have been interfered with By the Whites lately.[39]

Officials did not welcome the independent legal expertise made available to Indians. Indian Agent S. Hagan wrote, "I am not acquainted with [the] things they complain of," which surely indicates a reason for Indians to resort to independent counsel; but for Hagan, the petition simply meant that "some lawyer, I suppose is trying to make a little money out of the Indians."[40] McLean also did not like the involvement of lawyers: "The Department is aware that certain persons for their own ends are endeavouring to mislead the Indians in regard to this and other matters, but their interventions can lead to no good results."[41] Some officials not only chose to do little to defend treaty rights, but they also tended to criticize those who advocated treaty rights. In effect, Indian Affairs capitulated to Ontario's assault on Indian hunting – it would not pay lawyers to appeal cases and it dissuaded people from hiring their own lawyers. Rather than force the legal issues, department officials wrote provincial authorities asking for special consideration for particular convictions.

Although provincial officials had become increasingly aggressive about enforcement, intergovernmental correspondence signalled other important changes. Superintendent of Game and Fisheries Edward Tinsley wrote to Indian Affairs Secretary McLean: "In reference to the Golden Lake Indians I may say that they have been slaughtering deer for years, in season and out of season, and it must cease, as they have no right to go off their Reserve killing deer as they have been in the habit of doing."[42] Tinsley professed no desire to prosecute anyone, and on some occasions he had responded favourably to requests by Indian Affairs officials for leniency. Evidently, he attached little importance to the provisions of the legislation that recognized treaty rights and he advocated restricting unregulated hunting to Indian reserves. This position was more clearly expressed in 1912: "I have taken the stand that Indians, when off their respective Reserves, have no more rights than other people. The most persistent and destructive poachers the Department has had to contend with have been Indians, many of them boasting of their treaty rights empowering them to whatever they felt inclined."[43] Apparently, he had "endeavoured to be lenient with the Indians of the Province, but forbearance has ceased to be a virtue."[44] "Poaching" was the term applied to Indian hunting by those who did not consider provisions of a treaty as a relevant legal right. The proposition to restrict hunting rights to reserves, an expansion of provincial control, was not countered or disputed by Indian Affairs officials.

After 1910, the foundations for Ontario game protection policies became more intolerant of Indian interests and rights. Kelly Evans, founder of the Game Protection Association, a sportsmen's lobby, reported in 1911 for the Game and Fisheries Commission. While this commission failed miserably in dealing with the large American Fish Trust that had dominated and then over-exploited the Great Lakes fisheries, it succeeded at targeting Indian hunting. Commissioner Evans had definite views on "Indians" and held that "one of the principal factors in the destruction of game is the Indian living in the wilder regions."[45] His concerns were expressed in racial/cultural terms:

> In the main, also, it may be said that the Indian is not an energetic person, excepting when actually engaged in the pursuit of some wild creature, nor as a rule one possessed of great perspicacity in financial matters ... in general they are loath to undertake prolonged or steady work, and what money they make disappears with astonishing rapidity, so that during a great portion of the year food is with them a question of no little moment.[46]

Evans was trying to argue that Indian domestic hunting was in excess of reasonable needs. Many "depredations" occurred because Indians held a "supreme unconcern" for laws and because of commercial gains from selling big game or furs. His report recommended that there should be "one law applicable to white man and Indian alike in regard to open seasons and bag limits on public lands" but somehow acknowledged that "the privilege to the Indian of securing a permit to take all such game as the law allowed free of charge."[47] The *Evans Report* sought to restrict Indian hunting by placing it on the same basis as non-Native or sports hunting.

Concerning beaver and otter, Evans noted that the rights of Indians "to take these animals at their pleasure and even to dispose of their pelts to the white man, have not as yet been definitely disposed of."[48] For provincial officials, Indian trapping was another problem. Consistent with his racial views, Evans saw a definite economic role for Indians:

> The nature and habits of the Indian throughout the great bulk of the Province tend to prevent his entering upon the generality of those occupations which afford a livelihood to the white man. His domain is pre-eminently the woods; his craft, that of hunter, trapper, and woodsman. In general but small advantage accrues to the community through the existence of an Indian, other than through those functions which he can discharge in his native element, the woods, while, as before observed, the pursuit of trapping is not general calculated to attract the better class of white man in the wilder regions to undertake it, but on the contrary rather to serve as

> a means of gaining a competency for the shiftless and lazy. It would, therefore, appear that while there can be no great advantage in encouraging the white man to undertake trapping as a sole or chief means of livelihood, such advantage would exist in the case of the Indian, for not only would he thus be made to contribute materially to the public welfare, but his energies would be applied in the direction most suited to them.[49]

Essentially, he championed racial stratification: whites should be discouraged from living in the bush while Indians *belong* in the woods. Thus, racial determinism replaced mindful acknowledgment of federal jurisdiction and treaty obligations. The racism of this commission is a relevant aspect of the history of the development of provincial conservation policies. Gibson's earlier recommendation that Indians become guides for sportsmen was consistent with Evans's promotion of racial stratification.

The reworking of game and fisheries regulations in 1913 and 1914 reflected the thinking of the Evans Commission. The remaining Aboriginal and treaty rights provisions were dropped or regulated through orders-in-council. The original recognition of Aboriginal hunting rights in 1892 had been reduced, by 1913, to the discretionary policies of provincial officials,[50] after which, the combined effects of changes to the act and increased prosecutions amounted to a criminalization of Indian hunting. Subsequently, and as Evans had intimated, the fur industry would become a priority area for provincial regulation.

Regulating Indian Trapping: The Hudson's Bay Company Fur Seizures, 1910–16

In terms of fur-bearers, the Evans Commission reported (without statistical or anecdotal support) that nearly all species had been seriously diminished.[51] A policy of seizing the furs acquired by the Hudson's Bay Company (HBC) coincided with the commission's work. In order for the government of Ontario to completely regulate wildlife, with the view to bringing the traditional economy under its control, the provincial state first had to erode the influence of this old mercantile company.[52] With respect to commercial hunting, Evans recommended, "A few instances of really rigorous punishment applied to both white man and Indian concerned in such a deal would undoubtedly go a long way to check the present extent of this evil."[53] Rather than confront directly the question of Indian trapping in the Robinson Treaty territories, provincial authorities went after traders possessing furs. This stratagem amounted to an evasion of the full and free privilege of the Robinson Treaty nations. The right to sell had been thwarted by making purchasing illegal.

In February 1910, G. Train, an HBC post manager, was convicted of possessing a number of beaver skins and was fined $6,393.35 or sentenced to twenty years and six months in prison.[54] Subsequently, at the district court in Sudbury, HBC counsel Leighton McCarthy based his appeal on four points of law: (1) the Robinson-Huron Treaty of 1850, and the recognition of treaty rights in the Ontario Game and Fisheries Act that gave Indians the privilege to hunt and the right to sell; (2) the act attempting to regulate Indian hunting was *ultra vires* of the Ontario Legislature since the subject of Indians and Indian Lands was reserved to the exclusive jurisdiction of the Dominion parliament by the British North America Act (BNA Act); (3) the Ontario Game and Fisheries Act was *ultra vires* of the Ontario Legislature because criminal law is reserved to the Dominion parliament by the BNA Act; and (4) when the HBC surrendered it rights to Rupertsland it was granted the liberty to carry on its trade without hindrance.[55] Clearly, the severe prison sentence in this case indicated that the Ontario Game and Fisheries Act was not merely regulatory but at least quasi-criminal. The Crown counsel was not prepared to argue constitutional law, and it was agreed that a stated case would be prepared for the Ontario Court of Appeal.

The questions to be decided in the stated case were framed by McCarthy: which portions of the Ontario Game and Fisheries Act were *ultra vires*; what were the effects of the act on the right of Indians to hunt game and to sell skins; whether Indians could lawfully possess or sell game killed during the closed season; whether purchasers could lawfully obtain skins from Indians during the closed season; and whether the act affected the right of the company (as provided for by the deed of surrender) to purchase and possess skins.[56] The federal Deputy Minister of Justice, E.L. Newcombe, provided astute and useful comments on the questions for the stated case, writing, "It is, I think, quite probable that the Ontario Game Act is ultra vires as relating to criminal law," and advised that the *ultra vires* aspect of the Ontario legislation "should be very carefully argued in addition to the point that arises by reason of the treaty rights of the Indians."[57] In a subsequent legal opinion, he suggested some precision on which provisions of provincial legislation were *ultra vires* and that "the habit of hunting and selling the skins of animals" should be explicitly established; he then added, "I do not think we should be satisfied to rest the claims of the Indians on the Robinson Treaties except as an alternative. I think *it may well be argued that the Indian rights exist independently of these treaties*."[58] The Justice Department had indicated a need for evidence (hunting and selling animal skins), but then recommended pursuing an ongoing Indian right to hunt in an area ceded to the Crown by treaty as an argument against the jurisdiction of provincial game laws over Indian hunting. Moreover, Newcombe indicated that an "Indian" right was a stronger argument than a treaty rights argument, which he advised should be used only as an alternative. Disappointingly, the foundation (Aboriginal? inherent? customary?) for this particular assertion was not provided in his opinion. However, in terms of the history of legal interactions between Indigenous peoples and colonial authorities, Newcombe's legal opinion offered a strong justification for the opposition of Ontario's prosecution of Indian trappers. Even though the HBC fur seizures were still under consideration by a superior court, and the stated case had been guided by the Justice Department, Indian Affairs continued to give credence to Ontario's desire to control Indian hunting.[59]

The capacity of First Nations people to trap furs was primarily of commercial importance to the HBC. Nonetheless, the questions posed in the stated case attempted to clarify the effect of provincial game laws on the Robinson Treaties. The HBC earnestly supported a legal challenge to the province and had planned an appeal to the Judicial Committee of the Privy Council. Although these English legalists did not have the opportunity to argue an appeal of *R. v. Train* in the Judicial Committee of the Privy Council, the argument they had created complemented, corroborated, and expanded the defence that had been advocated by the Canadian legalists acting for the plaintiff. The memorandum of 28 October 1912 prepared by the eminent English legal firm Bischoff, Coxe, Bompas, and Bischoff for the HBC made a number of points demonstrating that the Ontario Game and Fisheries Act was *ultra vires*: (1) the act interfered with trade and commerce (a power more clearly within Section 91 of the BNA Act); (2) the jurisdiction over Indians and Indian lands was with the Dominion government; (3) the province's authority over property and civil rights (Section 92, Subsection 13 of the BNA Act) did not apply to game which is *ferae nature*; and (4) the fur trade could not be described as a matter of merely a local or private nature (Section 92, Subsection 16 of the BNA Act). This memorandum pointed out that the effect of Section 91(24) had been discussed by the Privy Council in the *St. Catharine's Milling* case and that the Privy

Council decision regarding jurisdiction over Ontario fisheries indicated that regulation through closed seasons was a Dominion responsibility (a relevant consideration with respect to the closed season for game).[60] This interpretation of the British North America Act, 1867 provided a jurisdictional argument that sought to protect Indian hunting by limiting the power of the province to regulate in matters concerning "Indians," game, and the fur trade. Sadly, this authoritative legal analysis was never properly assessed in a courtroom; it remained safely concealed until located in the archives. Nonetheless, its existence clearly demonstrates the capacity to make a cogent argument concerning commercial rights within the dominant legal conventions.

Train had been convicted in 1910, but the attorney general succeeded in delaying a hearing of the case until February 1913.[61] Thereafter, the judges reserved giving a decision, and by June 1914, it was apparent that Chief Justice Sir William Meredith had refused to make a judgment. According to HBC fur trade commissioner N.H. Bacon, "It is evident that the Judge has realized that he cannot deliver a judgment other than one which would be picked to pieces by the Law Lords in England [Privy Council]."[62] The problem of the disposition of *Rex v. Train* can be appreciated by Frank McCarthy's recollection for the Special Game Commission in 1931 that he had tried to raise a point of constitutional law "in 1912–13, when Sir William Meredith was sitting as Chief Justice, and it was so neat a point that he said 'Stop it,' and he never delivered the judgment, and he told me he never intended [to]."[63] In this instance, the problem was not so much that the law was being imposed upon treaty Indians but that the process had been suspended and the law was not allowed to be determined.

For the HBC, the process entailed a stated case which did not result in a stay of prosecutions.[64] The legal uncertainty surrounding the company's daily operations, the long delay before the appeal, the ongoing fur seizures, and the watchful interest that other provinces showed in Ontario's fight with the company created pressure for a hasty political arrangement.[65] In 1916, an arrangement was made between the HBC and the Ontario Game and Fisheries Branch. The HBC proposed that damage claims from illegal seizures would be dropped, fines would be remitted, and the company and the Game Branch would agree on reasonable regulations. The company's main lever in the negotiations had been the question of the province's jurisdiction over Indian harvesting. Negotiations had been conducted and legal issues concerning First Nations were resolved "politically"; needless to say, there was no involvement of the beneficiaries of the livelihood rights. The HBC agreed to take out fur dealer licenses and to complete monthly returns, and new regulations made special arrangement for treaty Indians (notably, royalty coupons permitted the trapping of beaver and otter). Ontario had designed a more regulated industry and had easily obtained Indian Affairs support for the specific terms affecting Indian trapping. The HBC had obtained some security and was freed from official molestation. It was also in the privileged position of issuing the royalty coupons to Indian trappers.[66] Certainly, the province came out of this political arrangement much further ahead than would have been the case if the jurisdictional problem had been resolved with a recognition of treaty rights. Apparently, Kelly Evans's desire for some "really rigorous punishment" was, to some extent, achieved.

The compromise ending the *Rex v. Train* standoff gave Ontario considerable control over the livelihoods of First Nations people. Through orders-in-council, Indian trappers in northern parts of the province were allowed to trap an individual quota of beaver and otter set by royalty coupons. Under a special individual system of identification, treaty Indians were permitted to trap without a license. Clearly, Ontario was legislating specifically for Indians. However, when the HBC agreed to a political compromise with the provincial government, the opportunity of legally defining the livelihood rights of Robinson Treaty nations, in particular, in the context of the early twentieth century was lost. In this era, the Hudson's Bay Company was the only entity with the interest, resources, and willingness to test legally the Robinson Treaty and the foresight to pursue issues of livelihood rights as far as the Privy Council. The refusal by the minister responsible for Indian Affairs to be represented by counsel at the stated case on the issue of Dominion jurisdiction over Indians suggests that the HBC's commercial self-interest was less problematic for the recognition of Indian treaty rights than the Dominion's relinquishment of a trust responsibility for Indian livelihood. The constitutional jurisdiction argument would have been more forceful had the minister of Indian Affairs defended Section 91(24) of the BNA Act. Moreover, federal reluctance made it easier for the court to procrastinate. Even if it is unknown to today's legal scholars and practitioners, the case of *Rex v. Train* was a pivotal event in the legal struggle for treaty rights recognition. While such law is removed from the purview of today's students and professors of law and practising lawyers, its existence very much influenced the actions of civil servants.

Provincial Trapping Regulations Challenged by Treaty Rights, ca. 1931

Many of the arguments that should have been legally determined in a superior court with *Rex v. Train* in 1913 resurfaced in *Rex v. Padjena and Quesawa* in 1931. A magistrate's conviction of two First Nations men for possessing beaver was quashed in divisional court by Judge J.M. McKay in 1930.[67] In this case, the judge held that the order-in-council regulating trapping was *ultra vires* because it abrogated rights under the Robinson-Superior Treaty and because of Dominion jurisdiction over "Indians" under Section 91(24) of the BNA Act. Judge McKay, reasoning much as had Judge Latchford, concluded that, "The said Robinson Treaty is binding on both the Dominion of Canada and on the Province of Ontario" and that "the Province of Ontario cannot abrogate the said Treaty."[68] Ontario appealed this case. At the magistrate's level, Deputy Superintendent General D.C. Scott's directive to the local Indian agent was to "ask for leniency on compassionate grounds rather than on legal rights," but with McKay's decision, the Department of Indian Affairs finally agreed to oppose the province's appeal.[69] The Bay Street law firm of Ludwig, Schuyler, and Fisher was hired. With the *Padjena* decision on the limitations of provincial game protection laws, the department finally supported a legal defence of the treaty.

Both the process and the outcome for the *Padjena* case bore a curious resemblance to the stated case concerning the HBC fur seizures (*R. v. Train*). Although sittings for the Crown's appeal at the Supreme Court of Ontario were delayed, Judge McKay's decision had little impact; First Nations trappers continued to be prosecuted, which led the Indian Affairs counsel M. Ludwig to speculate, "I am wondering whether the Attorney General's Department here has sent out instructions that Judge Mackay's [*sic*] decision is to be disregarded."[70] Again, the court was reluctant to render a judgment. Ludwig reported, "I understand the Chief Justice [Mulock] does not want to hear the case for the reason that his view is in favour of upholding the treaty obligation."[71] Oblique references were made to the earlier stated case of *Rex v. Train*. Justice Hodgins, who had heard the stated case on HBC furs, was reported as saying "precisely the same questions as are involved in this appeal [*Padjena*] were argued in the Court of Appeal in 1912 [1913] and that no judgment was delivered because the Court was of opinion the judgment might injuriously affect the real interests of the Indians and the then Chief Justice [Meredith, C.J.] suggested that the parties get together and come to some settlement, so that no judgment need be given."[72] Ludwig had discerned that in *Train*, the court was not ready to allow provincial legislation to override treaty rights. However, the view that the real interests of First Nations would be served by provincial game conservation legislation became an acceptable rationalization for avoiding a determination of the legal force of treaty livelihood rights.

Judge McKay's decision suggests that the 1916 deal made between the HBC and Ontario provided only a temporary evasion of the issue of treaty rights. Yet again the chief justice avoided providing a clarification of the legal process, stating "that this was argued fourteen years ago and no decision was given. It is a large question and one in which the public faith is involved. I think the court of today should hold, as it did that of fourteen years ago, that *it is inexpedient that this question be further litigated*."[73] Although *R. v. Train* never resulted in a written decision, and therefore could not be reported, it still had an impact on the *Padjena* case. Consistent with previous suggestions from lawyers and civil servants, the court had suggested during the appeal of *Padjena* that the two governments try to work out a satisfactory game law.

Conclusion: Powerless to Protect or Dishonour of the Crown?

In 1896, Hayter Reed identified an incongruity in that "the Indians acquired privileges under Treaty but to what extent they are allowed to exercise those privileges is left in doubt."[74] An enduring unwillingness to address that contradiction stymied efforts to engage in livelihood activities based on the exercise of treaty and Aboriginal rights until the Supreme Court of Canada began developing and providing a doctrine of Aboriginal harvesting rights. In the intervening hundred years, First Nations' hunting and other forms of harvesting were criminalized or at least interfered with. As Frank Beardy (Muskrat Dam band) wrote,

> In the early and mid 1920's, the provincial conservation officers began to make their appearance in this region. They enforced provincial game laws with intense ferocity. They confiscated and destroyed guns, nets, fish spears, canoes, along with other implements our people used for their daily subsistence. The people lived in fear and were under constant harassment of the amikogemag.[75]

The Province of Ontario acquired dubious authority to regulate Indian livelihoods because the federal government avoided the assertion of its jurisdiction. For the most part, the archival record is unable to document very many instances in which the federal Crown acted with honourable intentions. This legal history, a written documentary account of the failure to protect treaty hunting rights in the Robinson Treaty territories, also suggests that state-sponsored claims to conservation imperatives need to be carefully assessed in terms of the competition and re-allocation of resources.[76]

Despite compelling reasons, the Department of Indian Affairs was unwilling to make use of its federal authority to ensure provincial compliance with the treaty or defend its constitutional jurisdiction. Generally, the Department of Indian Affairs was feckless about defending treaty livelihood rights. Frequently, it discouraged First Nations and their advocates from pursuing legal action. Archival records indicate that a number of sophisticated legal arguments could have permitted Indian Affairs officials to advance livelihood rights through the courts, or to establish federal game legislation to protect treaty rights, or even to negotiate with the province for protection of Indian hunting. Instead, provincial regulation of the traditional economy of treaty Indians expanded, not so much because of the opportunity to seize upon an unclear division of powers, but because the federal government knowingly failed to defend its jurisdiction as provided for in the British North America Act, 1867.[77] Yet, in 1896, Indian Affairs Deputy Superintendent General Hayter Reed had asserted that treaties had the force of law. Apart from disregarding the law or responding to particular convictions, First Nations had no input into the implementation of treaty livelihood rights. The discussions between the provincial and the Dominion governments made no room for First Nations or their advocates. Nevertheless, they persisted with the desire to have their rights clarified.

Provincial encroachment on treaty rights and the compliant avoidance of the issue by Ontario courts meant that the legal status of Indian treaties and federal responsibility for Indians had been haphazardly de facto refashioned. These changes occurred without the consent of First Nations people; in fact, serious political agitation developed in support of their livelihood rights. While the abrogation of its jurisdiction by the federal Crown amounted to a failure to protect solemn treaty promises, in a more fundamental way, jurisdiction can be regarded as a secondary contradiction. Judge Latchford had seen through a convenient jurisdictional controversy, stating, "Nor is there a question of whether it is ultra vires or intra vires of the Ontario Legislature to prohibit the Indians of Lake Nipissing from having beaver skins in possession. The point is that *it is wrong* to violate a treaty; wrong on the part of a province or government as on the part of an empire."[78] Appeals to the integrity of treaties did not really sway authorities. Instead, provincial officials, such as Commissioner Evans, postulated a "conservation" imperative, sometimes predicated on explicit racial assumptions, but strategically designed to preserve so as to reallocate wildlife resources to sports hunters.

In terms of explaining the changing legal relationships between Aboriginal peoples and the Crown, any real desire to "find the law" should not be restricted to a perfunctory search for precedents in the reported case law, although the Internet and databases make that style of research simple, easy, and nonreflective.[79] To illustrate, no matter how skilled a case-law reader might be, the trial decision in *Padjena* provides not the slightest hint that the treaty rights had been contested mindfully in bureaucratic and legal forums. This little-known but several-decades-long jurisdictional dispute about the legal standing of a clearly worded section of the Robinson Treaties, resulting in the deliberate and legally sanctioned erosion of the lawful practice of treaty livelihood rights, was uncovered only by historical research conducted in several archives.[80] And as an unintended outcome, the findings of this research put Section 35 rights in a unique historical perspective: while legal principles were articulated in 1910 and 1931 to recognize and protect written Robinson Treaty rights, the courts demonstrated a strong preference to avoid ruling in favour of limiting the Province of Ontario's ability to encroach upon Indian treaties. Judge Latchford's reasoning during the dubious if not illegal incarceration of the Commandas, the initial even if somewhat ephemeral recognition of Indian hunting interests by Ontario legislation in the early 1890s, legal opinions developed by the Justice Department in the 1890s, Deputy Superintendent General Hayter Reed's assertion in 1896 concerning the legal standing of treaties, carefully worded memoranda from Indian Affairs law clerks, and the legal arguments advanced by McCarthy and the HBC's English solicitors with respect to the fur seizures all indicate that the treaty harvesting rights in this era could be adequately appreciated even from a strongly "colonial" legal mindset. In both the *Train* and *Padjena* cases, competent arguments were heard, but judgments were not given. Since judgments that have not been given cannot be appealed, the prospect of a Privy Council decision on treaty rights was precluded by the reticence of the Ontario superior courts. The *Padjena* trial decision was eventually reported some fifty-six years later. But without the benefit of the legal account and historical context of its appeal (i.e., archival records), it must stand out as a very perplexing legal anomaly. Given the long jurisdictional dispute between the Dominion government and the Province of Ontario, it is very understandable why Deputy Superintendent Duncan Campbell Scott would seek constitutional protection for Indian livelihood rights in the Natural Resources Transfer Agreements (ca. 1922–30) prior to the transfer of lands and resources to the prairie provinces, and yet this authority, a constitutional amendment in the form of the British North America Act of 1930, has been seriously misunderstood or ignored by lawyers. And consistently, it has been given historically unsound constructions by the courts.[81]

NOTES

This manuscript has had a long gestation period. It began in 1990 as a short research consultancy with Ontario Native Affairs Directorate later renamed Secretariat (ONAS) from which I authored a small study titled "Ontario's Appropriation of Indian Hunting: Provincial Conservation Policies vs. Aboriginal and Treaty Rights, ca. 1892–1930," A Report for the Ontario Native Affairs Secretariat (January 1991). In the Hudson's Bay Company Archives, Anne Morton and Judith Beatty expedited my research and inquiries concerning the prosecution of HBC employees and fur seizures by Ontario authorities. I would like to thank Lise Hansen, Victor Lytwyn, John Van West, Mark Stevenson, and David McNab, then with the Ontario Native Affairs Secretariat, for their comments and advice on this research. I also appreciate that ONAS was agreeable to the dissemination of this research (now much revised); nonetheless, the interpretations are my own and do not reflect the views of the Ontario Native Affairs Secretariat. Over the years, my efforts were enriched by the interest and advice provided by Peter Usher, James Morrison, Marianne Friesen, Don Purich, Skip Ray, Frances Thatcher, Dianne Newell, Laurie Meijer Drees, and Siomonn Pulla. Subsequent efforts to publish academically were entirely unsuccessful, and readers of this chapter should bear that in mind. Apparently, student reviewers at the *Saskatchewan Law Review* held that the submission was far too interdisciplinary and insufficiently legal, and similarly, reviewers for a 1994 submission to the *Canadian Native Law Reporter* found the manuscript seriously lacking in detail. Later, four reviewers, as well as the editors of the *Canadian Historical Review*, graciously provided profuse advice for fashioning a very different paper. In contrast to academic review in which both the disciplines of law and history found the manuscript rather wanting, others have found the research credible and relevant. The results were used by David C. Nahwegahbow in *Operation Rainbow* in the form of an affidavit for the Ontario Court of Justice General Division; Court File No. 584–95 (25 September 1995). Similarly, this 1991 report for ONAS was cited in volume 2 of the *Report of the Royal Commission on Aboriginal Peoples*, and its archival sources were heavily relied upon for its discussion concerning treaties and wildlife harvesting; Royal Commission on Aboriginal Peoples, *Report of the Royal Commission on Aboriginal Peoples*, vol. 2, *Restructuring the Relationship*, part 2 (Ottawa: Minister of Supply and Services Canada, 1996), 496–7, 509–11, 697n144. Similarly, the Honourable Justice Sidney B. Linden relied on the 1991 report for the Ipperwash Inquiry. See Jean Teillet, "The Role of Natural Resources Regulatory Regime in Aboriginal Rights Disputes," *Report of the Ipperwash Inquiry* (31 March 2005), 24–34. Practising lawyers seemed very receptive to this legal history; they continue up to the present day to request this sort of arhival-based assistance for litigation and negotiation purposes. The sharply contrasting responses to this empirically based, legal-historical argument underscore the divide between academic and applied research.

1 The term "Indian" is used in this chapter when it represents the historical concept.
2 Latchford to Attorney General J.J. Foy, 31 October 1914, in file 1914/1747, 4–32, [Criminal and Civil Files], RG 4 [Attorney General's Department], Ontario Archives [OA].
3 Latchford to Acting Attorney General I.B. Lucas, 13 November 1914, in file 1914/1747, 4–32, RG 4, OA.
4 Ibid. (emphasis in original).
5 A.M. Dymond to Acting Attorney General, 17 November 1914, in file 1914/1747, 4–32, RG 4, OA; specifically Dymond advised, "Mr. Justice Latchford is probably not aware of what has taken place in regard to the special case as I believe the negotiations between the Department and Sir William Meredith were confidential."
6 The Robinson-Superior and Robinson-Huron treaties are published in Alexander Morris, *The Treaties of Canada with the Indians of Manitoba and the North-West Territories* (Toronto: Belfords, Clarke and Co., 1880), 302–9. For a history of these treaties, see Arthur J. Ray, Jim Miller, and Frank J. Tough, *Bounty and Benevolence: A History of Saskatchewan Treaties* (Montreal: McGill-Queen's University Press, 2000), 35–44; for a detailed discussion of the context of the pre-Confederation treaties (1818–62), see J.R. Miller, *Compact, Contract, Covenant: Aboriginal Treaty-Making in Canada* (Toronto: University

of Toronto Press, 2009), 93–122. For an intensive study of these treaties, consult James Morrison, "The Robinson Treaties of 1850: A Case Study," a maunscript report prepared for Treaties and Land Research Section of the Royal Commission on Aboriginal Peoples (31 August 1996).

7 Section 91(24) provided federal jurisdiction for "Indians, and Lands reserved for the Indians," British North America Act, 1867. See Canada, Department of Justice, *A Consolidation of the Constitution Acts 1867 to 1982* (Ottawa: Communications Canada, Canadian Government Publishing, 2001).

8 Reed to Chief Game Warden E. Kinsley, 1 September 1896, file 84,041 pt. 1, vol. 2405, RG 10, Public Records of the Department of Indian Affairs, Library and Archives Canada [LAC].

9 For insights on this issue, see Cole Harris, "How Did Colonialism Dispossess? Comments from an Edge of Empire," *Annals of the Association of American Geographers* 94/1 (2004): 165–82.

10 Regrettably, the archival records do not provide insights concerning the possible motives for the federal government's capitulation. Speculation could suggest several possibilities: a fear of losing in the Privy Council which often favoured the provinces; overlapping partisan interests concerning federal and provincial governments; or the ability of strong provinces to get their way in the federation.

11 A history of conservation in Canada is not the intent of this article; rather, as a legal history, it simply suggests that the clash between proponents of conservation and recognition of treaty rights is not a recent development. Nonetheless, with respect to the conflict between conservation policymakers and First Nations' interests, see Frank J. Tough, "Conservation and the Indian: Clifford Sifton's Commission of Conservation, 1910–1919," *Native Studies Review* 8/1 (1992): 61–73.

12 Political opposition to the denial of treaty rights, expressed by numerous letters of protest and petitions, is beyond the scope of this chapter.

13 The significance of the early legal history has been overlooked as the legal literature considers only the reported case law of a later period. See David Knoll, "Treaty and Aboriginal Hunting and Fishing Rights," *Canadian Native Law Reporter* 1 (1979): 1–29; Dougald Brown, "Indian Hunting Rights and Provincial Law: Some Recent Developments," *University of Toronto Faculty Law Review* 39/2 (1981): 121–32; and Peter A. Cumming and Neil H. Mickenberg, *Native Rights in Canada*, 2nd ed. (Toronto: General Publishing, 1972), 207–26.

14 Nor is the situation simply a problem of the limitations of case law. Histories of conservation have not necessarily been attentive to Aboriginal

interests in fish, fur, and wildlife resources. It might have been accepted back in 1978, when Janet Foster, in *Working for Wildlife*, could largely ignore Aboriginal peoples or fail to reflect on the historical observations that portray Aboriginal hunters as destroyers of game, but equally in the 1998 edition, both in her preface and Lorne Hammond's afterword, no significance is attached to Aboriginal interests in either the preservation or harvesting of wildlife. Specifically, to disregard the existing treaty and Aboriginal rights recognized by Section 35 of the Constitution Act, 1982, and the significant changes in resource allocation that resulted with *R. v. Sparrow* in 1990 would seem to seriously misinform by omission. See Janet Foster, *Working for Wildlife: The Beginning of Preservation in Canada*, 2nd ed. (Toronto: University of Toronto Press, 1998).

15 R. v. Sparrow, Supreme Court of Canada [1990], 1 *Supreme Court Reporter* 1075.

16 Correspondence in 1882 and 1888 indicates that provincial authorities attentively avoided enacting game protection provisions that would conflict with federal jurisdiction over Indians. See file 37,328, vol. 2185, RG 10, LAC; and file 84,041 pt. 1, vol. 2405, RG 10, LAC.

17 For a discussion of early legislation, see Lise C. Hansen, "Indian Trapping Territories and the Development of the Registered Trapline System in Ontario," Historical Report, Ontario Native Affairs Directorate, 1989.

18 As an example of "protection" entailing social class biases along with particular views about the sporting capture of fish on a local scale, see Nancy B. Bouchier and Ken Cruikshank, "'Sportsmen and Pothunters': Class, Conservation and the Fishery of Hamilton Harbour, 1850–1914," *Sport History Review* 28 (1997): 1–18. For the findings of the game commission, see Ontario Game and Fish Commission, *Commissioners' Report, 1892*, G.A. MacCallum, Chairman (Toronto: Warwick and Sons, 1892).

19 An Act to Amend the Act for the Protection of Game and Fur-bearing Animals, Ontario Statutes, 1892, Chapter 58, Section 12 (hereafter, Ontario Game Protection Act, 1892). The changes to the legislation are evident in Bill 136 [1892], copy found in Box 49, RG 49, 1–7 H, Provincial Secretary Records, OA. The next year, An Act to Amend and Consolidate the Laws for the Protection of Game and Fur-bearing Animals, OS 1893, Chapter 49, placed Indian hunting rights in Section 27; a subsection was added which made provision for the use of orders-in-council.

20 Ontario Game Protection Act, 1892, OS, c. 58, s. 12.

21 Provincial Secretary J.M. Gibson to Deputy Superintendent General of Indian Affairs L. Vankoughnet, 31 May 1893, in file 84,041 pt. 1, vol. 2405, RG 10, LAC.

22 W.B. Robinson to Honourable Colonel Bruce, Superintendent General of Indian Affairs (24 September 1850) in Morris, *Treaties of Canada*, 17.

23 Gibson to Reed, 12 November 1896, in file 84,041 pt. 1, vol. 2405, RG 10, LAC.

24 Significantly, this assertion was not merely a personal view but a departmental position. Reed to Gibson, 21 November 1896, ibid. (emphasis added).

25 Nonetheless, market integration, prices, and new consumption possibilities can create incentives to overproduce. During the competitive period (ca. 1783–1821), when the North West and Hudson's Bay Companies raised purchase prices for furs and dropped the sale prices of trade goods, overproduction occurred. See Arthur J. Ray, "Some Conservation Schemes of the Hudson's Bay Company, 1821–50: An Examination of the Problems of Resource Management in the Fur Trade," *Journal of Historical Geography* 1/1 (1975): 49–68.

26 In a draft, consideration was given to requesting from the governor general "the appointment of a commission to bring about a settlement of the questions at issue," but instead the Justice Department was consulted. Superintendent General of Indian Affairs (James Allan Smart) to the Governor General (Sir James Campbell Hamilton Gordon), 5 July 1897, in file 84,041 pt. 1, vol. 2405, RG 10, LAC.

27 Legal Opinion, A. Powers, 5 July 1898, in file 1931/480, vol. 2422, public records of the Department of Justice, LAC; and a copy in file 84,041 pt. 1, vol. 2405, RG 10, LAC. I did not receive complete access to the Justice Department's file on hunting rights; in particular a legal opinion of 20 July 1897 was removed by access review on the grounds of solicitor-client privilege (file 480/1931, vol. 2422, RG 13, LAC [Robinson-Superior Treaty of 1850 and Robinson-Huron Treaty of 1850 Hunting and Fishing Rights of Indians, etc.]). In August 2016, I retrieved this file and learned that a formal review had been completed in 2004 *in consultation* with the Justice Department; most of the photocopy material that I had received in July 1991 had been excised from the newly "accessible" file. One can only speculate as to why a nearly one-hundred-year-old legal opinion concerning commercial rights would be excised in 1991. And the expunging of most of the remaining documents in 2004 implies a political/legal absurdity that reflects a deep and ongoing sensitivity concerning Aboriginal and treaty rights by agents of the contemporary federal state.

28 Law Clerk Memorandum (R. Rimmer), 31 August 1898, in file 84,041 pt. 1, vol. 2405, RG 10, LAC.

29 Legal Opinion, Powers, 5 July 1898, in file 1931/480, vol. 2422, RG 13, LAC. For the problem of clarity in the Ontario Game Protection Act see file

1898/1174, RG 4, 4–32, OA (Construction of Section 34 of the Ontario Game Protection Act).

30 Interested readers are encouraged to pursue the details in Ottawa-Correspondence, Memoranda and Printed Reports regarding Game Laws applied to the Ontario Indians, 1888–1905, file 84,041, vol. 2405, RG 10, LAC.

31 Gibson to Smart, 27 April 1899, in file 84,041 pt. 1, vol. 2405, RG 10, LAC.

32 Rimmer Law Memorandum, 31 August 1898, in file 84,041 pt. 1, vol. 2405, RG 10, LAC.

33 McLean to Bearite Bast, 23 July 1906, in file 420–8 pt. 1, vol. 6743, RG 10, LAC (emphasis added).

34 Ibid.

35 McLean to Charles John, 9 March 1907, ibid.

36 McLean to Stock, 28 August 1907, ibid.

37 McLean to Langworthy and McComber, 15 February 1910, ibid.

38 Petition to Honourable Frank Oliver from Delegates, 22 March 1911, ibid.

39 Chief Sagamak to Indian Agent Hagan, 15 January 1910, ibid.

40 Hagan to McLean, 5 February 1910, ibid.

41 McLean to Hagan, 8 February 1910, ibid.

42 Tinsley to McLean, 30 December 1909, ibid.

43 Tinsley added, "It has long since been decided that all the residents of the Province are amenable to the same laws, and they are not friends of the Indians who try to make them believe otherwise." Tinsley to McLean, 12 April 1912, in file 420–8 pt. 1, vol. 6743, RG 10, LAC.

44 Ibid.

45 Ontario Game and Fisheries Commission, *Final Report, 1909–1911*, Kelly Evans, Commissioner (Toronto: L.K. Cameron, 1911), 198 (hereafter, *Evans Report*).

46 Ibid., 199.

47 Ibid., 201.

48 Ibid., 210.

49 Ibid., 211.

50 The section concerning treaty rights was struck out after first reading of the bill in the 1913 session. By 1914, the basic statute structure had become entrenched: interpretative terms were defined; regulations could be made by order-in-council; game and fish regulations were combined under one act; many restrictions as to closed season, gear, and bag limits were established; various means to prevent evasion had been developed (restrictions on possession, sale, and transportation of game); licences controlled access; Indian and settler hunting had been restricted; and provisions were created for the administration and enforcement of the act.

51 *Evans Report*, 204.

52 The documentation on HBC fur seizures can be found in Archives of Manitoba, Hudson's Bay Company Archives, A.1/61; A.1/202; A.12/FT230/1; A.12/FT319/1a; A.12/FT319/1b; A.39/14/1; RG2/1/1; RG2/60/1; RG2/2/7; and RG2/2/8 (hereafter, HBCA).

53 *Evans Report*, 201.

54 As happened to the Commandas, the severe penalty imposed on Train reflected the nature of game protection. The use of summary convictions under the Ontario Game and Fisheries Act reveal several coercive features: those prosecuting the offence obtained one-half of the fine imposed; the defendants were compellable witnesses; and each pelt or animal was considered a separate offence. Convictions were permitted on the basis of *prima facie* evidence and the onus of proof was on the defendant when found in possession of game, fish, or gear. See Ontario Game Protection Act, OS 1893, c. 49, ss. 16, 18, 21, 22, and 23. By considering English origins, the repressive qualities of our early game protection can be appreciated; see P.B. Munsche, *Gentlemen and Poachers: The English Game Laws 1671–1831* (Cambridge: Cambridge University Press, 1981).

55 C.C. Chipman to HBC Secretary W. Ware, 8 April 1910, A.39/14/1, HBCA.

56 Draft 1911 Order-in-Council, copy in A.12/FT319/1a, HBCA.

57 Legal opinion on *Rex v. Train*, E.L. Newcombe, 22 March 1910, in file 420–8 pt. 1, vol. 6743, RG 10, LAC; and a copy also in file 480/1931, vol. 2422, RG 13.

58 Legal opinion, Newcombe, 2 September 1910, in file 420–8 pt. 1, vol. 6743, RG 10, LAC (emphasis added).

59 Official correspondence alleged that it "has been upheld by legal opinions to the effect that treaties could not confer upon the Indians other or larger rights in the matter of hunting, trapping and fishing than those that belong at Common Law to His Majesty's other subjects in general." Assistant Secretary to Francis W. Jacobs, 18 October 1912, in file 420–8 pt. 2, vol. 6743, RG 10, LAC. In contrast, the opinions in 1897 and 1910 recognized Indian hunting. Similarly, J.D. McLean claimed, "I have to say that it is held by the Provincial Government that the Indians are subject to the Game Laws of the Province to the same extent as whitemen. In this connection the Province has been upheld by judicial decisions and you should be careful therefore to observe these laws as otherwise you leave yourself open to the penalties contained therein." McLean to Robert George, 6 February 1913, in file 420–8 pt. 2, vol. 6743, RG 10, LAC.

60 See Memorandum: Ontario Game and Fisheries Act, Robert Younger and F.D. MacKinnon, 28 October 1912, in A.39/14/1, HBCA.

61 The case was definitely heard, and began on 10 February 1913. See Court of Appeal Minute Book No. 7 (1909–1914), Court Records, RG 22, OA; and Judge's Bench Book, Meredith J., RG 22-496-Box 4.

62 N.H. Bacon to A.M. Nanton, 12 June 1914, in G2/2/7, HBCA. The company was concerned that a Privy Council appeal would be blocked by retroactive legislation.

63 Minutes of Special Game Commission, Honourable W.D. Black Chair, Toronto, 10 August 1931, in file 420–8C, vol. 6747, RG 10, LAC.

64 HBC records document the details of ongoing harassment, but see file 1913/104, RG 4–32, OA (Re: seizure of Hudson['s] Bay Coy. Furs at Sioux Lookout and McIntosh); and file 441/1914, RG 4–32, OA (Complaint against Inspector McCurdy, Provincial Police in connection with the enforcement of the Game Act at Fort William).

65 The company was also under the impression that a successful court challenge finding the game act *ultra vires* would be nullified by legislation.

66 See Ontario, Department of Game and Fisheries, Regulations concerning trapping, Orders-in-Council, 6 and 10 October 1916.

67 Rex v. Padjena and Quesawa, Ontario Division Court, McKay, J. (10 April 1930), previously unreported, but now available in Brian Slattery and Linda Charlton, eds., *Canadian Native Law Cases: 1911–1930*, vol. 4 (Saskatoon: Native Law Centre, University of Saskatchewan, 1986), 411–14.

68 The judge argued that the same reasons that prevented the application of provincial game laws to Indian reserves should be extended so that Indians "are entitled under the terms of the said Treaty to hunt on the lands belonging to the Crown within the said territory, and that the said Game and Fisheries Act and regulations thereunder do not apply to them." *Rex v. Padjena*, p. 412.

69 Telegram from Scott to Indian Agent J.G. Burk, 24 January 1929, in file 420–8X pt. 1, vol. 6747, RG 10, LAC.

70 Ludwig to Department Secretary A.F. MacKenzie, 13 December 1930, in file 420–8 pt. 1, vol. 6743, RG 10, LAC.

71 Ludwig to Scott, 16 June 1930, in file 420–8 pt. 1, vol. 6743, RG 10, LAC.

72 Ludwig to MacKenzie, 15 October 1930, ibid. Years earlier, Judge Latchford had provided some insight into Ontario's sensitivities to treaty rights: "Although the Game & Fisheries Act is – as regards hunting by the Nipissing Indians as and where the Commandas were hunting – in manifest violation of the Treaty, the Ontario Government or any Department of it will, I think, be loath to take any action tantamount to admitting that the learned revisers of the Statute – most of them distinguished occupants of the Bench – and the members learned and otherwise of the Legislature, either ignored altogether the Robinson-Huron Treaty, or chose to regard

it as the Chancellor of Germany recently regarded an equally solemn (but not more solemn) obligation." Latchford to Scott, 18 November 1914, in file 420–8 pt. 1, vol. 6743, RG 10, LAC.

73 Newspaper report (30 May 1930), copy found in file 420–8X pt. 1, vol. 6747, RG 10, LAC (emphasis added). Apparently, the appeal was dropped after counsel for the attorney general revealed that the beaver were not trapped in the Robinson-Superior Treaty territory, thereby allowing both governments to sidestep the problem of Ontario's legislating with respect to Indians.

74 Reed to Gibson, 21 November 1896, in file 84,041 pt. 1, vol. 2405, RG 10, LAC.

75 Frank Beardy, "Commentary: It's Time to Re-examine the Treaties," *Wawatay News* 17/22 (22 November 1990).

76 For a scholarly analysis of the impact of conservation regulations on Aboriginal fishing rights, see Dianne Newell, *Tangled Webs of History: Indians and the Law in Canada's Pacific Coast Fisheries* (Toronto: University of Toronto Press, 1993).

77 The Department of Indian Affairs was advised by the Justice Department that immunity from provincial game laws for Indians could be provided "by legislation of the Dominion in the exercise of its paramount power with regard to Indians and lands reserved for the Indians." Legal opinion (Newcombe), 5 October 1917, file 480/1931, vol. 2422, RG 13, LAC.

78 This comment should be appreciated in the context of the First World War. Latchford to Scott, 18 November 1914, in file 420–8 pt. 2, vol. 6743, RG 10, LAC (emphasis added).

79 Two fine examples of legal analysis with historical depth are Sidney L. Harring, *White Man's Law: Native People in Nineteenth-Century Canadian Jurisprudence* (Toronto: University of Toronto Press, 1998); and Douglas C. Harris, *Fish, Law, and Colonialism: The Legal Capture of Salmon in British Columbia* (Toronto: University of Toronto Press, 2001).

80 The value of legal records as evidence of hunting rights litigation, even when the court did not recognize the treaty, has been demonstrated by William Wicken. In the *Sylliboy* case (1928), oral testimony was preserved. See William C. Wicken, "'Heard It from My Grandfather': Mi'kmaq Treaty Tradition and the Sylliboy Case of 1928," *University of New Brunswick Law Journal* 4 (1995): 146–61.

81 With respect to the problem of coming to a historical understanding of Indian livelihood rights, see Frank J. Tough, "The Forgotten Constitution: The Natural Resources Transfer Agreements and Indian Livelihood Rights, ca. 1925–1933," *Alberta Law Review* 41/4 (2004): 999–1048.

One Good Thing: Law and Elevator Etiquette in the Indian Territories

HAMAR FOSTER

A person could always pay enough to save his neck. That is one good thing about Indians.

William Stonia, testifying in *Reg. v. Haatq*, 14 December 1884

William Stonia's crude description of dispute resolution among the Gitksan was given in a murder case. A young Gitksan man named Billy Owen had drowned while in the employ of trader Amos Youmans, who had neither offered compensation nor reported the death to the family. When Haatq, Billy's father, learned of his son's death, he went to Youmans' store and killed him. Stonia witnessed the deed and was clearly puzzled by Youmans' failure to "pay enough to save his neck."[1]

Stonia's account of Gitksan law is at once overstated and incomplete; but it is a start, and to unpack his description one has to enter a multicultural legal world.[2] This is an exercise especially well suited to a book of essays that explores the many facets of the relationship between Indigenous and non-Indigenous peoples in Canada over the centuries. It is also a challenge not unlike looking at an optical illusion. What was subtle to the point of invisibility can very quickly become blindingly obvious: where there was only one reality, suddenly there are two. But to see the second one requires a shift in perception that may not happen; and if it does not, there will only be a white candlestick, and the dark faces flanking it will not come into focus.

I suspect that I am not the only person who neglected to park his cultural assumptions at the door when first exposed to accounts of frontier interactions between Natives and newcomers.[3] Not the only person, that is, who could see only the white candlestick. One of these

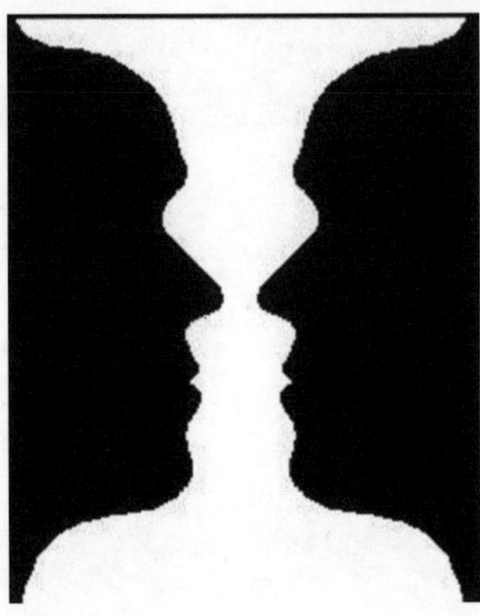

assumptions is that behaviour is not governed by law unless the laws are the sort with which we are familiar. In my case it was subliminally embedded by a childhood filled with cowboy comics and bad Hollywood movies, and the question of whether legal norms guided the actions of people who lived in stateless societies did not then occur to me. But if we do address this question I think we probably pass through three stages.

The first stage I have described already: we don't think much about it. We assume that fur trade and settler accounts of interactions with Indigenous people can be taken at face value. So when some sort of "depredation" is perpetrated by Indians against settlers, it appears simply as hostile behaviour motivated by interest or emotion. But when settler societies retaliate by capturing and trying those responsible, they are seen as not merely seeking vengeance or restitution but as applying settler law.[4] The archival and secondary literature is replete with examples: "savages" steal and engage in random attacks; settlers appropriate vacant land, act in self-defence, and punish according to a criminal code of some sort.

Why does this inference of asymmetry come so naturally? Partly, I think, because we associate law with written rules and legal institutions, and Indigenous societies in North America not only had no written languages but generally had no legislatures to pass laws, no police to enforce them, and no courts to interpret them. Ignorance also plays a part. If we do not educate ourselves about others we will invariably make incorrect, and often damaging, assumptions about them.[5] Another part, for some people, may be simple racism: the belief that tribal peoples are inferior and lack civilized concepts such as law.[6]

In the second stage, we seek to dispel our ignorance, to learn more about how things may have looked to the people on the receiving end of colonialism. When we do this it gradually dawns on us that Indigenous societies did engage in rule-directed behaviour towards others and that it is reasonable to describe some of this behaviour as involving legal norms. But the lack of recognizable institutions to promulgate, interpret, and enforce the rules remains a problem (how do you enforce laws without police?). So does the assumption that Indigenous law is an inferior sort of law. Provincial Secretary (and later Premier) John Robson was quite forthright about this: "The Queen's law," he told the Gitksan in 1884, "is better than yours."[7]

In the third stage, even the assumption of inferiority is subjected to critical scrutiny. Notwithstanding that most of us would not give up the benefits of a liberal democratic polity and the rule of law to live under the sort of legal order common in pre-contact North America, we begin to see that Indigenous law could be highly complex and was well adapted to the conditions in which it operated. We may also conclude that, in some respects, it may even have been superior to the colonial laws that replaced it.[8] Those of us who are not anthropologists may not reach this third stage, but in land claims litigation and treaty-making, you don't have to. Evidence of Indigenous law is admissible evidence of Aboriginal rights and title in Canada, whether judges and lawyers think it is inferior or not. And the existence of such law can be proved by expert evidence and by oral history.[9]

It is therefore a fact of some importance that the discourse of many fur traders, settlers, colonial officials, and journalists in nineteenth-century British Columbia was not (as one might expect) stuck at stage one but was comfortably at stage two. These people often referred to "Indian law" and, more specifically, to the "tribal law" of the various nations.[10] So did the judges. For example, when Judge Matthew Baillie Begbie spoke to the Tsilhqot'in chiefs who would be hanged after the "Chilcotin War" of 1864, he asked them what their law of murder was.[11] And after the murder case in which William Stonia testified in 1884 concluded, Justice Henry Crease reported to Ottawa that Youmans should have known that his marriage to a Gitksan woman would have made her people "more readily think that he was subject to their law." He added that Youmans should also have realized that he would not be spared if he did not report the death and make amends, even though "a well known tribal law" provided that his children would be looked after by the tribe.[12] This was not news in 1884. Nor was it news ten years earlier, in 1873, when a prominent Victoria lawyer told Indian Superintendent I.W. Powell that "Indians in their tribal condition have established almost universally a system of recompense for almost all offences" – and he called this system of recompense "law."[13]

Such statements are important because in the twenty-first century some of us, including some lawyers, may still be at stage one. Or perhaps such lawyers are simply adopting stage one as a forensic mask to be worn only in court or when preparing legal argument. If so, it is a mask that can leave a mark.[14] I discovered this when, as a result of my research and writing on the legal relations between "Natives and newcomers" in Canada, I was asked to be an expert witness in a lengthy Aboriginal rights and title lawsuit in the Supreme Court of British Columbia. A year or so after I filed my report and testified in the case – *Tsilhqot'in Nation v. BC* – I was approached at a bar function by a senior lawyer who had been involved in the litigation on the government side.[15] He asked me if I really believed all that "nonsense" about Tsilhqot'in law that I had put in my report.[16] At the time, I decided to treat his inquiry as an inappropriate rhetorical question and changed the subject. But if I may borrow from William Stonia, a person can always try for the last word. That is one good thing about lawyers.

Law and Property

I am certainly not the first person to reflect in print on the experience of giving evidence in an Aboriginal title lawsuit.[17] However, for some witnesses the experience was an unpleasant (or at least an unsatisfying) one, so I want to make it clear that the lawyers who cross-examined me in the *Tsilhqot'in* case were professional and courteous – I have no complaints to make about their conduct at all.[18] Some of the questions posed by counsel, however, appeared to be premised on a view of law that was firmly rooted in only one of the two legal traditions that were at issue in the case. Or, to put it more bluntly, a view of law stuck at stage one.

Before I testified, I had assumed that we had come a long way since the trial judge in the *Delgamuukw* case concluded that pre-contact Indigenous people probably did not act the way they did because of institutions. Rather, he said, they did so "because of survival instincts that varied from village to village," although they might well "have chosen to follow local customs when it was convenient to do so."[19] I hasten to add that I use this example not to denigrate the trial judge, who had probably seen many of the same bad Hollywood movies that had stealthily influenced my own early views.[20] Rather, I do it to stress that he said this in 1991; and if it was a highly suspect view of human social and cultural behaviour then, we should not still be thinking it nearly twenty-five years later.[21] Human beings who live in groups cannot do so for long if their only code of conduct or system of resource allocation is instinct and convenience.

One manifestation of this reductionism in the *Tsilhqot'in* case involved the question of whether the Indigenous peoples of what is now British Columbia had property laws. It was pointed out to me that in my report I had quoted, as evidence of Aboriginal property law, a dispatch of Governor Douglas. In it, Douglas asserted that the "native Indian population of Vancouver Island have distinct ideas of property in land and mutually recognize their several exclusive possessory rights in certain districts." I was then asked to reconcile this statement with something I had said in cross-examination the previous day, which was that the Indigenous peoples of British Columbia did not treat land "as a commodity." The point of the question appeared to be that I had been caught in a contradiction. As counsel for Canada put it, it was not clear to him "what the distinction is between having notions of property in land and … of land as a commodity."[22]

For me, the suggestion that if land is not a commodity it cannot be property not only emphasizes the cultural dissonance in the courtroom; it distorts the history of the common law. In the first-year property course I teach, a major theme is the gradual commodification of real property. A "feudal" tenant's land was originally neither inheritable nor devisable, nor was it capable of being alienated without consent. Was it therefore not property? I suppose a stickler might say no, it was not. But even so, the tenant was not without legal rights, first in his lord's court and then in the king's.[23]

At what point, then, would our stickler say that the tenant did become an owner? Would it be sometime in the twelfth century, when the king's courts began to enforce his heir's right to inherit? Or at the end of the thirteenth century, when he was permitted to alienate his holding without his lord's consent? Or perhaps in the sixteenth century, when Parliament finally empowered him to make a legal will and leave his land to someone other than the heir? Even then, however, the dynastic impulse to "magnify the blood" – by trying to ensure that land stayed in the family – fought a long, albeit losing, war against the forces of commodification, with such juridical monstrosities as the fee tail and the strict settlement competing with equally bizarre devices designed to "bar the entail."[24] Eventually, Parliament had to decide the matter. But the struggle between the market and other theories of property continues today over environmental values, human reproduction, the patenting of life forms, animal rights, and a host of other contentious issues.[25]

The point is this: Not only have the courts said that it is an error to require Aboriginal law to conform strictly to common law conceptions of property; those conceptions are contingent and change over time.[26] This was pointed out a century ago by a lawyer hired by the Dominion government to provide Ottawa with a legal opinion on the issue of Aboriginal title in British Columbia. In his *Report on the Indian Title*, T.R.E. McInnes complained that even the "ordinary lawyer looks askance at the Indian title" because it does not fit well with what he had been taught about land tenure. The problem, said McInnes, was that people associate ownership with alienability, whereas in earlier times possession was secured by law even though the possessor's power of disposition might be limited. McInnes even gave a relatively recent Canadian example: settlers in eighteenth-century Upper Canada who held land by certificates of occupation but who "were not always free to alienate such land."[27] And he said all this in a report submitted in August 1909.

Whether property rights are at stake or not, drawing the line between what is law and what is more reasonably regarded as something less can be difficult. Many definitions have been put forward, including ones designed to illuminate the role of law in stateless societies. A.S. Diamond, for example, insisted on a set of accepted rules to govern a community, sanctions to enforce the rules, and regularity in their imposition.[28] Others have argued that what is crucial is not the coercive enforcement of norms but their specification, which on its own may induce voluntary compliance.[29] The issue is an important one because, left unaddressed, the two solitudes that conduct Aboriginal title litigation simply sail by each other, like ships in the night. The Crown continues to operate on the "stage one" assumption that colonists have law and the Indians do not, and Indigenous witnesses, who are often acutely conscious of the potential significance of their testimony, tend to call all traditional customs and conventions "law."[30] Of course, even in non-Aboriginal legal orders, what is law and what is not law may not be clear until a court is asked to supply the answer.[31] But first one must ask the question.

Elevator Etiquette

Perhaps the most striking illustration of the gulf between the parties in *Tsilhqot'in Nation v. BC*, at least with respect to whether the documentary record yielded any evidence of Tsilhqot'in law, involves the difficult question of how one characterizes frontier violence. I spent a good deal of time in my report describing examples of violent exchanges between fur traders and settlers, on the one hand, and Indigenous people, on the other. Most of these examples I had described before.[32] Some had also been described by others, notably John Phillip Reid in his book *Patterns of Vengeance: Crosscultural Homicide in the North American Fur Trade*, which draws on examples from all over North America.[33] Many involve a chief or relative demanding that a particular person seek blood vengeance for a homicide; others involve offers of payment to avoid the need for blood vengeance. All reflect a legal tradition in which causation, collective responsibility, and compensation are fundamental, rather than fault, individual responsibility, and punishment. As a consequence, accident is not a defence, vengeance can be directed at any member of the offender's relevant kinship group, and, although our friend William Stonia overstated the case, compensation instead of vengeance was often an option.[34]

This is why Chief Ahan and Lutas, two of the Tsilhqot'in who had been involved in the Chilcotin War to which I referred earlier, came down to the coast in 1865 with a large load of furs. They had not been hanged with the others the year before because they had evaded capture, and they were concerned that the colonial authorities would be as relentless in seeking vengeance or compensation as the Tsilhqot'in would have been had the positions been reversed. They therefore made their offer of furs a liberal one and believed it would be accepted. It was not. A decade earlier, Governor Douglas had refused an even more dramatic offer of compensation for the life of a Hudson's Bay Company shepherd. He insisted instead that a sentence of hanging be carried out on Siam-a-sit, a young Cowichan man, notwithstanding that his mother had put forward her elderly husband to be hanged in his place. One for one was Indian law, she told Douglas. English law, however, begged to differ: both Siam-a-sit and, twelve years later, Chief Ahan were executed.[35]

Even more striking is a case from the Yukon at the end of the century. Three young Tagish men were appalled when they realized that Canadian criminal law required them all to die for killing only one white miner. A life for a life, or some form of acceptable payment for a life, was just. To them, three lives for one was, well, barbaric.[36] Two legal traditions, colliding in a courtroom, just as they would in *Tsilhqot'in Nation v. BC* a century later. But even if we were to concede that a system that required three deaths for one had displaced the Tagish rule, why would we deny that the Tagish rule was law?

I think the reason we tend not to see law in this sort of event lies, in large part, in the means of enforcement. In stateless societies, law enforcement depends both upon the sense of duty possessed by the person designated by law to be the enforcer and, if he is reluctant, upon the amount of persuasion brought to bear upon him by elders who are the carriers of the legal tradition.[37] And this may not look like enforcement if you do not consider the Indigenous perspective.

Take the killing of William Manning, almost the only settler in Tsilhqot'in territory in 1864, as an example. It took place after the bulk of the killings in the Chilcotin War, and the documentary evidence indicates that the killer, Tahpit, had been urged to do the deed by Chief Anaheim. At his trial Tahpit conceded he had killed Manning but said, as any man facing a capital charge might, that he had not wanted to: Anaheim had "forced [him] by threat."[38] On one view, this is a straightforward case of Anaheim bullying Tahpit into killing a white man, much as an urban gang boss might bully a new recruit into showing his loyalty by committing a serious crime. But why Tahpit? One explanation supported by the evidence is that the land appropriated by Manning belonged to Tahpit and his family and that he was therefore the legally appropriate person to assert the law of trespass against Manning, who had been warned that he must leave but did not.[39] As Judge Begbie noted in his bench book, Manning had located his homestead on "ground that had formerly been the property of Tahpit's tribe" and that he "had threatened and driven them off."[40]

When people such as Begbie use this sort of language, we need to pay attention. He was acknowledging that there might be some connection between the fact that Manning had squatted on the land of Tahpit's people and the fact that Tahpit was the person designated to kill him for it. Indeed, when he recorded the verdict against Tahpit in his bench book Begbie wrote immediately after it, "Land quarrel."[41]

Other BC examples abound. The killer of Chief Trader Samuel Black in 1841 was urged on by an old woman who was probably his aunt, and who demanded that he avenge the death of Chief Tranquille, whom Black was believed to have killed by magic. The nephew was himself killed months later by a posse of Hudson's Bay men and Okanagans.[42] Nearly half a century later "Kitwancool Jim" was commanded by his wife to kill a medicine man for the same reason: the medicine man had caused their son to sicken and die. When he reluctantly did so, Kitwancool Jim was seen as complying with Kitwancool (Gitanyow) law, but he was killed while escaping the agents of Canadian law, who took a different view.[43] Haatq, the killer of Youmans in 1884, did not need encouragement: he was the father of the young man who had died in Youmans' employ and about whose death Youmans had said nothing, let alone offered compensation. And as William Stonia and I have argued above – along with Haatq's defence lawyer, Attorney General Robson and Justice Henry Pering Pellew Crease – in killing Youmans, Haatq was not some sort of vigilante; he was acting consistently with Gitksan law.[44] Equally, the pressure Chief Anaheim put on Tahpit may look like schoolyard bullying, but that is to view such incidents solely from one perspective – to see, in other words, only the white candlestick.[45]

Not only might the person whose right or even duty it was to carry out a vengeance killing be reluctant, and therefore need the sort of encouragement I have just described, but sometimes a person was expected to give up his own life. This sort of situation arose when compensation for a death could not be agreed upon. Anthropologist Philip Drucker noted some time ago that among some tribes on the Northwest Coast, the life offered in exchange had to be equivalent in rank to the person killed and that the chosen one was expected to "don the ritual finery of his group and come out performing the dance associated with his highest crest until the injured group shot him down."[46] But this was a behavioural ideal and some were not up to it. John Phillip Reid supplies a striking example. In the early 1750s a young Chickasaw who killed a British subject was exhorted by his uncle to kill himself to satisfy the blood debt owed. The young man refused because he was afraid to die, so the uncle went into a public street and stabbed himself in his place, quickly dying of the wound.[47] It was that important.

Perhaps the best example of what to many settlers appeared to be lawless violence was the most common and provoked the most outrage: the apparently random killing of a white man who had no connection to the homicide being avenged. What had "law" to do with this? In fact, the killing of a member of one's group could generally be avenged (assuming compensation could not be agreed upon) not only by killing the perpetrator but, if he could not be caught, by killing *any* member of the perpetrator's legally relevant group. In other words, although individual liability attached to the person who was the actual cause of death, his household, his extended family, or clan – depending on the domestic law of that nation – might bear a collective responsibility as well. But the retaliatory killing was privileged – that is, it had to be accepted by the group subjected to it – only if the authorized avenger of blood killed someone who stood in the appropriate kin relationship to the original victim.[48] So the status of both avenger and avenged was important. On the other hand, if the homicide were international – between nations rather than within a specific nation – no privilege attached because what was "legal under the first nation's customs [might be] illegal to the second nation," and this was "a common cause of Indian wars."[49] It is perhaps unnecessary to add that it was a common cause of conflict with fur traders and settlers as well.

Thus, where a settler (of the British, American, or "white" nation) killed an Indian, the death could be avenged by killing *any* settler unfortunate enough to be in the wrong place at the wrong time. And the killer of the settler would not view himself or be viewed by his nation as having maliciously "murdered" an innocent person. The relevant legal principle was not individual responsibility for intentional or negligent homicide but group responsibility for *all* homicides caused by a member of one's nation. This was true even when an Indian was executed after a trial according to due process of settler law. No privilege attached to the settler executioner, and in many cases what the executed man had done was not illegal under the domestic law of his nation.[50] Government officials knew that such executions ran the risk that vengeance would be taken on an unsuspecting settler who had nothing to do with the case.[51] It may even be why some prisoners, when asked on the scaffold if they had anything to say, urged their fellows not to shed any more blood.[52] They may not have agreed that they had done wrong, but they knew whose laws would prevail in the end and what would happen if their executions were avenged.

Notwithstanding all this evidence of aggressive pressure being brought to bear on persons whom I would describe as responsible for law enforcement, not everyone sees it this way. For example, I was asked by counsel for Canada in the *Tsilhqot'in* case whether I would agree that, because the Tsilhqot'in were "a pre-literate culture with no central institutions of government," their rules were more like elevator etiquette than law. More specifically, I was asked whether the "elevator-riding rules" put to me – such as maintaining maximum distance from one another, facing forwards rather than backwards, and men allowing women to exit first – are analogous to what I was referring to as Tsilhqot'in law.[53] This question, remember, was put after extensive evidence had been presented concerning the strict requirement for compensation, the mutual recognition of exclusive possessory rights in land, and some of the elaborate rules for exacting vengeance that appear to have characterized the Indigenous legal tradition in British Columbia at that time.[54]

It is, I suppose, one interpretation. But somehow I doubt that Samuel Black – let alone Emily Post – would have agreed that his death was the result of a convention analogous to "ladies first." Nor do I think that the obligation that Gitksan law put upon Youmans to offer compensation to the family of his drowned employee or suffer blood vengeance had much in common with our own cultural disinclination to stand too close to another person on an elevator. And when Tsilhqot'in workers at Bute Inlet told the foreman, not long before they attacked the work camp, "You are in our country; you owe us bread," was this like a tip for the elevator operator? Or was it more like a demand for rent?[55] I know what I think the correct answer is, but legal history is one thing, the law another. If the parties choose to litigate, it is for the courts to decide.[56]

Perhaps my characterization of this issue is a little unfair. That is a temptation when provoked. But I am reminded of the first time I went to a school cricket match. I was thirteen, it was September 1961, and I had been watching the activity on the pitch for about ten minutes when I asked the dignified-looking gentleman sitting next to me when the match was going to start. "It started just before you arrived," he rather haughtily informed me. Ignorant of the rules of cricket and used to the rather more rowdy atmosphere of baseball, I had assumed that what I was observing was just some sort of warm-up. Once the rules were explained – actually, it took a little longer than that – I began to see the "form hidden in [the] apparent formlessness" of what I was observing.[57] A newly arrived Martian might have a similar experience watching her first soccer game: it would gradually become obvious that there was a reason that the only players who picked up the ball in their hands were the ones at each the end of the field. The eyes refocus, and random acts of aggression are transformed into rule-directed behaviour.

Conclusion

At a number of points, I was asked in cross-examination by counsel for Canada whether I had simply cherry-picked the historical record for examples of Indigenous law and ignored all evidence to the contrary.[58] This accusation was not surprising, but I think it misconstrues the opinion that I was providing to the court.

One of the questions I was asked to consider by counsel for the plaintiffs was how a legal historian would go about ascertaining whether a particular Indigenous group had a system of laws. My answer, in a nutshell, was that I would begin with two assumptions: first, that Indigenous groups had varying degrees of social organization and, second, that their members engaged in rule-governed relationships with others. The first assumption was expressed with eloquent simplicity more than thirty-five years ago by Justice Judson in *Calder v. AGBC*. When the settlers came, he said, "the Indians were ... *organized in societies* and occupying the land as their forefathers had done for centuries."[59] And long before the question of Aboriginal law achieved the legal importance it has today, Canadian courts had also given effect to the second assumption by holding that Indigenous "customs" could be regarded as laws capable of affecting even common law litigation.[60]

In other words, I was expressing the opinion that if you approach the documentary record assuming stateless societies cannot have laws, you are highly unlikely to find any. (It is rather like a novice fisherman who tries to catch eulachon with a salmon net and then ascribes her lack of success to the absence of eulachon rather than the size of the mesh.) You may even conclude that the demands for and offers of payment, and the extreme pressure put on individuals to take the sort of action taken by Tahpit and Kitwancool Jim, are nothing more than bullying or, to go to the opposite extreme, elevator etiquette. As Canada stated in its closing argument,

> [T]wo of [legal theorist John] Austin's fundamental points are so grounded in common sense and so obvious that they would have occurred to the Court even without ... being referred to Austin's work ... These two points are that: (1) "law" is the command of a sovereign power; and (2) there are rules and customs that govern people's lives that do not constitute "laws." Once these points are admitted ... one is led to the conclusion that the Tsilhqot'in did not have "laws" as we would define them.[61]

Indeed – the Tsilhqot'in did not have laws as counsel for Canada and Austin would define them. But Austin's definition of law has been contested since its inception.[62] Consider instead that vengeance killing and compensation and land tenure *might* be governed by very strict rules – rules that, like our own, would sometimes be violated – and you might discover a whole new layer of meaning. I would go further. I think that what you discover is an Indigenous legal tradition that stands in marked contrast to the Western legal tradition of which Canadian law is a part.[63] It is one in which, as I indicated earlier, causation, collective responsibility, and compensation are the fundamentals, rather than fault, individual responsibility, and punishment. But the two traditions are not wholly alien to each other. The system of land tenure on the Northwest Coast, for example, had much in common with what existed in England in the medieval period. That is, land generally descended by inheritance through families and generally could not be alienated *inter vivos* or devised by will. Indeed, had explorers and traders discovered the coast of British Columbia in the twelfth century rather than the eighteenth, Indigenous societies may not have seemed quite so strange.[64] And they almost certainly would have seen parallels between the emphasis on compensation in Indigenous law and the payment of *wergild* in their Anglo-Saxon homeland. I say this in part because Judge Begbie himself noted the resemblance a mere century and a half ago.[65]

No one has expressed the idea that we need to shift our perceptions if we want to truly understand Indigenous behaviour more clearly than John Phillip Reid. Discussing an incident in which some Paiutes "stole" a horse from one of the trappers with Peter Skene Ogden's Snake expedition in 1829, he says the following:

> We need not quarrel with Ogden for saying that the trapper's horse was "stolen." But we should ask whether the word has as much meaning as Ogden supposed when it is applied to only one side of the cross-cultural equation. What of applying it to the non-Indian ... side? While the Paiutes [who had neither agriculture, domesticated horses, nor effective hunting weapons, and who lived in a barren desert] were skulking about Ogden's camp, shooting arrows at the horses in the hope that their carcasses would be left behind, the Hudson's Bay people were trapping the beaver upon which the Paiutes partly depended for survival. Although we cannot be sure, as Ogden did not mention such matters, it is quite possible that the fur men were catching fish in the river, killing frogs along the banks, or picking the scarce berries from the bushes. Ogden ... would have

> considered it absurd if they had been told that the Indians considered that they were "stealing" the Paiutes' food. In their legal culture, beaver were wild animals belonging to no one and the berries were there for the picking. But what if the Paiutes made the legal argument that the horse was as much game as the beaver, or the moral argument that the trapper wanted to have only the pelt of the beaver or to ride the horse, while they could not survive without the meat from at least one of them? ... *When we employ the word "steal" to describe the conversion of the fur trader's horse by an Indian but not to the killing of beaver by that trapper, our meaning may be clear, but only because the law we apply is our law, the law of a single culture in what was a multicultural legal world.*[66]

Patricia Limerick may have had something similar in mind when she said that, when thinking about American Indian history, it "has become essential to follow the policy of cautious street crossers: Remember to look both ways."[67]

We need to do this even when examining the history of our own legal tradition. Morris S. Arnold, who is both a legal historian and a US federal court judge, makes this point in an essay in which he attempted to grapple with what, to modern eyes, is the impenetrable character of early medieval law. Because of the nature of proof at that time, legal questions and their answers rarely appeared on the record. Instead, God simply announced the result when the oath of one of the parties, usually the defendant, was tested in battle, the ordeal, or by wager of law. Even when juries gradually replaced these modes of trial they, like God, usually gave no reasons for judgment. What mattered was simply that the dispute had been settled. Arnold acknowledged that some might therefore conclude that there was no law involved, only a sort of "risk management." Others might be tempted to call it instinct – or even elevator etiquette. In his view, however,

> there can be commonly held social assumptions about the way a moral world is ordered, founded on logic and experience, that people accept in their daily dealings with each other, *and this entirely apart from whether there are places to resort to for their systematic and dependable vindication*. This natural law, as we may call it, counts, it seems to me and despite Austin, as much for law as the product of the most sovereign decree ever could.[68]

In this essay, I have barely scraped the surface of a topic that presents formidable challenges to the researcher. We really know very little about Indigenous law in the nineteenth century, particularly when confined to the documentary record.[69] Nonetheless, I hope I have shown that, whatever Indigenous law may have been, it was *not* elevator etiquette. Otherwise I have not lived up to the scholarly duty identified by S.F.C. Milsom, perhaps the most thoughtful student of the history of the common law since Maitland. The legal historian, he wrote,

> is generally tolerated by lawyers on a false basis: he is thought somehow to testify that all the wisdom of the ages is behind the present arrangements. But in fact the only distinctive service he can do for his own day is to raise doubts.[70]

I will poach from William Stonia one last time and interpret this as meaning that a person can always try to see things from another perspective.

That is one good thing about legal history.

NOTES

I am grateful to the Foundation for Legal Research for funding the project of which this essay forms a part, and to Matthew Schissel, Shane Sackman, and Micah Weintraub for their research assistance at various points along the way. I would also like to thank Benjamin L. Berger, Constance MacIntosh, Doug Harris, Katherine Cook, and John Borrows for their most helpful comments. A previous version of this paper was published in the *Advocates' Quarterly* 37 (2010): 66–86, and is republished here with permission.

1 William Stonia was a schoolteacher at the Forks of the Skeena River who was also employed by Youmans.
2 For a much more sophisticated analysis of the Gitksan tradition, there are now two excellent sources. Richard Overstall looks at Gitksan property law in "Encountering the Spirit in the Land: 'Property' in a Kinship-Based Legal Order," in John McLaren, A.R. Buck, and Nancy E. Wright, eds., *Despotic Dominion: Property Rights in British Settler Societies* (Vancouver: UBC Press, 2005), 22–49; and Val Napoleon examines the whole sweep of Gitksan law in "Ayook: Gitksan Legal Order, Law, and Legal Theory" (PhD diss., Faculty of Law, University of Victoria, 2009). See also Jo-Anne Fiske and Betty Patrick, *Cis dideen kat – When the Plumes Rise: The Way of the Lake Babine Nation* (Vancouver: UBC Press, 2000) for an analysis of the laws of one of the Gitksan's neighbours.

3 And these assumptions existed on both sides: especially during the early stages of Aboriginal/non-Aboriginal interaction, Indians were equally ignorant of, and confused by, European legal behaviour. But that is the subject of a different essay. Here, "we" means my fellow non-Aboriginals and me.

4 Of course, in the nineteenth century settlers did not invariably conduct a trial and fur traders almost never did. There was always an issue as to how much English due process Indians were entitled to.

5 One scholar who has thought about this issue describes the problem as follows: "First, we judge conduct by its exterior, present manifestation. Second, in doing so, we are unable to penetrate the historical rationality of present conduct. Third, in repetitive action, we see essentially habit and a lack of rationality." H. Patrick Glenn, "The Capture, Reconstruction and Marginalization of 'Custom,'" *American Journal of Comparative Law* 45 (1997): 613. I am indebted to Val Napoleon for this reference.

6 Harold Berman argues that we tend to think the nation-state is a necessary condition of law because "scientific" history was invented in the nineteenth century, in "the heyday of nationalism." See his "Introductory Remarks: Why the History of Western Law Is Not Written," *University of Illinois Law Review* (1984): 512.

7 This was said in the context of the *Haatq* case and is quoted in Hamar Foster, "'The Queen's Law Is Better Than Yours': International Homicide in Early British Columbia," in *Essays in the History of Canadian Law*, vol. 5, *Crime and Criminal Justice*, ed. Jim Phillips, Tina Loo, and Susan Lewthwaite (Toronto: Osgoode Society for Legal History, 1994), 44.

8 For example, in English and Canadian law there is no liability, civil or criminal, for purely accidental harm. Yet such liability makes sense in small hunter-gatherer or harvesting communities where the loss of a provider is a serious matter. Thus, even where there was no fault, compensation had to be made in either blood or property. There are in fact traces of this attitude in the early common law: a "blameless killer" was theoretically liable to forfeiture of property because his act had deprived the king of a subject: J.H. Baker, *An Introduction to English Legal History*, 4th ed. (London: Butterworths, 2002), 529. And today no-fault compensation is hardly an idea that is of purely historical interest. There are also much more fundamental similarities between Indigenous and Anglo-American law, notably when it comes to the "unwritten" variety, and actions in both legal worlds may be obligatory but enforceable only by persuasion and consent. Thus in the *Reference re Resolution to Amend the Constitution*, [1981] 1 S.C.R. 753, the Supreme Court held that, although the Canadian parliament has the legal authority unilaterally to request Britain to amend the constitution in a way

that affected provincial powers, a constitutional convention requires Ottawa to obtain a substantial degree of provincial consent, to be determined not by the courts but by the politicians. (I am indebted to my colleague, Ben Berger, for reminding me of this example.) See generally Jeremy Webber, "The Grammar of Customary Law," *McGill Law Journal* 54 (2009): 579–626, and the many sources referred to therein.

9 Delgamuukw v. British Columbia, [1997] 3 S.C.R. 1010, in which the Supreme Court stated that both the common law and the Indigenous perspective, including Indigenous law, must be brought to bear on the question of whether a plaintiff First Nation has Aboriginal title. Subsequently, in R. v. Marshall; R. v. Bernard, [2005] 2 S.C.R. 220, the court held at paragraph 65 that "[a]ll that is required [to establish Aboriginal title] is a demonstration of effective control of the land by the group, from which a reasonable inference can be drawn that it could have excluded others had it chosen to do so."

10 According to Desmond H. Brown, this was not initially the case in what is now southeastern Canada: see "'They Punish Murderers, Thieves, Traitors and Sorcerers': Aboriginal Criminal Justice as Reported by Early French Observers," *Histoire sociale/Social History* 35/70 (2002): 363–91.

11 Reported in Begbie to Governor Seymour, 30 September 1864, Colonial Correspondence (Begbie), F142F, British Columbia Archives.

12 Report to the secretary of state in *Reg. v. Haatq*, 18 December 1884, file 190, vol. 1421, RG 13, Library and Archives Canada [LAC].

13 Montague Tyrwhitt Drake to Powell, 11 November 1873, quoted in "The Queen's Law," 83. Drake was Haatq's defence counsel in 1884, and he told the jury that anyone in his client's circumstances would have felt not only justified but positively obligated to "follow the tribal laws" and exact blood for the death of his son. The people in this case were the ancestors of the Gitksan and Wetsuwet'en plaintiffs in the *Delgamuukw* case.

14 See John T. Noonan, Jr., *Persons & Masks of the Law* (New York: Farrar, Straus and Giroux, 1976), 20. By "mask," Noonan – who was appointed to the US Court of Appeals for the Ninth Circuit in 1986 – meant "a legal construct, suppressing the humanity of a participant in the process."

15 2007 BCSC 1700. My report, entitled *Tsilhqot'in Law*, was submitted 25 January 2005, and is Exhibit 0391. It was based exclusively on the documentary record and is to date my one and only appearance as an expert witness in an Aboriginal rights case. In 2014 the Supreme Court of Canada confirmed, for the first time in Canada's history, that a First Nation has unextinguished Aboriginal title to a significant portion of their traditional territory: see Tsilhqot'in Nation v. British Columbia, [2014] S.C.C. 44.

16 Or words to that effect. But I am pretty sure he said "nonsense."

17 See, for example, Arthur J. Ray, "Creating the Image of the Savage in Defence of the Crown: The Ethnohistorian in Court," *Native Studies Review* 6/2 (1990): 13–29.

18 I cannot say the same of some of Canada's closing arguments. By way of example, at one point it was implied that my impartiality is suspect because I repudiated in my testimony a view expressed in my 1989 MJur thesis: *Canada's Argument*, fn. 1284. However, no mention is made in this passage that I changed my mind in an essay published a decade before the Tsilhqot'in litigation.

19 Delgamuukw v. British Columbia (1991), 79 DLR (4th) 185 (BCSC), Part 14. "Instinct" is not really an explanation but a substitute for one, and this approach to Indigenous law and institutions was soon rejected by the Supreme Court of Canada. When that court heard the appeal in *Delgamuukw*, for example, the chief justice acknowledged that Aboriginal title is "grounded both in the common law and in the aboriginal perspective on land [which] includes … their systems of law": *Delgamuukw* (1997), paragraph 147. See also Douglas C. Harris, "Indigenous Territoriality in Canadian Courts," in *Box of Treasures or Empty Box? Twenty Years of Section 35*, ed. A. Walkem and H. Bruce (Penticton, BC: Theytus Books, 2003).

20 However, I did criticize the trial judge's decision, firmly but I believe respectfully, at the time: see "It Goes Without Saying: Precedent and the Doctrine of Extinguishment by Implication in *Delgamuukw v. The Queen*," *Advocate* 49/3 (May 1991): 341–57. A revised version was published the following year in Frank Cassidy, ed., *Aboriginal Title in British Columbia: Delgamuukw v. The Queen* (Montreal: Institute for Research on Public Policy, 1992): 133–60.

21 For a contemporary criticism of this aspect of the trial decision in *Delgamuukw*, see Michael Asch, "Errors in *Delgamuukw*: An Anthropological Perspective," in Cassidy, *Aboriginal Title in British Columbia: Delgamuukw v. The Queen*, 221–43 (see especially 224–5).

22 *Tsilhqot'in Nation v. BC, Transcript*, Day 216 (13 April 2005) at 00050–00056 (hereafter, *Transcript*). The dispatch in question was dated 25 March 1861 and was addressed to the secretary of state for the colonies. It is reproduced in *Papers Connected with the Indian Land Question, 1850–1875* (1875; repr., Victoria, BC; Queen's Printer, 1987), 19.

23 See generally S.F.C. Milsom, *The Legal Framework of English Feudalism* (Cambridge: Cambridge University Press, 1972).

24 The description of the fee tail as a "juridical monster" is Milsom's: see his *Historical Foundations of the Common Law*, 2nd ed. (London: Butterworths,

1981), 177. The details of these arrangements need not detain us. Suffice it to say that the fee tail was designed to prevent the "owner" from selling the land and thus disinheriting the heir, but there were ways he could "bar the entail," i.e., get around this obstacle. The strict settlement was a response to the latter and was a marvellous form of legalized intergenerational bribery that worked quite well: by the nineteenth century much of the land in England was locked up in entails. As Brian Simpson puts it in his introduction to vol. 2 of the University of Chicago's 1979 edition of Blackstone's *Commentaries*, it is "remarkable that in spite of Blackstone's exaltation of private individual property rights, the land owning class in reality had little use for them" (xi).

25 See generally Carol M. Rose, "Whither Commodification?" in *Rethinking Commodification: Cases and Readings in Law and Culture*, ed. Martha M. Ertman and Joan C. Williams (New York: New York University Press, 2005), 402–21.

26 See, for example, Amodu Tijani v. Secretary, Southern Nigeria, [1921] 2 A.C., 402–404 (per Lord Haldane). Indeed, it was the trial judge's "preoccupation with the traditional indicia of ownership" that attracted the criticism of Hall, J., in Calder v. AGBC, [1973] S.C.R. 313, xx. This point was made even more recently by Williamson, J., in Campbell v. British Columbia (Attorney-General), 2000 BCSC 1123, paragraph 107.

27 Hamar Foster, "A Romance of the Lost: The Role of Tom MacInnes in the History of the British Columbia Indian Land Question," in *Essays in the History of Canadian Law*, vol. 8, *In Honour of R.C.B. Risk*, ed. G. Blaine Baker and Jim Phillips (Toronto: Osgoode Society, 1999), 192. See this essay for more on McInnes's *Report* (and the two spellings of his name).

28 A.S. Diamond, *Primitive Law Past and Present* (London: Methuen, 1971), 195; referred to in Brown, "'They Punish Murderers,'" 367. A groundbreaking book in this general area is of course K.N. Llewellyn and E. Adamson Hoebel, *The Cheyenne Way: Conflict and Case Law in Primitive Jurisprudence* (Norman: University of Oklahoma Press, 1941).

29 For example, Jeremy Webber, "Grammar of Customary Law," 583–3, discussing the views of Lon Fuller, Gerald Postema, and others.

30 See, for example, Val Napoleon's discussion of the *Delgamuukw* trial, in "Ayook," 49–92. Citing legal theorist William Twining in support, she wonders whether "the seemingly impenetrable insularity of Western law as embodied in the Court" made Gitksan witnesses think that "they had to somehow legitimate their evidence by calling everything law." What is important, she concludes, is that "there was no space to explore this theoretical question in the *Delgamuukw* legal action. The plaintiff's legal counsel

did not take this up and the Crown's main strategy was to undermine Gitksan claims to law by arguing that what the witnesses called law was actually just tradition, and therefore not real law" (72). Nearly two decades later, that remained the Crown's strategy in the *Tsilhqot'in* trial.

31 To take a famous example: who knew that manufacturers owed a *legal* (as opposed to moral) duty of care to consumers with whom they had no contractual relationship until the House of Lords told us they did in Donoghue v. Stevenson, [1932] A.C. 562? And even then, the scope of this duty remained – and remains – unclear.

32 Primarily in Foster, "Queen's Law."

33 John Phillip Reid, *Patterns of Vengeance: Crosscultural Homicide in the North American Fur Trade* (Pasadena, CA[?]: Ninth Judicial Circuit Historical Society, 1999). I discovered Reid's work on law on the Oregon Trail in 1984 when I was a visiting scholar at Berkeley, and Professor John McLaren and I invited him to give the keynote address at a legal history conference we held at the University of Victoria in 1991. I also had the privilege of reading, in draft, some of the articles that later became chapters in *Patterns of Vengeance*.

34 Reid provides a striking example of the divergence of the two legal traditions. In 1805 a young Chippewa shot one of Alexander Henry the Younger's men at the North West Company's Pembina River post. Although it was an accident, the Chippewa youth expected, because he was the cause of the death, to be killed. He was therefore dumbfounded but grateful when Henry investigated the incident and concluded that there had been no intent to kill. Henry may have had a right to execute the young man according to Chippewa law, but his own "legal culture" said otherwise. Finding no intent, Henry "astonished not only the manslayer but probably every other Indian in the area by telling him he would not take his life" (Reid, *Patterns of Vengeance*, 45–7). See also Brown, "'They Punish Murderers,'" 380–4.

35 Foster, *Tsilhqot'in Law*, 32–4; and Foster, "Queen's Law," 63. Lutas, a young man, was pardoned and sent home.

36 See Alan Grove, "'Where Is the Justice, Mr. Mills?' A Case Study of *R. v. Nantuck*," in *Essays in the History of Canadian Law*, vol. 6, *British Columbia and the Yukon*, ed. Hamar Foster and John McLaren (Toronto: Osgoode Society, 1995), 87–127.

37 I say "he" and "him" because, in the records that I have examined, the duty of enforcement has invariably fallen on men.

38 Bench Book of Judge Begbie, GR 2025, vol. 4, British Columbia Archives. Until 1893 no one, Indigenous or non-Indigenous, charged with a serious offence could testify on oath; but Tahpit did speak at his trial.

39 And the penalty for trespass could be death: see, for example, Wilson Duff, ed., *Histories, Territories and Laws of the Kitwancool* (Victoria: British Columbia Provincial Museum, 1964), 36. The Kitwancool (Gitanyow) are a Gitksan people.

40 Bench Book of Judge Begbie.

41 Ibid.

42 Foster, "Queen's Law," 56–8; and Reid, *Patterns of Vengeance*, 87–9, 97–8, and 143–4.

43 See the romanticized account in Marius Barbeau, *The Downfall of Temlahem* (Edmonton: Hurtig, 1973), originally published in 1928.

44 The Gitksan chiefs wrote the government in September of 1884 to "lay before you our laws in regard to accidents and death [*sic*] that occur in company with others" (*BC Sessional Papers, 1885*, 279). It is an interesting conflation of Indigenous and English legal ideas, perhaps because local missionaries, who also wrote independently, were probably involved in its drafting.

45 As T.L. Merrill has written, because property is a norm, there is a consensus that it "cannot exist without some institutional structure that stands ready to enforce it. The usual assumption is that this institution is the state. But it is also possible that it is meaningful to speak of property rights in contexts governed by less formal enforcement mechanisms, such as social ostracism." This may well have been the fate of persons such as Tahpit if they failed to carry out their perceived duty. See "Property and the Right to Exclude," excerpted in Bruce Ziff et al., *A Property Law Reader: Cases, Questions and Commentary*, 2nd ed. (Scarborough, ON: Thomson/Carswell, 2008), 7.

46 Philip Drucker, *Cultures of the North Pacific Coast* (New York: Harper & Row, 1965), 73. When crossing a river on the way to his hanging, the killer of Samuel Black threw himself into the water and "drifted down the current, singing his war song … with little hope of escape." A number of the Okanagans in the posse shot him from the shore: A.C. Anderson, "History of the Northwest Coast," P-C 2, Bancroft Library, Berkeley.

47 Reid, *Patterns of Vengeance*, 48–50.

48 For an explanation of the concept of privilege in this context, see Reid, *Patterns of Vengeance*, 103, 116.

49 Ibid., 97.

50 I say "in many cases" because of course non-Indigenous people do not have a monopoly on lawlessness: sometimes Indians who were subjected to settler justice had acted illegally according to their own laws as well. For some examples see Foster, "Queen's Law."

51 One of the reasons that the trial judge recommended clemency for Haatq, whom he had sentenced to death, was that he had "no doubt that if Haatq be executed the usual vicarious revenge will be taken by some Indian relative on some straggling white." Report of the trial judge to the secretary of state in Reg. v. Haatq, 18 December 1884, file 190, vol. 1421, RG 13, LAC. Justice Crease's use of the term "vicarious" suggests that he had some understanding that a legal principle was at work, even if he had little respect for it. The death sentence was commuted to ten years' imprisonment. Haatq died in prison.

52 The Tsilhqot'in chiefs who were hanged in 1864 were recorded as making this request.

53 *Transcript*, Day 215 (12 April 2005), 00087–00095.

54 Most of these rules must be discerned by inference if relying solely on documentary sources, so some speculation is involved. For examples, see Foster, *Tsilhqot'in Law*, 8–9.

55 Quoted in R.C. Lundin Brown, *Klatsassan, and Other Reminiscences of Missionary Life in British Columbia* (London: Society for Promoting Christian Knowledge, 1873), 9.

56 For the trial judge's thoughtful and lengthy reasons for judgment in the *Tsilhqot'in* case, see above note.

57 Reid, *Patterns of Vengeance*, 195.

58 See, for example, *Transcript*, Day 216 (13 April 2005), 00040–00042 and 00062. I should add that one of the government lawyers has expressed concerns about whether it is "fair or realistic" to expect academics who have "formed close friendships and working relationships with individuals" in an Indigenous group, and whose careers may depend on such relationships, to "display the objectivity required of an expert witness when on the witness stand." See "Recent Developments in Aboriginal Rights and Title Cases," *Aboriginal Law Conference – 2009* (The Continuing Legal Education Society of BC, 3.1.10). Perhaps. But I had never worked with the Tsilhqot'in, had no such friendships or relationships, and my career does not depend on them. Yet the implication in these questions was that I, too, was incapable of objectivity.

59 Calder v. AGBC, [1973], 34 DLR (3d) 145 (SCC), 156 (emphasis added). On this aspect of the *Calder* case see Michael Asch, "*Calder* and the Representation of Indigenous Society in Canadian Jurisprudence," in *Let Right Be Done: Aboriginal Title, the Calder Case, and the Future of Indigenous Rights*, ed. Hamar Foster, Heather Raven, and Jeremy Webber (Vancouver: UBC Press, 2007), 101–10.

60 Some of the cases are discussed in Norman K. Zlotkin, "Judicial Recognition of Aboriginal Customary Law in Canada: Selected Marriage and

Adoption Cases," [1984] 4 CNLR 1. Perhaps the most pertinent example in the present context is Connolly v. Woolrich, [1867], 11 LCJ 197; aff'd [1869] 1 RLOS 253. This decision was cited with approval in 1993 by the BC Court of Appeal in Casimel v. ICBC, [1993] BCJ No. 1834, and concerned Amelia Douglas, wife of Sir James Douglas, and her family. In it, the Quebec courts upheld the validity of William Connolly's marriage *à la façon du pays* to his first, Cree wife at Rat River in Athabaska, notwithstanding that he had subsequently gone through a form of marriage according to Quebec civil law with Julia Woolrich. The court ruled that Connolly's married status under Cree law entitled the children of that marriage, one of whom was Amelia Douglas, to share in the estate. Connolly, who was James Douglas's superior in the HBC and his father-in-law, had succeeded John Stuart as chief factor in charge of New Caledonia in 1825 and presided over the establishment of Fort Chilcotin in 1829.

61 *Canada's Argument*, paragraph 617. The reference to Austin is to John Austin (1790–1859), who restricted the definition of law to the authoritative commands of a sovereign. I had referred the court to his writings.

62 Contrast the views of Justice Morris S. Arnold in "Towards an Ideology of the Early English Law of Obligations," *Law and History Review* 5/2 (October 1987): 505–21, and of the trial judge in Milirrpum et al. v. Nabalco Pty. Ltd. and the Commonwealth of Australia, [1971] 17 F.L.R. 141 (NT Sup. Ct.), 243–4 and 266–7. *Milirrpum* is an important early Aboriginal title case in Australia, and in it Justice Blackburn said he was not "much impressed" by the argument that there must be state enforcement before there can be law. "The inadequacy of the Austinian analysis of the nature of law," he wrote, "is well known." He added that, if a definition of law were necessary, he preferred defining it as "a system of rules of conduct [that] is felt as obligatory upon them by the members of a definable group of people" rather than as "the command of the sovereign."

63 On the latter tradition see Harold Berman, *Law and Revolution: The Formation of the Western Legal Tradition* (Cambridge, MA: Harvard University Press, 1983). For the former, see, for example, the work of my colleague at the Faculty of Law at the University of Victoria, John Borrows, and Val Napoleon, as noted earlier. As Douglas C. Harris has put it, look carefully at the evidence and you may catch "glimpses of a suppressed legal order struggling to survive the hegemony of the colonial legal order": *Landing Native Fisheries: Indian Reserves & Fishing Rights in British Columbia, 1849–1925* (Vancouver: UBC Press, 2008), 17. See also the introduction to his *Fish, Law and Colonialism: The Legal Capture of Salmon in British Columbia* (Toronto: University of Toronto Press, 2001).

64 As Brown notes, some French observers also noted similarities between ancient Old World cultures and Indigenous ones. Jesuit historian Joseph Lafiteau even quoted Herodotus "to show the resemblance between the matrilineal basis of Iroquoian and Huron society and the similar custom of the Lycians of Asia Minor." Brown, "'They Punish Murderers,'" 375–6.
65 See David R. Williams, *"The Man for a New Country": Sir Matthew Baillie Begbie* (Sidney, BC: Gray's Publishing, 1977), 107, citing an 1868 letter from Begbie to Governor Seymour. Reid suggests that Anglo-Saxon law codes might be the best guide to understanding the law of compensation in the Aboriginal transboundary west (Reid, *Patterns of Vengeance*, 19). Certainly, analogues existed among most of the Indigenous peoples of BC: see, e.g., Stuart Michael Piddocke, "Wergild Among the Northwest Coast Indians" (MA thesis, University of British Columbia, 1959), and "Law Enforcement," in Drucker, *Cultures of the North Pacific Coast*, 72–5.
66 Reid, *Patterns of Vengeance*, 27–8 (emphasis added).
67 Patricia Nelson Limerick, *The Legacy of Conquest: The Unbroken Past of the American West* (New York: Norton, 1987), 181. And, needless to say, Indigenous people could be as ignorant of Western legal norms as colonists were of Indigenous ones.
68 Arnold, "Towards an Ideology of the Early English Law of Obligations," 508 (emphasis added). In *Patterns of Vengeance*, Reid also cites Arnold (195–6).
69 Such scholars as Val Napoleon are doing much to remedy this.
70 S.F.C. Milsom, *Studies in the History of the Common Law* (London: Hambledon Press, 1985), 209.

Reclaiming History through the Courts: Aboriginal Rights, the *Marshall* Decision, and Maritime History

KENNETH S. COATES

Canadians and the Government of Canada were truly surprised by the 1999 Supreme Court decision in the *Marshall* case. Charged with fishing commercially without a license, and arguing that he had a treaty right to fish, Donald Marshall Jr. was found not guilty. In the process, the Mi'kmaq and Maliseet of the Maritimes secured a significant right to fish for commercial purposes and, in the surprisingly ill-defined language of the judgment, to earn "a modest income." The *Marshall* decision reinstated the legal authority of eighteenth-century treaties, empowered Atlantic First Nations economically, and transformed the region's political and resource management regimes. Equally important, the *Marshall* decision awakened the Maritimes to the history of treaties and Native-newcomer relations.[1]

Historian J.R. Miller's scholarship has, for more than twenty years, focused on two key elements, both highly relevant to the Maritime situation. First, he has consistently argued and ably demonstrated that the understanding of contemporary Indigenous affairs in Canada requires a sophisticated awareness of historical developments. Second, as his writings have repeatedly shown, the land and treaty claims of the modern era reflect deeply held Indigenous convictions about their entitlements, legal rights, and political standing as autonomous peoples. Aboriginal claims rarely emerge from changing legal and political environments; instead, they typically arise out of strongly and long-held beliefs about the legitimacy of their rights and claims. Jim Miller's research and writing has focused on two related goals: identifying areas of limited understanding/misunderstanding about Indigenous history and using historical analysis to build bridges between what are often very different views of the past.

The situation surrounding Mi'kmaw and Maliseet treaty and Aboriginal rights in the Maritime provinces provides a compelling illustration of the importance of Jim Miller's approach to the study and application of history. Given high-profile conflicts at Burnt Church and Indian River, and non-Indigenous protests throughout the region over the past decade, it is easy to forget how little attention Aboriginal claims and aspirations received in the region before the *Marshall* decision. While Mi'kmaw and Maliseet politicians, elders, and scholars spoke often about historical injustices and misallocated resources, their complaints generally went unanswered. In the Maritimes, most non-Indigenous people assumed the matter to have been settled through treaties that predated the Royal Proclamation of 1763 and that were deemed to have resolved, for all time, questions about Aboriginal rights and claims. Indeed, as recently as two years before the *Marshall* decision, most Maritimers would have argued that Aboriginal rights in the region had been well and truly settled.[2]

The *Marshall* decision affords an opportunity to explore two critical elements in Maritime history: the regular efforts by the Mi'kmaq and Maliseet to gain attention to their treaty rights and the marginalization of First Nations in the region's historical memory. In the first instance, First Nations people made numerous representations to governments seeking recognition of what they believed to be treaty rights. More generally, the social and economic invisibility of the Mi'kmaq and Maliseet resulted in a substantial removal of the First Nations from regional history.[3] Despite the efforts of a small number of historians and Indigenous scholars to build public understanding of First Nations history, the public at large were drawn more to a history of Acadia settlers, Loyalists, loggers, and perfidious central Canadians than they were to the issues of treaty rights, Aboriginal policy, and the harsh conditions facing Indigenous peoples in the region. Somewhat unusually for a region whose political history and historiography is rooted in a profound sense of grievance, the sense of injustice among the Indigenous peoples has remained outside the historiographical mainstream. Maritime historiography, after all, is dominated by superb threads of analysis relating to Maritime autonomy and political rights, the challenges of the region's working class, the economic crises associated with Confederation, and the frustrations of political marginalization. The study of Indigenous history and concerns has only rarely been integrated into the broader discussion of regional evolution.[4]

It is not that historians have been silent on Indigenous issues or ignorant of the experiences of the Mi'kmaq and Maliseet. The major works on the subject – Leslie Upton's *Micmacs and Colonists*,[5] Andrea Bear Nicholas's contributions,[6] William Wicken's excellent background study of Mi'kmaw and Maliseet claims – and other historical studies have made significant contributions to both regional history and the understanding of Native-newcomer experiences in the Maritimes.[7] In general, however, historians have dealt with Indigenous issues as substantially separate from other political, social, and economic currents in the region. Just as the Indigenous and non-Indigenous peoples in the region largely inhabited separate social, economic, and political spaces, so did the historical understanding of the Maritimes keep Indigenous anger and frustration distinct from regional political processes.

History, Treaty Rights, and the Public

Less than forty years ago, the study of Aboriginal treaty rights and claims scarcely registered on the national historical and historiographical consciousness. The general Canadian understanding – offset somewhat by political statements from Indigenous leaders and a small number of books like Harold Cardinal's *The Unjust Society*[8] – was that Indigenous Canadians had been treated well, certainly compared to the United States. The stated position of Prime Minister Pierre Elliot Trudeau that the Government of Canada was not interested in revisiting historical "might have beens" seemed to foreclose the idea of revisiting existing treaties or signing new ones. In fairly short order, started by Indigenous protests over the ill-conceived 1969 White Paper on Indian Affairs, the 1973 *Calder* decision on Nisga'a land rights in British Columbia, and the launch of comprehensive land claims negotiations with Indigenous groups in the Canadian North, the issue of treaty rights shifted from the national back burner to a key place in Canadian public affairs.[9]

At its root, the debate about Aboriginal treaty rights and claims rested on very different understandings of the past. Indigenous groups spoke of broken and unfulfilled promises, unresolved land and resource rights, and government lawlessness in dealing with their issues.[10] The national consensus was markedly different, emphasizing the absence of violence as had occurred in the United States and fair reserve and income support arrangements, as well as highlighting a peaceful treaty-making process, particularly in the West. The historical gap proved both crucial and formidable. It was difficult to motivate politicians and the country at large to respond to a perceived crisis when the general understanding was that Canada had handled its Indigenous affairs generously and properly. This consensus unravelled fairly quickly, however, as a new generation of historians shifted the focus of studies on Native-newcomer relations away from the fur trade and missionaries and towards government policy and the broader issues of the place of Indigenous peoples in Canadian society. The work of such scholars as A.J. Ray, Sylvia Van Kirk, Robin Fisher, Brian Titley, Jennifer Brown, Olive Dickason, John Tobias, Bruce Trigger, L.F.S. Upton, Frank Tough, Sarah Carter, and J.R. Miller challenged the historiographical understanding and offered a more nuanced and comprehensive view of the evolution of the place of Indigenous people within Canadian society.[11]

Several core and dramatic conclusions arose out of the new literature. First, it became clear that Indigenous people played an active role in shaping Native-newcomer relationships; they had not been passive pawns swept aside by the more powerful Europeans. Studies of government policy after Confederation and on the impact of residential schools (another area studied by J.R. Miller, who wrote the most important book on the subject) made it clear that the national authorities had not handled Indigenous affairs in the generous manner and spirit Canadians had assumed. Perhaps most importantly, the writing demonstrated that, in many different historical contexts, Indigenous people had been concerned about their rights to traditional lands and resources and pressed repeatedly their claims on governments. Equally, scholarship relating to the early treaties made it clear that Indigenous groups played an active role in encouraging, shaping, and monitoring treaty processes and rights. These pivotal documents had not emerged, as had long been thought, as a result of the benevolent hand of the federal government, reaching out to avoid conflict and dispossession of Native peoples, but rather as a consequence of direct Indigenous intervention in the settlement process.

While Canadian historians played a pivotal role in changing national assumptions about the role of Indigenous peoples in national history – an effort aided and reinforced by the speeches and statements of Indigenous leaders from across the country – more direct intervention loomed. In a series of highly controversial court cases, highlighted by the fundamentally important Delgamuukw legal process in north-central British Columbia, professional historians were drawn into the middle of the legal proceedings.[12] Court rulings on two major themes – the need to prove Indigenous occupancy of claimed territories and specific actions by governments or their agents that were not in keeping with the terms and/or spirit of the original agreements – made it clear that historians would play a central role in determining the outcome of the court cases. As happened with A.J. Ray in the *Delgamuukw* case, professional historians brought the documents, perspectives, and debates of the academy into the court, often to discover that the two cultures clashed as much as they complemented each other.[13]

Over the past quarter century, the confluence of Aboriginal rights, court proceedings, and engaged professional historians has transformed the historical profession, Indigenous law in Canada, and public understanding of the role of Indigenous people in Canadian history. High-profile court proceedings – including controversial rulings such as that issued by British Columbia Chief Justice Allan McEachern in the *Delgamuukw* case – attracted a great deal of media attention and sparked enormous public debate, particularly about the chief justice's characterization of pre-contact First Nations' life in British Columbia. The rulings and the government's response to the rulings typically attract lengthy and widespread attention, in part because legal precedents can and often are rolled out quickly across the country.[14] Equally, the imprimatur of the legal process, particularly when cases proceed all the way to the Supreme Court of Canada, offers a level of legitimacy and public attention that few historians can match.[15] Indeed, one could argue that the series of historically based court cases has done a great deal to shift Canadian attitudes towards Aboriginal rights in Canada. Importantly, however, not all of the shift has been towards a greater appreciation of the historical experience of Indigenous Canadians; the identification and enforcement of Aboriginal treaty and resource rights has also had the opposite effect of increasing challenges to the empowerment of Indigenous peoples.[16]

Mi'kmaw and Maliseet Rights

Indigenous people in the Maritimes were not, until the late 1990s, seen as being closely connected to the national treaty rights and claims processes. Their contact with Europeans – initially the French and, in the eighteenth century, the British – predated many of the better-known pivotal decisions relating to Aboriginal rights. The Royal Proclamation of 1763, for example, which committed the British authorities to signing treaties with Indigenous groups before occupying their lands, came after the initial settlements with the Mi'kmaq. The French had managed relations in the Maritimes with minimal conflict or formality before losing control of much of the region in the Treaty of Utrecht in 1713.

The British, in contrast, had difficulty controlling both the First Nations, who retained strong cultural and religious ties with the French, and the Acadians (French settlers and their descendants). Indeed, in the 1750s, the British went so far as to expel most of the Acadians from the region. Even the militarization of the region – the French at Louisbourg and the British at Halifax – did not end the uncertainty. The Mi'kmaq, in particular, found themselves drawn into the French-English conflict, living on lands internationally recognized as being British but still influenced by the French forces from New France. (The Maliseet in the Saint John River valley were largely removed from these eighteenth-century conflicts and pressures.)

Anxious to control the Mi'kmaq and to ensure their neutrality in times of war, the British signed a series of treaties with the local Indigenous peoples. Mascarene's Treaty (known as the Treaty of Boston and initially signed in 1725), a peace and friendship agreement, was signed in the region in 1726. A second major agreement, the Treaty of Halifax, was signed in 1752, again in an attempt to end hostilities associated with the bitter French-English conflict in the region. J.R. Miller summarized the treaty arrangements:

> Whereas the Treaty of Boston and Mascarene's Treaty (1725–26) had recognized an unimpeded First Nations right to gather, the 1752 agreement enshrined a right to trade, including at government-created and -subsidized truckhouses if they wished. Trade and peace were still closely linked.[17]

Events conspired to undermine the effectiveness of Mi'kmaw and Maliseet relations with the British. With the removal of the Acadians and the defeat of the French in New France in 1759–60, the military and political importance of the region subsided. New treaties of peace and friendship were signed. In fairly short order, however, the American Revolution unleashed sizeable British North American migration to the Maritimes, swamping the existing population, placing greater pressure on Indigenous use of land and resources, and altering the cultural balance in the area permanently. The Mi'kmaq, in particular, continued to press for recognition of their harvesting and commercial rights but with little support or interest from government officials.

The Mi'kmaq and Maliseet did not simply surrender to the new wave of immigrants. They remained in control of substantial portions of their traditional territories and, where they were able to do so, continued long-established harvesting activities. The newcomers, however, had little interest in the First Nations, pushing onto their lands and relegating them to the margins of the economic and social system. Importantly, the Indigenous people remained committed to traditional pursuits and, importantly, pressured governments to respect and attend to the treaty rights granted under the various eighteenth-century accords. As a Mi'kmaw petition of 1849 argued,

> Before the white people came, we had plenty of wild roots, plenty of fish and plenty of cord. The skins of the Moose and Cariboo were warm to our bodies, we had plenty of good land, we worshipped "Kesoult" the Great Spirit, we were free and we were happy.
>
> Good and Honorable Governor [John Harvey, lieutenant governor of Nova Scotia], be not offended at what we say, for we wish to please you. But your people had not land enough, they came and killed many of our tribe and took us from our country. You have taken from us our lands and trees and have destroyed our game. The moose yards of our fathers, where are they. Whiteman kill the moose and they leave the meat in the woods. You have put ships and steamboats upon the waters and they scare away the fish. You have made dams across the rivers so that the Salmon cannot go up, and your laws will not permit us to spear them.
>
> In our old times our wigwams stood in the pleasant places along the sides of the rivers. These places are now taken from us, and we are told to go away. Upon our camping groups you have built towns, and the graves of our fathers are broken by the plough and harrow. Even the ash and maple are growing scarce. We are told to cut no trees upon the farmer's ground, and the land you have give us is taken away every year …
>
> All your people say they wish to do us good, and they sometimes give, but give a beggar a dinner and he is a beggar still. We do not like to beg. As our game and fish are nearly gone and we cannot sell our articles, we have resolved to make farms, yet we cannot make farms without help. What more can we say? We will ask our Mother the Queen to help us. We beg your Excellency to help us in our distress, and help us that we may at last be able to help ourselves.[18]

For the First Nations in the Maritimes, the peace and friendship treaties were supposed to have secured for them a permanent place in the regional order. That failed to happen. The Mi'kmaq and Maliseet steadily lost control of their traditional lands and resource grounds, encountered increasing poverty, and found little interest in their appeals for either recognition of their treaty rights or general support for their economic and social concerns. A court challenge (*Rex v. Sylliboy*, 1928) failed to secure recognition of treaty rights to hunt and trap and seemed to limit future use of treaties to gain harvesting opportunities.[19] The Maritime region developed at a rapid pace – by the time of Confederation, it was the wealthiest part of the new Dominion of Canada – with increased population across Nova Scotia, Prince Edward Island, and New Brunswick. Government efforts at education, including the Shubenacadie residential school, and minor initiatives on other fronts had little constructive impact. The Mi'kmaq and Maliseet had been relegated to the margins in their own homelands.

Indigenous leaders did not simply accept the lot of their people. But petitions, representations, and protests to the British authorities and (after 1867) the Government of Canada, secured little satisfaction or even interest. No serious thought was given at the governmental level to reopening the treaties; from the government's point of view, issues of land and resources had been settled. The Mi'kmaq and Maliseet experienced a resurgence of political activism in the 1960s and 1970s, although with much less of an impact on the national scene than that in the rest of the country. A growing number of disputes, such as the Eel Ground reserve controversy in 1995 and the Christmas Mountain logging conflict the following year, made it clear that Indigenous people were unhappy with the status quo. For most Maritimers, however, these were isolated and local issues, with no real significance to the region or the country.

The situation changed – dramatically – with two court decisions in the 1990s. The regionally significant matter of Thomas Peter Paul and the much better-known Donald Marshall Jr. case destroyed any remaining sense that Indigenous Maritimers were content with their lot and undermined forever the argument that treaty rights were a dead issue in the region.[20] Both cases had a direct impact on regional and national understanding of the historical role and circumstances of Indigenous people in Canada.

Thomas Peter Paul, from the Pabineau Reserve in Northern New Brunswick, was arrested in May 1995 and charged with harvesting bird's-eye maple, a much-valued tree. He and other Maliseet had been harvesting the trees for some time, challenging the government to stop them from cutting trees on privately licensed land. Citing Mascarene's Treaty as his justification, Paul brought his arguments about existing treaty rights into the court. Provincial court judge Frederic Arsenault issued his surprising ruling on 28 August 1996, agreeing that the treaties protected Aboriginal resource rights. The appeal was heard the following year before Justice John Turnbull of the Court of Queen's Bench. Turnbull accepted – and enlarged – the decision, making a clear declaration that Mi'kmaq and Maliseet could harvest trees for commercial purposes, in keeping with the terms of the eighteenth-century treaties.

The ruling shocked governments and the public alike. Indigenous people had been empowered to assert their treaty rights and to use resources for commercial purposes. And a significant number did so. Non-Indigenous Maritimers reacted with dismay to the prospect of widespread and unregulated logging and to the possibility that the treaty rights might extend much further. The government appealed the decision yet again, this time to the New Brunswick Court of Appeal. The Court of Appeal dismissed the earlier court rulings, arguing that Justice Turnbull had erred in using historical material not placed in evidence before him and rejected the idea that commercial logging was a traditional activity conducted by Indigenous people in the region before contact. An attempt to have the case heard by the Supreme Court was rejected. First Nations reacted angrily to the decision, which they argued had removed from them long-ignored harvesting and treaty rights. Non-Indigenous politicians and commentators generally declared themselves pleased with the decision, which promised a return to order and the rule of the law in the forests of New Brunswick.

The shock and frustration associated with the Thomas Peter Paul decision was soon replaced by an even more dramatic court case, involving the familiar Donald Marshall Jr. Marshall had been involved in a false imprisonment case in the 1980s which, when fully investigated, revealed deep patterns of racism and misuse of power in Nova Scotia policing and legal processes. He returned to the public eye in the late 1990s, this time arising out of an arrest for fishing eels in Pomquet Harbour, Nova Scotia. With the high-profile and influential Bruce Wildsmith as his lawyer, Marshall pushed his case through a series of court reversals, arriving at the Nova Scotia Court of Appeal in 1997. The *Marshall* case hinged on a core assertion: that the original treaties, through the promise of the "truck houses," guaranteed the Mi'kmaq an ongoing right to harvest resources for commercial purposes. An appeal of the case was heard before the Supreme Court of Canada in 1998, attracting a reasonable amount of attention from First Nations groups, fishers' representatives, and government officials. Expectations were fairly slight, however, as the argument about the eighteenth-century treaties rested on slender terms within the treaty and a complex argument about the government's interpretation of those treaty provisions at the time they were signed. The government's position was that the treaty rights were simply an administrative expedient – the truck houses were places First Nations could trade if there were no other alternatives – and not a guarantee of an ongoing right separate from those enjoyed by other British subjects in the area.

The Supreme Court decision was rendered on 17 September 1999, to the delight of the First Nations and the dismay of the federal government and many non-Indigenous observers. By a vote of 5–2, the Supreme Court found in Marshall's favour, arguing that the eighteenth-century treaties covered fishing rights while maintaining that the rights were not unlimited. Rather, they were subject to conservation measures and were restricted to providing the First Nations with a "moderate income." The federal government, caught unaware by the sweeping nature of the decision, reacted slowly, adding to confusion in the fisheries. East Coast fishers, particularly in the lobster fishery, expressed dismay and worried about the future of their industry. Indigenous people in the Maritimes and across the country saw the decision as a further and continuing vindication of their claims to Aboriginal and treaty rights. Controversy swirled throughout the Maritimes, as the First Nations prepared to go fishing, as non-Indigenous fishers prepared to stop them, and as the Government of Canada decided what to do to control the situation. Confrontations erupted, particularly at Burnt Church, Nova Scotia, with standoffs edging towards violence through 1999 and 2000. The Supreme Court, seemingly dismayed by the public and often vitriolic response to the case, took the unusual step of clarifying their ruling in November 1999, stressing that the judgment applied only to the very specific issues at hand and did not extend the recognition of treaty rights to other resources, pending court hearings on these matters.

Historical Understanding and Treaty Rights

Legal scholars and political scientists have been examining these court cases, particularly the *Marshall* decision, in considerable detail. For historians, the court processes and outcomes reveal several very important aspects of the role of historical understanding and historians in the contested field of Aboriginal treaty and resource rights.[21] As A.J. Ray, one of Canada's leading practitioners of historical engagement with

Aboriginal legal processes, summarized the professional significance of the *Marshall* decision,

> *Regina v Marshall* highlights how the evolution of Aboriginal and treaty rights in Canada is an interactive process involving the First Nations, the public at large, the judiciary and the academic community. Each Aboriginal or treaty rights case raises general and particular historical questions that can significantly affect the lives of members of specific Native communities and those of their non-Aboriginal neighbours. Expert witnesses have to address the questions raised in reference to guidelines and procedures that the judiciary uses to assess their evidence and interpretations. In turn, the judiciary's understanding of Native history continually changes as a result of the participation of ethno-historical experts.[22]

Ray's study demonstrates how theoretical, conceptual, and methodological approaches intersect with the more narrowly structured legal environment. In addition, the engagement of historians in Aboriginal rights cases reveals broader and more general issues worthy of consideration. Judges and lawyers debate highly specialized questions, relating to the meaning and veracity of specific documents and the interpretive context within which the debates occurred. For other observers of the legal-historical processes, the debate over Aboriginal historical and legal rights reveals different patterns of interest to professional historians.

As the situation in the Maritimes proved, public understanding about Indigenous affairs can often be very limited. The situation varies across the country, from strong engagement (not always supportive) in British Columbia, the Prairies, and the North to limited interest in the Maritimes (before the Thomas Peter Paul and Donald Marshall cases). Treaty issues may be very much alive within First Nations communities, sustained by oral tradition and political activity, but they do not always surface in public discussions. When they do – even in western jurisdictions – the historical contexts within which these contemporary Indigenous debates are framed are rarely well understood. The standard historians' means of sharing and communicating new ideas, including scholarly books and articles, conference papers and university lectures, supplemented by occasional public engagement, have proven to be less than effective at changing public attitudes. The academic consensus – what Thomas Flanagan critically described as the "Aboriginal orthodoxy"[23] – on the rights of Indigenous peoples has been firmly established for more than twenty years. Yet public opinion polls suggest that general support for Aboriginal rights, derived from earlier commitment and past injustices, has fallen in that time. This pattern presents a significant challenge for historians who believe that the collective research and analysis of the profession should filter to society at large and should influence public attitudes towards Indigenous peoples and their rights.

Disputes about History

Aboriginal rights cases in Canada are rarely based on theoretical or conceptual arguments about the legal status of Indigenous peoples. Instead, the cases arise from one of several considerations: the failure of the Government of Canada (or its predecessors) to attend to their legal duties and responsibilities; the need for an Indigenous group to establish its use and occupancy; the failure to implement, enforce, or otherwise respect an earlier agreement with Indigenous peoples; or the argument that a law of government has not been properly applied or has not been applied at all. In a large number of instances, cases arise from highly specific challenges to the government and/or non-Indigenous interests, including the removal of land from a reserve, the inappropriate use of reserve land, disputes over membership or eligibility for Aboriginal rights, and the like.

Many of these cases – such as those started by Thomas Peter Paul and Donald Marshall – turn on historical understanding. The resolution of these cases requires a detailed understanding of the historical setting and context, access to appropriate written documents or oral testimony germane to the subject, and the historian's ability to assemble the material into a compelling and accurate narrative that makes sense to the court. Legal proceedings have become, as a result, historical and historiographical battlegrounds, with judges weighing both historical evidence and historical interpretation, and charged with relating the information both to the specific context under discussion and to the law of Canada. These can be extremely difficult processes, involving a great deal of work assembling the data, developing the arguments, and debating the evidence in court.

Historians as Participants

Because of the growing importance of historical understanding, historians have become ever more prominent in the Aboriginal rights processes. While some critics, notably Thomas Flanagan, Francis Widdowson, and Albert Howard,[24] decry the development of the "Aboriginal industry," the need to understand the historical circumstances and settings of literally thousands of cases has created greatly expanded opportunities for historical researchers and for experts willing to testify in court. The Thomas Peter Paul case did not involve extensive contributions from historical professions; indeed, the absence of a solid understanding of context and evidence proved to be a significant part of its downfall at the New Brunswick Court of Appeal. In the *Marshall* case, two historians, John Reid of St Mary's University and William Wicken of York University, worked with lawyer Bruce Wildsmith and the Marshall team. Stephen Patterson of the Department of History, University of New Brunswick, likewise served as an expert researcher and witness for the Crown in the case.

These three talented historians brought very different views to their work. Reid did not see the eighteenth-century treaties as constituting Mi'kmaw subjugation or surrender. Instead, he viewed them as agreements that reflected the balance of power in the region. Wicken argued that the British knew they had to make concessions to gain the peace they sought and that the Mi'kmaq would not have accepted the regulation of their harvesting activity. In addition, he suggested in court, issues of language and translation may have interfered with the shared understanding of the treaty terms and meaning. Stephen Patterson, brought before the court as a Crown witness, noted the deficiencies in the historical record and argued that the British used the treaties to bring the First Nations under government control, ensuring that the Mi'kmaq became subjects of the British Crown. The interpretations differ – as they usually do in the historical profession – and a sophisticated understanding of the historical, cultural, and political context backed each argument. The court decision turned, in substantial measure, on the justices' understanding of the historical arguments (although, as will be argued below, with the ironic twist that Dr Patterson's analysis was also used in part in making the ruling in favour of Marshall).

To a degree that few in the profession would have anticipated a few decades ago, historians have become actively engaged in legal processes, playing prominent roles as researchers and expert witnesses. It could not be any other way. The Canadian court system, particularly on matters related to Aboriginal rights and treaties, must come to terms with complex and highly controversial historical situations. Working through these processes in a historically sound manner is exceptionally difficult, since the assessments must determine what is legally right more than what is historically acceptable. To engage in this kind of analysis, particularly given how much rests on the outcome for all participants, without the use of trained historians would be unthinkable. It is now abundantly clear that Aboriginal and treaty rights cases will require ongoing engagement by the historical profession.

An important caveat is in order, however. Both technically and professionally, historians and other expert witnesses work for the courts, regardless of which side in the proceedings introduces them as witnesses. They are expected – as did Reid, Wicken, and Patterson – to stick to the evidence and to offer interpretations based on their professional understanding of the situation. Expert witnesses are not advocates for a particular position and may not even be fully aware of how their research and testimony relates to the specifics of the case being argued. Indeed, their responsibility is to the historical circumstances themselves, and to the standards of evidence, analysis, and interpretation in the historical profession at large. It is clear that the *Marshall* decision could not have proceeded as thoughtfully or as systematically without the engagement of historical professionals, who will continue to feature prominently in future cases of this type.

History Inside and Outside the Courtroom

While professional historians have engaged extensively with Aboriginal treaty and rights cases, an uncomfortable gap remains between the realities of the seminar room and conference presentations and the expectations of the courtroom. The *Marshall* case, in particular, proved to be a highly emotional exercise, involving legal and judicial review of an unclear and hotly contested theme in Indigenous and Maritime history. That three historians of the quality and stature of Reid, Wicken, and Patterson could bring divergent views to bear on the topic demonstrates the complexity of the historical situation, the paucity of documentation, and the very different contextual perspectives that the historians brought to the issue. As scholars will know, historiographical debates of this type can and do become heated, particularly when the subject at hand carries any of the highly emotional issues of race, gender, class, or region, to say nothing of extensive contemporary relevance and impact.

In legal proceedings, however, there has to be a winner, not just a healthy exchange of views. And the arbiter of victory is going to be a judge who may or may not understand the historical nuances, the complexities of evidence, and subtleties of contemporary academic analysis. Within the historical professions, disputes are engaged through commentators at conference sessions, anonymous peer reviews of research grants, critical or laudatory citations of published works, and formal books reviews. In Canada, these exchanges are generally (but not always) genteel and couched in careful language. On the other hand, in court proceedings, the stakes are often enormous. A winning argument can result in the acceptance of a long-demanded Aboriginal or treaty right. It can return wealth to a community or permanently remove the prospect of a decent settlement. A historian's participation can buttress Indigenous arguments – as Reid and Wicken did in *Marshall* – or support government arguments. Historians participating in legal proceedings, most of whom form strong opinions about the legitimacy of the cause they are discussing, carry an impressive weight on their shoulders.

Interestingly, historians carry their courtroom participation back into the profession. Historians deemed to be working on behalf of the government – and by definition against Indigenous claimants – often get sharply criticized for their participation. There is an assumption, far from true, that government-selected experts are somehow less sincere and more politicized than those testifying for Indigenous participants. In the *Marshall* case, Stephen Patterson faced considerable – even extreme – criticism for his role in providing expert testimony. He handled the response ably and professionally, but the critiques were unnecessary and inappropriate. His role in the court case was precisely the same as that of John Reid and William Wicken. He reviewed the evidence, interpreted it as he saw fit, and offered his services to the court. What the experience of the *Marshall* historians made clear is that the legalization of historical evidence and interpretation also politicizes and publicizes both the ideas and the participants. This rarely happens in the more genteel, isolated, and strictly academic discourses of the historical profession.

Judges as Historians

The Thomas Peter Paul and Donald Marshall Jr. cases raise serious questions about the ability of the judicial process to make sense of nuanced and complex historical circumstances. Court cases are evidentiary based. Judges look for clear and precise details that point to a specific outcome.

The understanding of historical situations, in contrast, is strongly contextual and interpretative. Understanding the past requires the careful handling of evidence, a comprehensive awareness of the historical context, and finely developed interpretative skills. Judges handle a baffling variety of cases and usually are presented with voluminous amounts of documentation, thousands of pages of expert testimony, and, often in Aboriginal cases, many hours of oral testimony. The material compiled and presented for the *Marshall* case was sizeable and would present a challenge for any historian to work through, without the added burden of coping with the complex legal issues around Aboriginal and treaty rights and knowing that the final decision would, one way or another, have a profound impact on First Nations and the surrounding community. A scholar facing the uncertainty of anonymous peer review or the potential disappointment of an often long delayed published review carries nothing like the expectations and pressures heaped on the back of a judge weighing an Aboriginal rights case.

In these two cases, the judges involved created historical controversy. The Thomas Peter Paul case attracted considerable attention because of the historical difficulties. The first judge accepted a thinly argued historical case, one not backed by solid documentation or analysis. The second judge, chastised later by the Court of Appeal for his handling of historical elements, added his own historical research and analysis to an already poorly handled historical case. In the end, the case was lost, at least in part, because the participants did not launch a proper case, drawing on detailed documentation and solid professional testimony. The situation was much different in the *Marshall* case, for each side brought professional historians and extensive research to the table. The Supreme Court decision, written for the majority by Justice Ian Binnie, included extensive use of the historical and historiographical testimony and clearly relied heavily on that information in reaching a conclusion.

Stephen Patterson, who believed that his testimony had been seriously misused by the Supreme Court, spoke out after the ruling: "I guess one is not supposed to say that the Supreme Court made errors, but it seems to me that strictly on the basis of historical fact, the justices in the majority decision may not have a view of the facts that would be adopted by an historian." Responding further to the decision, he said, "What I said was that the treaty gave the Micmac permission to bring the goods they had for sale to a truckhouse. What the judge did with that at the trial level was to say they had a right to trade at truckhouses and when the truckhouses ceased to exist any right that was implicit in the treaty disappeared with the truckhouses. But Binnie doesn't see that."[25] The Supreme Court recanted somewhat in its clarification of the initial ruling, but the main point here holds: historians testifying in court proceedings, regardless of the side that calls them to the stand, run the risk of having their analysis and evidence used by judges who are not trained historians and who might well misunderstand or misuse the information provided to them.

The Courts and Public Awareness

Historians have, at the core of their professional existence, the idea that historical awareness is essential to citizenship and understanding of one's place within the world. Each historian has his or her own way of attempting to achieve this end, although the vast majority remain most comfortable with traditional disciplinary means of sharing information. While a small number have added documentary films, websites, and other such media to their repertoire, the standard books, journal articles, and conference papers remain the main currency of the discipline. Court cases demonstrate the potential – in terms of both opportunities and risks – of dramatically different approaches. Because of Thomas Peter Paul and Donald Marshall Jr., the people of the Maritimes have a much stronger understanding of the historical circumstances of Mi'kmaq and Maliseet. There is much greater awareness about the eighteenth-century treaties and even more appreciation for the frustrations of First Nations peoples attempting to have their grievances heard and their challenges addressed. Indigenous issues are much more prominent on the provincial and regional agenda than ever before, in part because the shock of the *Marshall* decision awoke politicians to the dangers of continuing without a meaningful resolution of outstanding Indigenous issues.

For at least five years – from the first decision in the Thomas Peter Paul case to several years after the *Marshall* judgments and the calming of emotions around Aboriginal treaty rights in the region – Maritimers engaged extensively with issues around Mi'kmaw and Maliseet history. Extensive newspaper, radio, and television coverage arose out of the court processes, decisions, and subsequent controversies. Many of the media conversations were based, if only thinly, on comments about the historical background to the court decisions. Government actions, particularly related to logging rights and the sharing of the forests with Indigenous communities, ensured that the controversies remained alive and the debates current. Public figures became more attuned to the political presence of Mi'kmaq and Maliseet, many of whom continued to expect much more out of the legal and treaty processes than had been delivered. Lively debates, often angry and even extremely bitter at times, focused on the past, current, and future role of Indigenous people within Maritime society.

It is wrong to argue that the Thomas Peter Paul and Donald Marshall Jr. cases resulted in an immediate, deep, and positive appreciation for the history and cultures of the Mi'kmaq and Maliseet. Many angry words were spoken, and communities, particularly those reshaped by the controversies over the lobster fisheries, found themselves divided by the highly emotional controversies. Indigenous people found both support and pride in the judgments, for they vindicated a widely held Indigenous view of the history of treaties and their rights. Non-Indigenous supporters of Indigenous causes discovered historical validation for their defence of the eighteenth-century treaties and encouragement for their campaigns to improve Indigenous conditions. Governments, paying more attention to Indigenous issues, began to take the kind of steps in education and public policy that had become commonplace in central, western, and northern Canada. Somewhat lost in the debate is the reality that the *Marshall* decision recast the regional fishery in constructive and positive ways, paving the way for much greater Indigenous participation in all aspects of the East Coast fishery.

The provincial and federal court systems managed to do, in sum, what historians had been trying to accomplish for several decades. The courts were able to bring Mi'kmaw and Maliseet history and historical grievances into the public view. The courts did this best and most effectively when there was active participation by professional historians, even if the latter found the experience rather rocky and unsettling at times. The Supreme Court seemed surprised that its judgment created more waves than anticipated, for it, too, was learning about the social and cultural impact of Indigenous court decisions in the modern world. The *Marshall* decision, in particular, rewrote history, giving legal certainty to a still contested historical controversy and in the process revitalized regional interest in and knowledge of Mi'kmaw and Maliseet history.

Conclusion

Since turning his attention to the study of Native-newcomer relations in Canada, J.R. Miller has emphasized the importance of historical understanding as a key element in modern reconciliation. His studies on the Oka conflict, residential schools, the treaty process in Saskatchewan, and treaty-making across Canada provide carefully argued historical commentaries on highly emotional and controversial issues in Canadian Indigenous law and politics. In a field dominated by hyperbole and passionate arguments, Miller's work underscores the importance of moving beyond the heat and frustrations of contemporary political situations and of understanding the historical context and forces that created the contemporary conflict. While never shy about pointing out the deep injustices and social hostilities that pushed Indigenous people to the margins in Canada affairs, he has demonstrated repeatedly that carefully researched contributions on matters of historical contention can alter the tenor of the debate and shape public opinion.

The public debates and policy decisions arising out of the contemporary assertion of Mi'kmaw and Maliseet treaty rights have had a transformative effect on the Maritimes. Before the Thomas Peter Paul and Donald Marshall Jr. decisions, Aboriginal rights barely registered on the Maritime political landscape. Mi'kmaw and Maliseet leaders, elders, and community members understood the historical and political issues and pushed for recognition. Within the Maritimes at large, however, Indigenous peoples remained socially and economically isolated, largely locked out of the main resource sectors and rarely considered a cultural group of significant political importance. The treaty court cases changed the situation dramatically. Suddenly, Aboriginal rights, eighteenth-century treaties, and court decisions came to matter significantly in all debates about the future of the province and now have a much higher profile in regional political life. Unlike much of the country, where decades of intense debates preceded the search for political solutions, the Maritimes awoke suddenly to a legal and political reality shaped by the recognition of Mi'kmaw and Maliseet treaty rights. The legal contests have continued, both relating to the implementation of the *Marshall* decision and as a result of the legal foundations established by the Supreme Court judgment. The Joshua Bernard case, which relied on comparable argument but which failed before the Supreme Court, sought to extend the *Marshall* ruling to the forestry sector.

The *Marshall* decision reclaimed the Indigenous history of the Maritimes and brought the past back into the public realm. Across Canada, legal processes have been critical in defining Aboriginal rights and government obligations; in the Maritimes, more so than in other jurisdictions, the court challenges and judgments reminded an entire region of the contemporary relevance of historical understanding. Knowledge of history and extensive debate about judgments about historical events did not, however, bring consensus or a shared appreciation for the past. Instead, the *Marshall* decision reinvigorated First Nations' interest in history, challenged non-Indigenous understanding of the region's history, and created a new platform for political and legal debate. Aboriginal and treaty rights court cases are, at their heart, about attempts to define the present and future, to create a platform for Indigenous participation in contemporary Canadian society. As the Mi'kmaw and Maliseet situation shows, however, these contemporary court cases can, and do, transform our understanding of the past. By bringing to the public both the highly focused historical debates in the legal proceedings and the more general conversation that followed the decisions, the assertion of Mi'kmaw and Maliseet treaty rights has broadened historical understanding and forced the Maritimes to start the process of reconciliation on at least two critical fronts: with the Indigenous people of the region and with a history of the Maritimes that must now be reshaped to provide a more prominent place for Indigenous history and the record of Native-newcomer relations.

NOTES

1 The development of the *Marshall* decision is covered in Ken Coates, *The Marshall Decision and Aboriginal Rights in the Maritimes* (Montreal: McGill-Queen's University Press, 2000).

2 I moved to Saint John, New Brunswick, in 1997, taking up the position of dean, Faculty of Arts, at the University of New Brunswick at Saint John.

3 The most useful study on the evolution of Mi'kmaw engagement in the Maritimes is William Wicken, *Mi'kmaq Treaties on Trial: History, Land and Donald Marshall Junior* (Toronto: University of Toronto Press), 2002. See also William Wicken, John G. Reid, Maurice Basque, Elizabeth Mancke, Barry Moody, and Geoffrey Plank, *The Conquest of Acadia, 1710: An Interpretive and Contextual History* (Toronto: University of Toronto Press), 2004.

4 More recent scholarship, particularly by Margaret Conrad, has addressed this gap. See especially her work with James Hiller, *Atlantic Canada: A Concise History* (Toronto: Oxford University Press, 2006).

5 L.F.S. Upton, *Micmacs and Colonists: Indian-White Relations in the Maritimes, 1713–1867* (Vancouver: UBC Press, 1979).

6 One of her most interesting works is "Canada's Colonial Mission: The Great White Bird" (http://www.nativestudies.org/works.html). Professor Bear Nicholas's work focuses largely on language development and cultural persistence.
7 For a positive and analytical review of Wicken's *Mi'kmaq Treaties on Trial*, see Andrew Nurse, "History, Law and the Mi'kmaq of Atlantic Canada," *Acadiensis* 33/2 (spring 2004): 126–33.
8 Harold Cardinal, *The Unjust Society: The Tragedy of Canada's Indians* (Edmonton: Hurtig, 1969).
9 Sally Weaver, *Making Canadian Indian Policy: The Hidden Agenda 1968–70* (Toronto: University of Toronto Press, 1981).
10 A very good example of this perspective is Treaty 7 Elders and Tribal Council, with Walter Hildebrandt, Sarah Carter, and Dorothy First Rider, *True Spirit and Original Intent of Treaty 7* (Montreal: McGill-Queen's, 1995).
11 This scholarship is, of course, superbly summarized and analysed in J.R. Miller, *Skyscrapers Hide the Heavens: A History of Indian-White Relations in Canada*, 3rd ed. (Toronto: University of Toronto Press, 2000).
12 For an excellent reflection on the experience of a historian in an Aboriginal rights court, see A.J. Ray, "Native History on Trial: Confessions of an Expert Witness," *Canadian Historical Review* 84/2 (June 2003): 253–73.
13 A.J. Ray, "From the United States Indian Claims Commission Cases to Delgamuukw," in *Aboriginal Title and Indigenous Peoples: Comparative Essays on Australia, New Zealand, and Western Canada*, ed. Louis Knafla (Vancouver: UBC Press, 2011).
14 Robin Fisher, "Judging History: Reflections on the Reasons for Judgment in Delgamuukw v B.C.," *BC Studies* 95 (autumn 1992): 43–54; and Arthur J. Ray, "Creating the Image of the Savage in Defence of the Crown: The Ethnohistorian in Court," *Native Studies Review* 6/2 (1990): 13–29.
15 The details of the complicated and contentious decision on the *Delgamuukw* case can be found in Chief Justice Allan McEachern, *Reasons for Judgement in the Supreme Court of British Columbia Between: Delgamuukw, Also Known as Ken Muldoe, Suing on His Own Behalf and on Behalf of All the Members of the HOUSE OF DELGAMUUKW – Plaintiffs, and Her Majesty the Queen: Defendant* (Smithers; British Columbia Supreme Court, 1991).
16 This issue is covered in Greg Poelzer and Ken Coates, *From Treaty Peoples to Treaty Nation: A Road Map for All Canadians* (Vancouver: UBC Press, 2015).
17 J.R. Miller, *Compact, Contract, Covenant: Aboriginal Treaty-Making in Canada* (Toronto: University of Toronto Press, 2009), 63.
18 Quoted in Ruth Whitehead, *The Old Man Told Us: Excerpts from Micmac History, 1500–1950* (Halifax: Nimbus Publishing, 1991), 241.

19 Rex v. Sylliboy, Nova Scotia, County Court, 10 September 1928. Published in *Dominion Law Reports, 1929* (Toronto: Canada Law Book Ltd.).

20 For a detailed examination of these cases, see Ken Coates, *The Marshall Decision and Native Rights* (Montreal: McGill-Queen's University Press, 2000).

21 For an excellent and detailed analysis of the linkages between history, law, and the *Marshall* decision, see A.J. Ray, "Regina v. Marshall: Native History, the Judiciary, and the Public," *Acadiensis* 29/2 (spring 2000): 138–46.

22 Ibid., 146.

23 Thomas Flanagan, *First Nations? Second Thoughts* (Montreal: McGill-Queen's University Press, 2000).

24 Ibid., and F. Widdowson and Albert Howard, *Disrobing the Aboriginal Industry: The Deception Behind Indigenous Cultural Preservation* (Montreal: McGill-Queen's University Press, 2008).

25 "Supreme Court Misunderstood Testimony, Professor Says," *Times & Transcript*, 18 September 1999.

PART FIVE

Anthropologists, Historians, and the Indigenous Historiography

"We Could Not Help Noticing the Fact That Many of Them Were Cross-Eyed": Historical Evidence and Coast Salish Leadership

KEITH THOR CARLSON

The past several years have seen an escalation in tensions over land and identity within and between Coast Salish communities in the adjacent coastal regions of Washington State and British Columbia. The highly publicized disputes between the Duwamish and Muckleshoot near Seattle; the Yale and Stó:lō in the Fraser River Canyon; and the Musqueam, Squamish, and Tsleil-Waututh in the vicinity of Vancouver are only the most visible of these contestations. Although the immediate context for some of the discord can be found in the US Salish Tribes' efforts to secure recognition of federal treaty rights and the Canadian Salish First Nations' aspirations to secure modern treaties, the conflicts are at their heart competing visions over how collective identity is most appropriately defined and how political authority and leadership are most legitimately expressed. And in these disputes, legitimacy and appropriateness are adjudicated and assessed in relationship to history.

A host of social scientists have engaged in discussions over these matters, bringing a range of methodological and theoretical perspectives to bear on the Coast Salish past. But as Bruce Miller and Daniel Boxberger (two of the principal participants in these debates) observe, there is a "sometimes misleading assumption that anthropologists can easily deal with historical documents," and they point to the "valuable contribution that ethnohistorians and historians can make to the debate."[1] Interpreting this as an invitation, and recognizing the value in cross-disciplinary dialogue, I have chosen to engage the discussion less with reference to anthropological models than with a focused eye on the use and potential application of historical evidence in the construction and deconstruction of what is variously referred to as "traditional" or "pre-contact" or "Aboriginal" Coast Salish chiefly authority.

In particular, in concert with Miller and Boxberger and the more recent contributions by archaeologists Bill Angelbeck and Eric McLay,[2] I am seeking to assess both historical developments and historical narratives (written and oral) on their own terms. I am trying to further resituate the debate away from a discussion that mobilizes historical evidence in support of anthropological interpretation (and vice versa) towards one that recognizes not only the different ways in which classic ethnographers and historical personages created observations of the Coast Salish people, but also the way in which anthropologists and historians have used such information to create differing and often seemingly contradictory interpretations of the ethnographic and temporal "other." That is to say, a study of Coast Salish leadership holds the potential to reveal, and possibly reconcile, the still exaggerated opposition in the disciplines of history and anthropology between structure and event and between deductive and inductive reasoning.

Even as structuralism has fallen from academic favour, anthropologists still recognize the value of paying attention to the social structures that underpin society and that give culture meaning and coherence. Historians likewise, despite the rise of social history and postmodern theorizing, continue to demonstrate a predilection for events and the associated issue of change over time. Thus, as Marshall Sahlins has repeatedly elucidated, for too many anthropologists and historians "it seemed that 'event' and 'structure' could not occupy the same epistemological space. The event was conceived as antistructural, the structure as nullifying the event."[3] Whereas history was all dates, events, and the exploits of big men, with an emphasis on discerning change over time, anthropology was anonymous and principally interested in documenting those core features of society that remained stable over the passage of time. And yet, as Ray Fogelson has cogently argued, events (such as sudden disease-induced population decline) "dramatically affect social organizations, the perception of traditions, religious conversion, revitalization movements, and a host of other domains."[4]

Understanding the history of Indigenous peoples requires us to bring structure and event into dialogue with one another so we can assess the degree to which structure might sometimes accommodate and subsume an event, or conversely, the extent to which an event is occasionally so unprecedented and momentous that it causes structures to bend and change under its weight. We can do this, as Sahlins suggests, by inverting our theoretical praxis and recognizing that historical events can become ethnographically intelligible through the study of change rather than stasis. That is to say, instead of looking for continuity in change we need to be alert to instances of change in continuity.[5]

The Debate

The generally accepted ethnographic view of "pre-contact" or "traditional" Coast Salish society, as Wayne Suttles has pointed out, was that "there existed no political authority beyond the level of the village, [and] some have even denied the existence of village chiefs, seeing households as the largest autonomous unit." This model does not deny inter-village linkages and the power of kith and corporate-kin group ties built upon modes of economic exchange;[6] rather it asserts that such associations were characterized by "ties of marriage, exchange between affines, sharing of access to resources, and potlatching."[7] This orthodoxy faced a provocative challenge from the writings of Kenneth Tollefson in 1987 and 1989 when he applied evolutionary models to interpret historical evidence. Tollefson argued that prior to contact, the Puget Sound Salish had been organized into regional "Chiefdoms" and formal political confederacies.[8] Suttles and others, in Tollefson's view, had overemphasized social networks at the expense of real political bonds, and as such were just as incorrect as the earlier generation of ethnographers who had failed to see any meaningful connections between geographically isolated settlements. According to Tollefson, the problem was essentially historical and stemmed from the ethnographers' excessive reliance on twentieth-century informants and their associated ignoring of eighteenth- and nineteenth-century historical documents. The society that Suttles and others were describing was not traditional, Tollefson posited, but rather the remnants of an earlier, more sophisticated culture that had suffered contact-induced "defeat and forced removal." Historical evidence, on the other hand, allegedly documented strong centralized leadership from the era "before [Native] defeat and depopulation."[9]

Initially Tollefson's revisionist thesis seemed to gain traction among academics. It was picked up for inclusion in a prominent anthropology undergraduate survey textbook and also used as corroborative evidence by an archaeologist engaged in a similar debate in Southern California.[10] But in the end, it generally failed to shift the views of regional specialists. Eventually even Tollefson acknowledged that his conclusions were largely only applicable to one particular Coast Salish tribal community (the Snoqualmie near Seattle) and, even then, only at a particular historical moment (during the chieftainship of Pat Kanim in the 1850s), which was at least seventy years after first European contact[11] – but still sufficiently early for the Snoqualmie to argue that they met the criteria established by the US government to qualify for federal recognition as a "tribe" and therefore receive funding and political recognition.[12] This contemporary political context demonstrates vividly the highly politicized nature of discussions over historical expressions of Coast Salish collective identity.

While something of a scholarly consensus has re-emerged around the idea that Coast Salish people forged and maintained meaningful cross-tribal regional social networks prior to contact, not everyone has accepted the idea that these networks were principally material and ecological (i.e., not political) in nature. Jay Miller, in particular, argued that all of the more recent economic and political models of traditional Coast Salish society were fundamentally "flawed by misconceptions that wrongly emphasize Eurocentric stereotypes about personal individuality instead of situating families within their anchoring landscape." He sought to "return to basics" by bringing a more Indigenous epistemology to the debate and by rejecting what he regarded as a tendency within the established literature towards "overly democratizing a strong elite" through approaches that were "woefully irreligious."[13]

Suttles, of course, had earlier recognized and acknowledged the significance of non-material-based collective units derived from "participation in the yearly round of subsistence activities and periodic ceremonial activities." In particular, he had identified the centrality of such non-economic and non-political collectives as the inter-village communities of winter dancers – which at the time of Suttles's writing in the early 1960s were experiencing a renaissance.[14] Presumably, the fraternity of masked sx̱wó:oxeye dancers, and even the community of distinct spirit entities that Coast Salish shaman still describe as existing within every Coast Salish individual, also fell within this category. For as Suttles notes, none of these metaphysical communities was "necessarily identical with the residential units or the kin groups, some of them necessarily differing from them."[15] Bruce Miller and Boxberger likewise acknowledged that at certain times spiritual communities took situational precedence over the affinal ties forged through materialistic concerns. But for Jay Miller the spiritual networks, and in particular the radiating shamanic identification, were the most meaningful and consistently operationalized collective identities cutting across anchored watershed-based tribal communities.[16]

More recently, Stó:lō Nation's staff archaeologist, David Schaepe, has invited us to turn our attention to the unique geographic and archaeological features found in certain parts of Coast Salish territory for what they reveal about particular expressions of authority and collective identity. Schaepe shows how a previously unknown (to Western outsiders) network of massive rock walls linking immediate pre-contact-era settlements in the Fraser River Canyon demonstrates a profound degree of multi-village social and political cooperation most likely built upon the foundations of the corporate family group structure.[17] Schaepe's archaeological analysis, supported by Salish oral histories, also posits that construction of these walls and their coordinated use as defensive features during attacks suggest that centralized political leadership characterized that particular region for a period of time – perhaps similar to what Tollefson described for the Snoqualmie in the 1950s.

Most recently still, in 2011, Bill Angelbeck and Eric McLay have contributed to the discussion by analysing twenty-one separate oral accounts of what is arguably the single greatest instance of coordinated Coast Salish collective identity in the nineteenth century: the ca. 1830–55 multi-tribal Salish alliance that presented a united military force against the raiding southern Kwakwa̱ka̱'wakw Lekwiltok in what is today known as the Battle of Maple Bay. They conclude that the more than 1,000 warriors from roughly 50 Coast Salish communities who participated in the coordinated military exercise did so without any overarching political authority coordinating and directing their activities. The battle, they argue, therefore provides "a historical example of how a network form of cooperative political organization became regionally mobilized ... It illustrates ... how autonomous households mobilized networks of kin and other allies throughout the Coast Salish region ... to reveal that the scale of political cooperation was locally based, context dependent, and provisional."[18]

In the light of the still-unfolding nature of this debate, and the ongoing political tensions within and among contemporary Coast Salish communities, this paper is primarily interested in assessing whether introduced events have modified Coast Salish social structures (in a manner similar to either the geographic specificity Schaepe examines in the Fraser River Canyon or the temporal specificity described by Boxberger and Bruce Miller and by Tollefson for parts of Puget Sound) and, if so, determining the extent to which underlying social structures have informed the way such historical events were understood and responded to. In other words, were certain historical events so profoundly disruptive that they caused significant change in Coast Salish social structures – and in particular changes in Coast Salish systems of leadership? And if so, did they cause expressions of political authority within Salish territory to become more centralized or less centralized over time; if such change existed did it result in unidirectional change or perhaps some other more fluid expression of political authority?

The Earliest European Observers

An inductive approach to historical understanding necessarily starts with the earliest extant records. And indeed, much of the debate to date has revolved around determining which non-Indigenous observers were on site sufficiently early to observe traditional Coast Salish society. Tollefson, in particular, came under attack for suggesting that the American settlers of the early 1850s were on the scene before any significant contact-induced transformations in Coast Salish social structures had occurred. His detractors argued, quite correctly, that the Hudson's Bay Company (HBC) had been in contact with the Coast Salish for a generation prior to the Americans' arrival and, more to the point, had left records that "contain daily entries on the activities of the native people."[19] More important still, as Suttles pointed out, the Spanish had visited Salish territory even earlier. Indeed, Tollefson's assertions helped to inspire Suttles to conduct a review of the English translations of the Spanish records for their ethnographic observations. In the end, Suttles interpreted the Spanish documents as supporting his decentralized interpretation of Coast Salish authority, arguing that they provided "a loadstone showing that in this instance we are, after all, headed in the right direction."[20]

Certain vagaries and inconsistencies, however, exist within the early British and Spanish documentary sources that require comment. To take the Spanish records first, most English-language scholars interested in the Spaniards' observations have relied on Henry Wagner's widely accessible 1933 translations of the 1790s Spanish sources. Suttles uses Wagner to conclude that "on the matter of chiefly authority, the accounts of Quimper, Pantoja, and Cardero offer no support for any revisions of our views."[21] Indeed, Suttles titles his article after Manuel Quimper's observation that the First Nations of the Strait of Juan de Fuca "recognize no superior chief." From this reference and an absence of descriptions of centralized political leadership, it is easy to understand why Suttles would infer that the Coast Salish did not have regional leaders who controlled multiple villages comparable to the nearby Nuu-chah-nulth leader Wickaninnish at Clayoquot or Tatooch at Cape Flattery. While this is a reasonable interpretation of Quimper as presented by Wagner, it is not necessarily the only one. In addition, what Quimper did *not* report was not necessarily absent.

On the subject of meaning, Wagner's translation twice uses the expression "they recognize no superior chief" in relation to Coast Salish people. However, in one instance the reference appears in a paragraph in which Quimper is writing about both Salish and the Nuu-chah-nulth Dididat under the leadership of a man referred to as Janapé. It is possible to read the excerpt, therefore, as Suttles did – as implying that Quimper meant that this one particular Coast Salish community simply did not recognize Janapé the Dididat chief as their superior. The second time Quimper uses the expression is in describing the people of Bahia de Quimper (Port Discovery). In this instance, it is useful to quote the sentence in full: "They recognize no superior chief and carry on continual warfare with those on the north side [of the Strait of Juan de Fuca], thus accounting for the fact that the beaches are strewn with the harpooned heads of their enemies." From this sentence, one could infer that by stating that they recognized no superior chief, Quimper was reflecting the people of Port Discovery's contention that they themselves were the hegemonic power, that they were not subordinate to their northern neighbours. By way of comparison, had Quimper described Wickaninnish of Clayoquot (a man well known to have been a political powerhouse and regional leader), it is likely he would have concluded that Wickaninnish also did not recognize any superior chiefs, he being *the* hegemonic power.

But beyond these matters, in interpreting Quimper's statements, the issue of translation becomes crucial. Wagner (who incorporated into his published translation large portions of text from an unpublished 1911 translation done by G.F. Barwick and then relied on a team of graduate student research assistants to translate other sections of the documents) is notorious for inconsistencies. The extent of the inaccuracies becomes evident when one compares his translation with an independent one published three years earlier by Cecil Jane.[22] On one occasion, Wagner translates Pantoja's description of a group of Salish people from Georgia Strait in the following terms:

> We found *no notable difference* between their physiognomy and those of the other natives who had visited us in the strait. On the other hand, however,

> we could not help noticing the fact that *many of them were cross-eyed*, that they wore their mustaches short, and tufts of hair on their chins and their eyebrows were rather thick. Their clothes were reduced in general to coarse and well-woven blankets fastened by two pins on the shoulder, but only long enough to reach the knees. An occasional one wore a *deerskin*. What covered the man who appeared to be chief, merited special attention as he wore *a woolen blanket on top of these*, a hat in the *form of a truncated cone*, five *brass* bracelets on the right wrist, and a hoop of copper round his neck ... Later on two canoes appeared, and arrested our attention by the *evil appearance* of the four Indians who came in them, for they were *all cross-eyed* and of very disagreeable countenances.[23]

Compare this with Jane's translation of the same entry:

> We found *a noticeable difference* between their appearance and that of the other natives whom we had seen in the strait, but that which made the greatest impression on us was the fact that *many of them were blind in one eye, which was covered with a short skin.* They had pointed beards and very bushy eyebrows. Their clothes were generally no more than a cloak of rough wool and well woven, joined by two clasps at the shoulders and not hanging down below the knees. Here and there one was wearing a *skin*, that of the man who seemed to be the chief meriting special attention; he *wore under it another cloak of fine wool*, a hat with *an ornament like a shortened cone*, five *tin* bracelets on the right wrist, and one of copper around his neck ... There afterwards appeared at the anchorage two canoes which attracted our attention on account of the *hideous appearance* of the four Indians who were with them; *they were all pimply* and presented a most unpleasant sight.[24]

From Wagner we are presented with a description of Coast Salish people who were apparently the same as the Nuu-chah-nulth of Juan de Fuca Strait, who were strangely cross-eyed, and of evil countenance. Through Jane we are told the opposite, that these people were quite different from their Nootkan neighbours, most noticeably (and I will return to this issue) because they demonstrated characteristic signs of having suffered from smallpox.[25] Unfortunately, my Spanish is inadequate to allow me to assess the relative accuracy of the two translations vis-à-vis the original. However, at my request, a bilingual Spanish colleague, Luisa Munoz,[26] examined both translations in relation to the original handwritten Spanish and concluded that Jane was the more careful scholar.[27]

Lamentably for the purpose at hand, Jane translated only Quimper's journal and not Panjota's, so we cannot read a comparative published account of the alleged assertion that the Coast Salish "recognize no superior chief." However, upon scrutinizing a microfilm copy of Panjota's handwritten original, my colleague Munoz has determined that once again Wagner's translation left something to be desired. Pantoja's actual words are "El idioma de estos naturales varia mucho con el de los de fuera, no conocieron Superior. Estan en continua guerra con los del Norte por cuya razon tienen ... en sus playas cabezas de arponadas de sus enemigos." Munoz translates these as "The language of these naturals [Indigenous people] differs greatly from those on the outside [of the Straight of Juan de Fuca]. They, (the community) recognize none as superior, always being at war with those on the north side, which explains why the beaches are strewn with the heads of their enemies on poles." In other words, "superior" in this case may well refer to groups and not individuals, in which case what the Spanish appears to have meant is that the Coast Salish community at Port Discovery did not recognize the Nuu-chah-nulth tribes on the outside of the Strait of Juan de Fuca as their superiors.

Likewise, the second of Panjota's references to Coast Salish people allegedly recognizing no superior chiefs reads, "Acercandos el numero de naturales a 500, no conocieron superior," which Munoz translates as "The number of naturals [in this particular community] amounts to about five hundred. They do not recognize (other people or tribes) as superior." In the letter accompanying her translation, Munoz explains that in this sentence, the reference to not recognizing superiors appears to refer *not* to people within a village or community who did not recognize a given individual as their superior or chief, but rather to the people from one village considering themselves, and their leader, as superior to the people and leader from a neighbouring community: "As I understand it, they considered themselves the best tribe."[28]

Plainly, the Spanish records, especially as presented by Wagner, have limitations as tools for ethnographic reconstruction. And where they do provide relevant information, it can just as reasonably be read as challenging the traditional decentralized view of the Coast Salish people organized only at the family or village level as it can the opposite.

If the Spanish records are frustratingly confused and ambiguous, what are we to make of the subsequent fur trade documents? They raise at least two important questions: What, if anything, they can tell us about Coast Salish political structures, and in what context should the records be read in order to make them ethnographically meaningfully?

Regarding the issue of context, it is essential to note that after the initial Spanish and British explorations of the early 1790s (which are discussed in more detail later), the Puget Sound–Georgia Strait region was essentially ignored by Europeans until the mid-1820s. Complementary records suggest that perhaps a few Boston-based maritime fur traders sporadically visited the area in the late eighteenth and early nineteenth centuries, but these visitors apparently did not leave a record of their observations, nor do we know what impact their visits (if they indeed occurred) might have had. Thus, the earliest surviving detailed nineteenth-century European descriptions of Coast Salish people are those associated with Northwest trader Simon Fraser's 1808 exploration of the river that now bears his name, and those generated by James MacMillan during his 1824 exploration expedition up Puget Sound and into the lower Fraser Valley/delta on behalf of the HBC. Fraser, as well as two of MacMillan's clerks, John Work and François Annance, kept daily journals of their observations and experiences, and each of these has been preserved. Shortly thereafter, in 1827, Fort Langley was established on the lower Fraser River. Fort Nisqually was next built on the southern edge of Puget Sound in 1833. Incomplete journals from both these posts survive.

Historical scholarship on the early relations between Indigenous people and newcomers on the Northwest Coast has fit uncomfortably with the dominant narratives established by historians for the rest of North America. This is in large part because the chronology of interactions occurs so much later than in eastern and central North America, and because of the somewhat autonomous political developments of both the Indigenous people and the subsequent Pacific Slope colonial regimes. In his seminal survey *Skyscrapers Hide the Heavens*, for example, historian J.R. Miller has argued that the history of Native-newcomer relations in Canada can be understood within a paradigm that shifted from "cooperation, to coercion, to confrontation."[29] A similar model has been established for the United States in the writings of historians such as James Axtell.[30] But on the Pacific Coast, historians have instead followed a now well-worn path that was at first preoccupied with assessing the merits of the "enrichment thesis" (i.e., did the fur trade result in a flourishing of First Nations art and culture, or did it lead to the degeneration and exploitation of Indigenous people?), then with determining when contact-era cooperation turned into conflict, and finally when conflict-era "resistance" turned into "renewal."[31]

Among the most inspirational of the recent works are Cole Harris's *The Resettlement of British Columbia: Essays on Colonialism and*

Geographical Change, Alexandra Harman's *Indians in the Making: Ethnic Relations and Indian Identities Around Puget Sound*, and Lissa Wadewitz's *The Nature of Borders: Salmon and Boundaries in the Salish Sea*, which all argue that the theatre of power within which the fur trade and early settlement occurred was more complex and violent than previously appreciated. Informed by postcolonial theorizing, works such as these argue that European cultural imperialism was more subtle and multifaceted than previously conceived, but that Indigenous people were not without their own sources of competing power.[32] More directly relevant for the question at hand, perhaps, are studies of more easterly Indigenous groups of an earlier era. Extrapolating from the writings of Arthur J. Ray and others, one might conclude that those Coast Salish leaders living near European posts or trade centres may have taken advantage of the wealth and material advantage created by their position as middlemen in the trade to increase their authority and influence vis-à-vis their neighbours.[33] Analysis of changes in slave raiding among more northern and southern coastal communities resulting from the fur trade hints at the kinds of sociocultural impact of the fur trade among all Northwest Coast people.[34] But a review of relevant fur trade documentation creates an ambiguous image of Coast Salish leadership and political authority.

Simon Fraser arrived among the central Coast Salish in June 1808 after travelling down the river that now bears his name. Nearing the ocean, Fraser identified a single leader from a village near present-day Langley whom he described as exercising great influence over many people from various neighbouring communities. Fraser consistently referred to this person as "the Chief" and on one occasion explained how this leader "made us understand that he was the greatest of his nation and equal in power to the sun."[35] In another entry, relying on assistance from his upriver translator, Fraser described this particular leader as "the Chief of the Ackinroe"[36] – Ackinroe being the English corruption of the Nlakapamux/Thompson expression "*s?ecnkwu/ Se'á:tchenkō*," which they used to describe all the mainland Coast Salish Halq'emeylem speakers (and which Matilda Gutierrez of Chawathil explained was a pejorative term that implied that the Stó:lō were the grandchildren of Nlakapamux slaves).[37]

The alleged regional leader described in Fraser's journal lived in a series of connected longhouses that stretched for 640 feet (195 metres – or longer than six NHL hockey rinks). The chief's individual living quarters were distinguished from those of other family leaders by its size, at 5,400 square feet (501 square metres – or just under one-third the size of an NHL hockey rink) compared to 3,600 square feet (334 square metres) for the others. Upon Fraser's arrival, the chief invited him into his home and "entertained" the Europeans with "songs and dances of various descriptions."[38] According to Fraser, this man's leadership role was acknowledged by others throughout the ceremonies, for he stood "in the center of the dance or ring giving instructions, while others were beating the drum against the walls of the house."[39]

Social leadership and social space, of course, does not necessarily translate into political authority. But further indication of the extent of this leader's authority is suggested in his ability to direct the activities of a large number of people from multiple settlements. This became particularly clear when Fraser's welcome wore out and he was pursued back up the Fraser River by an increasingly large and hostile group of local Coast Salish – all led by "the Chief of the Ackinroe." In terms of specifics, Fraser even records that the chief successfully commanded several hundred people from a variety of villages to "drop behind" as they participated in the chase.[40] Following this demonstration of his authority, the now openly antagonistic Ackinroe chief and his followers shadowed Fraser's party all the way from a location near present-day Langley/Matsqui to a site beyond the modern town of Hope (a distance of over 100 kilometres). At each village where Fraser had been warmly received on his downward journey, he found that the Ackinroe leader was able to quickly turn the people against him. Fraser describes the way his nemesis accomplished this: "Still bent on mischief, the leader at landing began to testify his hostile disposition by brandishing his horn club, and by making a violent harangue to the people of the village, who already seemed to be in his favour."

While the evidence is insufficient to allow one to draw direct parallels between the levels of authority exercised by Fraser's Ackinroe chief and the Snoqualmie leader Pat Kanim of southern Puget Sound as described by Tollefson, or the multi-village leaders implied by the integrated Fraser Canyon rock walls studied by Schaepe, enough similarity does exist to warrant cautious comparison. Clearly, the Ackinroe chief not only thought of himself as a powerful leader, but he was able to demonstrate a degree authority throughout the entire lower Fraser watershed. What then does this mean for the standard interpretations of non-centralized leadership and political authority? For while it might be possible to explain the behaviour and apparent influence of Fraser's Ackinroe chief within a standard ethnographic understanding of status and kin ties among neighbouring communities, it appears that his degree of authority exceeded what would typically be attributed to a Coast Salish family or even village leader. Whether it was somehow institutionalized or rather a product of his personality in a particular historical context is impossible to tell.

In their respective journals from the 1820s, the immediate successors to Fraser in Coast Salish exploration, John Work and François Annance, consistently refer to Indigenous "Nations" and "tribes" (i.e., the "Nisqually Nation," the "Sanahomis tribe," the "Scaadchet tribe," the "Cahoutetts Nation," etc.). What they meant by "Nation" and "Tribe" is never entirely apparent. Aside from recognizing that the terms should not be correlated casually with those found in introductory anthropology textbooks from the mid-twentieth century, a careful contextualization of these modifiers is essential before attempting any interpretation. For instance, was there a standard early-nineteenth-century fur trader's notion of what nation and tribe meant? Did their use of such expressions reflect Indigenous realities, or were they indicative of what a Scotsman and a French Canadian explorer expected to see?[41] The fact that the journals describe clusters of villages as having a sense of collective identity suggests some sort of extra-village organization, but what form this took, and whether it was inconsistent with standard understandings of traditional culture – especially along the lines of that defined by Jay Miller – is unclear. Likewise, on the matter of leadership, fur traders John Work and François Annance both refer to certain men as "chief of this tribe" and others as "the principle chief of the tribe." Among certain tribes and nations, they also identify "a second chief," etc. Yet, contrary to what Fraser described in the same region sixteen years earlier, none of their alleged chiefs is shown to have any authority over people of other villages. Moreover, their identification of "3 or 4 chiefs" from a single village seems consistent with the standard decentralized ethnographic descriptions of apolitical household leaders related by blood and marriage but holding no real political authority.[42]

The existing *Fort Nisqually Journal* commences nine years after Work and Annance's expedition and thirteen years before the United States acquired unilateral sovereignty over the Puget Sound region. It provides detailed documentation for the years 1833 to 1859. Within the journal there are no explicit references to leaders with influence over broad geographical areas, but neither are there descriptions explicitly indicative of the contrary. The journal does describe leaders, or "chiefs," some of whom are clearly more influential than others. Frequent mention is made of "the" chief of such-and-such community (e.g., "Watskatch the Sannahomish chief") while on other occasions there are references to "a" chief of a particular community (e.g., "a Soquamish Chief") indicating the existence of more than one recognized leader. But references to "the" chief do not necessarily imply central leadership and authority. Rather, the designation often seems to simply refer to "a" previously mentioned chief. The degree of authority is never described explicitly; nowhere in the *Nisqually Journal* does the author attempt to explain Indigenous social structures or authority patterns. Again, the identification of people from multi-village "tribes" seems to indicate the existence of broad regional concepts of shared identity, but the many references to different leaders and the lack of mention of any single regional leader suggest non-centralized leadership.[43]

To place the Nisqually observations within a broader historical context, it should be noted that frequent entries describe Indigenous activities that appear related to the early-nineteenth-century prophet dance phenomenon.[44] In the 1830s, Coast Salish society was in a state of great social fluidity as people sought to accommodate new ceremonial expressions and prophetic teachings. We know that prophets were emerging in several areas of Coast Salish territory and introducing radical new ideas into Salish society. Some, as Suttles has documented, encouraged women to select their own spouses, thus undermining hereditary and hierarchical familial control while promoting gender autonomy and the diminishing of class divisions. Some of the prophets went on to consolidate significant political control (as in the upper Skagit watershed) while others seem to have confined their influence to social realms (middle and upper Fraser region). Several of the prophets professed divinely inspired knowledge of European religion, economy, and governance.[45] Certainly some family leaders opposed the prophetic teachings, while others no doubt worked to co-opt the movement and capitalize on the popularity and charisma of the prophets. Not only does the impact of the prophets need to be considered in any discussion of the historical expressions of Coast Salish political authority, but so too does whatever context it was that created the circumstances giving rise to the prophet movement – glimpses of which are found in the fur trade records.

While neither Fraser, Work and Annance, nor the keeper of the Nisqually journal ever attempt to describe the Coast Salish social structures,[46] in 1838, HBC chief factor James Douglas did provide what is possibly the closest thing we have to a fur-trade-era ethnographic description of the Puget Sound Coast Salish. Without defining or distinguishing among terms, Douglas described multi-village "communities" and "societies" (their names generally corresponding with Work's and Annance's "nations" and "tribes") occupying watersheds or islands. Collectively, all the Puget Sound Salish are described as "without a doubt ... one and the same people, deriving a local designation from their place of residence." Community or society "appellations" (such as Squaly amish, Puce alap amish, Sino amish, Sina homish, Skatchet, and Nowhalimeek)

> were regarded as the source of an imaginary line of demarcation, which divides the inhabitants of one petty stream, from the people living upon another, and have become the fruitful source of the intensive commotions, that so frequently disturb the tranquillity of the District. In fact, no national distinctions whether of character, of manners, of language or even diversity of interest could increase the animosity now existing between these branches of the same great tribe. The consequence of this state of mutual hostility is, a feeling of general distrust. Members of the distant communities cannot visit the Fort without endangering their personal safety, and therefore seldom make the attempt.[47]

It is difficult to draw firm conclusions from Douglas's descriptions. However, such observations are significant, for if, as Bruce Miller and Boxberger suggest, subsequent American documentation indicates that broader political entities and shared identities did not exist immediately prior to their creation by government officials during the Washington Territory treaty process in the mid-1850s, then something else in the preceding generation apparently caused a degree of decentralization: perhaps new leaders arising from the prophesy movement? Such an assumption is consistent with Jay Miller's thesis but also indicative of the importance of understanding introduced change alongside Indigenous response and agency.

Inter-community Hostility

Participants in the debate accept that Tollefson's description of Pat Kanim's political authority may be accurate, but they interpret it as resulting from the uniquely post-contact military necessity for collective security arising from nineteenth-century Lekwiltok (southern Kwakwa̲ka̲'wakw) raiding. Indeed, while Suttles sees "warfare as mainly another means of acquiring wealth, which was integral to the potlatch,"[48] he nonetheless explicitly links chiefly authority with conflict as expressed in the need for collective action against a common enemy – most significantly the Lekwiltok.[49] Bruce Miller and Boxberger likewise defer to Suttles's assertion that an absence of Spanish references to fortification is "evidence that in the 1790's Lekwiltok raiding into southern Central Coast Salish territory had not yet begun."[50] The evidence, however, is sufficiently murky that such firm conclusions are difficult to support.

Jay Miller criticizes Tollefson's description of Pat Kanim as being overly concerned with specific historical events and occurrences. For him, a better way to understand the Snoqualmie leader is to recognize that when faced with an external threat, traditional Coast Salish society was flexible enough to adapt enhanced features of centralized authority without those features becoming non-Indigenous in character. Nor did they necessarily have to become long-lasting or permanent. Yet, without a temporally sensitive context within which to appreciate instances of more centralized leadership, it is impossible to answer fundamental questions such as under what circumstances did centralized Coast Salish leadership occur, and were such factors strictly post-contact in nature? For this reason, it is important to determine whether the lack of Spanish references to Indigenous fortifications can actually be taken to mean that such fortifications did not exist, and if by extension, therefore, Lekwiltok raiding had not yet occurred, precipitating the need for centralized collective leadership.

Journals associated with Captain George Vancouver's voyages of 1791 to 1795 describe a specially designed, though recently abandoned, defensive village on the northern extreme of Salish territory, in southern Desolation Sound, near the Lekwiltok/Coast Salish border. This structure, known informally today among members of the Sliammon community as "Flea Village" due to the description in the British journals of numerous fleas living in the abandoned remains, seems to have functioned like a Salish Masada vis-à-vis the Lekwiltok:

> That [this region of Salish territory too] had been more populous than at present, was manifest by the party having discovered an extensive deserted village, computed to have been the residence of nearly three hundred persons. It was built on a rock, whose perpendicular cliffs were nearly inaccessible on every side; and connected with the main, by a low narrow neck of land, about the centre of which grew a tree, from whose

branches planks were laid to the rock, forming by this means a communication that could easily be removed, to prevent their being molested by their internal unfriendly neighbours; and protected in front, which was presented to the sea, from their external enemies, by a platform, which, with much labour and ingenuity had been constructed on a level with their houses, and overhung and guarded the rock. This, with great stability, was formed by large timbers judiciously placed for supporting each other in every direction; their lower ends were well secured in the chasms of the rocks about half way to the water's edge, admitting the platform to be so projected as to command the foot of the rock against any attempt to storm the village. The whole seemed so skillfully contrived, and so firmly and well executed, as rendered it difficult to be considered the work of the untutored tribes we had been accustomed to meet [in Georgia Strait and Puget Sound]; had not their broken arms and implements, with parts of their manufactured garments, plainly evinced its habitants to be of the same race.[51]

In addition, upon reaching the edge of Georgia Strait in 1808, Simon Fraser described what may have been a fortified village at Musqueam:

> Here we landed and found but a few old men and women; the others fled into the woods upon our approach. The fort is 1500 feet [457 metres] in length and 90 feet [27 metres] in breadth. The houses, which are constructed as those mentioned in other places, are in rows; besides some that are detached. One of the natives conducted us through all the apartments, and then desired us to go away, as otherwise the Indians would attack us.[52]

It could be argued that what Fraser interpreted as a "fort" was simply a series of connected Musqueam longhouses. In support of this position, anthropologist Mike Kew observes that Musqueam oral traditions make no reference to a fortified village, and had the village been fortified, it is unlikely Fraser's arrival would have caused people to flee to the forest.[53] These arguments are compelling. But on the other hand, Fraser was a fur trader who lived much of his life behind palisaded fort walls. As such, he knew what a fort was, and judging by other references in his journal, he was able to distinguish longhouses from fortifications. In his journal Fraser describes only two Salish villages as having been fortified. In addition to the structure at Musqueam, he described the Lilloet settlement in the upper Fraser Canyon in these terms:

> The village is a fortification of 100 by 24 feet surrounded with palisades eighteen feet high, slanting inwards, and lined with a shorter row that supports a shade [shelter], covered with bark, and which are dwellings. This place we understand is the metropolis of the Askettih [Lilloet] Nation.[54]

Placed in the context of this earlier description, I infer that what Fraser described at Musqueam was indeed a palisaded fort. His description of the Musqueam structure distinguishes between "the fort" and "the houses," the latter of which he describes as "constructed as those mentioned in other places." From this one might conclude that the sixty-foot-wide Musqueam longhouses were protected behind a ninety-foot-wide palisade. But again, such opaque descriptions highlight the inherent problems of drawing firm ethnographic conclusions from such historical evidence.

Other historical records, albeit from a somewhat later period, describe fortified Salish villages that are not inconsistent with Fraser's cryptic description. For example, in 1841 Charles Wilks described a village on the north shore of Whidby Island where longhouses were protected behind a giant palisaded wall. This wall was constructed of thirty-foot-tall (nine-metre-tall) plank pickets, which were firmly fixed into the ground, the space between them being sufficient to allow only a musket to point through. Wilks explains that fortifications of this sort reached 400 feet (122 metres) in length, within which the longhouses were situated.[55] In 1844, accompanying James Douglas on his voyage to establish Fort Victoria on the southern tip of Vancouver Island, the Reverend J.B.Z. Bolduc described a "little fortress" in Esquimalt Harbour formed by stakes planted in the ground.[56] Paul Kane likewise described a Clallam village that was protected behind a double row of strong pickets, the outer palisade being twenty feet high, and the second about five feet.[57] A.C. Anderson, another veteran of the fur trade, explained that in the 1840s, palisaded villages were common along the lower Fraser River. He describes the Kwantlen (from around the present site of Langley) as being so afraid of the Vancouver Island Cowichan that they "rarely venture to [the river's] mouth, and that Palisaded villages and other precautions against surprise show that even at home a ceaseless dread prevails." Anderson describes the uppermost Coast Salish village in the lower Fraser Canyon as "a palisaded fort," and he records that as soon as the fishing season ended, the local Coast Salish "retreated to their palisaded dwellings below."[58] Likewise, in the spring of 1858, Gibbs observed a fortified village at the junction of the Sumas and Fraser Rivers in the Fraser Valley.[59] But if these references largely coincide with the arrival of Europeans (and therefore potentially European architectural influences), David Schaepe's recent archaeological surveys of the lower Fraser Canyon rock wall structures suggest that wooden defensive palisades may also have long predated European visits and the associated early-nineteenth-century attacks by the Lekwiltok. Associated with a hilltop settlement at the mouth of the Fraser Canyon is a series of large linear postholes. These are ancient, well predating any European contact. Such features, coupled with the associated rock walls, Schaepe has concluded, are clear examples of collective action and centralized political authority.[60] Even more recently, archaeological examinations slightly farther north on the coast suggest that the Fraser Canyon fortification may not be unique in this regard.[61]

Some additional indication of the antiquity of Coast Salish fortified villages can also be gleaned from the historical record. In the mid-nineteenth century, George Gibbs observed a six-foot-deep, eight-foot-wide trench near Victoria which the local people explained was part of a defensive structure. From colonial governor James Douglas, Gibbs learned that such features were commonly found around Vancouver Island. An indication of the antiquity of these structures is suggested when Gibbs recorded that the local Indigenous people "had no tradition of their origin."[62] Similar accounts stating that the fortifications were so old that the local Indigenous population could not remember their original construction have been collected and cited by Grant Keddie, head of archaeology at the Royal British Columbia Museum, in a series of articles on "Aboriginal Defensive Sites" published in *Discovery Magazine*. For example, Keddie quotes Martha Douglas, Governor Douglas's daughter, describing two Coast Salish fortifications near present-day Victoria which the local Indigenous population considered ancient: "On asking the Indians about its origin they all say it was made by the old people who inhabited the country before them and they know nothing more about it."[63]

Gary Coupland argues that Northwest Coast warfare can be divided into two distinctive regional types: north coast (Kwakwa̱ka̱'wakw and north), and south coast (Salish). While revenge raiding was no doubt common to both groups, Coupland alleges that the former were primarily offensive and motivated by economic factors, while the latter were defensive and largely non-economic. This, Coupland states, is shown archaeologically by the large number of defensive sites among the Coast Salish, particularly around the border zone between the north and the south.[64] Whatever the merits of Coupland's economic determinist interpretation, the archaeological evidence there complements what Schaepe has documented in the lower Fraser Canyon and clearly shows that fortified structures did exist among the Coast Salish in the 1790s; the Spaniards, it seems, simply did not mention them, whereas the British referred only to ones that particularly intrigued them.[65]

The existence of pre-contact fortified villages, however, does not necessarily mean they were built and occupied by people whose leaders exercised centralized political authority over groups larger than an extended family. As Keddie points out, although "the very nature of a defensive village would demand greater social cooperation for group survival," accepting the idea that fortified Salish villages existed doesn't alone require that centralized leadership existed at the same time. Moreover, if the fortifications are indicative of the existence of some degree of political and social unity, they do not clarify the expression it took, or its extent – certainly they do not verify the existence of multi-village chiefdoms.

For insights into sociopolitical conditions, it is useful to ask against whom were the fortifications designed to protect? Historical geographer Robert Galois addresses this question while documenting how the Kwakwa̱ka̱'wakw were first exposed to significant European contact in the 1780s at the commencement of the maritime fur trade. He demonstrates that until 1800, most Kwakwa̱ka̱'wakw-European trade occurred overland across Vancouver Island via Nuu-chah-nulth middlemen.[66] After 1800, the centre of the maritime fur trade shifted from Clayoquot and Nootka Sounds to "Newitty," in Kwakwa̱ka̱'wakw territory on the extreme north end of Vancouver Island.[67]

Spanish and British sources place the southern boundary of Lekwiltok territory at Topaz Harbour in 1792. Spanish observers (filtered through Wagner's translations) also mention what appear to be regionally hegemonic leaders among the Kwakwa̱ka̱'wakw.[68] Of significance, as he travelled northward, Vancouver also observed a sudden and marked contrast between Salish and Kwakwa̱ka̱'wakw weaponry. Everywhere they went, the British encountered Salish armed with bows, arrows, and clubs. And while the tips of many Salish projectiles were made with reprocessed European iron, among the Lekwiltok, Vancouver found a veritable artillery of European-manufactured firearms, and numerous men so "dexterous" in the use of muskets that they could have "been accustomed to fire arms from the earliest infancy."[69]

Collectively, the archaeological and historical evidence suggests that it is likely that Lekwiltok raiding of Coast Salish communities predated the visit of Vancouver and Galiano-Valdes. One might assume that warfare increased significantly thereafter as a result of Kwakwaka'wakw numerical superiority and their monopolistic access to European weaponry.[70] Galois documents that by 1835 the Lekwiltok had annexed Coast Salish territory as far south as the islands off Campbell River, but it is unclear how fast this process occurred, or the extent to which direct annexation of northern Salish territory relates to raiding of more southernly Salish communities in Georgia Strait, the Fraser River, and Puget Sound.

What, then, should we make of the alleged link between Lekwiltok raiding and increased Salish centralization? Suttles discusses the numerous Spanish references to Coast Salish people armed with bows and arrows and wearing Indigenous armour (an observation corroborated by Vancouver). Suttles concludes from these sources that the "evidence on conflict therefore does not contradict the image we get from most ethnographies – of people who generally, out of enlightened self-interest maintained friendly relations with their neighbours, regardless of language boundaries, but were in conflict with more distant groups."[71] Although this interpretation has common-sense appeal, the archival record is actually ambiguous with regard to whether military aggression was related to geographic propinquity. In particular, there is no evidence to suggest that relations with neighbours were necessarily any less violent than those with more distant groups. The assumed relationship between collective defence and centralized leadership as expressed in shared concepts of political unity and regional identity, by extension, are just as difficult to assess from these records.

For example, as mentioned, Suttles quotes Quimper's description of the people of Port Discovery as "carrying on continual warfare with those on the north side, thus accounting for the fact that the beaches are strewn with the harpooned heads of their enemies."[72] On the basis of ethnographic evidence gathered from informants of the mid-twentieth century, Suttles suggests that the "north side" may refer to the slightly more distant Cowichan rather than the Songhees. The placement of Quimper's statement in the paragraph following his description of the Songhees people of the north side of the strait, and the fact that Quimper never ventured into Haro Strait to meet the Cowichan, indicates that it was actually more likely to have been the Songhees to which the Port Discovery people were referring. However, even if we accept that it might have been the Cowichan, should we consider them a "distant group"? By canoe in good weather, it is possible to travel from the Cowichan villages on Salt Spring Island to Port Discovery in a single day.

If the Spanish and British records are opaque on whether there existed an inverse relationship between geographic closeness and violence, the subsequent observations of HBC men are much less so. A generation after Captain Vancouver's voyage, the *Fort Langley Journal* documents a great deal of warfare among and between the central Coast Salish and their neighbours, particularly the Lekwiltok. From these records, it appears that contrary to Suttles's observation, and supportive of Jay Miller's approach, watersheds (and by extension languages) may actually have been the best indicators of collective identity and cooperative political action, for clearly they played a role in shaping responses to aggression. The *Journal* describes twenty attacks by various Salish warriors/raiders over a three-year period. An additional ten conflicts are mentioned involving various Coast Salish groups and the Lekwiltok. Most attacks involved multiple deaths, pillaging, and slave raiding. Moreover, they also demonstrate the shifting nature of Coast Salish alliances during this period. For example, 80 per cent of the conflicts among Halkomelem speakers pit Vancouver Island and mainland downriver speakers against people who spoke the central and upper mainland Fraser Valley dialects. The Cowichan of Vancouver Island, the most populous group and one described as having additional large summer villages near the mouth of the Fraser River, are by far the most common aggressors, and the upriver Chilliwack (whom records reveal to have moved more recently into the Fraser Valley from the neighbouring Chilliwack River watershed to the south and therefore only recently adopted the Halqemeylem language) are the most common recipients of their aggression.[73] Given the localized view of Coast Salish society offered to the men behind the fort's palisades, it is reasonable to assume that additional undocumented raids occurred beyond their observation. Conflicts that involved raiders having to pass in front of the fort in order to reach their objective are no doubt overly represented. While there is nothing in the records to suggest that any of these raids represented coordinated attacks by one community on another (indeed, they more likely represented isolated ventures by clusters of likeminded young men seeking opportunistic targets to demonstrate the veracity of their warrior spirit power), they do reveal that raiding and warfare were as likely to occur between neighbouring communities as they were among those slightly more distantly located. And they make clear that, taken as a whole, the Coast Salish people of the 1820s were involved in more internal conflicts than they were in contestations with the more distant Lekwiltok.

Smallpox

Any discussion of First Nations' history, as Ray Fogelson has argued, has to take into account the impact of introduced disease: "Drastically reduced populations are obviously decisive influences on the course of American Indian history, dramatically affecting social organization, the perception of traditions, religious conversion, revitalization movements, and a host of other domains. However, in the wake of numbing number counts, we have too few accounts of the native affective reactions and cognitive rationalizations of these catastrophic die-offs."[74] Reconstructions made from any of the early-contact-era records must take into account the fact that they describe Coast Salish communities earlier devastated by smallpox.[75] Thus we have to redefine what we mean by "contact."[76] What the earliest European observers documented was not traditional Coast Salish society on the verge of contact with Europeans. Introduced epidemic diseases had preceded direct contact by a decade.

In addition to Pantoja's cryptic observations of pox-scarred one-eyed smallpox survivors, Captain Vancouver and his crew describe numerous Salish people throughout Puget Sound and Georgia Strait as "horribly pitted" with smallpox scars. Vancouver and his officers report seeing human skeletons "promiscuously scattered about the beach in great numbers" and numerous abandoned villages "now fallen into decay; their inside, as well as a small surrounding space that appeared to have been formerly occupied, were overrun with weeds." The largest of these abandoned villages Vancouver estimated "had not been inhabited for five or six years, as brambles and bushes were growing up a considerable height."[77] What the earliest Europeans witnessed was a population that had just suffered massive and sudden population loss. The social and political implications of this loss have yet to be fully considered.[78]

If in "They Recognize No Superior Chief" Suttles is silent on the matter of disease, he does account for it in other publications.[79] However, he does so in a manner which consistently privileges Robert Boyd's analysis over that of Cole Harris.[80] Boyd's study is broadly based and has been criticized by Harris for lacking local and regional sensitivity.[81] Boyd dates the original epidemic as occurring sometime in the late 1770s and claims that it likely impacted all Northwest Coast Indigenous people.[82] Harris's study, on the other hand, dates the epidemic at 1782, and demonstrates that while it devastated the Chinook and Coast Salish, it did not reach the more northern Nuu-chah-nulth and Kwakwaka'wakw. Central to Harris's argument is the fact that Captain Vancouver recorded a marked increase in population density upon leaving Salish territory and entering Johnstone Strait. The Kwakwaka'wakw region is described as "infinitely more populous than the shores of the gulf of Georgia," and within it, Vancouver finds none of the promiscuously scattered human remains or empty villages that he described as common in the Salish Sea region. My own assessment of the primary documents confirms Harris's assessment of the date and geographic extent of the epidemic.[83] Robert Galois's complementary analysis likewise supports Harris's interpretation. After conducting an exhaustive review of the early maritime fur trade records, Galois concluded that the historical record was silent on smallpox among the Kwakwaka'wakw at this early time. Rather, a demographic decline consistent with the introduction of a deadly European crowd disease did not occur among the Kwakwaka'wakw until the 1820s.[84]

Accepting Boyd's argument for a Northwest Coast–wide pandemic as Suttles does is to implicitly create the impression that the non-centralized authority of the Salish is reflective of the same historical processes that shaped the more centralized social structures of the Nuu-chah-nulth and Kwakwaka'wakw. It fails to take into account the fact that ethnographic differences between the Salish and Nuu-chah-nulth/Kwakwaka'wakw may reflect the earlier devastation of Salish society by disease. The difficulty, however, is that the historical evidence is insufficiently robust to tell what effects the first smallpox epidemic had upon Coast Salish social and political organization. We know that smallpox was a major historic event in Coast Salish society and that its physical and emotional toll was terrible. But was the smallpox event so profound that it transformed the social structures that underlay Coast Salish society? Or, on the other hand, were the underlying social structures so well entrenched that, although devastating, the epidemic could not lead to structural change?

George Guilmet (and colleagues) raised similar questions in their 1991 article studying the "legacy of introduced diseases" among the southern Coast Salish. There they theorize that

> the indigenous cultures observed by members of the Vancouver expedition probably had already been modified by the presence of smallpox. Some cumulated cultural traditions may have been lost, and social institutions were perhaps simpler than before. In oral based societies ... the effect of the loss of [elders] as role models for children and adults had the potential of severely impacting social organization and stability. The loss of continuity in family and extended kin-based social units through the death of infants, spouses, grandparents, and other relatives may have led to significant social change ... The impact on the metaphysical and moral systems from the loss of shamans from disease, or from murder in the face of the unexplained death of patients ... should not be underestimated ... In addition to the impact on social organization and the philosophical system, disease-based depopulation probably diminished the ability of the local culture to maintain certain social institutions and accompanying rituals that required a minimum number of members of specific categories to be able to function normally.[85]

Lending credence to this sort of academic supposition are First Nations' oral histories and associated Indigenous interpretations of the impacts of the first major smallpox epidemic. Swinomish chief Martin Sampson wrote in the 1970s that Europeans "never saw the Indians at their full numbers and the peak of their culture. What they found was the broken remnant of a once-powerful people, reduced to this state by disease."[86] Albert Louie of Chilliwack, in 1965, explained that smallpox "killed, oh, half the Indians all around the Fraser River there."[87] Old Pierre of Katzie described in 1935 how "the wind carried the smallpox sickness among them. Some crawled away into the woods to die; many died in their homes. Altogether about three-quarters of the Indians perished."[88]

If the evidence for the Coast Salish area is sufficient only for preliminary speculation about the cultural and political consequences of smallpox, perhaps comparisons with other North American societies who suffered massive epidemics may provide valuable insights. For example, in conducting an ethnohistorical study of the Indigenous people of northwestern Mexico, Daniel Reff was puzzled by the stark contrast between the Spanish descriptions from the early 1500s and those of later observers. He notes that the earliest Spanish explorers "often mentioned or alluded to 'kingdoms' with sizable populations and complex economic and sociopolitical systems. By contrast, the later Jesuits made little or no mention of 'kingdoms' and generally described native populations in terms of small, dispersed rancherias, which lacked sophisticated economic and sociopolitical systems." These later Jesuit observations correspond with the current anthropological models describing northwest Mexican Indigenous society.[89] Reff attributes this discrepancy to epidemic diseases, many of which were introduced through Indigenous trade networks from distant European outposts. The disease, therefore, often preceded the arrival of those Europeans who carried the disease themselves. Reff concludes,

> Significant disease-induced reductions in population and the collapse of productive strategies must have had an impact on native social organization ... Anthropologists traditionally have inferred that aboriginal groups such as the Opata, Tarahumara, Yaqui, and Pima Alto lived in largely autonomous rancherias, headed by respected elders and war captains and organized in terms of bilateral kinship. This view of native social organization has been based almost entirely on historical materials such as kin terminologies from the eighteenth and nineteenth centuries and on ethnographic field work carried out in the last century. Researchers have largely ignored the comments of earlier Jesuit observers.[90]

Although Reff's study of cultural change among northwest Mexican Indigenous societies should not be applied casually to the Coast Salish, it nonetheless serves as a reminder of the extent to which depopulation can affect Indigenous social structures. The historical experience of the Coast Salish in this respect remains to be fully determined and is one of the outstanding challenges that historians of the region face.

Conclusion

There was a time when historians felt they could review documents and speak about contact and its effects with confidence. The event was alternatively the arrival of either European explorers or non-Native settlers; and everything subsequent represented a stage in the process of Indigenous social, economic, and political marginalization and cultural degradation. Stemming from this approach was the assumption that whatever the earliest newcomers described was necessarily Indigenous society at its pinnacle, and what came later was a compromised fragment of what had been. Such views, emerging as they did from the perspectives of European settlers themselves, acted as handmaidens for colonial policymakers and apologists who justified actions with teleological logic.

Likewise, not so long ago, anthropologists working on the West Coast were able to engage in memory ethnography and participant observation and feel confident that the structures their informants described as having characterized their grandparents' world accurately represented the way society functioned before contact induced change – before cultural contamination. Subsequent generations of humanists and social scientists, such as those involved in the debate over the historical expressions of Coast Salish leadership collective identity and political authority discussed earlier, have determined that the process was more complicated. Indigenous people had more agency than previously thought, and colonial agendas and actions were often more contradictory than a straightforward reading of policy documents allowed. And indeed, some of the consequences of contact and colonial policy were even contrary to what people at the time expected.

What is becoming clearer is that there is no conclusive answer to the debate over whether the Coast Salish were traditionally centralized or decentralized. If anything, the historical sources are perhaps most useful for what they reveal about the limitations of what we as historians can know about the Coast Salish past, highlighting as they do just how much we do not know. As such, these sources suggest ways in which we can reframe the questions we are asking about this early time period. For even without being able to confidently pierce the contact-era barrier created by smallpox to see how Salish societies were structured prior to this devastating disruption, the evidence from subsequent eras (and the insights gleaned from an examination of multiple social geographies within Coast Salish territory) speak to a remarkable degree of political elasticity and a corresponding willingness on the part of Coast Salish communities (variously defined) to accommodate a wide range of political expressions.

Such societal elasticity hints at the extent to which agency was wielded by familial collectives and Salish individuals. At times certain prominent men – either seizing opportunities created by sudden smallpox-induced depopulation, responding to the crisis of their more populous northern neighbours having access to Western firearms, embracing the economic opportunities associated with the fur trade, or taking advantage of colonial efforts to consolidate tribes and displace older prerogatives with the powers of government-recognized Indian chiefs – rose to prominence and exercised considerable political authority over a wide range of people and sometimes multiple settlements. Whether such also occurred prior to contact in response to other Indigenous events is impossible to tell, but certainly it is not impossible; and in some places at some times, it appears to have been likely. But so too is it impossible to determine if the seemingly more sporadic historical expressions of such centralized authority documented since 1790 are necessarily innovations or whether they harken back to what may have been more formal political institutions that existed pre-contact – similar to those expressed by Salish people's northern neighbours, who apparently escaped that first devastating epidemic in 1782. It is clear that since that time, whatever change has occurred within Coast Salish society towards centralization or decentralization has not been unidirectional. And there is nothing to suggest that we should expect it to be so in the future.

NOTES

This is a revised version of a paper I originally drafted in 1998. Several people have helped me refine my thinking since then. Foremost is J.R. Miller, who has repeatedly reminded me of the value of inductive research and the fruitfulness of cross-disciplinary dialogue to the understanding of the history of Native-newcomer relations. I am also especially grateful to Naxahetsi (Albert "Sonny" McHalsie) for the countless discussions we have had concerning the history of Coast Salish society; to the many Stó:lō and Sliammon Coast Salish elders who have shared aspects of their knowledge with me and especially to late Chief Wesley Sam of Soowahlie for sharing with me information about Coast Salish social structures that he learned from his grandfather Robert Joe; to Grand Chief (and recently BC lieutenant governor) Steven Point for taking time out of his busy schedule to share with me his ideas concerning the impact of Euroamerican culture on Coast Salish society; to Dave Schaepe for the conversations we had while looking for rock walls in the Fraser Canyon and then those we had subsequent to having found them; to Brian Thom for originally introducing me to the range and depth of Coast Salish anthropological discourse; to Bruce Miller, whose mentorship has been both motivating and inspiring; to Jay Miller for his enriching conversations and his insistence on attention to the non-material; to Mike Kew for answering many questions concerning the structure of Coast Salish families and for his thoughtful comments and encouragement after reading an earlier version of this paper; to Arthur J. Ray for reviewing and commenting on an earlier draft; and to the League of University of Saskatchewan Ethnohistory Graduate Students who patiently listened and then provided suggestions during a full evening of fleshing out ideas over beer.

1 Bruce G. Miller and Daniel L. Boxberger, "Creating Chiefdoms: The Puget Sound Case," *Ethnohistory* 41/2 (spring 1994): 267.

2 Bill Angelbeck and Erick McLay, "The Battle of Maple Bay: Dynamics of Coast Salish Political Organization through Oral Histories," *Ethnohistory* 58/3 (summer 2011): 359–92.

3 Marshall David Sahlins, "The Return of the Event, Again," in *Clio in Oceania, Toward a Historical Anthropology*, ed. Aletta Biersack (Washington, DC: Smithsonian Institution Press, 1999), 38–9.

4 Raymond D. Fogelson, "The Ethnohistory of Events and Nonevents," *Ethnohistory* 36/2 (spring 1989): 139.

5 Marshall Sahlins, *Historical Metaphor and Mythical Realities: Structure in the Early History of the Sandwich Islands Kingdom* (Ann Arbor: University of Michigan Press, 1981).

6 Bruce G. Miller, "Centrality and Measures of Regional Structure in Aboriginal Western Washington," *Ethnology* 28 (1989): 265–76; Keith Thor Carlson, "Stó:lō Exchange Dynamics," *Native Studies Review* 11/1 (1997): 5–48.

7 Wayne Suttles, "They Recognize No Superior Chief: The Strait of Juan De Fuca in the 1790's," in *Culturas de la Costa Noroeste de America*, ed. Jose Luis Peset (Madrid: Turner Libros, 1992), 252. For a detailed ethnographic discussion of Coast Salish social structures, see Wayne Suttles, "Private Knowledge, Morality, and Social Classes among the Coast Salish"; "Affinal Ties, Subsistence, and Prestige among the Coast Salish"; "Variation in Habitat and Culture on the Northwest Coast"; and "Coping with Abundance: Subsistence on the Northwest Coast," all of which are reproduced in Wayne Suttles, *Coast Salish Essays* (Vancouver: Talonbooks, 1987).

8 Kenneth D. Tollefson, "The Snoqualmie: A Puget Sound Chiefdom," *Ethnology* 26/2 (April 1987): 121–36. See also Kenneth D. Tollefson, "Political Organization of the Duwamish," *Ethnology* 28/1 (1989): 135–50.

9 Tollefson, "Snoqualmie," 123.

10 For example, Alice Kehoe's survey text *North American Indians: A Comprehensive Account*, 2nd ed. (Toronto: Prentice-Hall, 1992), and Jean Arnold's *The Origins of a Pacific Coast Chiefdom: The Chumash of the Channel Islands* (Salt Lake City: University of Utah Press, 2001).

11 Kenneth D. Tollefson, "In Defense of a Snoqualmie Political Chiefdom Model," *Ethnohistory* 43/1 (winter 1996): 145–71.

12 Miller and Boxberger, "Creating Chiefdoms." Though as Miller and Boxberger point out, pressure should be brought to bear on Western authorities to adjust their definitions of meaningful collective association to accommodate Indigenous realities, rather than expecting Indigenous people to prove they can meet European standards of political affiliation.

13 Jay Miller, *Lushootseed Culture and the Shamanic Odyssey: An Anchored Radiance* (Lincoln: University of Nebraska Press, 1999), 8. See also Jay Miller, "Back to Basics," *Ethnohistory* 44/2 (1997): 375.

14 A renaissance that, fifty years later, continues to gain momentum despite the increased emphasis on the local village community being fostered by American and Canadian government funding programs.

15 Wayne Suttles, "The Persistence of Intervillage Ties Among the Coast Salish," *Ethnology* 2/4 (October 1963): 512–25.

16 Miller, *Anchored Radiance*.

17 David M. Schaepe, "Rock Fortifications: Archaeological Insights into Pre-Contact Warfare and Sociopolitical Organization Among the Stó:lō of the Lower Fraser River Canyon, BC," *American Antiquity* 71/4 (2006): 671–705.

18 Angelbeck and McLay, "Battle of Maple Bay," 378, 380.

19 Miller and Boxberger, "Creating Chiefdoms," 274.

20 Suttles, "They Recognize No Superior Chief," 262.

21 Ibid., 261.

22 Cecil Jane, *A Spanish Voyage to Vancouver and the North-west Coast of America: Being the Narrative of the Voyage Made in the Year 1792 by the Schooners Sutil and Mexicana to Explore the Strait of Fuca* (London: Argonaut Press, 1930).

23 Pantoja in Henry Raup Wagner, *Spanish Explorations in the Strait of Juan de Fuca* (Santa Ana, CA: Fine Arts Press, 1933), 255–6. Emphasis added.

24 Pantoja in Jane, *A Spanish Voyage*, 48. Emphasis added.

25 The use of the expression "pimply" is less indicative of smallpox than is the characteristic blindness in one eye. Survivors of variola major were typically blind in one eye and often suffered from scar tissue hanging over the sightless orifice.

26 I am indebted to Luisa Munoz from Spain (who was studying at UBC while I was a PhD student) for the time she took out of her busy schedule to compare the Wagner and Jane translations to Quimper's original.

27 There are many instances where the Wagner and Jane translations differ. To cite just a few prominent inconsistencies, at one point Wagner claims "twelve canoes" approached the Spanish ship, while the Jane translation mentions "two." The occupants of Wagner's twelve canoes, "sold us some bows, arrows, clubs and three paddles for the canoe, as those who had let us have it went off without troubling to leave it provided with that accessory" (264). The men in Jane's two canoes "sold us some bows arrows, machetes and three small casks for the canoe, since those who had let us have the canoe had gone away without consenting to leave us these things" (55). Wagner quotes Pantoja as writing, "Although in these places

we do not find that pleasant view which a diversity of trees and young plants presents, nor the elegance of flowers and beauty of fruits, nor the variety of animals and birds; while the ear also misses the pleasant song of the latter, yet the observer will not fail to find many opportunities to admire the works of nature and divert his thoughts in contemplating the enormous masses of the mountains" (265). Jane's translation of the same passage reads, "It would certainly be impossible to find a more delightful view than that which is here presented by the diversity of trees and shrubs, by the loveliness of the flowers and the beauty of the fruit, by the variety of the animals and birds. When to this is added the pleasure of listening to the song of the birds the observer is afforded many occasions for admiring the works of nature and for delighting his senses as he contemplates the majestic outlines of the mountains" (57).

28 Luisa Munoz to author, 14 May 1998, author's personal collection.

29 J.R. Miller, *Skyscrapers Hide the Heavens: A History of Indian-White Relations in Canada* (Toronto: University of Toronto Press, 2000).

30 James Axtell, *Natives and Newcomers: The Colonial Origins of North America* (New York: Oxford University Press, 2001).

31 Those arguing enrichment include Joyce Wike, "The Effects of the Maritime Fur Trade on Northwest Coast Indian Society" (PhD diss., Columbia University, 1951); Wilson Duff, *The Indian History of British Columbia*, vol. 1, *The Impact of the White Man*, Anthropology in British Columbia, Memoir No. 5 (Victoria: Provincial Museum of British Columbia, 1964); and Robin Fisher, *Contact and Conflict: Indian-European Relations in British Columbia, 1774–1890* (Vancouver: UBC Press, 1992). Prominent opponents of the enrichment thesis include Barry M. Gough, *Gunboat Frontier: British Maritime Authority and Northwest Coast Indians, 1846–90* (Vancouver: UBC Press, 1984); and James R. Gibson, *Otter Skins, Boston Ships, and China Goods: The Maritime Fur Trade of the Northwest Coast, 1785–1841* (Montreal: McGill-Queen's University Press, 1992). Seminal in shifting attention away from the early to mid-nineteenth century was Celia Haig-Brown's *Resistance and Renewal: Surviving the Indian Residential School* (Vancouver: Arsenal Pulp Press, 1988).

32 Cole Harris, *The Resettlement of British Columbia: Essays on Colonialism and Geographical Change* (Vancouver: UBC Press, 1997); Alexandra Harman's *Indians in the Making: Ethnic Relations and Indian Identities Around Puget Sound* (Seattle: University of Washington Press, 1999); Lissa Wadewitz, *The Nature of Borders: Salmon and Boundaries in the Salish Sea* (Seattle: University of Washington Press; Vancouver: UBC Press, 2012).

33 See Arthur J. Ray, *Indians in the Fur Trade: Their Role as Trappers, Hunters, and Middlemen in the Lands Southwest of the Hudson Bay, 1660–1870*

(Toronto: University of Toronto Press, 1974); and Arthur J. Ray and Donald B. Freeman, *"Give Us Good Measure": An Economic Analysis of Relations Between the Indians and the Hudson's Bay Company Before 1763* (Toronto: University of Toronto Press, 1978). For examples of other more controversial studies which focus on non-economic factors, see Calvin Martin's *Keepers of the Game: Indian-Animal Relationships and the Fur Trade* (Berkeley: University of California Press, 1978); and Abraham Rotstein's "Trade and Politics: An Institutional Approach," *Western Canadian Journal of Anthropology* 3 (1972): 1–28. For a detailed critique of Martin's thesis, consult Kerry Abel and Jean Friesen, eds., *Aboriginal Resource Use in Canada: Historical and Legal Aspects* (Winnipeg: University of Manitoba Press, 1991).

34 Leland Donald, *Aboriginal Slavery on the Northwest Coast of America* (Berkeley: University of California Press, 1997). This work is an extension and elaboration of Donald's earlier article-length studies: "The Slave Trade on the Northwest Coast of North America," *Research in Economic Anthropology* 6 (1984): 121–58; Donald Mitchell, "Predatory Warfare, Social Status, and the North Pacific Slave Trade," *Ethnology* 73 (1984): 39–48; Donald Mitchell, "A Demographic Profile of Northwest Coast Slavery," in Marc Thompson et al., *Status Structure and Stratification: Current Archaeological Reconstructions* (Calgary: University of Calgary Press, 1985), 227–36; Leland Donald, "Slave Raiding on the North Pacific Coast," in *Native People, Native Lands*, ed. Bruce Alden Cox (Ottawa: Carlton University Press, 1988), 161–72.

35 W. Kaye Lamb, ed., *The Letters and Journals of Simon Fraser, 1806–1808* (Toronto: MacMillan Company of Canada, 1960), 104.

36 Ibid., 107.

37 Personal communication with Matilda Gutierrez of Chawathil, August 1998.

38 Lamb, *Letters and Journals of Simon Fraser*, 103.

39 Ibid.

40 Ibid.

41 For a thoughtful discussion of the way traders' expectations shaped the way they described and related to Indigenous people of the Pacific Slope, see Elizabeth Vibert, "Real Men Hunt Buffalo: Masculinity, Race and Class in British Fur Traders' Narratives," *Gender and History* 8/1 (April 1996): 4–21. François N. Annance, "A Journal of a Voyage from Fort George Columbia River to Fraser River in the Winter of 1824 and 1825," Hudson's Bay Company Archives, Archives of Manitoba, B/76/a/1.

42 T.C. Elliot, ed., "The Journal of John Work, November and December, 1824," *Washington Historical Quarterly* 3/3 (July 1912): 198–228.

43 G. Dickey, ed., *Journal of Occurrences at Fort Nisqually, 1833–1859* (Tacoma, WA: Fort Nisqually Historical Site, 1983).

44 For an ethnographic discussion of the Coast Salish prophet dance phenomenon, see Wayne Suttles, "The Plateau Prophet Dance Among the Coast Salish," in Suttles, *Coast Salish Essays* (Vancouver: Talonbooks, 1987), 152–98. See also June McCormick Collins, *Valley of the Spirits: The Upper Skagit Indians of Western Washington* (Seattle: University of Washington Press, 1974).

45 See Keith Thor Carlson, "Prophesy," in Keith Thor Carlson, ed., *A Stó:lō–Coast Salish Historical Atlas* (Vancouver: Douglas and McIntyre, 2001), 154–61.

46 Dickey, *Journal of Occurrences at Fort Nisqually*.

47 "James Douglas to Governor James Simpson, Fort Vancouver, 18, March, 1838," Appendix A, in E.E. Rich, ed., *The Letters of John McLaughlin from Fort Vancouver to the Governor and Committee*, First Series, 1825–38, vol. 4 (Toronto: Champlain Society, 1991), 280–1.

48 Suttles, "They Recognize No Superior Chief," 253.

49 Ibid., 252–3.

50 Miller and Boxberger, "Creating Chiefdoms," 274; Suttles, "They Recognize No Superior Chief," 261.

51 Lamb, *A Voyage of Discovery*, 604. See also Menzies's description of this same fortified village. Based upon his observations, Menzies estimates that the village had only recently been abandoned. Menzies also describes a particularly large ornate house in this village which he speculates must have been "the residence of the Chief or some family of distinction." C.F. Newcombe, ed., *Menzie's Journals of Vancouver's Voyage*, Victoria: Archives of British Columbia, Memoir No. 5 (1923), 66–7.

52 Lamb, *Letters and Journals of Simon Fraser*, 106.

53 Michael Kew, personal communication, Stó:lō Tribal Council grounds, Chilliwack, BC, May 1994.

54 Lamb, *Letters and Journals of Simon Fraser*, 82.

55 Charles Wilks, unpublished manuscript, British Columbia Archives and Records Service (henceforth BCARS), 322.

56 Reverend DeSmet, *Oregon Missions and Travels to the Rocky Mountains in 1845* (New York: 1847), 56.

57 Paul Kane, *Wanderings of an Artist* (London, 1859), 220.

58 A.C. Anderson, "Notes on the Indian Tribes of British North America and the Northwest Coast," copy on file at Stó:lō Nation Archives. Originally at BCARS.

59 George Gibbs, "Journal of an Expedition to Fraser River," WA-Mss S-1810, Beinecke Rare Book & Manuscript Library, Yale University, Hartford, CT.

60 David Schaepe, "Rock Fortifications: Archaeological Insights into Pre-contact Warfare and Sociopolitical Organization Among the Stó:lō of the Lower Fraser River Canyon, B.C.," *American Antiquity* 4/71 (2007): 671–705.

61 See two studies of immediate pre-contact Coast Salish defensive sites with an eye to their implications for political authority: William Angelbeck, "'They Recognize No Superior Chief': Power, Practice, Anarchism and Warfare in the Coast Salish Past" (PhD diss., Department of Anthropology, University of British Columbia, 2009); and Kisha Suprenant, "Inscribing Identities on the Landscape: A Spatial Exploration of Archaeological Rock Features in the Lower Fraser River Canyon" (PhD diss., Department of Anthropology, University of British Columbia, 2011).

62 George Gibbs, *Ethnology Manuscript Material, Number 1192* (Washington, DC: National Anthropological Archives, Smithsonian Institution, 1858), 223.

63 Martha Douglas's diary, quoted in Grant Keddie, "Aboriginal Defensive Sites, Part 2: Amateur Archaeology Begins," *Discovery, The Magazine of the Royal British Columbia Museum* 24/9 (February 1997): 5.

64 Gary Coupland, "Warfare and Social Complexity on the Northwest Coast," in *Cultures in Conflict: Current Archaeological Perspectives*, ed. Diana Tkaczuk and Brian C. Vivian (Calgary: University of Calgary, Archaeological Association, 1989), 205–14.

65 The first reference I can remember coming across that described fortified Coast Salish villages was by Cole Harris: "The fact that Vancouver's journals mention fortified villages and beacons, possibly watchtowers, 'so frequently erected in the more southerly parts of New Georgia,' and that there is abundant archaeological evidence of fortified, pre-contact sites around the Strait of Georgia implies that [Lekwiltok] raiding had been common before 1792." Descriptions of this sort, however, provide unique ethnographic challenges. More likely, the structures Vancouver referred to as being "so frequently erected in the more southerly parts of New Georgia" were not "fortified villages," as Harris states, but rather fish drying racks. Likewise, what Harris interpreted as "beacons, possibly watchtowers," were more likely poles used to hold nets used in catching waterfowl. Cole Harris, "Voices of Smallpox around the Strait of Georgia," in Cole Harris, *The Resettlement of British Columbia: Essays on Colonialism and Geographical Change* (Vancouver: UBC Press, 1997), 15.

66 Robert Galois, *Kwakwa̱ka̱'wakw Settlements, 1775–1920: A Geographical Analysis and Gazetteer* (Vancouver: UBC Press, 1994), 27.

67 Ibid., 28.

68 Wagner, *Spanish Explorations*, 222–3.
69 Lamb, *A Voyage of Discovery*, 613.
70 Galois, *Kwakwaka'wakw Settlements*, 235.
71 Suttles, "They Recognize No Superior Chief," 256.
72 Wagner, *Spanish Explorations*, 131.
73 See Keith Thor Carlson, "Intercommunity Conflicts," in Carlson, *A Stó:lō–Coast Salish Historical Atlas*, 46–7. See also Keith Thor Carlson, *The Power of Place, the Problem of Time: Aboriginal Identity and Historical Consciousness in the Cauldron of Colonialism* (Toronto: University of Toronto Press, 2010), chapter 5.
74 Ray Fogelson, "Ethnohistory of Events and Nonevents," *Ethnohistory* 36/2 (spring 1989): 139.
75 See Harris, "Voices of Smallpox," 3–30; Robert Boyd, "Commentary on Early Contact-Era Smallpox in the Pacific Northwest," *Ethnohistory* 43/2 (spring 1996): 307–28; Robert Boyd, "Smallpox in the Pacific Northwest: The First Epidemics," *BC Studies* 101 (spring 1994): 5–39; and also Keith Thor Carlson, "First Contact: Smallpox: 'A Sickness That No Medicine Could Cure, and No Person Escape,'" in Keith Thor Carlson, *You Are Asked to Witness: The Stó:lō in Canada's Pacific Coast History* (Chilliwack, BC: Stó:lō Heritage Trust, 1997), 27–40.
76 I have discussed this in more detail elsewhere: Keith Thor Carlson, "Reflections on Indigenous History and Memory: Reconstructing and Reconsidering Contact," in John Lutz, ed., *Myth and Memory: Stories of Indigenous-European Contact* (Vancouver: UBC Press, 2007), 46–68.
77 Lamb, *A Voyage of Discovery*, 528, 538, 539, 540, 568, 575, 578n3, 560.
78 An early attempt at assessing the social and cultural implications of smallpox on Coast Salish people is found in George M. Guilmet, Robert Boyd, David L. Whitehead, and Nile Thompson's pioneering work "The Legacy of Introduced Disease on the Southern Coast Salish," *American Indian Culture and Research Journal* 15/4 (1991): 1–32. See also "From the Great Flood to Smallpox," in Carlson, *The Power of Place, the Problem of Time*, 79–112.
79 See Suttles, "The Ethnographic Significance of the Fort Langley Journals," an epilogue in Morag McLaughlin, ed., *The Fort Langley Journals* (Vancouver: UBC Press, 1998). In a conversation shortly before his passing, Wayne Suttles expressed the opinion that in the Harris-Boyd debate "I am inclined to follow Boyd" (personal communication, 17 April 1997).
80 Robert T. Boyd, "Demographic History, 1774–1884," in Wayne Suttles, ed., *Handbook of North American Indians*, vol. 7, *Northwest Coast* (Washington, DC: Smithsonian Institution Press, 1990), 135–48.
81 Harris, "Voices of Smallpox."

82 For Boyd's more recent defence of his interpretation see "Commentary on Early Contact-Era Smallpox in the Pacific Northwest," *Ethnohistory* 43/2 (spring 1996): 307–28.
83 Carlson, *The Power of Place, the Problem of Time*, 79–112.
84 Robert Galois, *Kwakwaka'wakw Settlements, 1775–1920: A Geographical Analysis and Gazetteer* (Vancouver: UBC Press, 1994), 39–40.
85 Guilmet et al., "Legacy of Introduced Disease," 10.
86 Martin Sampson, *Indians of Skagit County*, Skagit County Historical Series 2 (Mount Vernon, WA: Skagit County Historical Society, 1972), p. I. Cited in Cole Harris, "Social Power and Cultural Power in Pre-Colonial British Columbia," *BC Studies* 115/116 (autumn/winter 1997/8): 69.
87 Albert Louis in conversation with Oliver Wells, 28 July 1965 (copy on file at the Stó:lō Nation Archives).
88 Old Pierre in Diamond Jenness, "Faith of a Coast Salish Indian," in *Anthropology in British Columbia – Memoirs 3*, ed. Wilson Duff (Victoria: British Columbia Provincial Museum, 1955), 34.
89 Daniel T. Reff, *Disease, Depopulation, and Culture Change in Northwestern New Spain, 1518–1764* (Salt Lake City: University of Utah Press, 1991), 13. I am grateful to Cole Harris for drawing my attention to Reff's publication.
90 Ibid., 245.

An Appealing Anthropology, Frozen in Time: Diamond Jenness's *The Indians of Canada*

DIANNE NEWELL AND ARTHUR J. RAY

Doubtless all the tribes will disappear. Some will endure only a few years longer, others, like the Eskimo, may last several centuries. Some will merge steadily with the white race, others will bequeath to future generations only an infinitesimal fraction of their blood. Culturally they have already contributed everything that was valuable for our own civilization beyond what knowledge we may still glean from their histories concerning man's ceaseless struggle to control his environment.

Diamond Jenness, *The Indians of Canada*[1]

When characterizing the pre-contact life of the plaintiffs' ancestors in his reasons for judgment in *Delgamuukw v. British Columbia* (1991), which concerned the comprehensive title claim of the Gitxsan and Wet'suet'en to their traditional, unsurrendered territory in north-central British Columbia, the chief justice of the British Columbia Supreme Court quoted the seventeenth-century English philosopher Thomas Hobbes.[2] Chief Justice Allan McEachern in ruling against the plaintiffs explained,

> It would not be accurate to assume that even pre-contact existence in [Gitxsan-Wet'suwet'en] territory was in the least bit idyllic. The plaintiffs' ancestors had no written language, no horses or wheeled vehicles, slavery and starvation was not uncommon, wars with neighbouring peoples were common, and there is no doubt, to quote Hobb[e]s, that aboriginal life in the territory was, at best, "nasty, brutish and short."[3]

This offensive statement drew a chorus of criticism from First Nations, legal, and academic communities.[4] Few scholars were more vociferous than the anthropologists, who faulted McEachern for regurgitating a centuries-old unsupportable, evolutionary, and Eurocentric anthropological perspective. What critics failed to point out, however, was that McEachern could have voiced the same sentiment merely by citing passages of Diamond Jenness's survey, *The Indians of Canada*. Although originally published in 1932, this unrevised[5] eighty-three-year-old sweeping endorsement of evolutionary anthropology by the then chief anthropologist at the National Museum of Canada is with us still. It remains in print, carries the imprimatur of the National Museum, is promoted as the "most comprehensive work available" on the subject, and goes largely unchallenged.

To date, the only extended critique of *Indians of Canada* is that of sociologist Peter Kulchyski, who in his 1993 article in the *Journal of Canadian Studies*, "Anthropology in the Service of the State: Diamond Jenness and Indian Policy," assessed the book in his critical appraisal of Jenness's role as a senior Canadian public servant advising the federal government on Indian policy.[6] Even the 2012 cradle-to-grave academic biography of Jenness by anthropologist Barnett Richling, *In Twilight and in Dawn*, while loaded with minute detail of Jenness's personal and professional life, mentions *The Indians of Canada* only in passing.[7] A major concern of ours is something that Kulchyski's important essay did not address: Why do the courts keep finding Jenness's type of anthropology so appealing so late in time?

The Indians of Canada: The Background

When *The Indians of Canada* first appeared in 1932, Diamond Jenness (1886–1969) – born and raised in New Zealand, educated at University of Oxford, and a specialist in Arctic anthropology – was the National Museum's newly appointed chief anthropologist and therefore a preeminent figure in the nascent field of Canadian anthropology. He had only just achieved his promotion when in 1928 the museum assigned him the task of writing both a general standard reference work/textbook on the topic of the Indigenous people of Canada and a summary version of it for the *Cambridge History of the British Empire* series. Jenness's biographer discovered that, for reasons both practical (he was about to leave on a major field trip to the Arctic) and scholarly, Jenness had been reluctant to write the book at that time: "Jenness griped that what eventually appeared in 1932 as *The Indians of Canada* was 'causing me all kinds of trouble,' confessing to [a colleague] that 'I am not qualified to write it, nor I think is anybody else. The worst of it is [the manuscript is] supposed to be finished inside of sixteen or eighteen months and the task really requires about ten years.'"[8] Despite these understandable misgivings, Jenness completed the project on target, likely because he narrowed the scope of the topic to First Nations almost exclusively.

The Indians of Canada has proved to be highly durable. The National Museum of Canada published it in 1932 as *Bulletin 65, Anthropological Series No. 15,* and began republishing it almost immediately, in 1934 (second edition), 1955 (third), 1958 (fourth), 1960 (fifth), and 1963 (sixth), and reprinted the sixth edition in 1967 and 1972. The seventh (and to date, the latest) edition was published, and for the first time in paperback, in 1977 and reprinted nine times thereafter, in 1980, 1982, 1984, 1986, 1989, 1993, 1996, 2000, and 2003, by the University of Toronto Press in association with the National Museum of Man, National Museums of Canada, and the government printers. The press published it as an e-book in February 2015. Editions two through six were unchanged in terms of content, other than the updating of information in the appendix on the linguistic map of Canada and the addition of a third appendix in editions four through six that briefly updated pre-contact information on specific regions of the country based on the application of new dating techniques (tree ring and carbon-14 analyses). By the seventh edition, the appendices and bibliography had disappeared.

The seventh edition was a special case. Historians Ian Getty and Donald B. Smith in the preface to a 1978 collection of essays on western Canadian First Nations observed that, in reviving *The Indians of Canada* in 1977, the University of Toronto Press was attempting to meet the "chronic shortage" of scholarly works to satisfy the growing public demand for First Nations' history. Getty and Smith note an irony in reissuing an outmoded book about the "Indian" as a vanishing race at a time when the Indigenous population was rebounding at a rate unparalleled in the rest of the population. But they could have gone further to suggest that a critical essay to help readers contextualize Jenness's outmoded 1932 study should have been included.[9] Far from including a much-needed critical introductory essay, the seventh edition and its later reprintings carry a back-cover publisher's blurb that claims Jenness's monograph "remains the most comprehensive work available on Canada's Indians." That message echoes the one contained in the foreword to the book by then director of the National Museum of Man, William E. Taylor, Jr., who, without ever discussing the contents of Jenness's study or cautioning readers, applauds the lasting relevance and scholarly stature of the book and declares, "Now a classic, it continues to be simply the best of its kind."[10]

Because *Indians of Canada* proved exceptionally enduring and continued for all those decades to be published by Canada's National Museum, it was highly influential. When writing in 1993 about Jenness's role as an advisor on national policy on Indigenous Canadians, Kulchyski reminds us that "for 50 years the standard reference, it [*The Indians of Canada*] was used to train untold numbers of anthropologists and others interested in Native Canadian Studies."[11] These "others" would have included several generations of lawyers and justices, including perhaps Chief Justice Allan McEachern, who earned his law degree in 1950. Kulchyski raises a legitimate question about the lack of critical examination of *Indians of Canada* and notes that "this relative silence over a figure of such stature is suspicious in its own right."[12] Several decades later this silence has yet to be explained.

The long-lasting influence of *Indians of Canada*, the failure of Jenness or anyone else at Canada's National Museum to revise it, or at the very least to add a critical introduction to the later editions, and the paucity of critical assessments of it by later generations of scholars raise several basic questions that we wish to address. What is the intellectual foundation upon which this study was based? What is the book's basic message about "Indians" in Canada? And why is it that Indigenous peoples still have to confront this type of old anthropological thinking when they seek to advance their Aboriginal and treaty rights in the courts today?

Scholarship about Indigenous peoples in Canada has evolved considerably over the decades since the original appearance of Jenness's survey. And, whereas in 1932, when Jenness produced it, this field was predominantly the domain of anthropologists (mostly archaeologists and field ethnologists), by the last quarter of the twentieth century, scholars from history, historical geography, political science, "Native studies," women's studies, historical sociology, and other fields had become actively involved. And the field of anthropology itself had changed, becoming more self-reflexive and critical, as the work led by anthropologists such George Stocking, Jr., and Clifford Geertz and historian of anthropology James Clifford has demonstrated. This broader and more critical scholarly involvement was in part the result of the growing political activism of Native North Americans in the late 1960s that generated such acclaimed popular writings as *Custer Died for Your*

Sins: An Indian Manifesto (1969), by the American Indian historian and activist Vine Deloria, Jr.; *Unjust Society: The Tragedy of Canada's Indians* (1969), by the young Cree leader from Alberta Harold Cardinal; and *Prisoner of Grass: Canada from the Native Point of View* (1975), by the Saskatchewan Métis scholar and radical activist Howard Adams. It was also fuelled by the subsequent claims litigation and treaty negotiations in Canada touched off by the Nisga'a title suit *Calder v. Attorney-General of British Columbia* (1973), which paved the way for the federal government's comprehensive claims process. Facilitating the growing body of critical ethnohistorical and claims research that followed has been the increasing accessibility in Canada of a range of archival records, most notably the massive archive of the Hudson's Bay Company, following its move to Canada from England in 1970.

By the time of the latest reprinting of *The Indians of Canada* in 2003, newer overviews of the history of Indigenous peoples in Canada were widely available. James Miller's pioneering synthesis, *Skyscrapers Hide the Heavens* (1989), was the trendsetting work. Miller's broad survey, and those of Olive Dickason (1992) and Arthur J. Ray (1996) that followed, emphasize Native-newcomer relations.[13] Miller and Dickason focus on the missionary and government aspects, whereas Ray stresses economic and Aboriginal and treaty rights dimensions. Written in an era of activism, cultural resurgence, and litigation, all three overviews, as well as the more specialized studies produced earlier – most notably those by Bishop (1974), Ray (1974), Fisher (1977), Van Kirk (1980), and Brown (1980) – paid considerable attention to Indigenous agency and, in the case of Van Kirk and Brown, were also studies written within the new subgenres of women's and family history.[14] By the 1990s, Native history in Canada was fast becoming one of the most vibrant and prolific topics in the Canadian history field. Class-action suits around Indian residential school abuse and the findings of Canada's 1996 Royal Commission on Aboriginal People, especially on the topic of residential schools, was the focus of some of the new research and writing. Memoirs and studies of the Indian residential experience include Celia Haig-Brown's pathbreaking interview-based monograph, *Resistance and Renewal* (1988), followed by the broad histories of the residential schools by James Miller, *Shingwauk's Vision* (1996), and John S. Milloy, *A National Crime* (1999).[15] The growing body of contemporary land claims and treaty negotiations, especially following the enactment of the patriated Constitution of Canada (1982), which recognizes and affirms existing Aboriginal and treaty rights for Indians, Métis, and

Inuit, perhaps contributed the most to sparking interest in all dimensions of the history and legal rights of these peoples. Examples of studies of prominent claims cases and the claims litigation process, often written by the experts involved, include Newell (1993), Mills (1994); Culhane (1998), Sterritt et al. (1998), Wickin (2002), Daly (2005), Miller (2011), and Ray (2012).[16] As is obvious from our opening quotation, the post-1950s cultural resurgence in Indigenous Canada and the present energetic and productive field of Indigenous history and ethnohistory, and the reasons for it, are phenomena that *The Indians of Canada* (1932) would never have predicted – on the contrary.

The Intellectual Context of the Original Edition: Salvage Ethnography

Jenness's classic study highlights and conforms to the nature of early North American anthropology and the dominance of Boasian ethnology in the early decades of the twentieth century. It is a "culture" history in the traditional anthropological meaning of that expression, that is, a regional cross-sectional study that offers the reader a glimpse of traditional First Nations' cultures as early-twentieth-century anthropologists imagined them to have been at the time of early European contact.

At the time that Jenness was writing his big survey, Franz Boas and his students dominated the emerging field of (North) Americanist ethnology.[17] Although not a student of Boas, Jenness shared many of his interests, and in 1916 he had been hired as a staff anthropologist at the Anthropology Division of the Geological Survey of Canada by (and would work under) one of Boas's most famous students, the distinguished American linguist Edward Sapir.[18] The Boasians were devoted to detailing the varied regional expressions of First Nations' cultures and explaining that diversity in terms of fundamental long-term historical processes, most notably acculturation, diffusion, migration, and culture-environment interaction.[19] They were especially drawn to questions about the likely Old World origin of the ancestors of First Nations and Inuit and to theories about intercontinental migration across the Bering Strait. Jenness's own work addressed questions about the origins and migrations of Native North Americans, especially Inuit. However, Boas was a theorist who encouraged theory building and testing in others, and Jenness was not.

Concerns about origins, migration, and diffusion had drawn some of the earliest North American ethnographic expeditions to the Arctic.

It was in the Arctic that Boas cut his teeth studying Inuit of Baffin Island (1883–4). Jenness did likewise, as a member of the Vilhjalmur Stefansson Canadian Arctic expedition (1913–16). The interest in ancient migrations from Siberia quickly drew Boas and many other researchers to Canada's Northwest Coast beginning in the 1880s.[20] Addressing fundamental historical questions such as these was of course a daunting challenge before the mid-twentieth century. The field of archaeology was in its infancy, and rigorous scientific dating techniques, most notably carbon-14 analysis, had yet to be developed.[21] Anthropologists had no choice but to gather evidence for diffusion, migration, and the timing of these processes from non-conventional sources. Among the most important sources of evidence were collections of material culture; field recordings of Indigenous myths, legends, and oral histories; physical anthropology;[22] and linguistic evidence collected in the field and preserved, studied, and in some cases displayed in major museums internationally.

The late 1800s and early 1900s was a time when major museums scrambled to collect material culture and amass ethnographic files.[23] There was a sense of urgency about this effort, for it was widely believed that Indigenous cultures were being rapidly and irreversibly transformed through the advance of foreign adventurers and settlers and the engines of economic development that would inevitably lead to their complete acculturation and assimilation. Many of the surviving societies, it was thought, would simply cease to exist once local populations died out from repeated epidemics and substandard health conditions in their communities. (Indeed, the First Nations population of North America reached its nadir in the late 1920s, on the eve of the publication of Jenness's *Indians of Canada*.) These fears encouraged archaeologists and ethnologists to rescue, or "salvage," elements of First Nations' cultures that they believed to be traditional, or pre-contact, in origin. In their salvage work, therefore, they scouted out groups that lived in places remote from centres of Euro-Canadian culture. By retreating deep into the "bush" and far into the North, salvage ethnologists believed they were effectively retreating backwards in cultural time, hence uncovering intact traditions.[24] This approach was predicated upon, and in turn reinforced, the notion that First Nations cultures had been "frozen in time" – unchanging – before the arrival of Europeans.

Salvage ethnology, like archaeology, was still in its infancy in Canada by the late 1920s when Jenness began assembling material for *Indians of Canada*. Only a few areas of the country would have received significant attention, a situation that doubtless lay behind Jenness's concern that neither he nor anyone else was qualified to write the book and that it would require more like a decade than a few years to produce. As the book's original bibliography suggests,[25] the areas with actual coverage were limited to the western Arctic, the central (mostly the Kwakiutl, today known as the Kwakwaka'wakw) and northern sections of the Pacific Coast, and the Northeast, especially southern Ontario and southern Quebec. Although salvage ethnologists preferred to work with remote groups, the southern areas of Ontario and Quebec were easily accessible from population centres and so were practical choices. Here, especially in southern Ontario, more archaeological work had been undertaken than anywhere else in the country. It also happened to be the former homeland of various Iroquoian speakers who had been heavily involved in the early days of European exploration and settlement. In contrast, the vast boreal forests of the Subarctic were virtually "untouched" by researchers. The key researchers in the eastern Subarctic were Frank Speck (another former Boas student), who studied Innu of Lake St John and their neighbours; Lucien M. Turner, who conducted research at Fort Chimo; and, in the northwest Subarctic, Frank Russell and J. Alden Mason, who worked in the Great Slave Lake area. In his history of ethnological research in the Subarctic Shield and Mackenzie borderland, ethnologist Ed Rogers found that in the initial era of research (1882–1920), few anthropologists penetrated the interior.[26] Most of this early work, regardless of its location, was collection-oriented and highly descriptive.

The notion of "culture areas," a concept that Jenness used to structure his survey of the Indians of Canada, has become so integral to popular and scholarly understandings of North American Indigenous society that it seems "natural." But the concept is in truth a creature of museum collecting in the late nineteenth century. As museums everywhere amassed their collections from ongoing salvage surveys, they faced the herculean task of organizing and presenting them to the public. Clark Wissler (another Boas student progeny) of the American Museum of Natural History and others developed the foundational notion that distinctive cultural areas could be defined in reference to distinctive regional physical environments. Under this scheme, the thinking was that the varied environmental settings strongly influenced the development and diffusion of culture elements and their integration into regional cultures by Indigenous groups. The interwar period was also the time when environmental determinism – the notion that the local physical environment had an overriding influence on cultural development – was popular in the humanities and social sciences, especially in the fields of history and geography. Although Boasian anthropologists rejected this simplistic notion in general, they recognized that environmental circumstances were important in that they offered up a specific array of possibilities for human development and set certain constraints, but argued that culture itself was a human creation.[27]

In his great tome, *The American Indian: An Introduction to the Anthropology of the New World* (1922), Clark Wissler divided North and South America into fifteen "culture areas" of which Canada encompassed six: the Pacific Coast, the Cordillera,[28] the Plains, the Western Subarctic, the Arctic, and the Northeastern Woodlands. In *Indians of Canada*, Jenness largely followed Wissler's culture area scheme, but he also innovated by subdividing the Northeastern Woodlands area into two areas: the "Migratory Tribes of the Eastern Woodlands" and the "Agricultural Tribes of the Eastern Woodlands."[29] He also substituted the term "Eskimo" for the Arctic area. As indicated by certain of the names for the areas employed by Jenness, the culture area model reflected cultural evolutionary perspectives of the day. True to the model, Jenness concluded that the cultures of some regions represented different stages of cultural development or evolution. In these and other ways, *The Indians of Canada* is a more or less definitive expression of late-nineteenth- and early-twentieth-century Americanist anthropology.

The Contents

In structure, content, and writing style, Jenness's *Indians of Canada* built on Frederick Hodge's encyclopedic *Handbook of Indians of Canada*, published by the Geographic Board of Canada in 1913, which was reprinted from Hodge's even earlier study, *Handbook of American Indians North of Mexico* (1907).[30] Jenness divided his survey into two main sections: the first, with seventeen broad thematic chapters, explored the pre-contact origins and life of First Nations and Inuit as a whole, and the other contains seven chapters, each of which is devoted to a review of the principal tribes of a "physiographic region" after contact with Europeans.[31] These physiographic regions corresponded with what he terms on his map "cultural areas."[32]

As is to be expected, Jenness directed his pre-contact, thematic chapters to the major interests and concerns of his circle of Boasian anthropologists. Boas and his students, and those who, like Jenness, shared

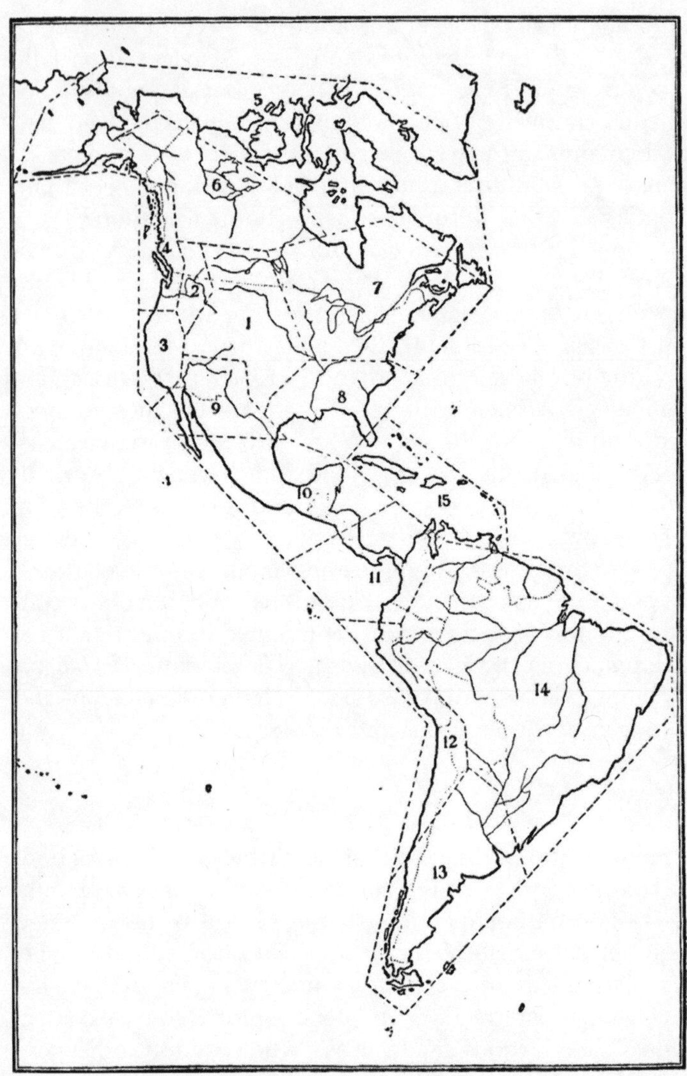

Clark Wissler's Culture Areas of North and South America.

Source: C. Wissler, *The American Indian: An Introduction to the Anthropology of the New World*, 2nd ed. (New York: Oxford University Press, 1922).

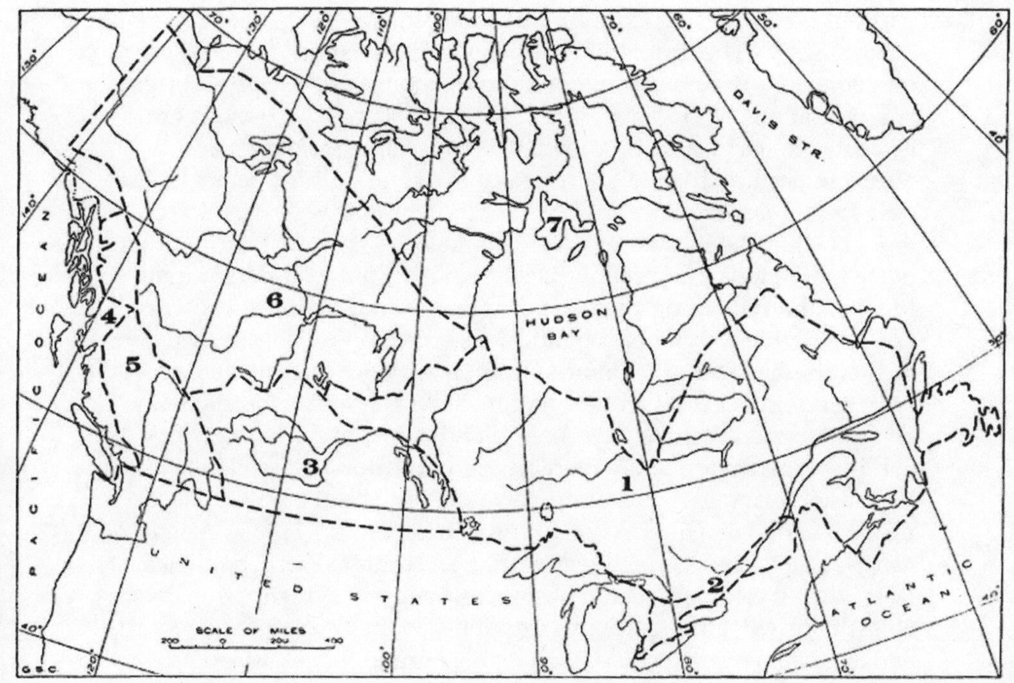

Diamond Jenness's Culture Areas of Canada. *1*, Migratory tribes of the eastern woodlands; *2*, Agricultural tribes of the eastern woodlands; *3*, Plains' tribes; *4*, Tribes of the Pacific coast; *5*, Tribes of the Cordillera; *6*, Tribes of the Mackenzie and Yukon River basins; *7*, The Eskimo.

Source: Jenness, *Indians of Canada*, 11.

their perspectives, vigorously challenged the popular notion of the day that racial differences could explain cultural differences. Jenness addresses the highly charged issue of race and culture in several of his introductory chapters, predominantly "Languages," "Archaeological Remains," and "Who Are the Indians?" In "Languages," in which he surveys the linguistic geography of Canada as it was understood by the late 1920s, Jenness offers a very Boasian-like cautionary note: "Race, culture, and language … are distinct features, no one of which affords a certain guide to the others. Each can change independently, so that similarity of physical type may conceal radical differences of culture or of language; and community of language, or of culture, may indicate no more than close contact between two peoples of different racial stock."[33] The chapters "Archaeological Remains" and "Who Are the Indians?" discuss prevailing theories about the pre-contact origins and migrations of "Indians" and "Eskimos." These discussions are, as he cautions, necessarily speculative, because archaeologists lacked the means to accurately date excavated human and cultural remains. Jenness speculates, correctly according to contemporary Western scientific thought, that the limited available evidence suggested that Inuit and other Indigenous peoples migrated from Asia but at different times.[34] Most of the remaining thematic chapters – on dwellings, dress, economic activities, social and political organization, social life, religion, music, drama, and art – offer sweeping surveys of core elements of Indigenous cultures as Jenness and his fellow anthropologists defined and understood them to have existed at the time of European contact.

It is commonplace today to think of ethnohistory, defined here as an interdisciplinary and multi-source-based history of non-literate peoples, as becoming a field in Canada only in the 1960s.[35] However, in *Indians of Canada*, Jenness was already using an ethnohistorical approach, at least when it came to breadth of sources. He drew evidence from available published ethnographies, unpublished field ethnology reports, and archaeological reports. Given that his primary goal was to provide a picture of Indigenous cultures as they were prior to or on the eve of contact, Jenness also consulted heavily the published journals and collections of letters by the earliest European explorers, fur traders, and missionaries for early "eye witness" ethnographic accounts and opinions. Jenness listed nearly fifty such sources in his bibliography, although few of them would have been scholarly editions and in any event, he uses their observations and conclusions uncritically.[36]

In the end, Jenness's thematic chapters introduced certain core perspectives that are problematic to this day. One is the notion that Indians were "primitives." As Adam Kuper reminds us, even though Boas had by the 1930s already led the way in turning American anthropology away from invoking evolutionary and racial theories to explain cultural differences, anthropologists including Boas continued to think of their discipline as being primarily concerned with the study of "primitive society."[37] In keeping with the notion of primitive society, anthropologists' classificatory models continued to group cultures along a continuum that ranged from primitive nomad, at one end, to high civilization, at the other. As noted earlier, the very use of the culture area model by Jenness reflects this outlook. This problematical sort of thinking about

Indigenous cultures as examples of stages of evolutionary development permeated Jenness's conclusions and predictions. In his chapters on material culture, technology, and economic life, for example, Jenness emphasizes the extreme technological backwardness of Indigenous cultures in Canada – the absence of "advanced" culture – compared to those of the European newcomers.[38]

Jenness's consistent use of absences to describe First Nations in Canada is quite striking, a finding we share with Peter Kulchyski.[39] Using absences as proof likely reflects the way contemporary culture-element distribution studies were conducted at the turn of the twentieth century. Researchers commonly entered the field with long lists of cultural traits and noted the presence or absence of elements on their lists as they surveyed various groups. Jenness promoted this notion of absence most forcefully in the chapter "Economic Conditions." In it, he emphasizes that all Indigenous people in Canada possessed only Stone Age technologies; absent were any of the technological achievements of the European newcomers.[40] For Jenness, the failure to move beyond what he viewed as a Stone Age technology blocked Indigenous people's abilities to make progress in most other areas of life. On this technological deterministic point, his writing is emphatic and metaphorical: "The slow, tedious manufacture of tools and household effects during the hours that could be spared from fishing and hunting greatly restricted his leisure for other pursuits, and powerfully strengthened all the other cogs that checked the wheel of progress."[41] Here, Jenness is drawing on the published journal of John Meares, one of the earliest Europeans to visit the coast of British Columbia, in 1788–9.[42]

To his "technological backwardness" argument Jenness added an important corollary, that all First Nations societies in Canada, no matter where on the evolutionary scale they fell, were incapable of adapting to changing circumstances in ways that allowed for their survival. Inuit of the Arctic and Subarctic littorals of Canada, with whom Jenness was most familiar, were the real exception, however. Jenness considered them, unlike the First Nations, to be "a hardy, resourceful people, fond of laughter and cheerful even in extreme adversities."[43] The very resourcefulness and personality of Inuit would allow them to adopt modern technologies easily and therefore to survive as a people much longer than "Indians," according to Jenness.

Seeing Euro-Canadian culture as dynamic and evolving and the cultures of Indigenous peoples as static, he goes on to conclude that First Nations of the Pacific Coast suffered more from contact than their East Coast counterparts and that this was due to the lateness of the arrival of Europeans on the Pacific Coast. This pronouncement echoed his dramatic conclusion about Pacific Coast cultures in the chapter on the social organization of the Iroquoian and Pacific Coast tribes. His stance here is that the Pacific Coast culture was too complex, too fragile: "Not a virile one like the Iroquoian, but a rich hot-house plant, nurtured by isolation in a particular environment, and incapable of withstanding a chill breeze from the outside world."[44] This point about the fate of Northwest Coast cultures is one to which we will return shortly.

That Jenness developed the theme of cultural backwardness throughout *Indians of Canada* was not simply the consequence of its being a common scholarly practice of the day: framing anthropological discourse in terms of a primitive-civilized comparative model. It also stemmed from Jenness's own reasoning that the backwardness of First Nations vis-à-vis Euro-Canadians was a major reason why First Nations had been largely displaced from their ancestral homelands, their cultures had plunged into decline, and their demographic survival had been rendered impossible. Jenness even extended this perspective on the connection of backwardness and the future fate of First Nations societies to the sphere of religion: "The nature-worship of the Indians was too vague, too eclectic to withstand the assault of a highly organized proselytizing religion like Christianity, or to serve as a rallying ground for the bands and tribes that struggled without guidance to adjust their lives afresh."[45] Neither in this particular discussion nor anywhere else in *Indians of Canada* did Jenness acknowledge that by the early twentieth century, the missionary effort of Christian churches in running Indian residential schools had become an aspect of the Government of Canada's forced assimilation policy for Indigenous peoples throughout the land.

Jenness continued to employ the primitive-civilized comparative framework in the second section of the book, which is devoted to the seven "physiographic" (cultural) regions he identified and mapped, with a series of thumbnail, post-contact ethnographies of the principal Indigenous groups within each. The nomadic hunter-gatherers of the Arctic and Subarctic he regarded as the most primitive, while the horticulturalists of the Northeast and the salmon fishers of the Pacific Coast he considered to be the most advanced. The buffalo hunting tribes of the Plains occupied an intermediate position on the Jenness scale of cultural development. This evolutionary scaling of the regions had already surfaced in the first section of the book, particularly in the chapters on the social organization of the "primitive migratory tribes" and of the Iroquoians and the Pacific Coast tribes.

For our present analysis of Jenness's approach to these ethnohistorical geographies, we focus on the Pacific Coast culture area as a prime example. Jenness's definition of the Pacific Coast covered an extensive area; it included the entire Northwest Coast culture area located in Canada and portions of the Western Subarctic and Plateau culture areas. As in the chapters concerning the tribes of other regions, the chapter on the Pacific Coast tribes is largely descriptive, but it also includes Jenness's prediction about the tragic fate awaiting these tribes. The discussion of each tribe closes with a paragraph about the massive population losses that had taken place after initial contact with Europeans.[46] By "tribes," he meant "linguistic groups," he explains, not groups of people who acted as independent political units.[47] His formulaic, one- or two-page ethnohistory of each tribe begins with written sketches of the geographic setting, then moves on to short descriptions of the economic and material culture. Portrayals of social life on the coast follow next, in which Jenness, not surprisingly, features two complex elements of Pacific Coast cultures – the potlatch and slavery – subjects which have always intrigued anthropologists. Descriptions of religious and ceremonial life follow, highlighting shamans and secret societies. Despite the cultural complexity that comes through in his descriptions, collectively these vignettes leave one with the deep sense of impending cultural doom for Pacific Coast people. It is a fate, as we have already seen, anticipated by Jenness in section one as inevitable, even natural.

Here as elsewhere in the ethnohistorical section, Jenness invokes his "backwardness" and "essential inability to adapt" theses to blame the victims for the disaster that had befallen them. Jenness acknowledged the complexity of Northwest Coast social organization; how could he not, given the careful attention Boas and a host of other anthropologists had been paying to it since the turn of the twentieth century? At the same time, he implicates that very complexity in the picture he paints of the irreversible downfall of Pacific Coast people after contact:

> Their complex social organization, so different from that of any European country, broke down completely. The grades in their society had no significance for the invading whites, and the potlatches that helped give these grades stability fell under the ban of the law. Slavery was abolished, and the new individualism that gave even the ex-slave an equal opportunity with the noble destroyed the balance and order in the "houses" and clans.[48]

There is so much to think about in this brief passage. For one thing, it references the potlatch ban, but in the passive voice. Jenness made no critical comments about federal laws such as the potlatch ban that was part of the policy to force assimilation on First Nations.[49] Echoing a conclusion reached in the thematic, pre-contact chapters of the book, Jenness argues in his coverage of the Pacific Coast that the more "advanced" societies of the area ended up being the most vulnerable to the destructive aspects (the "chill breeze" he mentions in section one) of Euro-Canadian civilization.

Jenness was well aware of the participation of the Pacific Coast peoples in the emerging regional economy of British Columbia, but he foresaw no future for them in such pursuits. Although First Nations communities had worked en masse for the coastal salmon canneries for half a century, he assumed that they could not hold their own against other workers, "the more industrious and efficient labourers from China and Japan," and that a similar fate awaited First Nations workers in BC's agricultural sector, where they could not compete with the Europeans and Chinese. "Socially [Indians] are outcasts, economically they are inefficient and an encumbrance," he concludes.[50] The fairly widespread, inaccurate notion that First Nations were traditionally not predisposed to commercial economic activities was dispelled in 1990 through the research of historian Sarah Carter, who, in looking at the failure of government treaty promises to provide land and infrastructure for successful First Nations reserve farmers in the Prairie West, reveals the deliberate government policy against First Nations' productivity that occurred between the 1880s and 1920s.[51] Based on his remarkable, pessimistic assessment, Jenness closes the chapter on Pacific Coast tribes with a chilling prophesy about their pending extinction: "The end of this century, it seems safe to predict, will see very few survivors."[52]

The notion of backwardness and an inability to adapt on the part of Northwest Coast people arose from the very nature of salvage ethnology, including and especially as practised by Franz Boas. Boas was deeply aware of the industrial work of First Nations communities of the Pacific Slope. He lived at the coastal canneries in the late nineteenth century in order to study them. In his letters he observed, and in his fieldwork accommodated, the seasonal migrations of entire First Nations' villages to the canneries, the intricate industrial and transportation networks thus formed, and the complex seasonal rhythms of Northwest Coast peoples' work and travel. Surprisingly, however, mentions of this work-travel complex are conspicuously absent from Boas's professional writings.[53] The same could be said for the professional writings of other prominent Northwest Coast anthropologists who worked in the area in the early years and, like Boas, depended on the presence of canneries and First Nations workers and fishers to facilitate their salvage ethnology research. These included Harlan I. Smith, Marius Barbeau, and Thomas McIlwraith.[54]

Considering that museums dominated anthropology in this era, we might also ask to what extent did museum-oriented anthropology of the day contribute to this kind of pessimism about the inevitable extinction of Indigenous people? As Susan Roy shows in her study of the history of BC's Musqueam First Nation and archaeology, museums had a vested interest in advancing these doomsday scenarios.[55] Yet in their professional writings on the Northwest Coast, the anthropologists upon whom Jenness relied for his 1932 survey of "Indians" in Canada did not go nearly as far as Jenness did when making dire predictions about the future of Native communities in this or any other culture area in Canada.

Jennessian Ethnohistory in the Age of Aboriginal and Treaty Rights Litigation

Jenness's 1932 survey, both in its descriptions and predictions, was not politically neutral. His position as chief anthropologist at the National Museum of Canada and a senior civil servant who published in federal government series meant that he was in a position of considerable influence in the formulation of federal government policy and the drafting of laws regarding Indigenous peoples. This may help to explain why Jenness's survey barely mentions government Indian policy, and even then only in the passive voice. The implication of this absence of discussion or debate seems to be that the policies and regulations of the late nineteenth century and early twentieth century were merely an aspect of the inevitable advance of a superior Western civilization.

Of the 442 pages of text and photos in *Indians of Canada,* Jenness devotes almost nothing – only a sixteen-page section and a few scattered references – to a description of Indian-white relations. But that is, of course, not to suggest that he came to no conclusions about such interactions, for he emphasizes throughout his work the theme that the decline of First Nations was the inevitable result of economic and social/cultural forces beyond their control because of interactions with whites. His actual chapter titled "Interactions of Indians and Whites" does not tell a story about the goals First Nations individuals and groups sought to achieve in their dealings with Euro-Canadian traders, missionaries, settlers, or government officials, which would become a common consideration of ethnohistorians beginning in the late 1960s followed by the broad surveys of Indigenous peoples in Canada by James Miller and others in the 1980s and 1990s. Rather, the story Jenness tells is one of the inevitability of cultural decline and demographic disaster for First Nations brought about by the destructive impact of the epidemic diseases, alcohol and firearms trading, game depletion arising from the early fur trade, and ultimately the loss of economic independence. Unlike the later histories, in Jenness's process-oriented history there are no individuals, or even government or missionary policies – or policymakers – to hold to account. The "Indians" were not to blame, but neither was anyone else.

To be sure, the 1920s was a time when the First Nations population appeared not to be rebounding from the near-fatal decline of the late nineteenth and early twentieth centuries. But it was also a time when federal Indian policy was aimed at the forced assimilation that was so tragically implemented through residential schools. In addition, the 1920s was the decade in which, due to growing First Nations activism around land claims and resource rights issues, especially by the Northwest Coast peoples with whom treaties had been promised by the state but not delivered, the federal government introduced measures to forbid under the Indian Act legal efforts to pursue those claims. Yet, in *Indians of Canada*, Jenness essentially was providing what Kulchyski refers to as a "litany of extinctions,"[56] writing for the Canadian public and policymakers the final chapter of First Nations societies as an inevitability.

Kulchyski's broader study of Diamond Jenness's influence on Canadian Indian policy finds that Jenness would maintain close relations with the state throughout his long career as a government anthropologist and that Jenness's "explicit policy writings" over time provided what Kulchyski concluded was "ideological support for and justification of state assimilationist policy towards aboriginal Canadians."[57] And he promoted a policy on assimilation that Kulchyski argues often exceeded state policy.[58]

This overzealousness about assimilation on Jenness's part was obvious in the 1940s, once it became known that the Indigenous population of Canada was experiencing a spectacular rebound. In 1947, the

Canadian government established a Special Joint Committee of the Senate and the House of Commons to revise the Indian Act in light of the changing demographics for First Nations. Jenness presented (in day-long testimony) his own twenty-five-year plan for "liquidating" the "Indian Problem." Its overall objective was "to abolish ... the separate political and social status of the Indians."[59] A scheme similar to the one proposed by Jenness in 1947 eventually surfaced in the 1969 White Paper on Indian Policy. The White Paper was a comprehensive solution to the "Indian problem" that sought to end the special legal relationship between Indigenous peoples and the Canadian state. It was introduced by the federal Liberal government of Pierre Trudeau in 1969 but retracted in 1971, in the wake of attacks on it by First Nations leaders and others. In 1973, following the *Calder* case, the government switched directions to develop a comprehensive claims process.[60] In his testimony before the 1947 committee, Jenness had cited the findings of his own *Indians of Canada*, with its already outdated conclusions about the fate of the country's Indigenous people, to support his assimilationist argument.[61] Kulchyski argues that Jenness's testimony reflected not only a particularly "ruthless approach" to assimilationist Aboriginal policy but also a remarkably poor understanding of the treaties negotiated between Canada (the Crown) and First Nations, in particular the fact that they involved treaty rights, guarantees that were intended to protect First Nations' cultures.[62]

Conclusion

We noted at the outset that Chief Justice McEachern's *Delgamuukw* decision became notorious for giving weight to Hobbesian thinking from the 1600s. Unfortunately, the evolutionary anthropological and philosophical perspectives highlighted in his judgment have not been limited to this particular case; they have turned up repeatedly in Aboriginal and treaty rights cases after the precedent-setting *Regina v. Sparrow* litigation concerning the right of the Stó:lō of the lower Fraser River to fish for social and ceremonial purposes.[63] After *Sparrow* (1990), which did not involve the question of an Aboriginal right to a commercial fishery, the Stó:lō took a landmark commercial fishing rights case (*R. v. Van der Peet*) to the Supreme Court of Canada. In their unsuccessful petition to the courts, the Stó:lō defendants claimed an Aboriginal right to a commercial fishery. The problem for them was that the testimony of their own anthropological expert, the acclaimed Northwest Coast specialist

Wayne Suttles, led the trial judge and Supreme Court of Canada on appeal to conclude that the defendants' ancestors were not sufficiently "advanced" culturally to have engaged in a commercial fishery before Europeans arrived on the scene. In his expert testimony, Suttles had classified the Stó:lō as having had a band level of social organization, or being (in the eyes of the court) a primitive society. When upholding the lower courts' rulings, the Supreme Court of Canada quoted the trial judge who had relied on Suttles's expert advice that

> the Sto:lo could not preserve or store fish for extended periods of time, and also that the Sto:lo were a band rather than a tribal culture; he [BC Provincial Court justice J. Scarlett] held both of these facts to be significant in suggesting that the Sto:lo did not engage in a market system of exchange. On the basis of these findings regarding the nature of the Sto:lo trade in salmon, the provincial court justice held that the Sto:lo's aboriginal right to fish for food and ceremonial purposes does not include the right to sell such fish.[64]

The reasoning of the courts in *Van der Peet* has been typical of that adopted in fishing rights litigation generally. All too often the court has made decisions based on evolutionary perspectives that imagine traditional Indigenous cultures were primitive compared to those of the European newcomers, especially in economic realms – in effect, they were allegedly pre-commercial societies – and in terms of land tenure practices and property concepts. It is clear why this antiquated anthropological thinking is so appealing to the court. Defining the Aboriginal "other" as primitive and incapable of making progress affords the intellectual rationale for judicial decisions that suggest legal remedies that do not radically alter the current economic order, an order which is a legacy of colonialism and its sustaining ideologies. In British Columbia, for example, such thinking justifies the restriction of First Nations fisheries to social/ceremonial uses and banning or severely limiting commercial harvesting even though there is conclusive evidence that production for exchange was a key dimension of traditional life for Northwest Coast peoples.[65]

There has been at least one voice on the Canadian bench that has warned against basing Aboriginal title decisions on ancient concepts about Indigenous cultures. When the Nisga'a appealed to the Supreme Court of Canada in 1973, for the first time in Canadian law the court acknowledged that Aboriginal title predated colonization.[66] But it was evenly divided on the question of whether Nisga'a title still survived. Three members of the Supreme Court agreed with the lower courts that the government's exercise of control over lands would have extinguished title; the other three found that title still existed and could yet be extinguished. Justice Emmett Matthew Hall, in drafting the opinion for the latter group, admonished the British Columbia Court of Appeal judge for his comment about the ancestors of the Nisga'a, that they were "undoubtedly at the time of settlement a very primitive people with few of the institutions of civilized society, and none at all of our notions of private property." Hall questioned the evidence behind this thinking: "[I]n so saying this in 1970, [Chief Justice Davey] was assessing the Indian culture of 1858 by the same standards that the Europeans applied to the Indians of North America two or more centuries before."[67] Hall then spelled out the extreme inappropriateness of reaching decisions on Aboriginal rights based on such outdated standards:

> The assessment and interpretation of the historical documents and enactments tendered in evidence must be approached in the light of present-day research and knowledge disregarding ancient concepts formulated when understanding of the customs and culture of our original people was rudimentary and incomplete when they were thought to be wholly without cohesion, laws or culture, in effect a subhuman species.[68]

That was in 1973. A decade later, the Gitxsan-Wet'suwet'en, who were inland neighbours of the Nisga'a, would in *Delgamuukw* initiate a title litigation in which the concerns Hall raised were central. And once again a British Columbia court would demonstrate an unwillingness to revise its outdated understanding of the history and culture of the province's First Nations.

While the appeal of Jennessian-style anthropology for the courts is understandable, the silence of academics about its ongoing sense of authority remains a puzzle. Arguably, the chorus of academic criticism about McEachern's ruling in *Delgamuukw* was to a considerable extent an exercise in distancing current scholars and scholarship from a dark past, as demonstrated in the repeated critical references to the trial judge's quotation from Hobbes. But no acknowledgment has been made of the fact that the legacies of that kind of thinking have been kept alive by the long-standing presence of an outdated, unrevised work of ethnology such as *The Indians of Canada*.

This silence, and the continual reprinting of *The Indians of Canada*, in its original, 1932 version without an accompanying critical essay, serves to raise a broader issue. The academy leaves an array of intellectual artefacts behind in the form of scholarly publications, museum collections, and standardized ways of thinking about Indigenous people, such as the culture area framework. Much as we might want aspects of our intellectual past to be buried and forgotten, the reality is that they live on. Surely, however, we have a responsibility to provide an ongoing critical commentary about how that legacy is used in the present. This obligation is especially urgent when old ways of thinking, ones that helped to legitimate oppressive colonialism, are employed – frozen in time – to sustain it in modern forms.

NOTES

1 Diamond Jenness, *The Indians of Canada*, 7th ed. (Toronto: University of Toronto Press, in association with the National Museum of Man, National Museums of Canada, and Supply and Services Canada, 2003; first published 1932), 264.

2 Thomas Hobbes, *Leviathan, or the Matter, Forme and Power of a Commonwealth Ecclesiasticall and Civill*, 1st ed., 1651 (printed for Andrew Crooke at the Green Dragon in St. Paul's Churchyard).

3 Chief Justice Allan McEachern, *Reasons for Judgment: Delgamuukw v. British Columbia* (Smithers: Supreme Court of British Columbia, 1991), 13. His ruling was not upheld on appeal to the Supreme Court of Canada, see *Delgamuukw*, [1997] 3 S.R.C. 1010.

4 See, for example, Frank Cassidy, ed., *Aboriginal Title in Canada: Delgamuukw v. The Queen* (Fernie, BC: Oolichan Books, 1991); Special Issue: Anthropology and History in the Courts, *BC Studies* 95 (autumn 1992).

5 To the second edition, members of the museum staff added a brief appendix containing a few archaeological references.

6 Peter Kulchyski, "Anthropology in the Service of the State: Diamond Jenness and Indian Policy," *Journal of Canadian Studies* 28, no. 2 (summer 1993): 21–50, http://search.proquest.com.ezproxy.library.ubc.ca/docview/203554292?accountid=14656 (account required). All page references here are to the electronic copy.

7 Barnett Richling, *In Twilight and in Dawn: A Biography of Diamond Jenness* (Montreal: McGill-Queen's University Press, 2012).

8 Ibid., 234.

9 Ian A.L. Getty and Donald B. Smith, "Preface," in Ian A.L. Getty and Donald B. Smith, eds., *One Century Later: Western Canadian Reserve Indians Since Treaty 7* (Vancouver: UBC Press, 1978), xi.

10 William E. Taylor, Jr., "Foreword," in Jenness, *Indians of Canada*, viii.

11 Kulchyski, "Anthropology in the Service of the State," 4.

12 Ibid., 2.

13 J.R. Miller, *Skyscrapers Hide the Heavens: A History of Indian-White Relations in Canada* (Toronto: University of Toronto Press, 1989); Olive P. Dickason, *Canada's First Nations: A History of Founding Peoples from Earliest Times* (Toronto: McClelland and Stewart, 1992); Arthur J. Ray, *I Have Lived Here Since the World Began: An Illustrated History of Canada's Native Peoples*, revised and expanded ed., (Toronto: Key Porter, 2010).

14 Charles A. Bishop, *The Northern Ojibwa and the Fur Trade: An Historical and Ethnological Study* (Toronto: Holt, Rinehart and Winston, 1974); Arthur J. Ray, *Indians in the Fur Trade: Their Role as Trappers, Hunters, and Middlemen in the Lands Southwest of Hudson Bay, 1660–1870* (Toronto: University of Toronto Press, 1974); Robin Fisher, *Contact and Conflict: Indian-European Relations in British Columbia* (Vancouver: UBC Press, 1977); Sylvia Van Kirk, *Many Tender Ties: Women in the Fur Trade* (Toronto: University of Toronto Press, 1980); and Jennifer S.H. Brown, *Strangers in Blood: Fur Trade Company Families in Indian Country* (Vancouver: UBC Press, 1980). Two studies published even earlier were A.G. Bailey's pioneering ethnohistory, *The Conflict of European and Eastern Algonkian Cultures 1504–1700: A Study in Canadian Civilization* (Saint John, New Brunswick, 1937), but it was largely unknown until its republication by University of Toronto Press in 1969; and Wilson Duff, *The Indian History of British Columbia*, vol. 1, *The Impact of the White-man* (Victoria: British Columbia Provincial Museum, 1964).

15 Celia Haig-Brown, *Resistance and Renewal: Surviving the Indian Residential School* (Vancouver: Arsenal Pulp Press, 1988); J.R. Miller, *Shingwauk's Vision: A History of Native Residential Schools* (Toronto: University of Toronto Press, 1996); and John S. Milloy, *A National Crime: The Canadian Government and the Residential School System, 1879–1986* (Winnipeg: University of Manitoba Press, 1999).

16 Dianne Newell, *Tangled Webs of History: Indians and the Law in Canada's Pacific Coast Fisheries* (Toronto: University of Toronto Press, 1993); Antonia Mills, *Eagle Down Is Our Law: Witsuwit'en Law, Feasts, and Land Claims* (Vancouver: UBC Press, 1994); Dara Culhane, *The Pleasure of the Crown: Anthropology, Law, and First Nations* (Vancouver: Talonbooks, 1998); Neil J. Sterritt, Susan Marsden, Robert Galois, Peter R. Grant, and Richard Overstall, *Tribal Boundaries in the Nass Watershed* (Vancouver: UBC Press, 1998); William C.

Wickin, *Mi'kmaq Treaties on Trial: History, Land, and Donald Marshall Junior* (Toronto: University of Toronto Press, 2002); Richard Daly, *Our Box Was Full: An Ethnography of the Delgamuukw Plaintiffs* (Vancouver: UBC Press, 2005); Bruce Granville Miller, *Oral History on Trial: Recognizing Aboriginal Narratives in the Courts* (Vancouver: UBC Press, 2011); and Arthur J. Ray, *Telling It to the Judge: Taking Native History to Court* (Montreal: McGill-Queen's University Press, 2012).

17 See Regna Darnell, *And Along Came Boas: Continuity and Revolution in Americanist Anthropology* (Philadelphia: John Benjamins, 1998).

18 Sapir was founding director of the Anthropology Division of the Geological Survey of Canada (1910–25). Jenness replaced Sapir in that position in 1927.

19 This emphasis on studying local cultural history has come to be known as historical particularism.

20 Boas conducted fieldwork under the British Association for the Advancement of Science and the Committee on North-western Tribes (1888–97), and led the Jesup North Pacific Expedition (1897–1902) to the Northwest Coast and Siberia, which was the most intensive early expedition on the Northwest Coast area.

21 Carbon-14 analysis started to come into use only in the early 1950s.

22 Although Boas and his students rejected race as an explanatory factor in cultural development, they did believe that racial studies could provide clues about past migrations from Siberia.

23 For an overview as it pertains to the Northwest Coast, see Douglas Cole, *Captured Heritage: The Scramble for Northwest Coast Artifacts* (Vancouver: UBC Press, 1985).

24 This concept is referred to as the space-time equivalence hypothesis. For further discussion see Matti Bunzl, "Foreword to Johannes Fabian's *Time and the Other*/Syntheses of a Critical Anthropology," ix–xxxiv, in Fabian, *Time and the Other: How Anthropology Makes Its Object*, 2nd ed. (New York: Columbia University Press, 2002).

25 Jenness stated in the first edition that his bibliography was not comprehensive. Nonetheless, there is every reason to suppose that it was representative of the scholarship of the day.

26 Edward S. Rogers, "History of Ethnological Research in the Subarctic Shield and Mackenzie Borderlands," in *Subarctic*, vol. 6 of *Handbook of North American Indians*, ed. June Helm (Washington, DC: Smithsonian Institution Press, 1981), 19–20.

27 Geographers termed this outlook "environmental possibilism."

28 It has since become common practice to refer to this region as the Plateau.

29 Other anthropologists who developed and popularized Wissler's original ideas created a distinction between physical and cultural areas. See most notably A.L. Kroeber's *Natural and Cultural Areas of Native North America* (Berkeley: University of California Press, 1939), and Harold E. Driver's *Indians of North America* (Chicago: University of Chicago Press, 1961). Kroeber was another former student of Boas. Today, based on the works of these anthropologists and on the Smithsonian Institution's fifteen-volume *Handbook of North American Indians* series, it has become common practice to think of the cultural geography of Indigenous Canada slightly differently from the way Wissler and Jenness did: we now speak of the Arctic, the Northwest Coast, the Plateau, the Subarctic, the Plains, and the Northeast.

30 Frederick Webb Hodge, ed., *Handbook of Indians of Canada* (1912; repr., King's Printer, 1913), Appendix: *10th Annual Report of Geographic Board of Canada*; reprinted from Hodge, ed., *Handbook of American Indians North of Mexico*, 2 vols., Bureau of American Ethnology Bulletin 30 (Washington, DC: U.S. Government Printing Office, 1907). *The Indians of Canada* also anticipates later handbook series, most notably the Smithsonian Institution's *Handbook of North American Indians* (1978–2008).

31 It is unclear why he used this term. Usually this expression is associated with geological regions. Jenness's areas were of a cultural and ecological nature.

32 The Smithsonian Institution handbook series is similarly structured, but whole volumes are dedicated to specific themes and culture areas.

33 Jenness, *Indians of Canada*, 22. He also concluded, incorrectly as it turns out, that Canada had not been occupied during the Ice Age (Pleistocene).

34 Many First Nations, however, reject this perspective.

35 The principal exception would be the work of A.G. Bailey in the 1930s.

36 Jenness included only those accounts that he cites in the book.

37 Kuper discusses the persistence of the notion of primitive society in anthropology. See *The Invention of Primitive Society: Transformations of an Illusion* (New York: Routledge, 1988), and *The Reinvention of Primitive Society: Transformations of a Myth* (New York: Routledge, 2005).

38 Chapters 3–8. Jenness attributed this to what he saw as the isolation of First Nations from centres of civilization. Jenness, *Indians of Canada*, 28.

39 See Kulchyski, "Anthropology in the Service of the State," 5.

40 Jenness notes that most Native groups had at least taken the "first step forward along the road to civilization" by moving beyond the "palaeolithic or Old Stone epoch." *Indians of Canada*, 33.

41 Ibid., 39.

42 John Meares, *Voyage Made in the Years 1788 and 1789, from China to the North West Coast of America* (London: Printed at the Logographic Press and sold by J. Walter, 1790).
43 Ibid., 263.
44 Ibid., 147–8.
45 Ibid., 258.
46 For his pre-contact population estimate Jenness relied on the James Mooney's classic, "Aboriginal Population of America," *Smithsonian Institution: Miscellaneous Collections* 80, no. 7 (1928). The historical demography of Native Americans was in its infancy, and scholars remain to this day divided in their estimates of the size of the pre-contact population of North America.
47 Jenness, *Indians of Canada*, 327n1.
48 Ibid., 350.
49 See Douglas Cole and Ira Chaiken, *An Iron Hand Upon the People: The Law Against the Potlatch on the Northwest Coast* (Vancouver: Douglas and McIntyre, 1990). The potlatch ban, introduced in 1884 and not dropped until the revision of the Indian Act in 1951, barred all public gift-giving ceremonies and was intended to cover the sun dance/thirst dance ceremonies of the Plains people.
50 Jenness, *Indians of Canada*, 350.
51 Sarah Carter, *Lost Harvests: Prairie Indian Reserve Farmers and Government Polity* (Montreal: McGill-Queen's University Press, 1990).
52 Jenness, *Indians of Canada*, 350.
53 See Newell, "Renewing 'That Which Was Almost Lost or Forgotten': The Implications of Old Ethnologies for Present-Day Traditional Ecological Knowledge Among Canada's Pacific Coast Peoples," *International Indigenous Policy Journal* 6/2 (2015), http://ir.lib.uwo.ca/iipj/vol6/iss2/6. Mentions of Boas's cannery involvement are to be found in his letters to his superiors and to his family. See Ronald P. Rohner, ed., *Ethnography of Franz Boas: Letters and Diaries of Franz Boas Written on the Northwest Coast from 1866 to 1931*, trans. Hedy Parker (Chicago: University of Chicago Press, 1969).
54 See Dianne Newell and Dorothee Schreiber, "Nuxalk Territories: Sites of Exploration and Science: Harlan I. Smith's Fieldwork in Bella Coola, 1920–1924," paper presented at the Annual Meeting of the American Ethnohistory Association, Eugene, OR, November 2008; Laurence Nowry, *Man of Mana: Marius Barbeau* (Toronto: NC Press, 1995); and John Barker and Douglas Cole, eds., *At Home with the Bella Coola: T.F. McIlwraith's Field Letters, 1922–4* (Vancouver: UBC Press, 2003).
55 Susan H. Roy, *These Mysterious People: Shaping History and Archaeology in a Northwest Coast Community* (Montreal: McGill-Queen's University Press, 2010).

56 Kulchyski, "Anthropology in the Service of the State," 5.

57 Ibid., 1.

58 Ibid., 3.

59 Canada, Special Joint Committee of the Senate and the House of Commons appointed to continue and complete the examination and consideration of the Indian Act, *Minutes of Proceedings and Evidence*, 25 March 1947 (King's Printer, 1947), 310 (hereafter "Minutes").

60 Canada, *Statement of the Government of Canada on Indian Policy*, Department of Indian Affairs and Northern Development, 1969. See Sally M. Weaver, *Making Indian Policy: The Hidden Agenda, 1968–1970* (Toronto: University of Toronto Press, 1981).

61 Minutes, 306. See also Kulchyski, "Anthropology in the Service of the State," 3.

62 Ibid.

63 Regina v. Sparrow, [1990] S.R.C. 1075.

64 R. v. Van der Peet, [1996] 2 S.C.R. 507, paragraph 7.

65 In *Regina V. Gladstone* [1996], which involved members of the Heiltsuk Band of British Columbia who had been charged with selling herring-roe-on-kelp caught without a commercial licence, the Heiltsuk won their appeal at the Supreme Court of Canada. The court recognized a commercial right to fish that is protected under Section 35(1) of the Constitution Act, 1982, and referred the critical question concerning infringement justification back to the trial court. Arthur Ray discusses some of the problems that arise in court when experts present ethnohistorical evidence based on older and newer scholarly perspectives: Ray, "Ethnohistory and the Development of Native Law in Canada: Advancing Aboriginal Rights or Re-inscribing Colonialism?" in *Métis-Crown Relations: Rights, Identity, Jurisdiction, and Governance*, ed. F. Wilson and M. Mallet (Toronto: Irwin Law, 2008), 1–26; and Ray, "Creating an Image of the Savage in Defence of the Crown: The Ethnohistorian in Court," *Native Studies Review* 6/2 (1990): 13–29.

66 Calder v. British Columbia, [1973] S.R.C. 313.

67 Ibid., 347.

68 Ibid., 346.

PART SIX

Conclusion

Aboriginal Research in Troubled Times

ALAN C. CAIRNS

On Being Reviewed

In 2000, the UBC Press published my *Citizens Plus: Aboriginal Peoples and the Canadian State*.[1] For me, this was a return to research and thinking about Aboriginal issues in which I had been involved in the mid-1960s as a contributor to what became the Hawthorn Report.[2] The Mohawk political scientist Gerald (now Taiaiake) Alfred devoted a column in the *Windspeaker*, "Of White Heroes and Old Men Talking,"[3] to discuss *Citizens Plus* and Tom Flanagan's *First Nations? Second Thoughts*.[4] He lavished praise on neither book. The only difference between his assessments was that he very severely criticized Flanagan's book, while *Citizens Plus* was only severely criticized.

What did Alfred say? After I was described as an old "grumpy geezer," the antithesis of a revered elder, he selectively misquoted a couple of my sentences which weakened the first sentence and deprived the second sentence of meaning.[5] He then concluded that I should "stop talking, and get out of our way." I assumed that "our" referred to Indigenous scholars, or perhaps Indigenous peoples more generally.[6] In either case, I interpreted this as a negative review.

Almost simultaneously, *Citizens Plus* was very favourably reviewed in *Quill and Quire* by Suzanne Methot, who awarded it a starred review, "indicat[ing] a book of exceptional merit."[7] This was reassuring. When I read the review, I did not realize that the reviewer, an Indigenous woman, had shown considerable courage in giving such a favourable review of a book written by a non-Indigenous person (discussed later). Alfred's review reinforced what I already knew, that the scholarly field of what Jim Miller calls "Native-newcomer relations" is fraught with dangers for the unwary, many of which he has singled out from personal experience.[8]

Politicization in a Scholarly Minefield

Why is this research area such a minefield? Why are passions so high and civility such a tender plant? A definition of politicization will be a useful beginning. By politicization, I mean that an academic publication on an Indigenous issue may not be evaluated solely or primarily on its merits as a piece of academic research but in a number of cases will additionally be viewed through a political lens. A scholarly article or book will be seen as aiding, or damaging, the pursuit of some political goal or social objective. Unless he or she is particularly obtuse, a prospective author will understand that dangerous territory lies ahead. If the research project proceeds, the language that is employed will be carefully considered, and the questions that are asked might not be the researcher's first choice. A cautious scholar may even conclude that the same subjects are best left for another day when passions have cooled, or that a safer, less politicized field has greater attraction. Typically, research is politicized when the subject matter or issue has contemporary consequences, society is deeply divided, and passions are involved. Becher and Trowler assert that "when people's identities are at stake, passions run deep. This may be one reason behind the tendency in areas in which values are highly charged – towards a disproportionate incidence of rifts and schisms."[9]

Nor are historical issues immune to being judged through a political lens. On the contrary, many historical subjects continue to have significant contemporary relevance and resonance. Research on slavery in the American South is not a safe subject simply because it happened long ago.[10] The study of Quebec history is profoundly political in the sense that varying interpretations of the past are felt to have different contemporary consequences.[11] Basil Davidson, who wrote extensively and supportively about historic African kingdoms and empires, did so as a willing servant of African nationalism and political independence in tropical Africa.[12] Such examples could easily be multiplied.[13]

Although the politicization of research and publication is not a rare phenomenon, each instance has elements of uniqueness.

The Assimilation Era

We can better understand where we are now in Aboriginal studies and policy if we know where we have come from. We are in the midst of a postcolonial transition period in Aboriginal research. The defeat of the 1969 federal government White Paper[14] by Indian organizations, and its subsequent withdrawal by Prime Minister Trudeau, ended what is appropriately called the colonial era.

In that period, research and publication took for granted that assimilation was desirable and in the nature of things. It was the goal passionately advocated in 1920 by Duncan Campbell Scott, deputy superintendent general of Indian Affairs (1913–32), when addressing a House of Commons Committee. "Our object," he asserted, "is to continue until there is not a single Indian in Canada that has not been absorbed into the body politic and there is no Indian question, and no Indian department, that is the whole object of this Bill."[15] This interpretation of the direction in which history was taking us was roundly endorsed in 1939 at a Toronto conference which brought together Canadian and American experts on Indian peoples.[16] Charles Loram, a professor in Yale University's Race Relations Department, asserted, "In the end, of course, the civilization of the white man must prevail … The only question is the rate at which [Indian culture] … should be eliminated or superseded or changed."[17]

In the 1940s, three of Canada's most eminent anthropologists, Thomas McIlwraith, Diamond Jenness, and Alfred Bailey, predicted assimilation in separate papers. In 1947, McIlwraith asserted that "Indians" had a choice of "conform[ing] to Euro-Canadian standards or perish[ing]."[18] In 1941, Jenness repeated what he argued in separate editions of his basic text published and republished over nearly a fifty-year period from 1932 to 1977,[19] that assimilation was the desirable and inevitable goal of Indian policy.[20] Bailey argued that the individualism of commercial capitalism had demoralized Indigenous people who were "wandering in an ocean of uncertainty, bereft of [their] eternal verities."[21] He believed that the ultimate outcome of social change was assimilation. In 1950, the Liberal minister of Indian Affairs, Walter Harris, asserted that the goal of Indian administration remained what it had always been, standard membership as citizens in the larger Canadian community.[22] Indeed, the 1969 federal government White Paper, and thus presumably its sponsors, Prime Minister Trudeau and Jean Chrétien, minister of Indian Affairs, saw assimilation as desirable and attainable if the appropriate measures were undertaken.

The believers in and advocates of assimilation were not immunized against the moral and intellectual climate of their era. Their beliefs and behaviour confirm the accuracy of Dean Inge's statement: "If you marry the spirit of your generation you will be a widow in the next."[23] Further, the discourse of assimilation had always been misleading or, more accurately, one-sided. Assimilation, I argued elsewhere,

> enjoyed a long hegemony largely because those who were opposed to it – especially the status Indian population – were silenced by their marginalization and by official policy. There was a potential debate throughout the assimilation era, but it was not joined. The majority society did not hear the other side.
>
> The monopoly of voice enjoyed by non-Aboriginal Canadians ill-served their understanding. Their unchallenged premises gave them a spurious confidence that history was on their side. Aboriginal people, of course, knew that the majority view of settler society was not their own. They knew the other side – its weapons, its arguments, its power – and they knew, depending on the waxing and waning of their own resistance, the extent and nature of their silenced dissent.
>
> The virtue of the contemporary period is that the debate about how we should relate to each other has opened up. We are closer to having an actual discussion than we have ever been.[24]

Nevertheless, as I argue here, while we now have the benefit of multiple participants, we also have various impediments that reduce the quality of our discussion of how we are to live together.

The Transition Period

The defeat and withdrawal of the *White Paper* ended the era of imperial scholarship in which assimilation was the goal. The politics of Indian Affairs was transformed through the defeat of the White Paper by organized and articulate Indian opposition. For the next four decades, the period in which the literature on issues exploded, the policy leadership of the federal government was either in abeyance or challenged when federal proposals were unacceptable to the organizations representing Indigenous peoples' concerns.[25] The literature which surfaced in this era confronted an environment of insecurity, unpredictability, and politicization.

The road to the assimilation future was sidetracked by three factors. First, there was no indication that reserves were disappearing. Indeed, the Hawthorn Report (1966–7) assumed their ongoing existence into the distant future.[26] This assumption was not surprising because the Hawthorn inquiry was commissioned as a response to the malaise about the direction of Indian policy, including the troubling fact that reserves were not winding down, as assimilation theory assumed they would. Second, enfranchisement, the process by which status Indians gave up their legal position and became ordinary Canadians, had minimal appeal and accordingly provided no evidence that an incremental erosion of the number of legal status Indians was under way. Finally, the demise of the European empires, which had governed much of humanity for generations, undermined the support for internal colonialism in countries with settler majorities. Much of internal colonialism's legitimacy had been derivative. It had been parasitical on the larger external world of empire, where European powers justified the global imperial hierarchy in which they were at the apex by a mixture of racial and cultural arguments. The end of overseas empire, "one of the most remarkable features of the twentieth century,"[27] undermined this historic paradigm in world politics and spilled over to undermine its Canadian counterpart of internal colonialism. For example, Little Bear, Boldt, and Long locate Indian peoples' "quest for greater autonomy [as] part of a wider movement encompassing a number of countries' indigenous groups."[28]

The winding down of the imperial era in Canadian Indian policy, and the assimilation assumptions which had pervaded it, had major consequences which are often overlooked. From the Canadian state's perspective, assimilation had been the obvious response to the minority Indigenous peoples within its borders whose presence preceded the arrival of Europeans. Further, assimilation was a much more obvious objective in internal colonialism, where the shape and future of the domestic society was at stake, than it was for overseas colonialism, where cultural and other diversities did not challenge the home front.

As Rogers M. Smith and Charles Taylor point out, the state is in the business of making citizens.[29] In his description of the theory and practice of the modernizing state, James C. Scott notes its propensity to regulate the domestic environment it encounters in order to simplify its tasks.[30] The result is pressure for a common citizenship, common education, a population whose members can be tabulated in terms of easily identifiable categories, and so forth. The purpose served by these and other policy thrusts is to simplify the task of governance. Hence an unregulated diversity is seen as administratively awkward.

From the vantage point of the state, the historic policy of assimilation makes sense; hence the residential schools make sense.[31] Hence D.C. Scott's famous statement of absorbing every "single Indian" into the body politic[32] can be seen as part of the logic of the state; equally revealing is Trudeau's classic statement in 1969 that it was "inconceivable that in a given society one section of the society [could] have a treaty with the other section of the society. We must all be equal under the laws."[33] Hence the support for a Christianizing policy via the vehicle of missionary activity; hence the enfranchisement policy; hence the 1969 White Paper; hence the province-weakening, nation-building goals of the Charter directed to transform the psyche of Canadians.

What the preceding suggests is more than a malevolent non-Indigenous elite arrogantly wielding power, although that is part of the picture; it is also a polity/society responding to what it considered to be the dictates of statehood, according to the assumptions of the time. Among its other virtues from the state's perspective, assimilation would hugely simplify the task of governing. By contrast, hundreds of thousands of Indigenous peoples living in small communities, possessed of special status and with their own governing arrangements and ambivalent attitudes to Canada, was obviously far down on the list of desirable futures for the state. Assimilation, therefore, prior to its overt repudiation by Indigenous peoples, was a natural policy for the Canadian state. Accordingly, its disappearance as the goal of Indian policy, or of Indigenous policy in Canada more generally, had profound consequences for the decades which followed.

Before we too loudly lament the slow progress following the withdrawal of the White Paper in alleviating what Noel Dyck called the "Indian problem," and which might now be better labelled the Canadian problem, we should underline the complexity of the contemporary situation.[34] As already noted, the process and result of assimilation were conceptually clear. Ultimately, Indian peoples would disappear into the majority society. The relations of the state to its newly assimilated Indian people, now citizens, would be the same as its relation to other Canadians. Heterogeneity would he replaced by homogeneity. In the assimilation era, heterogeneity was kept at bay by keeping First Nations outside the non-Indigenous community through a separate bureaucracy, separate policies, and the absence of the franchise. While we now know the assimilation goal was unrealistic, that is not my concern at the moment, which is rather to contrast the complexities of the present situation (where we do not have a clear destination and the impediments to rapprochement are profound) with the simplicities of the assimilation era from the vantage point of the Canadian state. Further, Canadians were ill-prepared for the new postcolonial world which confronted them. Canadians and their governments inherited no intellectual capital appropriate to the new reality of Indigenous nationalism diffused across the country in small communities at the same time as a significant exodus to urban centres was under way.

Although it was not immediately clear, the post–White Paper challenge required a more complicated understanding of citizenship to accommodate Indigenous peoples who were increasingly describing themselves as belonging to nations. Further, the 1982 Constitution Act created a new constitutional category, Aboriginal Peoples of Canada, which included Indian, Inuit, and Métis peoples. Aboriginal policy now had to deal with different histories, different population numbers, and different geographies, including both on- and off-reserve members of First Nations. Also, the combination of the defeat of the White Paper and the political awakening of Indigenous peoples meant that the federal government no longer had an automatic leadership role. Realistically, it was now on the defensive, momentum was on the Indigenous side, and the moral climate favoured Indigenous peoples.

Two major policy directions surfaced in the 1960s. The authors of the Hawthorn Report (1966–7) argued that reserves were here to stay, that a major exodus to urban centres was under way, and that Indians should be thought of as "Citizens Plus." This status would simultaneously recognize that Indians were full-fledged Canadian citizens and also had a "plus" bundle of rights and recognition based on the "they were here first" fact. A few years later, the federal government White Paper (1969) advocated the elimination of separate legal status and the transformation of "Indians" into standard Canadian citizens. The White Paper, in effect, had repudiated the Hawthorn proposals, while organized First Nations' opposition repudiated the White Paper and led to its withdrawal.

In policy terms, the legacy of the 1960s was the recognition that the historic goal of assimilation had been repudiated, that Indigenous peoples with a separate legal status were here to stay, and that the specifics of the accommodation of Indian (and later all Aboriginal) peoples had to be worked out.

The Changing Context of Scholarship

In contrast to the previous eras when assimilation was a clear goal, and also in contrast to the clarity of independence as the goal of Third World nationalism, the post–White Paper era in Canada lacks sufficient coherence and clarity of objective to be summed up by a single label.

With a handful of exceptions, the Third World colonies of the European imperial powers gained independence in the decades immediately following World War II. In contrast to the postcolonial acceleration of history in the Third World, as more than a hundred new states emerged from the ashes of imperialism, escape from the legacy of a colonial past by Indigenous peoples in majority settler countries has been halting, incomplete, and inconclusive. The reasons for the greater difficulty of escaping from internal colonialism than from the overseas reality of colonies distanced from the imperial centre are both simple and profoundly important.

The overseas colony achieves independence, sometimes peacefully, sometimes after a bitter struggle, and enters the international community as an independent state. The availability of statehood facilitates the ending of overseas colonialism by holding out an outcome acceptable to both the departing imperial power and the nationalist movement which displaces it. An expansive international state system facilitates the living apart of the former colony, now a state, and the former imperial overlord, still a state, although a shrunken one as its former colonies leave its embrace. The exit option available to the departing imperial powers is not available to settler majorities in domestic colonialism.

Superficially, it might seem that the accommodation of small Indigenous nations sharing space with majority non-Indigenous settler peoples would be easier than the escape from Third World colonial status. In fact, it is much harder. Unlike assimilation, which leaves the structure of the domestic state untouched, modified only by an enlarged citizen base, and unlike the achievement of independence, which separates the former imperial power from its colony by the vehicle of autonomous statehood in the international community, the search for reconciliation within the same country of Indigenous minority nations and settler majorities and their governments is likely to lead to an impasse.[35]

Reconciliation in a settler colony such as Canada presupposes a cohabitation of the settler majority and Indigenous nations within the same state. They cannot escape from each other. The internal Indigenous nations have to settle for what appears as a shrunken goal when contrasted with Third World possibilities. The settler state may have to make accommodations that take it away from its preferred citizenship regime, from an institutional-constitutional inheritance, and from the very idea of a state that it has imbibed from its history. In these circumstances, stalemate is the most likely outcome.

The period from the defeat of the White Paper to the present is the setting for a thus far unending search for a rapprochement in Canada. The field is flooded with scholars from a dramatically increased variety of disciplines – law, political science, history, public administration, philosophy, and more recently, sociology. Concurrently, the major Indigenous organizations representing Indians, Inuit, and Métis have become much more voluble participants as constitutional politics responding to Quebec nationalism opened up arenas for making claims. Further, the Royal Commission on Aboriginal Peoples published its massive report in 1996, although it had minimal impact on the federal government. Finally, by the first decade of the twenty-first century, an Indigenous scholarly community had emerged. Although its members are disproportionately in the field of law, they are also scattered through the social sciences and humanities. The probability is that the Indigenous academic community outside of law will continue to grow, in part as a response to the faculty requirements of Indigenous studies departments scattered across the country.[36]

The contemporary world of Indigenous-settler relations is a transition era, characterized by a frustrated nationalism diffused among Indigenous peoples. Where we are now in Indigenous / non-Indigenous relations is not a resting place for either Indigenous peoples or the Canadian state. This reality is a pervasive backdrop to all research dealing with Indigenous peoples and their relations with the larger society and the Canadian state. No matter what our research is, we cannot escape our knowledge of this larger unfinished business. The stakes are very high on both sides, and passions are engaged. All who do research and publish in this politicized area are aware that they are local participants in a global post-imperial arena that seeks to reorder relationships between Indigenous peoples and the states in which they live. Scholars, both Indigenous and non-Indigenous, are conscious that what they say or write matters. Binnema and Neylan correctly assert that "interpretations of Native history have direct bearing on the present and future lives of Native peoples."[37] The same can be said of other disciplines caught up in the fluidities and ambiguities of the present era. Even if our research does not deal directly with contemporary concerns, we cannot entirely escape the contemporary intellectual and moral climate. This is doubly true when individuals confront the major policy issues on the agenda of the relationship between Indigenous peoples and the Canadian state.[38]

The postcolonial world, which it is the task of scholars to explore and explain, differs dramatically from its predecessor. While we now know that the small group of early scholars then interested in Indigenous issues read the future incorrectly, they had the luxury of doing their research and publication in a secure environment. The future was thought to be known. Indigenous peoples might die out or get absorbed into the general population. In the meantime, they were on the sidelines. Status Indians lacked the franchise. Inuit were far away, still relatively isolated, and only minimally aware of discussions by others of their future. There was at the time an ambiguity whether Métis were or were not an Indigenous people, an issue not resolved until the insertion of Section 35 into the 1982 Constitution Act.

The scholars in that era had a standard, easily understood storyline that was not challenged by Indigenous scholars or by Indigenous readings of their work. Further, the storyline, which presupposed the appropriateness of majority white rule over Indigenous peoples in Canada, was reinforced by the overpowering global presence of the European empires, which, in even stronger terms, communicated the message of the normality of rule by small numbers of Europeans over millions of subjects.

In that era, the handful of anthropologists doing research in Canada were part of a global community that included Malinowski in the Trobriand Islands and Radcliffe-Brown in the Andaman Islands, with the only difference that Canadian anthropologists were closer to home. In the first half of the twentieth century, anthropology followed the flag, analysing the subjects of Western imperialism abroad and Indigenous minorities at home in Western societies. The question which troubled Clifford Geertz in the aftermath of imperialism, "What gives us the right to study them?" was not asked.[39] As Jim Miller points out, history, law, and sociology had minimal interest in Indigenous issues before the White Paper, and anthropology had been primarily engaged in salvage anthropology, an interest in First Nations' life prior to the coming of Europeans.[40]

In *Natives and Newcomers*, Bruce Trigger writes that the "present work seeks to demonstrate that Canadian historical studies as a whole have suffered from the chronic failure of historians and anthropologists to regard native peoples as an integral part of Canadian society." Writing a quarter of a century ago, he asserted that "historians still tend to study native peoples only in terms of their relations with Europeans during the early periods of European settlement."[41]

Legal studies up to the late 1960s were, if anything, even more remiss about including Indigenous peoples' research and writing. When Gerard LaForest attended law school in the late 1940s, "there was not even a passing reference to Aboriginal title." In 1962, he became interested in Aboriginal title and had to go back to "Clement's book on constitution," the last edition published in 1916.[42] When Tom Berger "went to law school in the mid fifties we never discussed, and the law teachers never discussed, Aboriginal rights ... never discussed Indians ... [Basic] questions were never asked in law schools in those days – not in any law school in the country."[43]

Scholarship on Indigenous issues in the contemporary postcolonial era differs profoundly from this picture. First, the scholarly community is much larger; second, its composition is much more diversified by discipline; third, Indigenous contributions are being recognized and heard. In 1984, Little Bear, Boldt, and Long observed that the stimulus for their edited volume *Pathways to Self-Determination* sprang from their frustration "that the Indian perspective is largely missing from published materials on issues affecting Indians," which led to Indian resentment of what "they perceived as academic paternalism and as assimilationist bias in much of the literature ... They hold that no one can know as much as Indians themselves about what policies are valid for them."[44] (Accordingly, most of the contributors to the volume are First Nations leaders.) The basis for Little Bear and colleagues' complaint is gone, as there is now a significant, growing Indigenous scholarly community. Furthermore, there is now an official constitutional category – Indians, Inuit, and Métis – making up the Aboriginal Peoples of Canada[45] and a large and growing urban Indigenous population. Indigenous nationalism is a major factor.[46] The final and most important characteristic of scholarship in the contemporary era is that the long-run goal remains unclear.

The 1969 White Paper, with its defeat and subsequent withdrawal by the Trudeau government, was a watershed not only with respect to the debate it triggered on the future position of First Nations, and subsequently Inuit and Métis, in Canadian society, but also in the academic response to this new world.[47] As Miller points out, a quarter century after the White Paper there had been an explosion of courses and programs dealing with Indigenous peoples at the University of Saskatchewan where he taught,[48] a development replicated in universities around the country. One of the most significant developments in Indigenous research and studies is the huge increase in the literature on Indigenous peoples, past, present, and future, and from a variety of disciplinary and sub-disciplinary perspectives, which has become unmanageable. The flood of literature is beyond the capacity of a single scholar to master. The result has been a retreat into specialization, fragmenting what in simpler times was a more manageable body of literature. We may know more in the aggregate than formerly, but what "we" know is scattered through different minds nesting in different disciplinary and sub-disciplinary programs.[49] Further, the disciplines which had paid almost no prior attention to Indigenous issues suddenly entered a field where passions were high, the historic Indian policy was in tatters, and the future was less clear than had been imagined in the assimilation era.

The Perils of Scholarship in Troubled Times

The explosion of academic and popular interest in Indigenous peoples, their past, their contemporary condition, and their alternative futures is an overwhelmingly positive achievement. Our knowledge is more comprehensive. Our vantage points are more diversified. Non-Indigenous scholars no longer have a monopoly of the research process. On the other hand, there are many impediments to research for both Indigenous and non-Indigenous scholars, which are byproducts of a transition era in which the goals towards which we are headed are shrouded in ambiguity.

In 1994 and 1995, the *Canadian Historical Review* hosted – one might say – a debate between historians about recent literature on Native-newcomer relations. In "Desperately Seeking Absolution: Native Agency as Colonialist Alibi?" two graduate history students at the University of Toronto, Robin Brownlie and Mary-Ellen Kelm, criticized recent writings of Douglas Cole and Ira Chaikin on the potlatch (*An Iron Hand upon the People: The Law Against Potlatch on the Northwest Coast*), an article by J.R. Miller ("Owen Glendower, Hotspur, and Canadian Indian Policy"), and an article by Tina Loo on the potlatch ("Dan Cranmer's Potlatch: Law as Coercion, Symbol, and Rhetoric in British Columbia, 1884–1951"). Cole and Miller replied separately, and Kelm responded to their reply. The debate underlines what Kelm and Brownlie variously described as "the politically charged field of Native-Newcomer relations" and "a politically charged environment,"[50] observing that "writing First Nations' History is a politically fraught activity."[51] Neither Cole nor Miller was oblivious of the fact that what they wrote might have consequences outside the academy and that there were (and are) prevailing narratives which act as lenses through which scholarly work on Indigenous issues will, by some, be judged.

The debate was about Native agency, how significant it was, and how it should be reported. All contributors agreed that Native agency was a "good thing," as it made Indigenous peoples actors in the great drama in which they were pitted against the forces of colonialism – the Indian agent, the missionary, and so forth.

However, Cole and Chaikin were criticized for not underlining the anti-potlatch law as an "assault on indigenous culture."[52] Cole and Chaikin argued that various factors, "not least Native resistance, thwarted the full implementation of governmental intention."[53] Miller was charged with arguing that the pass system and the anti-potlatch law were not rigorously enforced, and that residential schools required a nuanced judgment, not a blanket condemnation. Loo argued in her essay that the law could be beneficial, as Native people on occasion would use the law to their own advantage. Among other things, resistance to the potlatch, she asserted, had the virtue of stimulating political consciousness.

Brownlie and Kelm's position was that too great an emphasis on "agency" appeared to soften the impact of colonialism by minimizing its negative effects. Cole, Chaikin, Miller, and Loo, claim Brownlie and Kelm, go too far because they use "evidence of Native resilience and strength to soften, and at times to deny, the impact of colonialism, and thus implicitly to absolve its perpetrators."[54] This trend of reporting and perhaps exaggerating the potency of agency contains "an insidious tendency to turn Native agency into colonialist alibi."[55] The authors they criticized were accused of having a Eurocentric bias, especially Cole and Chaikin,[56] and of perhaps even having some sympathy for the motives and goals of the colonial officials who administered the regime. Brownlie and Kelm, by the very title of their critique, "Desperately Seeking Absolution," in effect suggested that Cole, Chaikin, Miller, and Loo were easing their consciences by implying that the administration of Indian peoples was not as dreadful as its contemporary image suggested. The debate had theological overtones, with the charge "Desperately Seeking Absolution" levelled at Cole and the others, and the counter-criticism that Brownlie and Kelm were motivated by a "sense of contrition ... a wish to do penance by 'redressing past injustices,'" leading them to "label as 'insidious' articles and books that do not share their own sense of sin and contrition, their own desire for confession and penance."[57]

Looking back, what is striking is that the space between the two sides was very small. Both agreed that "agency" existed. The difference between them was over the relative impact of agency (grassroots capacity from below) and of colonialism (the power of the state from above) in the lives of Indigenous peoples. One might have left it at that and simply said that reasonable people might disagree on the issue. As Miller shrewdly observed, we should neither underemphasize agency nor overemphasize Native victimhood.[58]

In a sense, however, the debate was not about substance but about the proper positioning of academic contributions in deeply contested territory and the legacy of a past about which no one could be proud. Kelm and Brownlie leaned towards the idea of the scholar as missionary. To them, the historian's job was more than doing history. It was serving a cause. Their political positioning is indicated by their references to the "legal system of a foreign power ... foreign legal authorities" and "authority of foreign governments on their [Indian] lands."[59] They refer to "the agenda behind historical writings,"[60] and Kelm refers to the need to address the "politics of scholarship."[61] Miller, cognizant of the difficulty of predicting the consequences of what historians write, modestly concluded that "perhaps historians should settle for getting it as right as they can."[62] Given that the substantive difference between Cole, Chaikin, Loo, and Miller and their critics was limited, the debate in fact was about different ways of doing history and about scholarly predispositions. Kelm and Brownlie were servants of a cause. Cole, Chaikin, Loo, and Miller were not.

As the historians' debate suggests, non-Indigenous scholars are not immunized against the pressures to be careful in what they say or write. At a minimum, they realize that the intellectual and political climate in which they write is charged with passion. They understand that they are positioned in the transition era between the defeat of the White Paper and the goal of greater autonomy for self-governing Indigenous peoples, the details of which are very slowly emerging.

Anthropology, the discipline which historically claimed an especially sensitive understanding of Indigenous peoples based on anthropologists' immersion in Native societies and the resultant intimate contact with Native peoples, also finds its autonomy challenged in the contemporary period. Noel Dyck refers to the "practices of self-censorship" widely adopted by anthropologists working within the field of Indigenous-state relations.[63] He reports that for some critics "independent ethnographic inquiry into the evolving field of Indian administration came to be identified in some quarters as being 'problematic,'" a view congenial to "political figures who appreciated the benefits of being able to exercise discreet control over public understanding of their activities."[64] Overall, Dyck portrays the research field of Indigenous-state relations as challenged by restrictions on access to Indigenous communities, by self-censorship, and by "political correctness" (his words).[65] The result threatens to be an impoverished anthropology in this subfield and a lessened supply of dispassionate understanding.

The political scientist Menno Boldt, who in *Surviving as Indians* is sympathetic to First Nations' concerns, nevertheless felt compelled to deny that he was entering forbidden territory. He resisted possible allegations of paternalism, denied the "insider thesis" (i.e., that his identity as a non-Indigenous person would preclude understanding), and concluded that his writing on Indigenous issues was justified because the "principle of a common humanity requires scholars to transcend the boundaries of their identity to find common human ground."[66] The minimum consequence of the pressures to which Boldt responded is a careful use of language, saying what a scholarly conscience impels one to say in cautious, non-inflammatory phrases. In some cases, "Telling It Like It Is" (Dyck's phrase) might jeopardize the goal of Aboriginal self-government – which, according to Dyck, most anthropologists support – "by revealing the degree of social breakdown, malaise and abuses of power in a number of native communities."[67]

A disturbingly clear expression of how one anthropologist sees his role is presented by Daniel Boxberger:

> Contemporary Coast Salish anthropologists are working within the context of Boldt and *Delgamuukw*, and our entree into Native communities depends upon the communities' perception that our research has some practical application in respect to land, resources, and self-determination. Not only does our relationship with Coast Salish communities depend upon this perception but our moral and ethical commitments demand it. My hope is that we are witnessing a shift from a politically motivated research agenda directed by the nation-state to a politically motivated research agenda directed by the Fourth World state.[68]

Many academics were drawn into the constitutional politics of the 1980s and 1990s, when the constitution was the centrepiece on the public agenda. The place of Indigenous peoples in the constitution was one of the focal points for constitutional commentary. Not surprisingly, scholars, especially in law and political science, were drawn into the fray. This generated a burst of introspection about how this participatory role should be played and the difficulties of playing it. The almost unvarying message that surfaced was the difficulties researchers experienced in a climate of constraints. There was a high degree of unwillingness to say anything that might be construed as unsympathetic to Indigenous aspirations, such as impediments to or limitations of grandiose self-government ambitions for the small populations, under 500, of most First Nations, or in the practical difficulties of self-government without a land base. The constraints affected politicians who were afraid of appearing reactionary and accordingly did not voice "sincere and sometimes reasonable concerns about enhancing the various rights of aboriginal peoples."[69] Academics were warned that high costs may follow any "deviation from the generally sympathetic orientation towards native rights."[70] The authors of these disturbing observations go on to note that the "few scholars who have dared to express doubts about the appropriateness, and indeed authenticity, of aboriginal claims have been attacked and even ridiculed, regardless of the substance of their concerns."[71] A legal scholar who pointed out certain difficulties he saw in the proposed implementation of self-government was clearly apprehensive that, as a non-Indigenous person, his concerns might put him in the wrong camp.[72] Two other non-Indigenous authors, after pointing out certain "pitfalls" of First Nations' government, wished to make it clear that they were only pointing out "problems." They wrote, "It is for the Indian people, not non-Indian academics like ourselves to weigh the advantages and problems of Indian government and decide on its acceptability."[73] (It would be a useful study to trace the emergence of the practice of Euro-Canadian scholars defining themselves as non-Indians or non-Indigenous. Scott, Jenness, and McIlwraith did not do so in the imperial era.)

Although the evidence is fragmentary, it appears that there are tacit understandings that Indigenous scholars will not criticize each other. Emma LaRocque, a Métis women and professor of Native Studies at the University of Manitoba, describes the cross-pressures she encounters:

> I am painfully aware that social and political realities place Native academics in unusual circumstances. In the first place, we are still a very small

> community, making it difficult to treat each other's works critically … Moreover, there seems to be an unstated expectation that women not criticize women, or that Native scholars not criticize Native scholars. This … detracts from the important theoretical work that needs to be done, and it hampers intellectual vibrancy. Aboriginal scholars walk a tightrope between keeping a wary eye on western-defined canons and negotiating cultural and/or community interests.[74]

Indigenous feminist scholars who criticize the abuse of power by men in First Nations communities are harshly reprimanded and even threatened for breaking ranks. "Aboriginal women stigmatized as feminist," reports Joyce Green, "have endured political and social ostracization and threats of violence and of other punitive tactics."[75] A number of Indigenous women, fearful that their loyalty might be questioned and of retaliation back home for what they wished to tell the RCAP commissioners, insisted on giving their evidence in camera. The commission speculated that their requests were either "because they feared community disapproval if they spoke out in public, or because they did not wish to talk about social dysfunction in their communities in a public forum."[76] An Indigenous woman who supported the Charter asserted that speaking persistently of women's problems led to being "labeled as a dupe of the colonizing society."[77]

In the midst of the constitutional discussions of the 1980s over the right of self-government, Marie Smallface Marule, a member of the Blood tribe, lecturer in Native American studies, and a prominent administrator in Indigenous organizations, stated, "We must beware of the traitors in our midst – those of our people who have already accepted elitism, materialism, and individualism, who are trying to convince us that the Canadian way is the only way. Yes, it may be inevitable that our greatest enemies are within our ranks."[78] Although he does not use the word "traitor," Taiaiake Alfred makes a similar point about "leaders who promote non-indigenous goals," referring to "greedy corrupt politicians [who] are seduced by the mainstream … who are looking, sounding, and behaving just like mainstream politicians."[79] Calvin Helin, the author of the recent book *Dances with Dependency*, which is highly critical of First Nations leadership, cited numerous instances in which criticisms of various reserve practices had a price tag, including reprisals, lawsuits, denial of benefits, and expulsion from the reserve.[80] He documents the perils that await band members who expose corruption and other abuses of power. He refers to some band councils that "rule by out-and-out intimidation."[81] Helin, a member of the Tsimshian Nation, understands the constraints that inhibit plain speaking but asserts that the taboos against truthful reporting and analysis ill serve First Nations communities. He is well aware that in exposing corruption and other abuses of power, he is breaking the taboo against speaking out.

He attributes the abuses of power in some First Nations communities to the absence of accountability to the community and the politically exaggerated sensitivity of the Indian Affairs Branch (IAB), which fears to intervene. Helin's critique extends beyond band councils to include the IAB and what he calls the "Indian industry."[82] He sums up the situation with the thesis that "Aboriginal people are ... reluctant to speak publicly about these issues because they do not wish to provide grist for the political right in Canada who many people feel are racist, and have no real interest in actually trying to make the situation better ... Generally, non-Aboriginal observers have been reluctant to raise this issue as well because in the current climate of political correctness, they might automatically be labeled as racists."[83]

In at least in one case, book reviewing is also subject to pressure to distribute praise and criticism according to political criteria. In 2001, Suzanne Methot, a Cree reviewer for *Quill and Quire* who had reviewed every "major book written by or about Aboriginal people in Canada" over the previous four years, reported the pressures to which she was subject. She is proud of her independence, by which she means a willingness to review each book on its merits. Hence she sometimes writes negative reviews of books written by Indigenous authors and even rave reviews of "books written by non-native authors on aboriginal subjects." Methot willingly pays a price for her integrity. "I've paid for my independence and for my honesty," she writes. "I don't get invited to the conferences. I will never get a grant from a program juried by Aboriginal people. I will never again work in-house at an aboriginal publication."[84]

I admit that an aggregation of specifics, which could be added to, does not constitute a theory with across-the-board application. I also recall Alfred's suggestion that as a "grumpy geezer" my views should be discounted, and I should "get out of our way." One way, perhaps, of "getting out of the way" is to note that the most serious critiques of the politics of reserves come from Joyce Green, a Métis professor at the University of Regina; from Jean Allard, a former member of Ed Schreyer's cabinet in Manitoba and a Métis; and from Calvin Helin, a member of Gitlan Tribe of the Tsimshian Nation. Their critiques – from different perspectives, but in all cases based on personal knowledge – cannot be denied because of some alleged bias attributed to their source. Helin, Green, and Allard have made major contributions to our understanding of the realities of reserve life. All three are Indigenous and thus bring their own experiences or life histories to their contributions.

Helin's views have already been noted at length. Green's edited collection, *Making Space for Indigenous Feminism*, provides a litany of observations of the suppression, subordination, and maltreatment of women in various Indigenous societies around the world. She laments the lack of space for rigorous exchanges of ideas and suggests "that Aboriginal feminists do not enjoy enough security to participate routinely in the freedoms of speech, thought and association that are considered minimums for expression of citizenship in contemporary Canada." Indeed, the conference that led to the book was limited to invited participants so that free discussion could occur.[85] In my third example, Allard describes reserves as a system that invites abuse and does so successfully. The frequent results are an impoverished community and an elite class with access to public funds filtered through chief, council, and others linked to them. The IAB is negligent in enforcing any accountability. Chief and council are frequently draconian in their treatment of community members who highlight abuses and seek to introduce reforms. Reserves, Allard writes, "are, in effect, lawless societies."[86] Government processes are contaminated because "there is no real separation between politics and administration on reserves [with the result that] ... whoever is elected is in control of just about everything on a reserve!"[87]

Given the preceding – the hesitations of some writers and the candour of others – it is surely undeniable that research is urgently needed on the politics of reserve life, on the relations between chiefs, councils, and the reserve population, on the winners and losers, and on who leaves and who stays. We need to know the success stories as well – how many, where, how, why – so that the lessons learned can lead to improvement.

The Royal Commission on Aboriginal Peoples: The Strategy of Avoidance

The Royal Commission on Aboriginal Peoples deserves special attention. After all, it was a "royal commission," which presupposes objectivity. Royal commissions are given special research and reporting responsibilities typically because the problems they analyse are too difficult for the ordinary political process to handle, or perhaps because they are too divisive to be handled by Parliament or the bureaucracy. To suggest that bias, or selectivity, was at the heart of RCAP is to argue that even a policy instrument whose raison d'être assumes objectivity is not immune from the political climate of the post-imperial era. To argue that the Royal Commission on Aboriginal Peoples was an opportunity missed may not surprise most students of public policy. However, to assert that the commission's report displayed a remarkable selectivity in its inclusion and exclusion of certain realities is a more serious accusation. Further, that selectivity was purpose-driven. It was undertaken on behalf of a vision of the future position of Aboriginal peoples in Canada that the commission sought to foster, a vision whose plausibility would have been weakened by a more candid presentation.

The RCAP's downplaying of three social facts – the large and growing urban population, the one-third of individuals who declared an Aboriginal ancestry but did not have an Aboriginal identity, and the extent and significance of intermarriage – was the servant of parallelism. Parallelism is the view that Indigenous nations and the Canadian nation coexist side by side, sharing geography but minimal community.

The report dramatically downplayed the significance of the urban dimension of the contemporary Indigenous population, in spite of the fact that nearly 50 per cent of the Indigenous-identity population lived in cities, compared to 31 per cent of the Indigenous-identity population living on reserves. Further, slightly less than half of individuals self-identifying as "Indian" lived on reserve.[88] Confronted by this reality, the commissioners focused their attention on the reserve-based population. The well-known Native studies professor at Trent University, David Newhouse, asserted that it was difficult to "get urban aboriginals on the agenda" of commissioners who were "more interested in traditional native life and problems."[89] The commission chose to focus disproportionate attention on communities more insulated from the majority society, the better to support its thesis that reserve communities were the bastions of Indigenous difference whose reinforcement was central to the commission's vision.

This bias of attention was justified by the report's questionable portrayal of reserve life as idyllic when contrasted with an urban existence. The RCAP reported its optimistic vision of the future of "healthy, sustainable communities that create the conditions for a rounded life ... [contrasted with] forced emigration to the margins of an essentially alien urban environment. Even if such communities have to be subsidized in the long term to give their citizens access to standards of health and education equivalent to those of other Canadians, the costs, both social and financial, are likely to be significantly less than those occasioned by a rootless urban existence."[90]

Surprisingly, and regrettably, the report noticed only in passing that one-third of individuals with an Indigenous ancestry did not declare an Indigenous identity. It noted "some evidence that [they have] socio-economic characteristics quite similar to Canadians as a whole, while those who do identify as Aboriginals have quite different socio-economic characteristics."[91] However, it relegated this information to a footnote and did not follow it up. To say the least, this was a remarkable, indeed inexplicable, omission in a report with a key focus on the revitalization of Indigenous culture and identity. The commissioners, either by oversight or deliberately, deprived their inquiry of what would appear to be relevant information and understanding central to their mission: the loss of identity. The report also displayed minimal interest in intermarriage, normally a subject of great concern for small populations living in the midst of much larger societies. This omission was extraordinary, given that intermarriage rates off-reserve were over 60 per cent.[92]

It could be argued that the dismissive treatment of intermarriage, the unwillingness to accord urban Indigenous peoples a degree of attention proportionate to their numbers, and the complete failure to pay any attention to the one-third of those whose Indigenous ancestry was not accompanied by an Indigenous identity reflected no more than the inevitable inability of even a royal commission to do everything. This explanation, however, is unconvincing. The RCAP spent twice as much money as any other royal commission in Canadian history.[93] Further, it had enough resources to undertake thirty-two studies on treaty issues.[94] Given these facts, it is difficult to claim that these three areas were deprived of attention because of budgetary austerity.

If the omissions or scanty treatment are not accidental, the question becomes, what purpose do they serve? The answer is that their exclusion or minimal attention was intended to stress the separateness and distinctiveness of the Indigenous peoples of Canada. Serious attention to intermarriage would have ill served the claim to separateness and distinctiveness. Indeed, it might even have been seen as an example of assimilation, an outcome hostile to the commission's philosophy of distinctiveness in the service of separateness. To draw the reader's attention to the ancestry population that did not carry an Indigenous identity would again have made the thesis of distinctiveness less convincing.

Such a study might even have turned into an assimilation success story, an analysis the commission preferred not to risk hearing. Finally, the relative neglect of the nearly 50 per cent of the Indigenous-identity population in urban settings, contrasted with the attention paid to the reserve-based 31 per cent of that same population, again strengthened the commission's thesis of parallelism: Indigenous nations coexisting side by side with the Canadian nation. Intermarriage, urban Indigenous peoples, and the large non-identifying population with Indigenous ancestry all underlined interdependence – the living together of Indigenous and non-Indigenous peoples – rather than parallelism.

These realities conflicted with or at a minimum challenged the primacy of the Indigenous nation and the nation-to-nation relation that was reiterated throughout the report. Here too, however, the report is if not deceptive at least confusing. On the one hand, the centrality of nation is a recurrent assertion, implying a contemporary reality.[95] On the other hand, the report admits that very few Indigenous nations now exist, although they once did, prior to their fragmentation by government policy. Accordingly, it emerges that nations are a project for the future. Indeed, the report disapproves of the many small bands (often with only a few hundred people) calling themselves nations. Real nations, albeit still small ones, with populations of 5,000–7,000, will emerge only after a complicated process of commission-recommended consolidation that will see over 600 bands, plus Inuit and Métis communities, collapsed into 60 to 80 nations, capable of relating to Canada on a nation-to-nation basis.

The RCAP's optimistic, indeed utopian, strategy of highlighting nations which were to emerge in the future deflected attention from the reality on the ground that most reserve communities have populations of hamlet or village size. The likelihood that all, or even a majority, of these small communities could be swallowed up in a massive comprehensive consolidation was, at best, minimal. What to do with the recalcitrants who resisted the consolidation process was left for a future generation to decide. The royal commission's failure to examine seriously the facts of intermarriage, to give the large urban Indigenous population attention proportionate to its numbers, and to analyse the ancestry population that did not self-identify as Indigenous weakens the reliability of its report.

If the interpretation of the preceding few pages is correct, the RCAP did not manage to extricate itself sufficiently from the political pressures that play in the tortured policy areas of Indigenous-state relations.

It failed to do what Noel Dyck described as the goal of quality independent advice, suggested by the phrase "Telling It Like It Is!" Instead, we have a report that in these three important subject areas significantly underinforms or misinforms its readers. The report provides one more telling example that the study of Native-settler relations is beset with pressures that, if succumbed to, politicize research.

Conclusion

We are all conscious of the political currents that swirl around the social sciences, history, and law when they tackle Indigenous subjects. We delude ourselves if we think that academic discussion of subjects where we, as a people, are deeply divided can easily be undertaken in a spirit of equanimity, governed by a disinterested, dispassionate search for truth. In controversies dealing with serious discontents, our behaviour is not that of an astronomer examining a distant planet. Accordingly, the debates we conduct are often passion-ridden, frequently to their detriment.

We are all caught in the legacy of colonialism which characterized Indigenous-settler relations at least up to the 1950s. It is impossible for this historic reality to be expunged from our memories and identities.[96] Accordingly, scholars involved in Indigenous research and publication are aware that theirs is difficult, even treacherous territory. The evidence is widespread, as earlier sections of this essay have indicated.

The basic source of the pressures which play on us is the ongoing struggle of Indigenous peoples to escape from a colonial past. As discussed earlier, it was far easier for the overseas colonies of the European powers to achieve independence than for Indigenous minorities in Western societies to achieve a rapprochement with the majority population in the midst of which they live. Simply put, there is a conflict, a basic incompatibility, between the contemporary version of the modern democratic state and the aspirations of many Indigenous peoples in Canada and elsewhere. One result is a frustrated nationalism which shows no signs of disappearance. The unending presence of a frustrated nationalism inevitably politicizes research. The researcher, accordingly, has to be aware that what he or she writes may have consequences, positive or negative, for the objectives of Indigenous peoples. In these circumstances, it is not a rare event for a scholar to get caught in the crossfire.

The inability to escape from a colonized past manifests itself for many Métis, Inuit, and First Nations members in according limited legitimacy to the major institutions of the constitutional order, in according limited legitimacy to Parliament, in disaffection from federal and provincial governments, in weak voter turnout, in their status as "uncertain citizens" (John Borrows's phrase),[97] in ambivalent attitudes to the Charter, and in an overall constitutional alienation. These realities suggest that many Indigenous people are in but not of Canada. While some of these disaffections may erode over time, some frustrations will surely linger on for an indefinite future, subject to periodic fluctuation.

These are classic breeding grounds for the politicization of research, which will be reinforced by the increasing number of Indigenous professors, many of whom will be strong advocates for the advancement of their people. A division of research interests between Indigenous and non-Indigenous academics is likely to arise over time, following a difficult transition period.

If politicization is going to be a permanent part of our academic future, we need to think clearly about how we see ourselves as scholars. In an era of identity politics, sympathy for and empathy with Indigenous peoples as they struggle to advance themselves will be widespread. Some scholars, both Indigenous and non-Indigenous, will become part of an intelligentsia who support Indigenous causes. Intermittently, they will experience conflict between what their research tells them and the cause with which they have identified. Even if, as Cole Harris suggests, "honest scholarship controls its biases," it cannot control biases that are "implicit or invisible."[98] These include disciplinary assumptions, the cultural environment, the spirit of the times, and the deepest recesses of our personalities. As Evie Plaice observes, we should be asking ourselves "what it is we are currently engaged in that might in time look just as draconian and misplaced" as Duncan Campbell Scott's ideas are to us. "After all, Scott's ideas were shared by most of his liberal Canadian contemporaries."[99]

To recognize these and other factors which shape our thoughts does not free us from their influence. We can, nevertheless, recognize that there is a division of labour between scholar and activist. If this division is observed, then knowledge is our best contribution.[100] David Apter, the American political scientist, summed up the evolution of his thinking over a long career by stating, "I began my career firmly dedicated to the proposition that philosophers only interpreted the world when the job was to change it. I now believe that the only way to change the world is to interpret it."[101] Amidst the cacophony of voices, we must find a place for the scholar who, in the simple but elegant language of

Julien Benda, is "the man of study ... the man who, silently seated ... reads, instructs himself, writes, takes notes."[102]

NOTES

1 Alan C. Cairns, *Citizens Plus: Aboriginal Peoples and the Canadian State* (Vancouver: UBC Press, 2000).
2 H.B. Hawthorn, ed., *A Survey of the Contemporary Indians of Canada*, 2 vols. (Ottawa: Queen's Printer, 1966 and 1967).
3 See Taiaiake Alfred, "Of White Heroes and Old Men Talking," *Windspeaker* 18/2 (June 2000): 4.
4 See Tom Flanagan, *First Nations? Second Thoughts* (Montreal: McGill-Queen's University Press, 2000).
5 "Possibly I am wedded to ideas of statehood and of political community that are anachronistic. Possibly a too cautious pragmatism, the product of inertia, impedes my ready acceptance of constitutional visions that focus on how we can escape from each other and too little on how to our mutual benefit we can cooperatively work together in a country, that, overall, is not a discredit to those of us who lure here." Alfred deleted the underlined part, making the second sentence meaningless.
6 Alfred, "Of White Heroes and Old Men Talking."
7 Suzanne Methot, review of *Citizens Plus: Aboriginal Peoples and the Canadian State*, by A.C. Cairns, *Quill and Quire* 66/3 (March 2000): 56.
8 J.R. Miller, *Reflections on Native-Newcomer Relations: Selected Essays* (Toronto: University of Toronto Press, 2004). Miller discusses several controversies about his work in the introduction. For a lengthy exchange over divergent views of the appropriate scholarly approaches to research and publication dealing with Native-newcomer relations, see Robin Brownlie and Mary-Ellen Kelm, "Desperately Seeking Absolution: Native Agency as Colonialist Alibi?" *Canadian Historical Review* 75/4 (December 1994): 543–56; and Doug Cole, J.R. Miller, and Mary-Ellen Kelm, "Desperately Seeking Absolution: Responses and a Reply," *Canadian Historical Review* 76/4 (December 1995): 628–43. It is appropriate for me to confess that much of what I have to say repeats many of Jim Miller's observations in *Reflections on Native-Newcomer Relations*. For example, we are both concerned about the difficulties of research in the troubled area of how Indigenous peoples and other Canadians are to live together harmoniously. We share similar observations/concerns about Indigenous peoples' "suspicion of non-Native researchers" (Miller, *Reflections on Native-Newcomer Relations*, 29), about political

correctness (61–3), about academic self-censorship (63, 64, 76), about the dilemmas of the "voice" appropriation issue (63, 99), about the perils of the "insider" thesis that you have to be one to know one (68, 69, 70), about the Tri-Council Policy statement and the fear of increasingly complex and demanding requirements to be met before undertaking research that involves people as informants or subjects (29–30). See also Noel Dyck, "Canadian Anthropology and the Ethnography of 'Indian Administration,'" in *Historicizing Canadian Anthropology*, ed. Julia Harrison and Regna Darnell (Toronto: UBC Press, 2006), 90–1; and the excellent survey of major problem areas noted in "'I Can Only Tell What I Know': Shifting Notions of Historical Understanding in the 1990s" (Miller, *Reflections on Native-Newcomer Relations*, 61–81).

9 Tony Becher and Paul R. Trowler, *Academic Tribes and Territories: Intellectual Enquiry and the Culture of Disciplines*, 2nd ed. (Buckingham, UK: Society for Research into Higher Education and Open University Press, 2001), 126.

10 Peter Novick, *That Noble Dream: The "Objectivity Question" and the American Historical Profession* (Cambridge: Cambridge University Press, 1988), 472–91.

11 Ron Rudin, *Making History in Twentieth-Century Quebec* (Toronto: University of Toronto Press, 1997).

12 See Basil Davidson, *The African Awakening* (London: Cape, 1955); Basil Davidson, *Africa in Modern History: The Search for a New Society* (London: Allen Lane, 1978); and Basil Davidson, *The Black Man's Burden: Africa and the Curse of the Nation-State* (New York: Times Books/Random House, 1992).

13 See Novick, *That Noble Dream*.

14 Canada, *Statement of the Government of Canada on Indian Policy*, Presented to the First Session of the Twenty-eighth Parliament by the Honourable Jean Chrétien, Minister of Indian Affairs and Northern Development (Ottawa: Department of Indian Affairs and Northern Development, 1969).

15 Scott's statement deserves lengthy citation. "I want to get rid of the Indian problem. I do not think as a matter of fact, that this country ought to continuously protect a class of people who are able to stand alone. That is my whole point. I do not want to pass into the citizens' class people who are paupers. This is not the intention of the Bill. But after one hundred years, after being in close contact with civilization it is enervating to the individual or to a band to continue in that state of tutelage, when he or they are able to take their position as British citizens or Canadian citizens, to support themselves, and stand alone. That has been the whole purpose of Indian education and advancement since the earliest times. One of the

very earliest enactments was to provide for the enfranchisement of the Indian. It is written in our law that the Indian was eventually to become enfranchised." Cited in John Leslie and Ron Maguire, eds., *The Historical Development of the Indian Act*, 2nd ed. (Ottawa: Treaties and Historical Research Center, Research Branch, Corporate Policy, Department of Indian and Northern Affairs, 1979), 114.

16 C.T. Loram and T.F. McIlwraith, eds., *The North American Indian Today* (Toronto: University of Toronto Press, 1943).

17 Ibid., 5, 7, 8.

18 Corn Buchanan, "Canadian Anthropology and Ideas of Aboriginal Emendation," in Harrison and Darnell, *Historicizing Canadian Anthropology*, 100.

19 Diamond Jenness, *The Indians of Canada*, 7th ed. (Toronto: University of Toronto Press, 1977).

20 Buchanan, "Canadian Anthropology and Ideas of Aboriginal Emendation," 96–7.

21 Ibid., 98.

22 Cairns, *Citizens Plus*, 18.

23 Cited in Alan C. Cairns, *Prelude to Imperialism: British Reactions to Central African Society 1840–1890* (London: Routledge and Kegan Paul, 1965), xiii.

24 Cairns, *Citizens Plus*, 5.

25 Noel Dyck, "Canadian Anthropology and the Ethnography of 'Indian Administration,'" in Harrison and Darnell, *Historicizing Canadian Anthropology*, 83.

26 Cairns, *Citizens Plus*, 162–3.

27 Anthony Best, Jussi M. Hanhimaki, Joseph A. Maiolo, and Kirsten E. Schulze, *International History of the Twentieth Century and Beyond*, 2nd ed. (London: Routledge, 2008), 81.

28 Leroy Little Bear, Menno Boldt, and J. Anthony Long, eds., *Pathways to Self-Determination: Canadian Indians and the Canadian State* (Toronto: University Toronto Press, 1984), 25.

29 Rogers M. Smith, *Civic Ideals, Conflicting Visions of Citizenship in U.S. History* (New Haven, CT: Yale University Press, 1997), 32; and Charles Taylor, "How to Be Diverse: The Need for a Looser 'Us' to Accommodate 'Them,'" review of *Rethinking Multiculturalism* by Bhikhu Parekh, *Times Literary Supplement* 20 (April 2001): 4. As Deborah Yashar writes, "State institutions and policies ... seek to forge national citizens," and "citizenship regimes ... have defined who is a citizen, how citizens should interact with the state, and what rights citizens might claim." Deborah J. Yashar, *Contesting Citizenship in Latin America: The Rise of Indigenous Movements and the Postliberal Challenge* (New York: Columbia University Press, 2005), 282.

30 James C. Scott, *Seeing Like a Mate: How Certain Schemes to Improve the Human Condition Have Failed* (New Haven, CT: Yale University Press, 1998).

31 "The main goals of the residential school program were to Christianize, assimilate and transform the child's way of life so that it approximated European standards as closely as possible." In John H. Hylton, *Aboriginal Sexual Offending in Canada*, 2nd ed. (Ottawa: Aboriginal Healing Foundation, 2000).

32 Leslie and Maguire, *Historical Development of the Indian Act*, 114.

33 Pierre Elliott Trudeau, "Remarks on Indian, Aboriginal, and Treaty Rights," Vancouver, British Columbia, 8 August 1969.

34 Noel Dyck, *What Is the Indian Problem?* (St John's: Institute of Social and Economic Research, 1991).

35 According to Fleras, it is close to conventional wisdom that the challenge of Indigenous demands to the liberal democratic state is pervasive, profound, and close to intractable. Augie Fleras, "Politicizing Indigeneity: Ethno-politics in White Settler Dominions," in *Indigenous Peoples' Rights in Australia, Canada, and New Zealand*, ed. P. Havemann (Auckland: Oxford University Press, 1999), 188–9, 195–7, 223–5. See also Cairns for a discussion and summary of the literature in agreement with Fleras in a special journal issue on Aboriginal citizenship: "Afterward: International Dimensions of the Citizen Issue for Indigenous Peoples/Nations," *Citizenship Studies* 7/4 (December 2003): 497–512.

36 For a helpful, sympathetic analysis of contemporary Aboriginal constitutional thought, see Dalie Giroux, "Éléments de pensée politique autochtone contemporaine," *Politique et Sociétés* 27/1 (2008): 29–53.

37 See Ted Binnema and Susan Neylan, eds., *New Histories for Old: Changing Perspectives on Canada's Native Pasts* (Vancouver: UBC Press, 2007), i–ii.

38 Large research projects are influenced by the climate of opinion at the time of the research and writing. When the Hawthorn research project of the mid-1960s, which led to the two-volume *Survey of the Contemporary Indians of Canada*, was getting under way, there was no discussion of an "Indian" component in the cadre of senior researchers. At the time, the omission was not controversial, as there were very few Indian university graduates, and even fewer with graduate degrees. Oddly, the issue of representation, pressed by the federal government before it gave its final approval for the project to proceed, had nothing to do with the presence or absence of an Indian member of the senior research group. The pressure, reflecting French Canadian nationalism, concerned the absence of a senior French Canadian, which was resolved with the appointment of Marc-Adelard Tremblay as associate director. Thirty years later, the RCAP went

out of its way to stress the Indigenous component on the commission. It was co-chaired by an Indigenous commissioner (Georges Erasmus) and a non-Indigenous commissioner (René Dussault). Four of the seven commissioners were Indigenous, including one distinguished Métis scholar, Paul Chartrand. There were two co-research directors, one Indigenous (Marlene Brant Castellano) and one non-Indigenous (David Hawkes). Whenever possible, research reports were to be doubly assessed by an Indigenous and a non-Indigenous reviewer.

39 Clifford Geertz, *After the Fact: Two Centuries, Four Decades, One Anthropologist* (Cambridge, MA: Harvard University Press, 1995), 107.

40 Miller, *Reflections on Native-Newcomer Relations*, 283. On history, also see James Walker, "The Indian in Canadian Historical Writing," *Canadian Historical Association, Historical Papers* (1971): 21–47.

41 Bruce G. Trigger, *Natives and Newcomers: Canada's 'Heroic Age' Reconsidered* (Montreal: McGill-Queen's University Press, 1985), 4, 48.

42 Gerard LaForest, "Reminiscences of Aboriginal Rights at the Time of the Calder Case and Its Aftermath," in *Let Right Be Done: Aboriginal Title, the Calder Case, and the Future of Indigenous Rights*, ed. Hamar Foster, Heather Raven, and Jeremy Webber (Vancouver: UBC Press, 2007), 54.

43 Frank Calder and Thomas Berger, "Frank Calder and Thomas Berger in Conversation," in Foster, Raven, and Webber, *Let Right Be Done*, 43.

44 Little Bear, Boldt, and Long, *Pathways to Self-Determination*, ix.

45 "In this Act 'Aboriginal Peoples of Canada' includes the Indian, Inuit, and Métis Peoples of Canada." Section 35 of the Constitution Act, 1982.

46 Hence the priority of the nation as the key vehicle in RCAP's Report for the advancement of Aboriginal peoples. For example, "the Aboriginal nation [is] ... the core around which the Commission's recommendations are built." And "Aboriginal peoples are political entities that, because of their treaties, the recognition of their rights in Canada's constitution, and the nature of their social and cultural cohesion, need to be recognized as nations, negotiated with as nations, and thereby empowered to implement their own solutions within a flexible Canadian federation." Canada, *Report of the Royal Commission on Aboriginal Peoples*, 5 vols. (Ottawa: Canada Communication Group Publishing, 1996), 1015–16.

47 See Miller, *Reflections on Native-Newcomer Relations*, 279–95.

48 Ibid., 281–2.

49 Becher and Trowler suggest that from a "system-wide perspective, recent years have seen a diversification of the academic profession into even smaller and more different worlds than was previously the case" (*Academic Tribes and Territories*, 17; see also p. 45).

50 Robin Brownlie and Mary-Ellen Kelm, "Desperately Seeking Absolution: Native Agency as Colonialist Alibi?" *Canadian Historical Review* 75/4 (December 1994): 543, 556.
51 Kelm in Cole, Miller, and Kelm, "Desperately Seeking Absolution: Responses and a Reply," 639.
52 Brownlie and Kelm, "Desperately Seeking Absolution: Native Agency as Colonialist Alibi?" 548.
53 Cole, Miller, and Kelm, "Desperately Seeking Absolution: Responses and a Reply," 632.
54 Brownlie and Kelm, "Desperately Seeking Absolution: Native Agency as Colonialist Alibi?" 545.
55 Ibid.
56 Ibid., 547.
57 Cole, Miller, and Kelm, "Desperately Seeking Absolution: Responses and a Reply," 633–4.
58 Ibid., 638.
59 Brownlie and Kelm, "Desperately Seeking Absolution: Native Agency as Colonialist Alibi?" 553.
60 Ibid., 543.
61 Cole, Miller, and Kelm, "Desperately Seeking Absolution: Responses and a Reply," 640.
62 Ibid., 639.
63 Dyck, "Canadian Anthropology and the Ethnography of 'Indian Administration,'" 87.
64 Ibid.
65 See also Noel Dyck, "Telling It Like It Is: Some Dilemmas of Fourth World Ethnography and Advocacy," in *Anthropology, Public Policy, and Native Peoples in Canada*, ed. Noel Dyck and James E. Waldram (Montreal: McGill-Queen's University Press, 1993), 192–212.
66 Menno Boldt, *Surviving as Indians: The Challenge of Self-Government* (Toronto: University of Toronto Press, 1993), xviii.
67 Cairns, *Citizens Plus*, 37–8. In a speech to an academic audience in the 1990s, I referred to some concerns that I thought should be considered on the road to Aboriginal self-government. To my surprise, I was subsequently congratulated by several people, not for the cogency of my remarks, but for my courage in making them. This has happened on several occasions.
68 Cited in Dorothy Kennedy, review of *Be of Good Mind: Essays on the Coast Salish*, ed. Bruce Granville Miller, *BC Studies* 158 (summer 2008): 121. Dorothy Kennedy, the reviewer of *Be of Good Mind*, in which Boxberger's

chapter appears, remarks that "Many of the contributors … subscribe to the notion that the process of interpreting factual knowledge into palatable current weaponry is the fob of the anthropologist and historian. Can a seeker of the truth respect this new expediency?"

69 Brian Schwartz, *First Principles, Second Thoughts: Aboriginal Peoples, Constitutional Reform and Canadian Statecraft* (Montreal: Institute for Research on Public Policy, 1986), 325.

70 Roger Gibbins and Rhada Jhappan, "The State of the Dirt in Native Studies in Political Science," paper presented at the Tenth Biennial Canadian Ethnic Studies Association Conference, Calgary, 18–21 October 1989, photocopy.

71 Ibid. For further elaboration of these points, see Alan C. Cairns, "Ritual, Taboo, and Bias in Constitutional Controversies in Canada, or Constitutional Talk Canadian Style," in *Disruptions: Constitutional Struggles from the Charter to Meech Lake*, ed. Douglas E. Williams (Toronto: McClelland and Stewart, 1991), 210–14. See also Alan C. Cairns, "Why Is It So Difficult to Talk to Each Other?" *McGill Law Journal* 42/1 (February 1997): 78–82.

72 Merry Wilkins, "Take Your Time and Do It Right: Delgamuukw, Self-Government Rights and the Fragmatics of Advocacy," *Manitoba Law Journal* 27/2 (2000): 250n4.

73 J. Rick Ponting and Roger Gibbins, "Thorns in the Bed of Roses: A Socio-political View of the Problems of Indian Government," in Little Bear, Boldt, and Long, *Pathways to Self-Determination*, 122.

74 Emma LaRocque, "Métis and Feminist: Ethical Reflections on Feminism, Human Rights and Decolonization," in *Making Space for Indigenous Feminism*, ed. Joyce Green (Black Point, Nova Scotia: Fernwood Publishing, 2007), 62.

75 Joyce Green, "Taking Account of Aboriginal Feminism," in Green, *Making Space for Indigenous Feminism*, 24. Another publication, *Aboriginal Domestic Violence in Canada*, prepared for the Aboriginal Healing Foundation, reported "an emerging *culture of violence*" in "many Aboriginal communities" and stated that "domestic violence and abuse have become a part of the way of life of many communities … The levels of abuse are simply astronomical … Many communities are virtual war zones … dangerous to move about at night and sometimes even dangerous to stay at home. Increasingly, nowhere is safe. Of course, not all Aboriginal communities are as bad as this, but a shocking number of them are becoming as bad." Michael Bopp, Judie Bopp, and Phil Lane, Jr., *Aboriginal Domestic Violence in Canada*, 2nd ed. (Ottawa: Aboriginal Healing Foundation, 2006), 7, 10, 11.

76 Royal Commission on Aboriginal Peoples, *Public Hearings: Exploring the Options –Overviews of the Third Round* (Ottawa: Canada Communication Group, 1993), 4. See also Cairns, *Citizens Plus*, 74, for additional references to violence against women.

77 Joyce Green, "Constitutionalizing the Patriarchy: Aboriginal Women and Aboriginal Government," *Constitutional Forum* 4 (1993): 118.

78 Marie Smallface Marule, "Traditional Indian Government: Of the People, by the People, for the People," in Little Bear, Boldt, and Long, *Pathways to Self-Determination*, 45.

79 Alfred, "Of White Heroes and Old Men Talking," xiv, v.

80 See Calvin Helin, *Dances with Dependency: Indigenous Success through Self-Reliance* (Vancouver: Orca Spirit Publishing, 2006), 151–6.

81 Ibid., 153.

82 For the latter, see ibid., 17, 36–9, 104, 115, 160–1; and indirectly, Jean Allard, "Big Bear's Treaty: The Road to Freedom," *Inroads* 11 (2002): 135–6.

83 Helin, *Dances with Dependency*, 157.

84 Methot, review of *Citizens Plus*, 42.

85 Green, *Making Space for Indigenous Feminism*, 17. See also pages 23, 25, 30, 54, and 56 for the violence and insecurity characteristic of Indigenous women's lives.

86 Allard, "Big Bear's Treaty," 146.

87 Ibid. See also Helin, chapter 9, "The Welfare Trap and Political Pathologies," in *Dances with Dependency* for a passionate critique of corruption, nepotism, and abuse of power, among other aspects of reserve life. See Helin also for the maltreatment of would-be reformers trying to employ the same civic rights as other Canadians. "Ordinary Indians living on reserves," Allard writes, "can be controlled by financial inducements, or brought to heel by the threat of physical harm, loss of jobs or welfare benefits, eviction from their homes, banishment from the reserve." Allard, "Big Bear's Treaty," 159. See in general Helin, chapter 6, "Challenging the System," in *Dances with Dependency* for the maltreatment of those who do. On the related topic of sexual offences, see Hylton, *Aboriginal Sexual Offending in Canada*.

88 John Richards, *Creating Choices: Rethinking Aboriginal Policy*, Policy Study 43 (Toronto: C.D. Howe Institute, 2006), 9.

89 John Gray, "Absent Aboriginals: Not a Word About Natives," *Globe and Mail*, 4 May 1997.

90 Canada, *Report of the Royal Commission on Aboriginal Peoples*, 5 vols. (Ottawa: Canada Communication Group Publishing, 1996), 2:2, 1023.

91 Ibid., 1:24n7.

92 Stewart Clatworth and Anthony H. Smith, *Population Implications of the 1985 Amendments to the Indian Act: Final Report* (Perth: Living Dimensions, 1992), iii.

93 Oddly enough, the commission asserts that a "breakdown of expenditures" can be found in appendix I (Canada, *Report of the Royal Commission on Aboriginal Peoples*, 5:304). However, there is no appendix I. It appears to have been deleted.

94 Canada, *Report of the Royal Commission on Aboriginal Peoples*, 2:1, 94–5n4.

95 For example, Aboriginal peoples "constitute nations today … the Aboriginal nation [is] … the core around which the Commission's recommendations are built." Canada, *Report of the Royal Commission on Aboriginal Peoples*, 2:2, 1015.

96 As this chapter was being written, the Canadian version of a Truth and Reconciliation Commission was under way. The first volume of the Report of the Royal Commission on Aboriginal Peoples had the task of portraying the past as an indictment of the newcomers' treatment of Indigenous peoples. The title of Daniel Paul's book *We Were Not the Savages* (1993; repr., Halifax, NS: Fernwood Publishing, 2000) correctly identifies which side has to make amends to the other.

97 John Borrows, "Uncertain Citizens: Aboriginal Peoples and the Supreme Court," *Canadian Bar Review* 80 (2001): 15–41.

98 Cole Harris, "Arthur J. Ray and the Empirical Opportunity," in *New Histories for Old: Changing Perspectives on Canada's Native Pasts*, ed. Ted Binnema and Susan Neylan (Vancouver: UBC Press, 2007), 264.

99 Evie Plaice, "A Comparative History of 'Cultural Rights' in South Africa and Canada," in Harrison and Darnell, *Historicizing Canadian Anthropology*, 113.

100 Bryan Schwartz, after noting the tendency for academics to take the Aboriginal "side," asserted that "there are enough skilled politicians, technical employees, and consultants available that academics are not needed to act as servants and mouthpieces for competing interests. Their function ought to be to supply independent criticism and creative suggestions." Schwartz, *First Principles, Second Thoughts: Aboriginal Peoples, Constitutional Reform and Canadian Statecraft* (Montreal: Institute for Research on Public Policy, 1986), 326.

101 David Apter, "The Passing of Development Studies – Over the Shoulder with a Backward Glance," *Government and Opposition* 15 (1980): 275.

102 Ray Nichols, *Treason, Tradition, and the Intellectual: Julien Benda and Political Discourse* (Lawrence: Regents Press of Kansas, 1978), 22.

Contributors

Kerry Abel was formerly professor of history at Carleton University and now is an independent scholar. She is the author of *Drum Songs: Glimpses of Dene History* (2005 [1993]) and *Changing Places: History, Community, and Identity in Northeastern Ontario* (2006), among others.

Jonathan Anuik is an assistant professor in the Department of Educational Policy Studies at the University of Alberta. His research interests are First Nations, Métis, and Inuit education policy and history as well as the pedagogy of education history in Canadian teacher education.

Jean Barman is professor emerita in the Faculty of Education at the University of British Columbia. She serves as a consultant on history and heritage to a number of cities and organizations and has published extensively on the history of British Columbia, including *The West Beyond the West* (2007 [1996]).

Alan C. Cairns is an officer of the Order of Canada, professor emeritus of Political Science at the University of British Columbia, and past president of the Canadian Political Science Association. His numerous publications have influenced Canadian constitutional and political thought on subjects ranging from federalism and governance to Aboriginal rights. His publication *Citizens Plus: Aboriginal Peoples and the Canadian State* (2000) remains one of the most important in the field.

Keith Thor Carlson is professor of history and research chair in Aboriginal and community-engaged history at the University of Saskatchewan. He is an honorary member of the Stó:lō Nation and the author of

The Power of Place, the Problem of Time: Aboriginal Identity and Historical Consciousness in the Cauldron of Colonialism (2010), among others.

Kenneth S. Coates is Canada research chair in regional innovation in the Johnson-Shoyama Graduate School of Public Policy, University of Saskatchewan. He is also director of the International Centre for Northern Governance and Development. He has published extensively on Indigenous rights and policy issues and the history of the Canadian North.

Brendan Frederick R. Edwards is with Library and Archives of the Royal Ontario Museum, after teaching at universities abroad and in Canada. His doctoral studies were supervised by J.R. Miller. He is the author of *Paper Talk: A History of Libraries, Print Culture, and Aboriginal Peoples in Canada Before 1960* (2005) and a number of essays, including contributions to volumes 2 and 3 of the *History of the Book in Canada* (2005, 2007).

Hamar Foster, QC, is an emeritus professor of law at the University of Victoria, where over the years he taught criminal law and procedure, trial advocacy, evidence, property law, legal history, and the law respecting Aboriginal title and rights. He has been researching and writing about comparative criminal law, Indigenous law, and legal history since the 1970s.

P. Whitney Lackenbauer is a professor of history and co-director of the Centre on Foreign Policy and Federalism at St Jerome's University in the University of Waterloo. He is the author of *The Canadian Rangers: A Living History* (2013), the coauthor of *Canada and the Changing Arctic: Sovereignty, Security and Stewardship* (2011), and has edited a number of collections including *Blockades or Breakthroughs? Aboriginal Peoples Confront the Canadian State* (with Yale Belanger, 2014).

Dianne Newell is professor emerita of history at the University of British Columbia and past director of the Peter Wall Institute of Advanced Studies. She specializes in Canadian social history and science and technology studies with interdisciplinary approaches. Her books include *Judith Merril: A Critical Study* (with Victoria Lamont, 2012); *Fishing Places, Fishing People: Traditions and Issues in Canadian Small-Scale Fisheries* (edited with Rosemary Omer, 1999); and *Tangled Webs of History: Indians and the Law in Canada's Pacific Coast Fisheries* (1997 [1993]).

Arthur J. Ray, FRSC, is professor emeritus of history at the University of British Columbia. He specializes in the historical geography of Indigenous people and the history of Aboriginal and treaty rights litigation. His publications include *Aboriginal Rights Claims and the Making and Remaking of History* (2016); *Telling It to the Judge: Taking Native History to Court* (2011); *An Illustrated History of Canada's Native People: I Have Lived Here since the World Began* (2005 [1996]); and with J.R. Miller and Frank Tough, *Bounty and Benevolence: A History of Saskatchewan Treaties* (2000).

Myra Rutherdale taught at universities across Canada before settling at York University. Her publications include *Women and the White Man's God: Gender and Race in the Canadian Mission Field* (2006); *Contact Zones* (edited with Katie Pickles, 2005); and a study of midwifery in Canada, *Caregiving on the Periphery* (2010). Sadly, she passed away in 2014 before publication of this volume.

Donald B. Smith is professor emeritus of history at the University of Calgary and the author of a number of biographical studies of Indigenous people and those who pretended to be Indigenous. Most recently, he published *Mississauga Portraits: Ojibwe Voices from Nineteenth-Century Ontario* (2013).

Frank J. Tough (University of Alberta) was a colleague of Jim Miller's at the University of Saskatchewan (1984–98); they collaborated with Arthur J. Ray on a report for the Office of the Treaty Commissioner (Saskatchewan) which was revised and published as *"Bounty and Benevolence": A History of Saskatchewan Treaties* (2000). Within frameworks that synthesize legal and economic history, his major publications have used arcane archival sources to elucidate the origins of contemporary treaty and Aboriginal rights disputes.

Bill Waiser, SOM, FRSC, DLitt, is distinguished professor emeritus at the University of Saskatchewan. He is the author of more than a dozen books, including the award-winning *Saskatchewan: A New History*. His latest book, *A World We Have Lost: Saskatchewan before 1905*, was released in 2016.

We gratefully acknowledge the assistance of the University of Saskatchewan in the preparation of this volume.

Index